PSYCHOPHYSICS

PSYCHOPHYSICS

Introduction to Its Perceptual, Neural, and Social Prospects

S.S. Stevens

Edited by Geraldine Stevens

With a New Introduction by Lawrence E. Marks

Transaction Books
New Brunswick (U.S.A.) and Oxford (U.K.)

Second printing 2000

New Material in this edition copyright © 1986 by Transaction Publishers, New Brunswick, New Jersey 08903. Original edition copyright © 1975 by John Wiley & Sons, Inc. Transaction paperback edition published by permission of John Wiley & Sons, Inc.

Library of Congress Catalog Number: 85-24555
ISBN: 0-88738-643-1 (paper)
Printed in the United States of America

Library of Congress Cataloging in Publication Data

Stevens, S.S. (Stanley Smith), 1906-1973.
    Psychophysics : introduction to its
perceptual, neural, and social prospects.

    Reprint. Originally published: New York : Wiley,
c1975.
    Bibliography: p.
    Includes indexes.
    1. Psychophysics. I. Stevens, Geraldine.
II. Title. [DNLM: 1. Psychophysics. WL 702 S846p 1975a]
BF237.S65   1986   152.1   85-24555
ISBN 0-88738-643-1 (pbk.)

Introduction to the Transaction Edition

Lawrence E. Marks

S.S. Stevens's *Psychophysics* first appeared just a decade ago, two years after the author's sudden and untimely death; fortunately, Stevens had virtually completed the manuscript, which Geraldine Stevens prepared for publication, applying to it both her fine editorial skills and an acumen concerning matters psychophysical that far exceeds what she modestly acknowledges in the preface. In 1975, at the time of its publication, *Psychophysics* was a landmark work, and a landmark I believe it shall remain. No volume of a mere 300 or so pages could possibly survey and explicate all of his accomplishments; nevertheless this his last work does manage to capture the fundamental themes that underlay not only Stevens's experimental research but his vision of what psychophysics—and psychology—are and can be.

Within the first few pages, indeed within even the first few paragraphs, the reader will understand that this is no mere compendium of pristine psychophysical methods, no mere tabulation of sensory thresholds, just noticeable differences, or power-function exponents, no mere recounting of arcane observations on sensation and judgment, but a lively account by one of experimental psychology's seminal figures of his lifelong scientific quest for general laws governing human behavior. E.G. Boring once noted that psychophysics is traditionally considered to be one of the dreariest subjects in the history of experimental psychology; but Boring wrote this in 1942, when students of sensation and psychophysical judgment could not hold Stevens's *Psychophysics* in their hands. Not just methods, not just thresholds, not just exponents of power functions, *Psychophysics* the book, like psychophysics the discipline, considers the responses of organisms—here, mostly human organisms—to their environment. Much of the wisdom in this volume lies in its exposition of an approach that can apply quite generally to the study of human behavior.

Stevens's *Psychophysics,* like Gustav Fechner's *Elemente der Psychophysik* (1860) written a little more than a century earlier, reveals its author's vision of psychology, especially experimental psychology. Stevens and Fechner were in some respects worlds apart: Fechner, the European steeped in philosophy, built his psychophysics atop a theoretical substrate that permitted him to experiment only as far as theory dictated; whereas Stevens, the pragmatic and empirical American, hurtled on to see where measurement might take him. Yet both men were pioneers of psychophysics, kindred spirits in their view that measurement and the quantitative study of sensory processing bear wide significance for understanding mind and behavior.

Stevens, like Fechner, perceived psychophysics in a broad sense as well as a narrow one as a discipline virtually coextensive with psychology itself. In his introductory chapter to the *Handbook of Experimental Psychology,* Stevens wrote: "Measurement is an especial preoccupation of psychophysics—not only of psychophysics in the narrow sense of the term, but of psychophysics in its older and broader spirit, which tries to discover rules relating the responses of organisms to the energetic configurations of the environment" (1951, p. 1). Toward the end of the chapter he continued, "In a sense, there is only one problem of psychophysics, namely the definition of the stimulus. In this same sense there is only one problem in all of psychology—and that is the same problem. The definition of the stimulus is thus a bigger problem than it appears at first sight. The reason for equating psychology to the problem of defining stimuli can be stated thus: the complete definition of the stimulus to a given response involves the specification of all the transformations of the environment, both internal and external, that leave the response invariant" (pp. 31-32).

Measurement and invariance go hand in hand, both being central to psychophysics. And because psychophysics was, in Stevens's eye, a microcosm of psychology, so are measurement and invariance central to psychology at large.

Although Stevens's name became closely associated with measurement, especially with psychophysical scaling, the key concept is that of invariance. In my view, invariance plays several central roles: To explicate these roles, it is handy to borrow the terminology of Morris (1938), which Stevens himself often cited (e.g., 1939, 1951). To my reckoning, invariance makes three appearances: in the semantics of science, in the syntactics of science, and in the pragmatics of science. First of all, invariance underlies the very semantic content—the subject matter—of science,

which in psychology comes down to the pursuit of "the complete definition of the stimulus." Second, invariance underlies the syntactic tools—
the mathematical properties of scales of measurement—that scientists apply to their observations. Finally, invariance underlies one of the primary
pragmatic goals of science—the scientific dream, namely, the construction
of simple and broadly general theories of nature.

The major problem posed by psychophysics, avers Stevens, is to discover the stimulus; the goal of psychophysics is to learn which aspects of
stimuli affect perceptual or other behavorial responses, and, perhaps
most importantly, to identify the sets of different stimulus conditions that
leave responses invariant. This metascientific view of Stevens's parallels in
a basic way James J. Gibson's (1966) view, and perhaps it is neither ac-
cidental nor wholly surprising that the past decade has witnessed a growing recognition among students of perceptual processes that perception
largely involves the detection of or reaction to what Gibson termed *higher-
order invariances* in the makeup of environmental stimuli. Behind the flux
of sensory experience, beneath the apparent chaos of light, sound, and
other stimulus energies, there are invariant, albeit complex, structures in
the stimulus array, and these invariant structures are mirrored in invariant
perceptual experiences.

If it is the job of our perceptual systems to identify invariances in the
world of stimuli, so too is it the job of scientists to identify invariances in
the universe of scientific discourse. If I had to choose a single achievement
as Stevens's most significant, it would surely be his classification of four
fundamental types of scales of measurement. Of course, his is a scheme
that applies to measurement everywhere in science, a scheme that rests
ultimately on the mathematical invariances proper to each type of scale,
whether nominal, ordinal, interval, or ratio scale. Essentially, what
determines each type of scale is the set of transformations that leave intact
some crucial, invariant property of the objects being measured—for
nominal scales, the property is the identity of each object; for ordinal,
interval, and ratio scales, it is the rank order among objects, the relative
size of the intervals between objects, and the ratios between objects.

However cleverly and carefully a scientist observes nature, however
wisely and astutely one organizes those observations, the scientific desire
remains unfulfilled until observations and laws are subsumed under
general principles and theories; and principles and theories are general to
the extent that the universe manifests invariances. It is the search for
unities amidst diversity that fires many a scientific imagination. Invariance
is at once the subject matter of science and the heuristic mode of the
scientist's inquiry, and astute readers, regardless of background or dis-

cipline, can learn a great deal by following this almost autobiographical account of Stevens's search for invariant and unitary laws governing the invariances of human psychophysical behavior.

Running through the pages of this book is the endeavor most closely associated with Stevens's name, the search for and the discovery of the invariance known as the psychophysical power law. The power equation relating sensation to stimulus is the mathematical embodiment of what is commonly called Stevens's law, the rule that, for every sensory modality, equal ratios of sensation magnitude correspond to equal ratios of stumulus intensity. The empirical operations—those particular psychophysical methods—that led to the formulation of the power law are operations by which subjects match numerals to the magnitudes of sensory experiences. The method of magnitude estimation is the best-known example. Here again lies a parallel between the behavior of the scientist and that of the scientific subject: Measurement, says Stevens, involves the matching of numbers to objects or events according to a rule. By asking subjects to match numerals to sensations, the scientist can match numbers to sensations and thereby measure them. Such matching is sufficient for measurement. Nothing more is needed.

If the two decades that preceded Stevens's *Psychophysics* saw the rise of the new psychophysics, the decade since its first publication has seen no slackening in the use of the methods Stevens espoused. The ratio methods —magnitude estimation, magnitude production, cross-modality matching —continue in unabated use to teach us about sensory mechanisms, about perceptual processes, and yes, as undoubtedly would have pleased Stevens, about the social consensus. (For a collection of papers treating applications of psychophysics to the measurement of social attitudes, see the symposium volume edited by Wegener, 1982.)

Also unabated is interest in—and continuing controversy about—the power law. The power law, Stevens's law, is a simple and powerful rule, extremely general as well as extremely useful. And as the ensuing chapters make clear, this pair of characteristics—simplicity and generality—are the benchmark of scientific laws and theories in Stevens's eyes; these are requisite properties of any proper scientific grail.

If the quest for the general psychophysical law pervades this work, if the sword Stevens uses to clear the path is experimental measurement, the driving force is Stevens's vision of nature. Quests demand a singlemindedness, and in the present case the motivation is an unwavering belief in the uniformity of nature, whose laws and rules are unfailingly simple and ultimately will submit to clear thought and direct empirical attack. This is a classical physicist's view of nature; like Einstein, Stevens rejects the notion of a God who plays dice. To those engaged in psychological research, where the moment-to-moment and person-to-person fluctuations in performance cause many to despair, the lesson of *Psychophysics* is clear: Measure carefully, reduce variability, and eventually nature will reveal her heretofore secret, underlying uniformities. Seek the psychophysical law and one discovers a power equation, with exponents determined more and more precisely as data accrue. Seek the rules of perceptual discrimination and one finds a neural quantum, the discrete, indivisible unit or step underlying the detection of a sensory change.

Clearly, *Psychophysics* is a work whose purview far transcends psychophysics, as indicated by its subtitle, *An Introduction to Its Perceptual, Neural, and Social Prospects.* The striking and central word here is *prospects,* for *Psychophysics* looks ahead as well as back. The scientific enterprise always entails its tomorrows as much as it summarizes its yesterdays. To the diligent reader *Psychophysics* can serve as a guide to roads in the future just as it retraces Stevens's path over the half-century past; to willing eyes the scenery can be exciting, even enchanting, all along the way. As Paul Valéry (1894) wrote in his *Introduction to the Method of Leonardo,* "What a man leaves after him are the dreams that his name inspires and the work that make his name a symbol of admiration."

REFERENCES

Boring, E.G. *Sensation and perception in the history of experimental psychology.* New York: Appleton-Century-Crofts, 1942.

Fechner, G.T. *Elemente der Psychophysik.* Leipzig: Breitkopf and Härtel, 1860.

Gibson, J.J. *The senses considered as perceptual systems.* Boston: Houghton-Mifflin, 1966.

Morris, C.W. Scientific empiricism. *International Encyclopedia of Unified Science,* 1938, 1, 63-75.

Stevens, S.S. Psychology and the science of science. *Psychological Bulletin,* 1939, 36, 221-263.

Stevens, S.S. Mathematics, measurement, and psychophysics. In S.S. Stevens (ed.), *Handbook of experimental psychology.* New York: Wiley, 1951, pp. 1-49.

Valéry, P. *Introduction à la méthode de Léonard de Vinci,* 1894. Paris: Nouvelle Revue Française, 1919.

Wegener, B. (ed.), *Social attitudes and psychophysical measurement.* Hillsdale, N.J.: Erlbaum, 1982.

Contents

Preface

I have just read over S. S. Stevens' last piece of writing—the book you hold in your hands. Though he did not live to read it—and he often said that he would never sign a contract for a book until he had read it—he did write it, every word of it. Or at least all but one footnote that I finally composed in the hope that it would lay to rest the insistent question of why the power law exponent for loudness is .33 here and .67 there.

The relation of sound power to sound pressure is a difficult concept, much too complicated for me, and only by tightly grasping every psychophysical thread in my unscientific clutch could I hold onto the facts long enough to get it written. I hope the reader has grasped the relation of pressure to energy. It is crucial to an understanding of auditory psychophysics; and in comparisons of power function exponents from one sense modality to another it may spell the difference between exultation and despair.

My contribution to psychophysics is made clear by the author, late in Chapter 1, where he referred to me as his most faithful observer. Thirty-odd years in the observer's booth does not make one a scientist. I have, however, read every word with as much understanding and care as I could muster, checked and cross-checked handwritten manuscript and sources, drafted and redrafted figures, and tried in every way to ensure that the book would be as true to its author's intent as a devoted editor could make it.

The sad thing, of course, is that I could not resolve the inevitable problems that surface in any book with the sureness with which an author makes decisions in his own subject matter. I was fortunate to have the skilled and generous help of three friends, Richard J. W. Mansfield, Joseph C. Stevens, and David V. Cross, who read the manuscript and contributed to the difficult resolutions. All three had worked at Harvard during some part of the 20-year span in which psychophysics grew from a method for measuring thresholds of sensation to a scientific basis for scaling sensations and perceptions. And, as I write this preface, Peter Stevens is sweeping through the manuscript and polishing any neglected facets.

Two good friends returned from "retirement" to lend a hand with the final editing and drafting of illustrations, Edith L. Annin and Mable Field. To all the friends who held my hand in this difficult task, my loving gratitude.

GERALDINE STEVENS

CHAPTER 1

The Psychophysical Law

It has taken some homely and simple procedures to reveal beautiful and elegant relations in the behavior of the sensory system. Recently invented procedures have shown that whenever the stimulus increases, the intensity of the sensation grows in accordance with a common basic principle. In every sense modality, sensation is a power function of stimulus. The principle seems clear and straightforward now, but it was a zigzag path with many wrong forks that led finally to the discovery that equal stimulus ratios produce equal sensation ratios. That is the basic principle that underlies the psychophysical law. The ratio invariance tells us that the psychophysical law is a power function.

It is not easy, after the fact, to single out exactly those blocks and diversions that deflected progress, my own included, from a straight course toward the psychophysical law, for experience has meaning only against the background of the *Zeitgeist,* which permeates our thinking and determines what, in any given time period, is in fact thinkable. I find that I can think now about quantitative relations among sensations that were scarcely conceivable four decades ago—relations that were deemed quite beyond imagining a hundred years ago. Barriers of belief had to be breached in order to forge a fresh paradigm.

It was not only that laboratory traditions were encrusted with rules and procedures that blocked the way, but before it became possible to think more clearly about the measurement of sensation, the nature and meaning of measurement had to be understood in a revised light. What by common consent was unmeasurable a century ago has now been measured, and in the process there has emerged a restructuring of psychophysics that provides a new perspective on the ancient problem of the relation of stimulus to sensation. Many features of the new psychophysics have evolved so gradually that to me much of the progress seemed more like an onward flow than a sudden leap. But then, the *Zeitgeist* changes only slowly. It takes a generation for a new conception to win its place in the textbooks.

A contrary *Zeitgeist* was not the only impediment, however. Another hazard arose from the natural tendency of scientists to find fascination in complexity. Simplicity is easy to overlook. The history of both mathematics and science has taught us repeatedly that it is often most difficult to discover the simplest things. Before the theory of measurement could support a new psychophysics, some far-reaching simplifications had to be introduced both at the conceptual level and at the level of method and procedure.

TWO CONFLICTING LAWS

Psychophysics may be said to have been born when scientists began to think seriously about the possibility that they might measure sensation. That was back in the 1850's. Long before then, however, many people had marveled at the richness of sensory experience and had described how sensations differ in quality. Seeing is different from hearing; taste is different from touch; pain is different from smell. But each of those sensations can also vary in intensity or degree, so that a sensation of brightness may be said to be weak or strong. But how weak, or how strong? Is it possible to measure the strength or magnitude of a sensation, or is sensation too personal and too intimately an affair of the mind to be quantified?

Most scientists who addressed that question decided that no direct measurement could be made of a subjective magnitude. A few scientists conceded that some kind of indirect measurement might prove possible, but the possibility of any direct kind of measurement was ruled out as patently absurd. As it turned out, however, a simple and direct kind of measurement was later invented and put to interesting uses. Yet for almost a century psychophysics tried to solve its central problem—the measurement of sensation—by indirect methods, methods that inspired great ingenuity but that proved inadequate to the task.

The development of the direct methods has changed many things. It has made possible the quantification not only of sensory magnitudes, but also of other interesting matters concerned with human judgments. Opinions about the prestige of different occupations and the seriousness of different crimes provide two examples of the kinds of subjective opinions that have been scaled by the direct methods of psychophysical measurement. The direct quantification of the social consensus has inaugurated serious explorations in what we might call social psychophysics.

More important to psychophysics itself, the new direct methods resolved a conflict that had flared off and on for more than two centuries. The issue concerns the form of the psychophysical law, the equation that tells how the strength of the external stimulus determines your impression of subjective intensity. The two contending laws are known as the logarithmic law and the power law.

Curiously enough, the two conflicting laws made their first appearance in connection with a friendly game of chance. More than two centuries ago a paradox in a gambling game led to one of the first conjectures about the law that governs the subjective value of stimuli. If we regard money as a stimulus and the subjective value attached to its ownership as a response, then the problem becomes a stimulus-response relation. How does subjective value grow when the number of dollars is increased? What is the mathematical form of the law? That is the basic question, but first let us turn to the gambling problem.

TWO LAWS OF UTILITY

Imagine for a moment that we decide to play an old and famous game named after St. Petersburg. You are to flip a coin as often as necessary until it comes up heads. If it comes up tails only once, you pay me a penny. If it falls tails twice, you pay me 2 pennies, if three times, you pay 4 pennies, and so on—doubling your payment for each appearance of tails. Now, in order for me to persuade you to play the St. Petersburg game, you would want me to pay you something. How much? For what stake would you be willing to play? Ten pennies? Twenty pennies? Many people have been willing to take the risk of playing the game for amounts such as those.

But if the coin came up tails time after time, as indeed it might, the payment you owed me would double each time. If it came up tails eleven times in succession, you would owe me 1024 pennies, and if the coin continued to come up tails your debt could reach an enormous amount. Therein lies the paradox. Why would anyone risk a potentially enormous loss for a relatively small gain?

In the year 1728 a 24-year-old mathematician named Gabriel Cramer puzzled over the paradox and hit on a possible solution. Let us suppose, he said, that the subjective value of money, what economists now call *utility,* grows less rapidly than the numerical amount of money, the number of pennies or dollars. In particular, let us suppose that the subjective or psychological value grows only as the square root of the number of pennies. A square-root relation would mean, for example, that in order for the satisfaction you felt to double, I would need to give you four times as many pennies. Given such a nonlinear relation between the money stimulus and the mental appreciation of it, we would have, thought Cramer, a possible explanation of the St. Petersburg paradox. Risking 90 pennies, says the square-root relation, is not nine times as bad as risking 10 pennies, it is only three times as bad, for the square root of nine is three.

We know about Cramer's conjecture only because Daniel Bernoulli, another noted mathematician, mentioned the idea in a footnote attached to his famous paper of 1738 in which he proposed his own solution to the paradox. Bernoulli's hypothesis, which he reached quite independently, resembled Cramer's in one important respect. Both men concluded that the subjective value of each penny becomes less as the number of pennies increases. In the jargon of the economist, money exhibits a decreasing marginal utility.

But Bernoulli chose a logarithmic function to represent the decreasing marginal utility, whereas Cramer had chosen a power function with an exponent of one-half, which is the square root. In Fig. 1 we see a graph of the

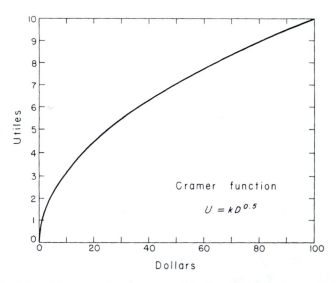

Fig. 1. The form of the power function proposed by Cramer in 1728 to express the relation between subjective value (utility in utiles) and amount of money. The exponent is 0.5, which means that the function expresses a simple square-root function. In other words, the subjective value grows as the square root of the number of dollars, so that it takes a fourfold increase in dollars to double the subjective value. (From Stevens 1959a. Reprinted by permission of John Wiley & Sons, Inc.)

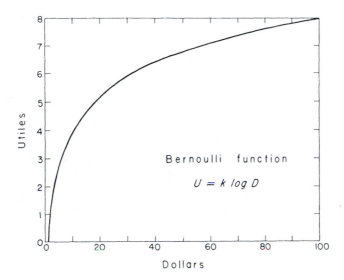

Fig. 2. A logarithmic function of the kind Bernoulli proposed in 1738. It was supposed to express the relation between subjective value in utiles and number of dollars. (After Bernoulli 1738.)

power function that Cramer used to explain the growth of utility (ordinate) as a function of gains in wealth (abscissa). A graph of the logarithmic function proposed by Bernoulli is shown in Fig. 2. Both curves are similar in one important respect. They are both concave downward in a manner consistent with the principle that has appeared so obvious to nearly everyone, namely, that the value of one added dollar seems less when you have a thousand than when you have only two or three. Nevertheless, there are important differences between the two functions, even though both are concave downward.

Bernoulli derived his logarithmic function by first making a simple assumption. The added utility, he said, grows smaller as the number of *dollars* grows larger—a simple inverse relation. Cramer's power function derives from an assumption that is just as simple and perhaps even more plausible. This alternative assumption states that the added utility grows smaller as the total *utility* grows larger. Again a simple inverse relation, but this time it is between the added utility and the total utility, not between the added utility and the total number of dollars.

Which alternative provides the better formulation? Bernoulli's logarithmic function has commanded the greater attention and has exerted the wider influence. "To this day," wrote one commentator, "no other function has been suggested as a better prototype for Everyman's utility function" (Savage 1954). Perhaps that author had overlooked Cramer's power function—easy to overlook—for it was written in Latin and appended as a note to Bernoulli's original article. In any case, Cramer's idea has exerted almost no influence among those who theorize about utility. But experiment, not assumption, can settle such issues, and experiments have suggested that Cramer was the one who diagnosed the matter correctly.

The correctness of Cramer's power function can be demonstrated by experiment. A simple one that I have often carried out with students in a classroom follows a procedure suggested by experiments in sensory psychophysics (Galanter 1962). The student is asked to attempt his own subjective estimate of utility in answer to a proposal like this: "Suppose I were to tell you that I have a special fund for the purpose, and that I am going to give you $10. That would make you happy, would it not? Now think this over carefully: how much would I have to give you to make you twice as happy?"

The results of such experiments support a crucial point. A 2-to-1 change in the anticipated satisfaction, or utility, is typically estimated to require a change in the size of the gift by a factor of about 4. In other words, it requires about $40 to double the utility of $10, which is what Cramer's conjecture predicts. Classes of students have given factors ranging from about 3.5 to 5 (Galanter 1962). Those are average or median values, of course, for people do not always agree with one another in their estimates. But the interesting point is that by a procedure of direct estimation, a group of people give median estimates of "value" that grow approximately as the square root of the number of dollars. The students in those experiments have confirmed Cramer's conjecture of 1728—the one illustrated graphically in Fig. 1.

Let us turn now to the indirect psychophysical procedures invented in the 1850's. There we encounter the second round in the contest between the logarithmic law and the power law.

PLATEAU'S PARTITION SCALE

In a field very different from games of chance, that of visual perception, the blind Belgian physicist J. A. F. Plateau undertook to determine how the subjective lightness of a surface changes with stimulus intensity (the reflectance of the surface). We have no evidence that Plateau knew about Cramer's conjecture, or that he conceived his perceptual problem to be in any way similar. Whatever the circumstances, we know that Plateau went beyond mere conjecture and conducted an experiment. The clear lines of his thought, however, became snagged on a misconception.

Plateau took it for granted that, as he said, "we have no ability to judge directly the ratio of two sensations." Having made that assumption, he found himself looking perforce for an indirect approach. If we cannot judge when one sensation is twice as intense as another, said Plateau, perhaps we can at least judge when the contrast between pairs of reflecting surfaces appears equal. If we could create equal contrast steps of lightness, perhaps we could build up a lightness scale starting from zero. That procedure, he reasoned, would provide an indirect measurement of sensation.

Plateau devised an ingenious procedure. He gave each of eight artists a black and a white and asked each of them to paint a gray that appeared to lie halfway between black and white. Remarkably enough, although each painter worked in his own studio, each presumably under very different illumination, the grays they painted turned out to look very much alike, "presque identiques." From that remarkable fact—the invariance of the bisection point under changing illumination—plus the assumption that the bisection point corresponded to a sensation ratio rather than to a sensation difference, Plateau concluded that apparent lightness grows as a power function of the light intensity given off by the reflecting surface. Actually, since the logarithmic law also predicts an invariant bisection point, Plateau's experimental finding would not preclude a logarithmic law unless more was known. Of course, Plateau may have known more. He may also have measured the actual reflectance of the paintings.

In any case, Plateau knew that more experiments were needed to determine additional contrast steps between black and white, so he asked his friend Delboeuf to carry on the study by mixing black and white to produce shades of gray on rotating color wheels. In a long and tedious effort, Delboeuf (1873) produced a series of intervals or partitions—equal-appearing contrast steps—but his partition scale seemed to accord better with a logarithmic law than with the power law that Plateau had proposed. Plateau therefore decided that his conclusion must have been defective, and he renounced the power law. A sad reverse for psychophysics!

That capitulation on Plateau's part left the field to the logarithmic law that had been conceived a few years earlier by another physicist. As he lay abed on the morning of October 22, 1850, G. T. Fechner was wondering how to connect the inner world of sensation with the outer world of stimuli. There must be some lawful relation, he thought, and the possibility occurred to him that each time the stimulus is doubled there is added a constant increment to the sensation. A relation of that kind would agree with a logarithmic law, as we see graphically in Fig. 3.

After Plateau abandoned the power law, psychophysics found itself saddled with the logarithmic function for almost a century. A few dissenters protested from time to time, and a few sporadic attempts were made to establish one or another different form of the psychophysical function. There

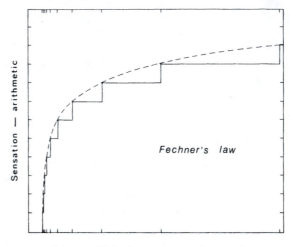

Fig. 3. Fechner's law is a logarithmic function. When the stimulus increases geometrically (for example, by doubling at each step), the sensation, according to Fechner, increases arithmetically (in steps of constant size). The dashed line connecting the steps shows a logarithmic function similar to that shown in Fig. 2.

was no thread of continuity in those efforts, however, and each worker seemed often to ignore the work of his predecessors. The early advocates of alternative psychophysical laws produced argument and speculation, but they did few experiments.

Fechner, meanwhile, through careful experiments and ingenious arguments, had convinced himself of the truth of his early morning inspiration. The logarithmic form of the psychophysical law seemed to him so secure that in 1877 he defied his critics with these words:

> The tower of Babel was never finished because the workers could not reach an understanding on how they should build it; my psychophysical edifice will stand because the workers will never agree on how to tear it down.

Fechner was right in a way. His "edifice" was never torn down; it was, as we shall see, merely abandoned in favor of a more serviceable structure.

FECHNER'S JND SCALE

Like Plateau, Fechner stated quite frankly that he saw no way to measure sensation directly. We can, Fechner acknowledged, say that this pain is stronger than that pain, or that this light is brighter than that light. But mere comparison is not enough. "A real measure of sensation," Fechner said, "would demand that we be able to call a given sensation twice, thrice, or so-and-so many times as intense as another—but who would say such a thing?" (Fechner 1860).

So what did Fechner do? If he could create units of sensation, he decided, he could count them up. If the units were all of equal size, then by counting the units he could measure sensation. It was as simple as that.

Fechner's attention had been called to the work of E. H. Weber, who in 1834 proposed what we now call Weber's law. He, and others before him, had noted that in order for a change in a stimulus to become just noticeable, a fixed percentage must be added. In other words, what it takes to make a perceived difference is a relative matter. To a small stimulus only a small amount need be added. To a large stimulus a large amount must be added. Thus Weber's law says that the just noticeable difference (JND) grows larger in direct proportion to the size of the stimulus.

Fechner accepted Weber's law and added a new feature. He proposed that each time a JND is added to the stimulus the sensation increases by a jump of a constant size. There, in equal sensation increments, he thought he had found the equal units needed to measure sensation. The combination of Weber's law and Fechner's assumption led directly to a logarithmic law for the growth of sensation.

To see what Fechner's scale of sensation would be like for loudness, for example, we may think of the scale as a ladder. Now let us imagine an experiment. Suppose I turn on a very faint sound, so faint that you cannot hear it. I increase its intensity until it stands just at your absolute threshold, where you can barely hear it. That gives us the first step on the ladder. I now increase the intensity until you say yes, that is louder—louder by a JND, which gives us the next step on the ladder. From there I increase the intensity again until it produces another JND, making another step up the ladder. In that way we can proceed step by step until we reach the loudness whose value we want to measure. What is that value? It is, according to Fechner, the number of steps up the ladder. Thus the procedure of counting the steps is conceptually very neat indeed, however messy it might prove to be in actual practice. But what about the size of the steps? There is little profit in trying to count the steps on the ladder if they are not equal in subjective size. For Fechner all the steps were subjectively equal by assumption, indeed by fiat.

Thus it was that Fechner proposed to measure sensation by way of indirect experiments—a kind of assault from the rear. Instead of asking a person to make a direct estimation of the relative magnitudes of his sensations, Fechner conducted scores of discrimination tests in which he measured the JND. That key concept, the JND, appears innocent enough if all we want to know is a person's ability to tell one stimulus from another. But the JND becomes loaded with potential deception when it is regarded as something more than a measure of sensitivity. Why? Because when we undertake to measure a JND, we in fact measure the confusions of the subject as he tries to cope with small stimulus differences. The JND is a poikilitic measure, a name given it because it is a measure of variability or "noise"—those nasty perturbations that set limits on our sensory resolving power.

Fechner, believing that he had devised a unit of the subjective scale, proceeded to measure the JND at various places along the scale and then to count up the number of just noticeable steps. In that way he thought he could measure the total subjective magnitude. Confusion and variability in the judgment of small differences thus became Fechner's unit of measurement. The notion of using confusions as a unit has seemed fanciful to some scientists, but many have taken it seriously. L. L. Thurstone based his well-known measurement of attitudes on what he termed Fechner's "logic." Thurstone improved the mathematical machinery but left intact the assumption that out of variability and confusion we can forge the units of measurement.

The decision to transform a measure of variability into a unit of measurement marked the beginning of quantification in psychophysics, but its sequel was mainly an orgy of methodology, in the proper sense of the word methodology—which means the study of method. What came to be called the classical psychophysical methods consisted of three different variations on a procedure for measuring the JND. William James made the forthright judgment that "Fechner's book was the starting point for a new departure in literature, which it would perhaps be impossible to match for the qualities of thoroughness and subtlety, but of which, in the humble opinion of the present writer, the proper psychological outcome is just *nothing*" (James 1890, I, p. 534).

Fechner had his defenders, however, and his form of the psychophysical law became the standard version expounded in nearly all the textbooks. And October 22nd is celebrated by psychophysicists as Fechner Day.

CATEGORY SCALE OF STELLAR MAGNITUDE

In the polemic battles waged to support his logarithmic law, Fechner cited not only the failure of Plateau's partition scale to sustain a power law, but also the verdict of a partition procedure that goes back more than 2000 years. From time immemorial men have watched with fascination the stars and the wandering planets, and it is little wonder that the night skies over ancient Greece inspired thought and scientific study. In about 150 B.C. the astronomer Hipparchus invented a quantitative scale to keep track of stellar magnitude—the brightness of the stars. To the star that appeared the brightest he assigned the first magnitude. To those ranking lower in brightness he assigned the second, third, and so on, down to the sixth magnitude. The sixth magnitude was the faintest he could see. In other words, Hipparchus devised a six-point category scale with which he subdivided or partitioned the star brightnesses into equal-appearing steps. He then assigned each star to its appropriate step or category.

That procedure of visual estimation was used by astronomers for many centuries, until at last photometers were invented to measure the actual amount of light coming from a given star. The astronomers then found that the old visual category scale was related to the starlight intensity by a function that was approximately logarithmic, as shown in Fig. 4. Fechner, of course, was delighted. We now know, however, that the category scale is not a scale of sensory magnitude. Rather, it belongs to a class called partition scales, and its form is not logarithmic as Fechner thought.

The astronomers, for their part, stopped using the visual procedure of category estimation in favor of objective photometry, but they kept the upside-down scale of Hipparchus. To this day the astronomers continue to measure light output in "stellar magnitudes," but the astronomer's scale has been adjusted to conform exactly to a logarithmic function. The difference from step to step on the logarithmic scale of stellar magnitude is now defined as 4 decibels (or four-tenths of a logarithmic unit).

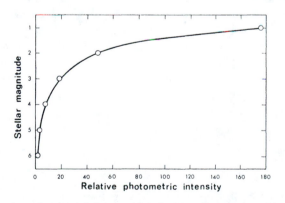

Fig. 4. Showing how the visual judgment of stellar magnitude varies with the photometric intensity of the starlight. The curve is based on about 20,000 observations on the part of many early astronomers. The curvature of this category scale is approximately logarithmic. Because there are hundreds of times more faint stars than bright ones, the category scale of stellar magnitude is much more curved than the category scale obtained with uniformly distributed stimuli. (Data from Jastrow 1887.)

If Fechner's confidence in the scale invented by Hipparchus was in fact misplaced, what went wrong? Hipparchus used a procedure that gave him a workable scale for astronomical observation, but the game was spoiled for sensation measurement. By basing his scale on a judgment of subdivisions or apparent differences instead of a judgment of ratios, he gave us a partition scale instead of a magnitude scale. A true magnitude scale would enable us to tell how many times brighter one star appears than another. The partition scale cannot answer questions about ratios. But before we pursue that problem further, let us look more carefully at what we mean by a sensory continuum, and at the two classes into which sensory continua divide.

METATHETIC VERSUS PROTHETIC

Everyone agrees that sensations come in so many and such varied forms as to elude complete description. No formula can capture all the richness of the daily sights and sounds and tastes and smells and feelings to which our sense organs admit us. Nevertheless, once we make a few basic distinctions, there emerge some simple principles that relate specific aspects of sensation to certain properties of stimulus forces. A chief distinction is the one between quantity and quality, or magnitude and kind, or size and sort. No pair of common words quite fits the distinction; but what it means concretely is that sweet is different from sour, although both may vary from strong to weak.

It is only fair to point out that psychophysics, the science of sensation, has little to say as yet about qualitative variations among sensations. The qualities of the sensory world confront us with a succession of baffling and discontinuous leaps as we go from one sense modality to another—and no one quite knows why. The various colors, tastes, smells, and pressures seem not to lie on a continuum, but to exist in more-or-less complete independence of one another. Sometimes a crude ordering among them seems possible, but for the most part the sensory qualities are just what they are, and the best we can do is to name them.

More attractive opportunities present themselves for those aspects of sensation that appear to lie on a continuum of some sort. There we can order sensations on a scale from faint to intense, or on some other dimension, and for numerous continua we can devise a form of measurement that is stronger than mere ordering. It would, of course, simplify our problem if a common set of rules governed all perceptual continua, but that turns out not to be the case. At least one basic distinction must be made between two kinds of continua.

The prototypes of the two kinds of perceptual continua are exemplified by loudness and pitch. Loudness is an aspect of sound that has what can best be described as degrees of magnitude or quantity. Pitch does not. Pitch varies from high to low; it has a kind of position, and in a sense it is a qualitative continuum. Loudness may be called a *prothetic* continuum, and pitch a *metathetic* one. The criteria that define those two classes of continua reside wholly in how they behave in psychophysical experiments, but the names themselves were suggested to me by the nature of the physiological processes that appear to underlie some of the sensory continua.

Sensory discrimination may be mediated by one or the other of two processes: the one additive, the other substitutive. Additional excitation may be added to an excitation already present, or new excitation may be substituted for excitation that has been removed. An observer can tell, for example, when a light pressure on the arm becomes a stronger pressure, and he can also tell when the stimulus is moved from one location to another, say, from his wrist to his elbow. Different sets of general laws govern those two types of sensory reaction—the "more than" and the "different from."

The metathetic, positional, qualitative continua seem to concern *what* and *where,* as opposed to *how much.* They include such things as pitch, apparent position, apparent inclination, and apparent proportion. They were once thought to include visual saturation and visual hue, but experiments now suggest otherwise (Indow and Stevens 1966). All in all, the metathetic continua seem to comprise a smaller and less orderly class of perceptual variables than the prothetic continua.

THE PSYCHOPHYSICAL POWER LAW

The prothetic continua have yielded gratifying rewards for the efforts that have been made to scale their magnitudes. In the years since 1953 more than three dozen continua have been examined, always with the same outcome: the sensation magnitude ψ grows as a power function of the stimulus magnitude ϕ. In terms of a formula, we may write

$$\psi = k\phi^\beta$$

The constant k depends on the units of measurement and is not very interesting; but the value of the exponent β serves as a kind of signature that may differ from one sensory continuum to another. As a matter of fact, one of the important features of a sensory continuum lies in the value of its exponent.

So rarely does it happen in behavioral studies that a simple quantitative law can be shown to hold under many diverse circumstances that the widespread application of the power law has become a matter of considerable interest. By 1953 I had managed to show that a power law governs our reactions to both light and sound, but since that time experiments in the Harvard Laboratory of Psychophysics have demonstrated a power law for taste and smell, warmth and cold, vibration and shock—in fact, a power law seems to govern nearly every sensory continuum for which the stimulus magnitude can be varied by known amounts. The universality formerly claimed for Fechner's logarithmic law seems to have fallen to the psychophysical power law.

Table 1 lists some of the perceptual continua on which the power law has been shown to hold, together with a representative value of the exponent. Of course, no modality can be fully described by a single exponent; the value of the exponent can vary parametrically with certain conditions of stimulation.

The exponent of the power function determines its curvature. If the exponent is exactly 1, the function follows a straight line on ordinary linear graph paper. The output, the reported sensation, then varies directly with the intensity of the stimulus. But when the exponent is greater than 1, the line representing the function is concave upward, ascending on an ever-steepening slope. When the exponent is less than 1, the line curves the other way. The curvature then is downward and the line becomes ever more horizontal.

Those important relations are illustrated in Fig. 5, where we see examples of three perceptual continua, each having a different exponent. Electric current through the fingers produces a sensation that grows more and more rapidly as the current increases, whereas brightness grows less and less rapidly with increasing physical intensity. As we might expect, the apparent length of a line seems to grow very nearly in direct proportion to the physical length. Six inches looks about twice as long as 3 inches—not exactly, perhaps, but fairly closely.

A very nice feature of the power function shows up in the form it assumes when we plot the curve in log-log coordinates (logarithmic scales on both axes). The graph of a power function then becomes a straight line. All the curvature disappears. And as an added bonus, the slope of the straight line becomes a direct measure of the exponent. In terms of logarithms, the power law equation becomes:

$$\log \psi = \beta \log \phi + \log k$$

That formula describes a straight line in log-log coordinates, and the exponent β becomes the slope of the line.

Table 1. Representative exponents of the power functions relating subjective magnitude to stimulus magnitude

Continuum	Measured exponent	Stimulus condition
Loudness	0.67	Sound pressure of 3000-hertz tone
Vibration	0.95	Amplitude of 60 hertz on finger
Vibration	0.6	Amplitude of 250 hertz on finger
Brightness	0.33	5° Target in dark
Brightness	0.5	Point source
Brightness	0.5	Brief flash
Brightness	1.0	Point source briefly flashed
Lightness	1.2	Reflectance of gray papers
Visual length	1.0	Projected line
Visual area	0.7	Projected square
Redness (saturation)	1.7	Red-gray mixture
Taste	1.3	Sucrose
Taste	1.4	Salt
Taste	0.8	Saccharine
Smell	0.6	Heptane
Cold	1.0	Metal contact on arm
Warmth	1.6	Metal contact on arm
Warmth	1.3	Irradiation of skin, small area
Warmth	0.7	Irradiation of skin, large area
Discomfort, cold	1.7	Whole body irradiation
Discomfort, warm	0.7	Whole body irradiation
Thermal pain	1.0	Radiant heat on skin
Tactual roughness	1.5	Rubbing emery cloths
Tactual hardness	0.8	Squeezing rubber
Finger span	1.3	Thickness of blocks
Pressure on palm	1.1	Static force on skin
Muscle force	1.7	Static contractions
Heaviness	1.45	Lifted weights
Viscosity	0.42	Stirring silicone fluids
Electric shock	3.5	Current through fingers
Vocal effort	1.1	Vocal sound pressure
Angular acceleration	1.4	5-Second rotation
Duration	1.1	White noise stimuli

We can see how those features work out if we make a log-log plot of the three functions shown in Fig. 5. We find that the differences in curvature in Fig. 5 become differences in slope in Fig. 6. The high exponent for electric current through the fingers gives a steep slope; the low exponent for visual brightness gives a flat slope. The nearly linear function for apparent length in Fig. 5 becomes a slope that is close to 1.0, or 45 degrees, in the log-log coordinates of Fig. 6.

More important than those graphical conveniences, the power function tells us that there exists a beautifully simple relation between stimulus and sensory response. We can sum it up in seven words. Equal stimulus ratios produce equal subjective ratios. That statement about ratios captures the essence of the psychophysical law. To see what it means in concrete application, consider some examples. It requires approximately an eightfold increase in energy to double the apparent brightness of a light, no matter where we start from in the first place. It requires an increase in current of only about 20 percent to double the apparent intensity of electric current through the fingers, and the value 20 percent remains the required increase all up and down the scale. The general rule is this: on all continua governed by the power law, a constant percentage change in the stimulus produces a constant percentage change in the sensed effect.

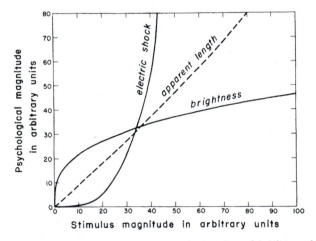

Fig. 5. The apparent magnitudes of electric shock, length, and brightness follow different curves of growth, because their power law exponents are 3.5, 1.1, and 0.33, respectively. Note how the curve is concave upward or downward, depending on whether the exponent is greater or less than 1.0. The power function for apparent length is almost straight in these linear coordinates because its exponent is close to 1.0. The units of the scales have been chosen arbitrarily in order to show the relative form of the curves on a single graph. (From Stevens 1961.)

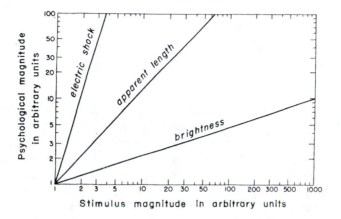

Fig. 6. When the curves in Fig. 5 are plotted against logarithmic coordinates, they become straight lines. The slope of the line corresponds to the exponent of the power function that governs the growth of the sensation. That is because the power function $\psi = \phi^\beta$ can be written as $\log \psi = \beta \log \phi$. Hence in log-log coordinates, β is the slope of the line. (From Stevens 1961. Figures 5 and 6 reprinted by permission.)

It has often been said that if something is scientifically important, it is simple. But nature seems somehow to hide her simplicities from us, for it has also been said that simplicity is the hardest thing of all to achieve. In the power law we seem, after a hundred years of detour, to have achieved a simple rule that enjoys pervasive application. The simplicity of the power law stands on a par with that of the logarithmic law, which the power law displaces. Fechner said of his logarithmic law, "It bears that simple character that we are accustomed to find in fundamental laws of nature" (Fechner 1860, p. 68). Perhaps an equally bold claim can now be made for the power law.

WHY A POWER FUNCTION?

If nature has favored the power function over competing alternatives, some compelling reason must lie behind the choice. I am not sure that our understanding of that profound problem has yet fully ripened, but in thinking about the power law we need to remind ourselves that the power function is a common form throughout all of physics. In fact, most of the laws of physics are power functions. Why is that so? It results, at least in part, from the way the physicist chooses to describe his universe. He finds it convenient to choose a set of primary quantities, usually length, mass, and time, and to develop a scale for each of them. Each scale is made to satisfy what is called the ratio requirement, which means simply that measured ratios are independent of the scale units. On the scale of length, for example, if a boy is half as tall as his father when measured in inches, he is also half as tall when measured in centimeters. That ratio requirement seems simple enough, but it has a far-reaching effect. When the primary quantities are combined to form a secondary quantity, such as force, the ratio requirement imposes a particular functional form, a form that decrees that only powers of the primaries can combine. Thus force, which by Newton's law equals mass times acceleration, can be expressed in terms of the three primaries as the multiplication of three terms: length and mass raised to the first power and time raised to the minus second power. The exponents attached to the primary quantities are said to express the dimensions of the secondary quantity, in this case, the dimensions of force.

Our present task, however, is not to pursue an examination of physics but to inquire whether power functions seem plausible in the perceptual domain. Since, in order to survive, we must be able to move about effectively, perception must to a certain degree achieve stable and veridical representations. It must tell us how matters stand out there. But the universe is in constant flux. We move about and other things also move. Day turns into night. Sound sources approach and recede. How can perceptual stability be achieved in the face of the ongoing flux?

We can perhaps formulate a better question by asking what aspect of the universe most needs stability. For example, is it the differences or the proportions and ratios that need to remain constant in perception? Apparently it is the proportions—the ratios. When we walk toward a house, the relative proportions of the house appear to remain constant: the triangular gable looks triangular from almost any distance. A photograph portrays the same picture whether we view it under a bright or a dim light: the ratio between the light and the shaded parts of the photograph seem approximately the same even though the illumination varies. The perceived relations among the sounds of speech remain the same whether the speech is soft or highly amplified. In other words, the perceptual domain operates as though it had its own ratio requirement—not a mathematically rigid requirement, as in physics, but a practical and approximate requirement.

The usefulness of perceptual proportions and relations that remain approximately constant despite wide changes in stimulus levels is immense. Think how life as we know it would be transformed if speech could be understood at only a single level of intensity, or if objects changed their apparent proportions as they receded, or if pictures became unrecognizable when a cloud dimmed the light of the sun.

By making the perceived aspects of stimuli depend on power functions of the stimulus dimensions, nature has contrived an operating mechanism that is compatible with the need for reasonable stability among perceptual relations.

ON THE REWRITING OF HISTORY

Now let us return to the story of how the power law came about. The new psychophysics, it seems, has provided the answer to Fechner's original problem, the stimulus-response relation that he contemplated as he lay abed on October 22, 1850. Whenever a new development manages to solve a problem of long standing, two things usually happen. For one thing, the scientific effort turns with vigor to those new tasks to which researchers can apply the fruits of the new perspective. For another, a backward search begins to find in the historical past those antecedents that may have anticipated or aided the breakthrough. In short, a scientific discovery opens a new future and creates a new past.

We have already seen how Cramer's long-forgotten conjecture about a square-root function for utility has now taken on new interest as perhaps marking the first application of a power function to a subjective response. In other words, the history of science, which had formerly bypassed Cramer's speculation, must now be recast so as to move that event forward into prominence. This is not the place to go deeply into the history of psychophysics, but I should remark that I have counted half a dozen other scholars who in one way or another conjectured a psychophysical power function, but who lacked adequate empirical evidence to sustain the principle. And there is perhaps an even larger number of investigators whose experiments produced evidence for a power function, but who seem to have overlooked the fact.

RATIOS VERSUS DIFFERENCES

The emergence of the power law has required the marriage of two partners: an adequate experimental procedure and an appropriate conceptual schema. Several times in the history of psychophysics we encounter one of those partners without the other. Cramer conjectured an appropriate schema, but he was a mathematician, not an experimenter, and it seems that he produced no empirical evidence. Plateau perceived correctly the role of ratios in a power law schema, but his belief that observers could not judge ratios led him to adopt an inadequate method—the judgment of differences, or contrast steps.

The first investigator to experiment with the judgment of ratios appears to have been Merkel (1888), who asked observers to produce the "doubled stimulus," as he called it—in other words, to produce a 2-to-1 ratio of sensations. Merkel had hit upon an adequate method, and his ingenious apparatus, with which the observer could produce ratios of brightness, was fully equal to the task of revising the Fechner law. Unfortunately, however, Merkel seems to have had no clear conception of how to construct a scale of sensation, and his efforts exerted little influence on psychophysics. In the next century, the scholarly Titchener (1923) made disparaging reference to Merkel and his method of doubling. Titchener said, "We are reminded that he is, by mental constitution, a physicist rather than a psychologist. . . ."

Titchener himself favored the notion that sensation can be measured by allowing the observer to judge differences rather than ratios. The difference method derives from Plateau's experiment with the artists, but Titchener called it the method of equal sense distances. The judgment of differences or distances results in a partition scale of one sort or another. Although the method produces useful results when applied to a metathetic continuum such as pitch, when applied to prothetic continua the method suffers severe limitations.

It was the invention of the telephone, with its attendant development of electrical instruments, that set in motion a revival of Merkel's procedure of ratio production. Merkel had produced a sound intensity by dropping a small metal ball from a given height onto a block of ebony. He controlled the sound intensity by varying the height of the fall—a control that was uncertain at best. The invention of electrical oscillating circuits and telephone receivers injected a new order of precision and convenience into auditory experiments.

Beginning in the 1930's physicists and psychologists utilized the new instruments to elicit ratio judgments of loudness. In a torrent of new experiments two main procedures were used. Pairs of sounds were presented and the observer estimated the ratio of the loudness—a version of the method of ratio estimation (Richardson and Ross 1930). In a more ambitious application of ratio estimation, students in a classroom listened to a sound whose loudness was then decreased in successive steps. For each step the students estimated what percentage of the original loudness remained (Ham and Parkinson 1932).

The method of ratio production was extended to other ratios, so that the observer adjusted the variable sound to appear half as loud as a given standard sound, as well as twice as loud. Ratios other than 2-to-1 were also used (Geiger and Firestone 1933).

The foregoing are representative examples of studies undertaken in the early 1930's. Except for one study, the results based on ratio judgments stood in fairly good agreement. So good, in fact, that the general form of the loudness function seemed to be determined, at least to a fair approximation. The one discrepant study has never been explained, even though some of us later tried to replicate the experiment with the aid of the same type of early equipment (Stevens, Rogers, and Herrnstein 1955). Our results on ratio judgments conformed to those of the majority, leaving us at a loss to know what went wrong with the one maverick study. Nature puts few bounds on the number of ways in which an experiment can go awry.

In the meantime a new procedure had been invented, a procedure based on the fact that a sound seems louder when you listen with both ears than when you listen with only one. Fletcher and his colleagues at the Bell Telephone Laboratories made the assumption that listening with two ears gives twice the loudness. Looking with two eyes does not give twice the brightness, as you can easily verify, but the ears seem to be connected together in a different manner. Fletcher reasoned that if a tone in two ears is made to sound as loud as the same tone in one ear, then he would know what ratio of stimulus intensities corresponds to a 2-to-1 ratio of loudnesses. He also obtained ratio information by way of a similar assumption about two tones in the same ear. Provided the tones are not so close in frequency that they interfere with each other, their loudnesses may be assumed to add (Fletcher and Munson 1933).

Like several other investigators, I tried my hand at putting all the various ratio determinations together in the hope of producing a definitive loudness scale—a scale whose unit I called a sone (Stevens 1936). The loudness scale based on the pooled ratio judgments was not a function that could be described by a simple formula, although in general form it happened to look more like Cramer's square-root function than like Fechner's logarithmic function.

By 1938, nearly a decade of research based on ratio judgments had established one important point. Contrary to the pronouncements of Plateau and Fechner—and of nearly every other scientist who had addressed the question—human observers can judge the ratio of two sensations, and they can do so with fair consistency (Stevens and Davis 1938).

By contrast, when we asked observers to judge differences or intervals, the results presented us with a puzzling discord. We followed a procedure like that used by Plateau. Tones at three levels of intensity followed one another in sequence, and the observer adjusted the level of the middle tone to make it appear equidistant from the top and bottom levels. In other words, the observer bisected the loudness interval between the faintest tone, at 80 decibels, and the strongest tone, at 100 decibels (Newman, Volkmann, and Stevens 1937). The striking feature of the bisections was their consistent disagreement with the bisection points predicted by the loudness scale based on ratio judgments. The actual bisections always fell below the predicted bisections. In terms of sones—the unit of subjective loudness— the lower interval always contained fewer sones than the upper interval.

Why the systematic discrepancy? Why does partitioning not agree with ratioing? As we shall see in Chapter 5, that problem still confronts the psychophysicist. The judgment of differences differs profoundly from the judgment of ratios, but nobody has thus far explained the discrepancy to the satisfaction of everybody else. In the book on hearing that Davis and I published in 1938 I suggested that in the bisection experiment the observer may fail to keep separate two possible attitudes. Under one attitude he tries to set the middle stimulus to half the distance between the top and bottom stimuli. Under the other attitude he tries to set the middle stimulus to produce equal ratios—so that top is to middle as middle is to bottom. In actual practice the observer may compromise between those two attitudes—the setting of equal differences and the setting of equal ratios. A compromise would perhaps explain the bisection results, but, as we shall see in Chapter 5, partitioning can take many forms, and it is not certain that one explanation suffices for all circumstances.

In the meantime it should be noted that partitioning has proved quite successful on metathetic continua. The paradoxical discrepancy between difference judgments and ratio judgments appears to afflict only the prothetic continua.

Should the loudness scale be based on ratios or on differences? Most authors have chosen to base the scale on ratio judgments, but Garner (1954) undertook an extensive study of the bisection method and proceeded to construct a loudness scale that agreed with judgments of equal differences. That scale differs markedly from the sone scale, of course, and the disagreement between the two scales points up the curious discord between judgments of ratios and judgments of differences.

SERENDIPITY

In 1953 I was not yet prepared to accept the idea that ratioing must necessarily disagree with differencing, or, as I prefer to call it, partitioning. Consequently, I undertook a series of experiments to try to replicate Garner's findings. Although I seemed to obtain slightly better agreement between bisection judgments and ratio judgments than Garner had obtained, nothing I tried was able to eliminate the fundamental discrepancy. But more about that in Chapter 5.

I also discovered a curious effect of stimulus order. Where the observer set the bisection point depended on whether he listened to the sounds in ascending order or in descending order. The path followed in an ascending series sounds strikingly different from the path followed in a descending series. There occurs a kind of hysteresis effect. The question then arose whether the same hysteresis effect would occur if the observer bisected the distance between two brightnesses. The same effect did in fact occur with brightness bisections. Moreover, brightness resembled loudness in the way bisection judgments disagreed with ratio judgments.

Even more interesting, however, when I tried the method of ratio production, the ratio productions obtained with brightness resembled the ratio productions obtained with loudness. Could it be that there was a brightness scale having the same form as the loudness scale? If so, what was that form? That question led to a new exploration. I had been asking observers to produce ratios by adjusting one stimulus to make it appear half as strong as a standard stimulus. That fractionation method, as I called it, had become a much used procedure. But its limitation seemed to be that any single halving informed me about only a small segment of the loudness scale or the brightness scale. What I wanted was a method that would tell me the overall form of the scale, from a weak stimulus to a strong one. I expressed that idea to a colleague who objected that he had no loudness scale in his head from which he could read such values directly. That was a novel thought, however, and I persuaded him to explore it with me.

I turned on a very loud tone at 120 decibels, which made my colleague jump, and which we agreed would be called 100. I then turned on various other intensities in irregular order, and for each stimulus he called out a number to specify the loudness. I plotted the numbers directly on a piece of graph paper in order to see immediately what course was being followed by the absolute judgments, as I first called them. The experiment seemed to work so well that I proceeded to enlist other observers. The plots of the magnitude estimations, as I now call them, that were produced by the first half-dozen observers are shown in Fig. 7. Each observer's estimations were plotted on a separate graph, because in that purely exploratory exercise I used different stimuli and explored different tentative hypotheses as I went along. Besides, I had no assurance that it would be proper to average the data from different observers. The general agreement among the responses of the first few observers persuaded me that I had probably hit upon a promising method, and that the potential of the procedure ought to be explored seriously.

Although I continued to study the responses of individual observers and to make plots of the individual responses, I began also to pool the data for a group of observers by computing median values. The arithmetic mean

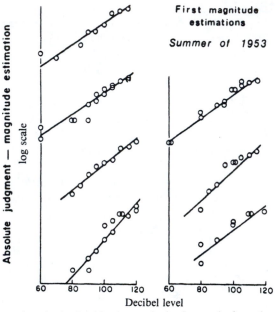

Fig. 7. First results obtained with the method of magnitude estimation. Each point represents a single numerical estimate. The stimulus was a tone at a frequency of 1000 hertz. The different intensities were presented in irregular order after a first intensity, 120 decibels, had been given and designated as the loudness 100.

was clearly not appropriate, because the distributions were skewed. It later became plain, after enough data had been examined, that the geometric mean is the most useful average for magnitude estimation.

Perhaps because each individual observer's data had been studied from the outset, I was quite startled ten years later to find that the power law was under attack because certain observers did not produce strict power functions in an experiment on the judging of lifted weights. Some of the judgments, said the authors, "were found not to follow Stevens' law although averaging over observers does yield a power function. Stevens' power function thus seems to be an artifact of grouping" (Pradhan and Hoffman 1963). An average is indeed an artifact, for it may coincide with no single measurement. When the average family is said to comprise 3.6 persons we do not expect to find parts of children. That number 3.6 is "an artifact of grouping." The scientist averages several measurements whenever he thinks the errors that pull the measurements this way or that can be made to cancel one another. If all observers deviate from a power function in a similar way, averaging their responses does not produce a power function. On the other hand, if the deviations of observers are more random than systematic, then averaging produces a power function. Actually, in several extensive studies the judgments of individual observers have been shown typically to follow the power law. Those judgments that deviate do not appear to do so in a systematic way. Averaging seems, therefore, to be in order (J. C. Stevens and Guirao 1964; Marks and J. C. Stevens 1966; Berglund et al. 1971).

But let us return to 1953. The next question was whether the new procedure of magnitude estimation would work with brightness. I arranged some apparatus that allowed the observer to view a circular milk glass surface mounted in a black screen. The milk glass was illuminated from behind by an ordinary projection lantern so that the observer saw nothing but a luminous circle of light. The intensity (luminance) of the target was controlled by inserting attenuators (neutral filters) in the beam of the lantern. As in the auditory experiment, I first turned on a very strong stimulus and told the observer that it represented the brightness 100. I then turned on a series of different intensities, each for a second or two, in irregular order, and the observer assigned a number to each brightness as he perceived it. The medians of the responses obtained from 18 observers are shown in Fig. 8.

That first brightness experiment, giving median values that fell very close to a straight line in log-log coordinates, forced a turning point in my thinking. It suddenly seemed possible that nature might be trying to say that a simple principle lay behind all the noise and variability of the data

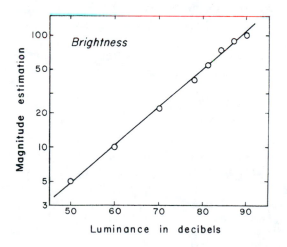

Fig. 8. First application of the method of magnitude estimation to the scaling of brightness. Each point is the median estimation by a group of 18 observers, each of whom judged each stimulus twice in irregular order. The straight line in the log-log coordinates represents a cube-root power function.

and behind the apparent disagreements among different kinds of procedures. Perhaps both brightness and loudness are governed by the same simple power law. That possibility inspired new experiments, and before the year was out I presented a paper before the National Academy of Sciences suggesting that a cube-root law governs the sensory response to light and sound* (Stevens 1953). Research that began as a study of the bisection puzzle ended with the formulation of the power law. Serendipity was in full charge during that summer of 1953.

MAGNITUDE ESTIMATION

As a method, magnitude estimation showed great promise, but it took almost another year of trial and error to find out how best to use the procedure. I soon discovered that the procedure of presenting a standard stimulus at the top of the range, to be called 100, caused unwanted effects. A series of experiments made it plain that if a standard is used, it should be placed near the middle of the range rather than at one end.

In an experiment with the standard placed near the middle of the range and called 10, I obtained the data represented by the circles in Fig. 9. For each judgment the observer pressed one key to hear the standard and another key to hear the variable. I next tried extending the range of the stimuli to be judged. The median results for a 90-decibel stimulus range are shown by the squares in Fig. 9. The top stimulus was 120 decibels, a sound so loud that one observer objected and left the experiment. Note that the median magnitude estimations depicted by the squares extend over a total range of more than 1,000 to 1.

Those two experiments with a standard called 10 and located near the middle of the range produced the most interesting results I had obtained up to that time.

But there remained a serious question: should a standard be used? Or should the observer be left free to choose his own scale unit, or modulus, with no help from the experimenter? To me the need to present a standard stimulus and to designate its value appeared so obvious that I doubt that I would ever have questioned the practice except for an insightful observation

---

* The cube-root law actually governs the sensory response to light and sound when the stimulus is measured in terms of energy flow; when the sound stimulus is measured in terms of sound pressure, however, the exponent for loudness is 0.67, as given in Table 1. To a first approximation, sound energy is related to the square of sound pressure. Thus 10 decibels of energy or 20 decibels of sound pressure equals one log unit. Because there is no simple, direct means of measuring energy flow, most experiments on loudness designate the stimulus intensity as sound pressure level. [Editor's note.]

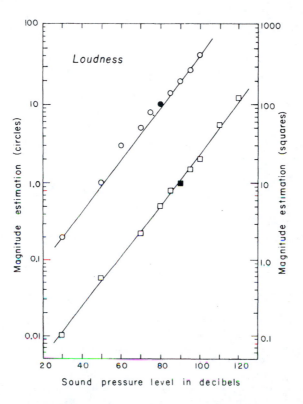

Fig. 9. Magnitude estimations of loudness. A standard called 10 (filled symbol) was set at 80 decibels (upper curve) and at 90 decibels (lower curve). The points are the medians for 2 estimations by each of 18 observers. The straight lines through the points have been drawn with the slope (exponent) two-thirds. With the stimulus expressed in terms of sound energy, the lines would describe a cube-root function.

by my wife—my most faithful observer and collaborator. While typing some prose in which I was exhorting the experimenter to avoid placing any constraints on the observer's use of numbers, she asked me why I constrained the observer into using a particular modulus by calling the standard 10.

That question led to a new experiment in which the instruction was simply to assign numbers to a series of loudnesses. Thus, after a year's effort, the procedure of magnitude estimation had finally been reduced to its simplest possible form. Why is it so hard to discern the simplest way?

The outcome of the "no standard" procedure is shown in Fig. 10. Those data defined the most satisfactory power function for loudness that had yet been produced (Stevens 1956a). Most of the 32 observers seemed

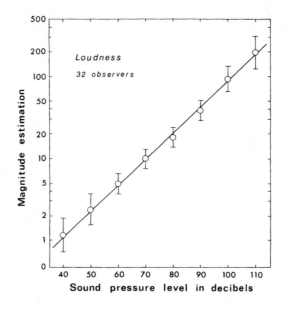

Fig. 10. The loudness function for a tone of 1000 hertz. The straight line in the log-log coordinates has a slope (exponent) equal to 0.64. These data are from the first experiment (in 1954) to utilize the then novel procedure of allowing each subject to choose his own standard or modulus. To the first stimulus presented, the subject assigned whatever number seemed appropriate. The vertical line through each point shows the interquartile range of the 64 judgments, two by each subject. Since each subject used a different modulus, the data were first normalized by equalizing the geometric mean judgment of each subject. (Some of these data were originally published in Stevens 1956a.)

reasonably well pleased with the elimination of the standard. One observer who had previously served in several experiments in which a standard modulus had been prescribed had this to say about the free modulus:

> I felt freer to use numbers over a wide range. I liked the idea that I could just relax and contemplate the tones. When there was a fixed standard I felt more constrained to try to multiply and divide loudnesses, which is hard to do; but with no standard I could just place the tone where it seemed to belong.

That comment expresses the main distinction between the free number matching involved in magnitude estimation and the more constrained multiplying and dividing that is required in the method of ratio estimation.

In trying out the new, unconstrained form of magnitude estimation I gave each of the 32 observers an arbitrary intensity as the first stimulus, and the observer assigned to it whatever number seemed appropriate. It is interesting to see what numbers the observers chose for that first assignment. Figure 11 shows that they did not choose numbers at random, for there was a fairly high correlation between the number chosen and the stimulus presented. The line through the first choices in Fig. 11 represents the cube-root power function. The trend of the points suggests an interesting hypothesis. Given a large enough number of observers, it might prove possible to verify the power law with each observer assigning only one number to one stimulus.

It should be remarked that a large store of accumulated evidence has now demonstrated that the loudness function for the 1000-hertz tone is not a pure power function. The slight departures from the straight line in Fig. 10 are apparently real (Robinson 1957; Stevens 1957a). That and other considerations have led me to propose that, as a reference sound, 1000 hertz should be abandoned in favor of a ⅓-octave band of noise centered at 3150 hertz. At that higher frequency the loudness function agrees more closely with a strict power function (Stevens 1972a).

There is no such thing as a perfect method for measuring anything, sensation included. Magnitude estimation has faults, but it has the great

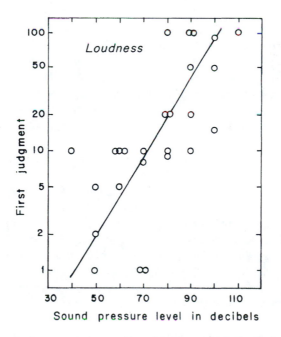

Fig. 11. When each observer was free to choose his own modulus, the choice varied with the intensity of the first tone presented. The first intensities were selected in a haphazard way by the experimenter. The line represents a cube-root function with the exponent one-third.

advantage of convenience. All measurement involves the matching of an aspect of one continuum to an aspect of another continuum. In the method of magnitude estimation the observer brings one of the continua with him as the system of numbers that he has learned and practiced so very thoroughly in memorizing the multiplication table, in counting his change, and in measuring many things. With the number system thoroughly drummed into him, the observer can match numbers from that continuum to items on any other continuum with which he is confronted. The method calls merely for the presentation of a series of stimuli in irregular order, preferably a different order to each observer. The instructions may be modeled on this example:

> You will be presented with a series of stimuli in irregular order. Your task is to tell how intense they seem by assigning numbers to them. Call the first stimulus any number that seems appropriate to you. Then assign successive numbers in such a way that they reflect your subjective impression. There is no limit to the range of numbers that you may use. You may use whole numbers, decimals, or fractions. Try to make each number match the intensity as you perceive it.

Because everyone is not familiar with the process of number matching, it has sometimes proved helpful to initiate the new observer by presenting him with an easy experiment, such as the judgment of the apparent length of lines. The lines, six to ten in number, should cover a wide range of lengths—say, a ratio of about 30 to 1, or more. After judging such lines, presented briefly in irregular order, most people seem to achieve a firm grasp of the knack of assigning numbers to match apparent magnitude. An exercise in judging the apparent size of circles of different areas has also proved a good way to instruct subjects in the principles of magnitude estimation.

How many observers are needed? That depends on how much they disagree. For simple sensory scaling it has been found that groups of 10 observers usually give stable geometric means. Each stimulus intensity is ordinarily presented twice only, because more presentations have been found to give little or no added information. In most such experiments the variability is well behaved. It grows approximately in proportion to the magnitude judged. Note in Fig. 10 that the vertical lines are all of nearly the same length in the logarithmic coordinates. In those coordinates a constant length means a constant percentage variability.

When the magnitude estimations are corrected to a common modulus and are plotted on a logarithmic scale, the distribution of the judgments resembles the bell-shaped normal curve. The log-normal form of the distribution means that averaging can best be done by computing the geometric means of the magnitude estimations. That method of averaging involves the averaging of the logarithms, which has an additional advantage. Despite the different numbers that the different observers may have assigned to the first stimulus, no normalizing is needed prior to averaging. The slope (exponent) of the power function remains unaffected even though each observer uses a different unit or modulus for his subjective scale.

MAGNITUDE PRODUCTION

It is perhaps doubtful whether there exists any procedure of measurement known to science that is fully devoid of systematic error, and magnitude estimation is no exception. Interestingly enough, a principal systematic error in magnitude estimation shows itself best when the procedure is reversed, so that instead of matching numbers to stimuli the observer

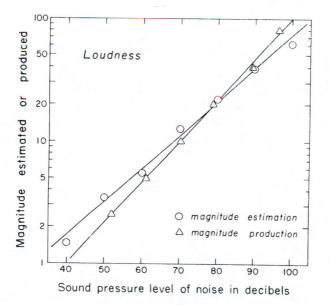

Fig. 12. The matching of numbers to loudness (magnitude estimation) and the matching of loudness to numbers (magnitude production). The stimulus was a band of noise 250 to 2000 hertz wide. Ten observers made matches. Magnitude estimation gave a flatter curve and thus a lower exponent than magnitude production. (From Stevens and Greenbaum 1966. Reprinted by permission.)

matches stimuli to numbers. It is then revealed that the exponent obtained by magnitude estimation falls systematically below its proper value.

In the reversed procedure, called magnitude production, the experimenter may read a series of numbers in irregular order, and for each number the observer adjusts a stimulus to produce a matching sensation. It usually works best if the experimenter uses numbers that are spaced geometrically. For example, each number may be twice as large as the one below it. An appropriate range of numbers may need to be determined by preliminary trials, because the range of producible stimuli is always limited.

A typical pair of experiments that employed both estimation and production gave the results shown in Fig. 12. There we see that magnitude estimation (circles) produced a power function with an exponent (the slope of the line) that falls slightly lower than the slope produced by magnitude production.

A similar effect occurs in all matching experiments—an effect so pervasive that it has often been described and has been called by several different names. I have referred to it as the *regression effect*. One way to think about the regression effect is to regard it as a tendency for the observer to shorten the range of whichever variable he is allowed to adjust. If he controls the numbers, he shortens the range of numbers; if he controls the stimuli, he shortens the range of stimuli. On the average, he seems to regress toward the mean. He errs more often in the direction of the center of the scale than in the direction of the extremes—a kind of centering or conservative tendency that is analyzed more fully in Chapter 9.

The ubiquitous presence of the regression effect has an important implication. It means that any single kind of matching experiment, for example, magnitude estimation, will give an answer that is slightly biased. The exponent of the power function obtained by magnitude estimation falls, on the average, slightly lower than the actual exponent of the continuum. By the same token, the exponent obtained by magnitude production averages slightly too high.

When both estimation and production can be carried out in a balanced experimental design, we obtain two exponents, one too small and the other too large. It seems sensible therefore to average the two exponents. An appropriate average for that purpose is the geometric mean of the two exponents.

On many perceptual continua it turns out that a balanced experiment cannot be arranged, because there is often no way to place the stimulus under the control of the observer. Largely for that reason, the method of magnitude estimation has become the scaling procedure most often used. I can think of no circumstance in which magnitude estimation could not be applied.

CROSS-MODALITY COMPARISON

Early in 1954, soon after I had encountered the great similarity between brightness and loudness, as manifested in their common cube-root relation to stimulus energy, I gave a talk before the Institute of Radio Engineers. In order to portray the brightness-loudness similarity I prepared a common decibel scale for vision and hearing, as shown in Fig. 13. The decibel was invented by transmission engineers in order to provide a unit for measuring gains and losses in the transmission of energy. Since both light and sound involve the flow of energy, the decibel provides a convenient unit with which to describe both visual and auditory stimuli (Stevens 1955a). The decibel is a tenth of a logarithmic unit. It could be called a decilog and sometimes is. A table of decibels and common logarithms is given in Appendix A.

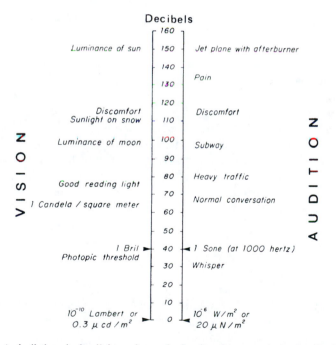

Fig. 13. A decibel scale for light and sound, showing the approximate levels of luminance and of sound intensity produced by various sources, together with a few representative levels. The points indicated by arrows are exact levels fixed by definition. The other levels are approximate only. The reference values at 0 decibel are close to the absolute threshold. The reference for light is expressed in both lamberts and candelas per square meter. The reference for sound is given in terms of both power in watts per square meter and pressure in newtons per square meter.

On a decibel scale we need to choose a starting place—a reference value corresponding to zero decibel. For visual and auditory stimuli it is convenient to choose a reference value that is close to the absolute threshold, or slightly below. In that way the most useful decibel values all become positive and there is no need to deal with negative values.

Since an increase of 60 decibels represents a millionfold change of energy flow, Fig. 13 makes it plain that both the eye and the ear respond to enormous ranges of stimuli. When a stimulus level rises to a value a million million times (120 decibels) higher than the absolute threshold, both the eye and the ear experience discomfort. Comfortable stimulus levels for both vision and hearing lie in the vicinity of 70 decibels. Values such as the comfort level can be given only approximately, because they depend on individual judgment and they also depend on the frequency of the stimulus. On the other hand, values fixed by definition can be stated more precisely. Thus I have proposed to fix the subjective units for the two sensation scales at 40 decibels. A bril and a sone are, respectively, the brightness and loudness experienced by a normal (median) observer when the stimuli (white light and a 1000-hertz tone) are at 40 decibels above reference level.

The impressive similarity shown in Fig. 13 between vision and hearing led me to entertain the notion that some sort of direct comparison ought to be possible. The idea seemed a bit fanciful at first, but why not ask observers to produce a sound that seems as loud as a given light is bright? I suggested to a student, J. C. Stevens (who despite our common name is not related to me), that he might try to incorporate that exercise in his thesis research. The first efforts seemed rather discouraging, however, mainly because the Psycho-Acoustic Laboratory was not yet equipped with the optical apparatus and dark rooms required for such a study. A decade later, though, after we had learned much more about cross-modality matching, an excellent study was completed in which observers matched brightness directly to loudness, and loudness directly to brightness (see Chapter 4).

Cross-modality matching turned out to be so successful a procedure that I gradually arrived at two convictions—tentative, of course, like all scientific convictions: (1) any continuum can be matched to any other continuum; and (2) the procedures that involve number matching—magnitude estimation and magnitude production—are merely special cases of cross-modality matching. In other words, the number continuum serves as just another kind of stimulus continuum.

As I now see it, the direct matching of an apparent magnitude on one continuum to an apparent magnitude on another continuum emerges as the paramount procedure of the new psychophysics. Cross-modality matching provides the foundation for the sensory power law.

SUMMARY

Before going on to examine some of the foregoing topics in greater detail, let me try to summarize what we have learned about the psychophysical law.

The early history of psychophysics recounts a tale of conflict, a tug-of-war effort to resolve an antimony that was brought about by the clash of two competing laws, the logarithmic law and the power law. Both laws can be traced to origins in the speculations of mathematicians regarding the relation between number of dollars and a person's subjective assessment of the value or utility of each added dollar. The dependence of subjective value (utility) on stimulus magnitude (dollars) was conjectured by Cramer (1728) to be a power function with the exponent ½ (square-root relation) and by Bernoulli (1738) to be a logarithmic function.

The conflict entered its first experimental phase in the 1850's when two physicists sought to determine the relation between stimulus intensity and sensation magnitude by means of two different indirect procedures. Plateau asked eight artists to paint a gray that appeared midway between black and white, and from the results of that partitioning exercise he concluded that apparent lightness increases as a power function of the stimulus reflectance. Additional partitionings of the gray scale did not support the power function, however, and Plateau abandoned his hypothesis. Fechner meanwhile had conjectured a logarithmic law for the dependence of sensation on stimulus, and he proposed to demonstrate his law by measuring just noticeable differences and by counting them off as though they could be regarded as equal units of sensory magnitude. Among other bits of evidence for his view, Fechner cited the astronomers' 6-point scale of stellar magnitude, a scale that turned out to be approximately logarithmic.

Sensory continua fall into two classes, metathetic and prothetic. The one concerns position or quality; the other quantity. Most continua belong to the quantitative prothetic class. The evidence shows that partition procedures (such as those of Plateau or Hipparchus), which aim to create a simple interval scale, can achieve a linear scale only on metathetic continua. On metathetic continua the variability tends to be constant when measured in subjective units (e.g., pitch in mels—see Chapter 5). The counting off of JND, as advocated by Fechner, proves a satisfactory scaling procedure on a metathetic but not on a prothetic continuum.

On prothetic continua—those continua concerned with intensity or amount, the variability—and hence the JND, tends to increase in proportion to the magnitude. Consequently, the counting off of prothetic JND leads to a logarithmic function. When partition procedures (including bisection and category scaling) are applied to prothetic continua, there results a biased function, a function that is curved relative to the scale of magnitude determined by ratio scaling procedures.

Scales of perceptual magnitude may be created by asking observers to match numbers to stimuli. Beginning in 1953, it was shown that on prothetic continua the perceived magnitude increases as a power function of the stimulus magnitude. Each modality has its own exponent, although the value of the exponent may change with adaptation, contrast, and other parameters of an experiment. The exponent of the power function determines the curvature of the function. The basic principle that underlies the power law is that equal stimulus ratios produce equal sensation ratios. The emergence of that principle opens a new future for psychophysics and also discloses a new past. The forgotten scholars who conjectured power laws move back into the stream of history.

The method of ratio production inaugurated by Merkel lay long forgotten, but it was reinvented in the 1930's and became a popular method for loudness scaling. Ratios of loudness were also determined by ratio estimation, by one-ear versus two-ear loudness balances, and by the addition of widely spaced tones. The loudness scale based on those several kinds of experiments did not accord convincingly with a power function. The method of magnitude estimation applied to brightness in 1953 produced a convincing power function and led to the formulation of a cube-root law for brightness and eventually for loudness.

When the method of magnitude estimation is complemented by its inverse, the method of magnitude production, a regression effect is disclosed. Each of the two methods is afflicted with an opposite bias, and the use of both methods may permit the cancellation of the bias.

The matching of numbers to stimuli, and vice versa, constitutes a special case of a more general procedure called cross-modality matching. With the development of cross-modality matching, it has become apparent than any continuum can be matched to any other continuum. Cross-modality matching thus becomes the most basic procedure of scaling. Some of its uses are described in Chapter 4.

CHAPTER 2

Sensation
and
Measurement

The early efforts to measure sensation followed indirect routes. Plateau used partitions into equal-appearing contrast steps; Fechner used units of resolving power or just noticeable differences, the JND. The idea that measurement must involve the counting of steps or units still prevailed in the 1850's, and the psychophysicists of that date were looking for something to count.

Psychophysics now makes the assumption that division into countable steps or units is not required, for sensation is analogous to many other scientific constructs to which measurement is commonly applied. Consider temperature, for example. No one expects to slice temperature into units that can be added or subtracted or counted like beans. How then do we determine the temperature of a body? We study the body's behavior. We place the body in contact with other materials or systems and we note what effects the body produces. How cold is the air outside? We place a thermometer outside the window where the air can act upon it. When the temperature of the thermometer itself matches that of the air we read the height of the mercury. Of course, it required many centuries for scientists to disentangle the complexities of temperature measurement in order to reduce it to a relatively simple matching operation. In fact, we have now progressed to the point where ratios as well as differences of temperature can be given operational meaning on the Kelvin scale.

It is much the same with sensation: the magnitude of a person's sensation may be discovered by a systematic study of what he does in a controlled experiment in which he operates on other systems. He may, for instance, adjust the loudness in his ears to match the apparent intensity of various concentrations of salt solution applied to his tongue. In that way his matching behavior can tell us how the growth of loudness compares with that of saltiness. Psychophysics has developed several procedures to carry out such cross-modality matches, as described in Chapter 4.

One of the curiosities of history is the seeming assurance with which so many scholars and scientists have said that sensation cannot be measured. Those who have made that claim comprise a long and distinguished list, including, of course, Fechner and Plateau. Some authors have asserted the impossibility of sensory measurement as though it were a truth too obvious for argument. Others have suggested reasons for their pessimism. The well-known claim of William James is perhaps the most quotable: "Our feeling of pink is surely not a portion of our feeling of scarlet; nor does the light of an electric arc seem to contain that of a tallow candle in itself."

That sentence was written many years ago. The fact that sensations cannot be separated into component parts, or laid end to end like measuring sticks, once stood as a telling argument against the measurability of sensation. But that was before we had come to understand that measurement is not limited to counting. It was in fact before scientists had become fully aware that mathematics and the number system can be regarded as a formal schema, a game of signs and rules, man-made and in a basic sense arbitrary, like the rules of chess. The emancipation of mathematics, its complete decoupling from matters of empirical, earthy fact, was destined to fashion a new outlook on the problem of measurement.

THE BRITISH INQUIRY

The new outlook began to crystallize in the 1940's. It was then that a new theory of measurement was formulated in direct response to the challenge raised by the problem of measuring sensation (Stevens 1946). The challenge had taken explicit form when the British Association for the Advancement of Science appointed a distinguished committee of physicists and psychologists to consider the problem. Appointed in 1932, the committee undertook to assess the possibility of "quantitative estimates of sensory events." In other words, is it possible to measure sensation?

As a concrete example the committee chose to consider the sone scale of apparent loudness, as exemplified in the loudness scale presented by Stevens and Davis (1938). After debating off and on for seven years the committee made its final report, but the members reached no consensus regarding the measurability of sensation. Why not? My own diagnosis of the snags that prevented agreement focuses on the inability of the members to agree on the meaning of the two key terms: measurement and sensation.

During the same period, but quite unaware of the labors of the British committee, I too had been snagged on the same two concepts. There seemed scant prospect that my work in psychophysics would move ahead if the meanings of sensation and measurement remained obscure. Actually, the concept of sensation presented the smaller challenge. But the concept of measurement required an intellectual about-face—a difficult maneuver under the best of circumstances.

Why was measurement such a difficult concept? Do we not all make measurements? Is measuring not an everyday chore for many of us? Indeed it is. But familiarity with daily applications does not guarantee an understanding of the deeper principles involved. As a matter of fact, through the centuries scholars have debated and disagreed over the meaning of measurement. A foremost authority on the subject, N. R. Campbell, who happened also to serve on the British committee mentioned above, pronounced harsh judgment on his fellow physicists. "The most distinguished physicists," he said, "when they attempt logical analysis, are apt to gibber; and more nonsense is talked about measurement than any other part of physics" (Campbell 1938).

ORIGINS

Some of the difficulties can perhaps be sidestepped if we first consider how measurement came into being. In primitive forms, of course, it predated written history. Men practiced measurement for thousands of years before there was any theory of measurement. Practice nearly always precedes theory. Early man solved the practical necessity of measurement and only in later ages did anyone reflect upon the meaning of what he had done. The first necessity was to measure numerosity—to create a procedure for the counting of people and cattle and coconuts.

The fascinating detective work needed to unravel the main features of man's earliest struggles with number and measurement has beckoned many scholars, especially some of the linguists, because the number words have exhibited an amazing stability over the centuries. Through the names of the numbers not only can we trace the affinities of the many world languages, but we can also recreate some of the intellectual struggles that led to gradual growth of the number domain. For a fascinating cultural history of numbers, see Menninger (1969).

Some of the oldest number words bear witness to the stage of development when number concepts consisted merely of one, two, and many. The word three itself in some languages has seemed to carry the sense of "beyond." A transcendent meaning is preserved in the expression "thrice blessed," and in the French *très* (very) which is closely related to *trois* (three). The forms and meanings of the oldest number words suggest that early man made out with very few numbers and added new ones only when a real need arose. Even in the present day, for example, to the Ainu people of Japan anything more than a thousand is "many." Apparently no larger numbers are needed by those people.

The number sequence grew by tentative and slow accretion. It was not created fully formed by a single man of genius; instead it grew from the early distinction, "I—you," which became "one—two," and then painfully on to three. When it got to four it halted, at least in many languages; and four was for a time the limit of counting. The sequence later pressed on to ten, where it seems to have hesitated again for a period before pushing on to a hundred, and then on to a thousand. At the limit of a thousand the number sequence stood still for a long time. Its progress was halted until social and commercial developments imposed further demands.

Thereafter the number sequence ceased to grow on its own, so to speak, as the natural outgrowth of man's practical activities. Instead, man began to perceive the nature of his creation, and so he deliberately drove the number sequence onward, up to a million and a billion, far beyond the reach of the demands of his everyday life. For now the number sequence had evolved into an abstraction, an ingenious intellectual creation worthy of study in its own right, apart from its mundane role in the measurement of numerosity.

In its early forms the number sequence grew by force of the demands imposed by the need to measure numerosity, the numerosity of fish, pigs, paces, moons, enemies, and all the other items that needed counting. Measurement came first. The counting of things made up the primary endeavor, and number words arose as names for degrees of numerosity. The idea of number as a disembodied abstraction, standing apart from the things numbered, cannot be said to have been current at that early stage. Indeed it was a tremendous intellectual feat to create the abstraction "number," as opposed to number of something.

The modern number system, as it is called, became divorced from counting only in very recent times—after centuries of disputation and trial. The mathematician no longer thinks it proper to test his calculations by showing that they agree with what can be done with pebbles or beads or lines drawn in the sand. But the empirical testing of arithmetic was once so much taken for granted that some kinds of numbers were long barred from acceptance. We now take the negative numbers for granted, but they were formerly outlawed, for how could something be less than nothing? And the square root of a negative number. How could there be such a thing? We still call it an imaginary number, even though wonderfully ingenious uses have been found for it in electrical engineering and other endeavors.

NUMERICAL SYMBOLS

Just as social necessity generated number names in an ever-expanding sequence, a parallel necessity forced men to write them down in order to
record inventories and keep the books on commercial transactions. Like
the spoken numbers, the written numerals evolved slowly through many
different forms, differing greatly from one culture to another. Borrowing
has been common. At the present time, we in the West speak a variety of
different tongues; but we write each of those languages with the aid of the
Roman alphabet; and for our numbers we all use the numerical symbols
borrowed from India by way of the Arabs.

There was a time when our ancestors had number words but no
numerals. Many cultures did not bother to invent their own numerals, but
took the easier path of borrowing. Actually the western peoples have borrowed two different numeral systems, the Roman numerals and the Indian,
or so-called Arabic, numerals. The use of the Roman numerals was coextensive with the Roman Empire, and their application in commerce out-
lived the empire by approximately a thousand years. The penetration of the
new Indian numerals into western Europe took place around 1500 A.D. The
penetration was not easy, for it had to overcome a deeply rooted affection
for the Roman numerals, which had served so long in custom and commerce. But the changeover did occur, and with such profound effects that
the date 1500 stands as a pivotal divide in the intellectual history of western
man.

Thereafter trade and commerce expanded rapidly. Money came more
and more to replace barter. The rising merchant class found itself aided by
a powerful tool, for the new Indian system of numerals, with its symbol for
zero, made it possible for the merchant to keep his accounts more easily,
and without cutting notches into tally sticks. Even more important, with
the Indian system he could make his own computations without calling on
a specialist in the art of reckoning. If you wonder why a specialist was
needed for computations, try multiplying two numbers expressed in Roman
numerals, say, XXIX times CVII. Without a zero, the Roman numeral had
no "place value." Instead, value was given by symbol and order. Consequently, computations required extraneous aids, such as the abacus or
the "counting bank," which was a reckoning table ruled with lines and
equipped with "counters" or pebbles.

When we turn our attention to the earliest form of our own numerals,
derived from the Brahmi numerals of India, we find an interesting resemblance to several other kinds of numerals. Like the first three Roman
numerals, I, II, III, the first three Brahmi numerals were __ = ≡. In other
words, they were built on the cardinal principle of providing a number of
strokes equal to the value represented by the numeral. That principle of

cardinality also reveals itself in other numeral systems. We find, for example, that the Egyptian system of numeration used the cardinal principle extensively, representing each of the numbers, one through nine, by the appropriate number of strokes. In that graphic system of numerals, the man measuring the numerosity of the camels in a caravan could put down one stroke for each camel. When he reached ten he made a symbol like an inverted U. For 11 he added a stroke beside the inverted U, and so on. Twenty was indicated by two inverted U's, thirty by three, and thus the principle of cardinality was preserved through the higher numbers.

Now, the cardinal principle reflects man's earliest ·attempts at measurement. What is more important, it illustrates one of the most fundamental operations of measurement, the operation of matching. The ancient Egyptian matched number of strokes to number of camels, and he thereby measured the numerosity of the herd. Or he matched number of strokes to number of paces stepped off from house to river, and thereby measured the distance. On his papyrus he wrote the results of his measurements with the aid of numerals that featured the simple and graphic cardinal property, one stroke for each unit—a one-to-one matching.

With those numerals, cumbersome as they seem to us, the ancients not only recorded their measurements, but they explored what we would now call arithmetic, posing problems and solving them, despite the awkwardness of their notation. The abstract concept of number shows its first hesitant appearance in those mathematical exercises, but many centuries would pass before number would be conceived as an abstraction capable of staying aloft on its own, with no support from the elemental measurements that gave it birth.

What we learn from the fascinating history of numbers is that the elementary and universal need to assess numerosity was the mother of measurement. A primitive matching operation, the matching of item to numeral stroke, seems to have been man's first use of a numerical system to express quantity. In those simple origins we encounter the germ of two important developments, one of them fortunate and liberating, the other constraining and obstructive.

The happy development was the number system itself, perhaps man's greatest abstract creation. The less happy development was the conception that true measurement is possible only when the operations can be shown to mirror the basic operations that can be performed with pebbles. We will return to that problem.

THE NUMBER SYSTEM

The measurement of numerosity gave rise to what we know as the natural numbers, the numbers we use when we count. The term digit refers to a finger and a small natural number. But the natural numbers, as positive whole numbers, continue on past 20 where we run out of fingers and toes. Yet it seems that the numerosity of our fingers determined the base of our system of counting, the decimal system. If we had had no thumbs, the base would presumably have been eight, which would have had many advantages, for eight is a power of two. Mental calculations would be easier on base eight, and in the age of computers (which operate on the base two) numeration on a base that is a simple power of two would aid the fit between man and machine. But anatomy has decreed the base ten.

The first addition to the realm of number was the fractions, what are called the positive rational numbers. The creation of the fractions had its origin in the need to measure not only countable things like pebbles, but "continuous" things like the length of a line or the liquid in a vessel, things that can vary in magnitude. Although the unit fractions date back at least as far as 1700 B.C., the recognition that fractions can serve as fully accredited members of the number domain was slow in coming. In about 300 B.C. Euclid was forming the ratios of two natural numbers, such as ¾, but he seems not to have regarded those ratios as numbers. Why?

That question poses the deeper question, what is a number and what criteria must a new kind of number satisfy in order to be admitted to the number domain? The early mathematicians saw no distinction between the abstraction we now conceive as number and the empirical world whose properties can be reflected by number. The divorce had yet to take place separating the abstract, formal, schematic model, now known as number, from the empirical world of pebbles, fingers, and paces. The ancients had no conception of a syntactics, a discipline devoted to signs and rules having no necessary reference to the empirical world. That conception emerged only in very recent times after many new kinds of numbers had forced their way into use—numbers for which the mathematician could no longer invoke an empirical test to certify their proper behavior.

The negatives were resisted, as we have already noted, because they were regarded as absurd and fictitious. Nothing can be less than nothing. Not until the time of Descartes (about 1600) did the negatives become fully naturalized citizens of the number domain. Somewhat earlier, the irrational numbers had been introduced into Western Europe, numbers like $\sqrt{2}$ that cannot be expressed as the ratio of two integers. And the imaginaries, exemplified by $\sqrt{-1}$—numbers that arose through what seemed a mere "empty play upon symbols"—also became accepted and found use in mathematics.

The point to this abbreviated account, given in more detail elsewhere (Stevens 1951), is to show how the number concept detached itself from the primitive measurement of numerosity and sallied off into the realm of abstraction, abjuring any necessary concern with empirical reality. In the great dichotomy that now divides abstract schematics from concrete empirics, we see how number has found its place on the side of the purely schematic enterprise, a creature and tool of the mathematician. The schematic structure erected through the various extensions of the number domain excites our interest for many reasons. For one thing, we have need for a schematic model to represent the outcome of our empirical measurements.

FUNDAMENTAL MEASUREMENT

If the liberation of the purely mathematical concept of number, resulting in its complete decoupling from any concern with empirical measurement, gave impetus to the development of mathematics, and indirectly of science, a similar benefit did not accrue from the retention of a constrained conception of measurement. The classical conception of measurement proved especially costly to psychophysics. In order to see how the classical conception of measurement could work to impede the progress of some aspects of science, let us first consider the nature of what has been called fundamental measurement.

The central features of fundamental measurement stand out most clearly in the measurement of numerosity—the quantity of countable things like beans. All the principles of so-called additivity are reflected in the manipulations that we can perform on piles of beans. We can determine the equality of two piles. We can double the numerosity by combining the two equal piles. We can show that the order in which the piles are added makes no difference; in fact, we can show that numerosity obeys all the axioms that govern addition in ordinary algebra. We are not surprised at the close correspondence between addition and the manipulation of beans, because it was just such manipulations that gave rise to elementary mathematics in the first place.

So far so good. The number system and the rules of arithmetic are merely serving as a useful model for the concrete manipulations that we can perform with collections of beans. But the next step presents a certain peril. It was initiated by Helmholtz (1887) when he turned the matter around, so to speak, and implied that unless the concrete operations could be mirrored by the mathematical laws of additivity, the operations did not qualify as measurement. In other words, instead of the mathematical model being made to agree with empirical operations, as had happened when arithmetic was in its infancy, the model has come to dictate what kinds of operations qualify as measurement.

It is true that a few other magnitudes represent attributes that are empirically isomorphic with the numerosity of collections of objects. Among such magnitudes are weight and length. If we take proper care we can manipulate weights and lengths in such a way that the axioms of addition can be shown to apply to the manipulations, at least up to a point. The agreement between axioms and manipulations can never be perfect, because axioms are formal, logical statements, whereas length and weight are empirical variables whose measurement is always subject to some degree of error. Thus we can never prove for real weights that two weights, each equal to a given weight, are equal to each other. The concept of transitivity applies exactly in arithmetic, but it applies only approximately when we weigh objects.

What Helmholtz tried to do was to examine the logical foundations of measurement. In that endeavor he was a pioneer destined to lead a succession of scientists who have grappled with the theory of measurement, and who have tied measurement to the axioms of addition. It is interesting that Helmholtz himself was not yet prepared to accept the view that axioms and postulates are merely formal assumptions and therefore essentially arbitrary. Indeed, Helmholtz saw the axioms of arithmetic as being similar to the axioms of geometry, which were, as Helmholtz put it, "to be established or refuted through experience." In that view Helmholtz was mistaken, it seems, for the mathematicians have taken the bold step of changing the axioms of geometry, revealing thereby the exciting possibility of new kinds of geometry. Axioms and postulates, we now understand, are merely the demands we lay down when we formulate a formal system. They are the rules to be obeyed, like the rules of chess. As such, they are a human creation and therefore alterable if we so will.

Those who followed Helmholtz managed to tie measurement even more rigidly to the formal rules of addition, so that fundamental measurement was thought to be impossible unless additive operations could be carried out. One member of the British committee pronounced the extreme view. He said that "any law purporting to express a quantitative relation between sensation intensity and stimulus intensity is not merely false but is in fact meaningless unless and until a meaning can be given to the concept of addition as applied to sensation" (Final report, p. 345). Sensation, it seems, must be cut into pieces that can be added and subtracted, like beans, or combined like weights in a scale pan.

THE NEW GENERALIZATION

Think how different has been the development of mathematics from the development of the concept of measurement. Mathematics discovered more than a century ago that power lay in freedom. Increased richness and power lay in the invention of new kinds of numbers and in the ever wider generalization of rules and principles. The extension of rules and principles into new domains motivates much of the research in modern mathematics.

Quite opposite has been the development of measurement. There the purist has maintained that no wider principle is valid than the principle of addition. In order for measurement to rest secure, he demands that it demonstrate its capacity to mimic the rules of addition as embodied in the postulates of ordinary arithmetic.

The difficulty, of course, is that many things need to be measured whose nature precludes the demonstration of additivity. Not only in psychophysics, but also in much of psychology and the social sciences, there is a need to scale new kinds of variables and to measure the previously unmeasured. Procedures modeled on the counting and adding of beans do not suffice for the measurement of such concepts as the social status accorded a person by reason of the degree of his education. A man's social status resides in the views and opinions of other people. If status is conferred by a consensus judgment, it cannot be measured by so-called additive procedures. But there exist other approaches, provided the concept of measurement can be broadened and generalized to include them.

If we generalize our conception of measurement, perhaps it will gain power, just as mathematics has extended its reach and vitality by ever wider generalizations.

How widely can the concept of measurement be generalized? My own efforts to push outward the bounds defining measurement have brought me through successive stages to the view that measurement occurs whenever an element from one domain is matched, equated, or conjoined to an element of another domain. The matching operation becomes the key. At the heart of measurement is the same kind of operation we encountered when early man created numerals by matching number of strokes to number of camels or other objects. It is the same kind of operation that is involved when a subject is asked, for example, to squeeze a hand dynamometer to signify by the force of his handgrip the apparent intensity of a light shining in his eyes.

Of special importance, however, is the case in which number is one of the elements that is coupled or conjoined to some object, item, or circumstance. When number is involved, we are led directly to the definition of measurement that is often cited: Measurement is the assignment of numbers to objects or events according to rule (Stevens 1946). The rule of assignment can be any consistent rule. The only rule not allowed would be random assignment, for randomness amounts in effect to a nonrule.

Given the generalized conception of measurement, we may next inquire, what special kinds or subclasses of measurement can be created? Viewed in that perspective, we see that so-called fundamental measurement, the type that was modeled on the rules of additivity, amounts only to an important special case. It specifies particular rules in the form of operations that lead to the assignment of numbers to special magnitudes—numerosity, length, weight, and a few others.

MEASUREMENT AS A SCHEMAPIRIC ENTERPRISE

It is helpful, as we have seen, to regard measurement as a two-part endeavor, consisting on the one hand of manipulations and on the other of models. You do something, you perform a sequence of operations, and afterwards you invoke a model or a schema to stand for what you have done. The model used in measurement is usually the system of numbers bequeathed to us by mathematics. The empirical operations may vary enormously, however, depending on what is to be measured. It should be noted, though, that the simple reading of a dial or the use of a calibrated measuring stick is not measurement in the basic sense. Think what you would do if there were no dial and you had to start from scratch to arrange the measurements that could be used to calibrate a dial. How, for example, would you go about it if, like Isaac Newton, you wanted to build and calibrate a thermometer in order to assign numbers to temperature in a useful way? As it happened, Newton did not do too well, at least not as compared to his other triumphs.

We find, then, that in the business of measurement the number system of mathematics can provide the schema; experimental manipulations can provide the facts, the empirics. Properly combined, the empirics and the schema can form a schemapiric union that results in useful measurement.

Our understanding of the profound difference between the empirical manipulations of science and the schematic structure of mathematics took many centuries to develop, mainly because the operations of both measurement and mathematics had seemed at first to be one and the same process. We have seen how the earliest scales of measurement were arrangements for the counting of goods and chattels, friends and enemies. The numbers themselves, with their rules of combination and all the paraphernalia that grew into modern mathematics, originated as a simple model designed to mirror what was done with collections of objects when the purpose was to measure numerosity.

Since arithmetic was invented to serve the purpose of measurement, it is not surprising that the basic arithmetical operations, such as addition, have a form that is similar (isomorphic) to the elementary manipulations by which we count a pile of pebbles. The isomorphism between arithmetic and counting was tight and coherent like the fit of a good glove. The conformity was so precise, in fact, that many centuries passed before anyone suspected that the properties of the schematic model could be abstracted and made into a logical symbolic system that could stand on its own, quite apart from the practical procedures of measurement. Helmholtz, we recall, was not prepared to admit the wholly abstract nature of arithmetic. He argued that we must put the axioms of arithmetic to empirical test. Nevertheless the long-contested divorce was finally decreed, a divorce that divided the formal, schematic aspects of mathematics from the empirical manipulations of the "concrete" disciplines. Thereupon it became clear that the schemapirics of measurement must be separated into two parts—the schematics of mathematics and the empirics of laboratory operations. Mathematics can mirror manipulations, but it no longer legislates their freedom. We now recognize that measurement extends to wherever we can invent systematic rules for pinning numbers on things.

The number system originated by our ancestors becomes a schematic model, to be used in whatever way we please. It is a rich model, as we all know, and one or another aspect of its structure can often be made to portray one or another property of the objects or the events that we try to measure. That is why it is a useful convention to define measurement as the assigning of numbers to objects or events in accordance with a systematic rule. There are different kinds of rules, of course, and so there are different kinds of measurement; but for each kind of measurement there obtains some degree of isomorphism between the two domains, the relations among objects and the relations among numbers.

For the empirical properties of the world, then, numbers may serve as the schematic model. The most important of the schemapiric unions concern four kinds of relations.

1. *Identity*. Numbers may serve as names or labels to identify items or classes.
2. *Order*. Numbers may serve to reflect the rank order of items.
3. *Intervals*. Numbers may serve to reflect differences or distances between items.
4. *Ratios*. Numbers may serve to reflect ratios among items.

Corresponding to each of those four uses of numbers, there is a type of scale—nominal, ordinal, interval, and ratio. The scales are listed in Table 2

Table 2. Scales of measurement. Measurement occurs when we use a schema (usually numbers) to represent empirical operations. The schemapiric outcome is called a scale. The four main scale types are shown below. Each type of scale uses different features of the number system because numbers can express identity, order, difference, or ratio. The key that defines the type of scale lies in the permissible number transformations, that is to say, the ways in which we can alter the numbers and still represent all the empirical information, with no loss. (Adapted from Stevens 1946.)

Scale	Operations we perform	Permissible transformations	Some appropriate statistics	Examples
Nominal	Identify and classify	Substitution of any number for any other number	Number of cases Mode Contingency correlation	Numbering football players Model numbers
Ordinal	Rank order	Any change that preserves order	Median Percentiles Rank-order correlation	Preference lists Hardness of minerals Rank lists
Interval	Find distances or differences	Multiplication by a constant Addition of a constant	Mean Standard deviation Product-moment correlation	Temperature Fahrenheit Temperature Celsius Calendar time Standard scores
Ratio	Find ratios, fractions, or multiples	Multiplication by a constant only	Geometric mean Percent variability	Length, weight, numerosity, duration, and most physical scales Temperature Kelvin Loudness in sones

with definitions and examples. The key to the nature of the different scales lies in a powerful but simple principle: the principle of invariance. After we have carried out a set of manipulations (such as comparisons, matchings, balancings, orderings, etc.), we usually assign a set of numbers to reflect the outcome of the operations. Once the numbers have been assigned we can ask a crucial question: in what ways can we change the numbers without losing any of the empirical information? What transformations of the scale numbers are permissible? In other words, under what transformations does the useful information remain invariant and undisturbed?

As Table 2 shows, each of the four scales has its own group of permissible transformations. For our present purposes, the group of greatest interest is the one that defines the ratio scale, for that is the type of scale most useful to science. On the ratio scale we are allowed only one kind of change. We can multiply by a constant, as we do when we convert inches to centimeters or miles to kilometers. Any more radical change than a uniform stretching or shrinking of the scale by a constant multiplier would distort the picture that the ratio scale serves to portray.

The measurement of sensation on the most interesting type of scale—the ratio scale—would require, therefore, a procedure for assigning numbers to sensations in such a way that any transformation other than multiplication by a constant would cause loss of information. Such a scale would fulfill the criterion of a ratio scale, and with it we could tell how sensory magnitude grows with the stimulus input. The numbers on a ratio scale would allow us to specify, for example, when one sensation is twice as intense as another.

The theory of measurement outlined above was developed in 1940, but I managed to publish it only after World War II. In those days the widely held view that true measurement exists only when the experimenter is able to perform a physical addition was blocking progress in psychophysics. The requirement of empirical addition seemed to some people to preclude the measurement of subjective brightness or loudness. But the fact of the matter was that the measurement of loudness had already been accomplished to at least a fair degree of precision, and a unit for the loudness scale had been proposed (Stevens 1936). The remaining task was to formulate a theory of measurement capable of accommodating the measurements that scientists were actually producing.

In the history of science it has usually happened that men have measured first and developed the theory afterwards. Empirics before schematics. That rule was illustrated by the measurement of loudness, where the early loudness scale had become a scientific reality before a measurement theory had been generated capable of designating what kind of scale it was. The theoretician concerned only with schematics often finds work on a kind of clean-up squad whose duty it is to provide neat and tidy models to typify and organize the empirical research that has gone before.

In psychophysics the actual empirical measurement of sensation has advanced so rapidly that it has left many of the schematizers and model makers behind. But that, no doubt, is only a temporary state, and we may look forward to the time when the theorists will have adjusted their formal schemas to square with what goes on in the laboratory when the human subject serves as a matching comparator.

SENSATION AS CONSTRUCT

Since each of us can testify that sound may rise or fall in loudness and that lights may grow dim or bright, the problem of mapping the path along which sensation grows or declines ought to prove solvable. Nevertheless, one can scarcely raise the question of measuring sensation without rousing a troop of myths and prejudices that surround the issue of privacy. Ever since the philosopher Descartes tried to distinguish between mind and matter, we have had to contend with the dualistic view that man's higher mental processes constitute a thing apart, inaccessible to science and measurement. Regardless of how successful quantification may prove to be in all the rest of science, in psychophysics it has yet to shake off all suspicion, for there lingers in many of us a feeling, not only that human experience is somehow inscrutable, but also that measurement, because of some flinty rigor, may lacerate the human spirit if we probe too deeply with the aid of scales and numbers.

Actually, however, in the study of sensation there need be no question of violating the privacy of immediate experience (whatever that may mean), because the sensation that science deals with is the type of human reaction that lends itself to public scrutiny. Remember how the blind physicist Plateau measured the sensation of lightness and created a partition scale. Plateau did not need to experience the lightness himself. He worked with the results produced by the eight artists who painted the middle grays. When he needed eyes he asked someone else to look.

What science means by sensation is a construct, a conception built upon the objective operations of stimulation and reaction. We study the responses of organisms, not some nonphysical mental stuff that by definition defies objective test. Especially in the search for general sensory laws does it become obvious that the term "sensation" derives its meaning from behavioral reactions—verbal responses, dial turnings, key pressings, or even the painting of grays. The reactions are those made by organisms under circumstances that cause them to respond to stimuli. That behavioral principle, faithfully adhered to, enables us to make quantitative order out of the actions of our sensory systems when they respond to the stimulus configurations of the environment.

We call sensation a construct because in a very real sense we construct the concept out of the observations we make on behaving organisms. We call the electron a construct for a similar reason—because it is a notion that we put together from observations made in laboratory experiments. We do not see the electron the way we see a tomato. Instead, what we observe are many subtle effects, and when we find effects of just the right kind we decide that something was there—something we call an electron. In an analogous way, when certain effects occur we decide that the subject is experiencing a sensation. The main difference between the constructs of physics and those of psychophysics is that psychophysical constructs pertain to people, called observers or subjects, and are therefore said to be subjective.

SUBJECTIVE VERSUS OBJECTIVE

If we remember that subjective pertains to subjects, in particular, to the response of human observers, we can usually avoid those metaphysical issues that often arise when discourse centers on so-called subjective experience. The distinction between subjective and objective resembles the distinction between stimulus and response. The usefulness of the distinction is confirmed over and over in the laboratory. Thus a subject may be instructed to sit before a table and to lift a weight placed in front of him on the table. If asked to respond to the objective weight stimulus, the subject can emit many different kinds of behavior, verbal and otherwise. Convention dictates that it is the verbal responses that are called subjective, although any other response, such as moving the weight from hand to hand, for example, could with equal propriety take on the label subjective, because the action pertains to the subject. But semantic convention assigns the term subjective mainly to the responses that the subject makes with his vocal cords.

When something is said to be merely subjective, the phrase often carries the pejorative flavor of something suspect or untrustworthy. And indeed subjective responses to stimuli often show great variability. But just as the meteorologist must pursue his study of the shifting clouds in the sky, undeterred by their restless evolutions, so must the psychophysicist study the subjective judgments of people, despite the fact that the judgments sometimes waver. If we want to know about a subject's sensations, we have no choice but to study the subject's so-called subjective reactions, which may or may not be verbal.

Fortunately, some kinds of verbal reactions serve the purpose better than others, especially when the goal is to measure sensation. When the subject lifts the weight, for example, instead of asking him for an open-ended description of its apparent heaviness, we may ask the subject to assign a number to represent the heaviness. In other words, we can employ the method of magnitude estimation. One of the curious misconceptions that hinders the fuller use of numerical judgments is the widespread belief that people must necessarily perform poorly if they try to match numbers to the magnitudes of sensations. As we have seen, though, they perform very well indeed, and with a facility that often astonishes both the subjects and the experimenter.

ILLUSIONS

Because our perceptions of the external world seem remarkably faithful to the state of the reality around us, we often find ourselves shocked or amused by so-called illusions. Mostly they concern visual phenomena. The moon rises large as a tub over the horizon but seems to shrink as it ascends the sky. A stick looks shorter lying horizontal than it does standing vertical. Those and the many visual illusions that fill the textbooks strike us as queer, partly because the illusory effect can be readily verified. But an interesting question arises, is any perception true, or completely veridical? When the placement of a saw cut becomes critically important, should the carpenter trust his eye?

In a very important sense, all perception can be said to be illusion. Perception seldom agrees perfectly with the picture of the world that we obtain when we construct that picture with the aid of rulers, gauges, and meters. The so-called physical operations of measurement tell us that the stimulus is different from what we perceive. But it is usually a question of degree. We find it convenient to proceed on the basis of a practical semantic rule that reserves the word illusion for the more outrageous and obvious discrepancies between what the ruler or the meter says and what perception says.

The other illusions (percepts) find themselves incorporated into the perceived scenery to which we have become adapted, and we cease to call them illusions. When I first tried to walk about with bifocal glasses—an experience that comes to many people around the age of 48—the ground near my feet seemed displaced from its accustomed location, and I once tripped over a curbstone and cut my knee. A few years later, however, the ground resumed its proper place in perception, and it became possible even to ski with bifocal glasses.

MULTIDIMENSIONALITY

All sensations exhibit a multiplicity of aspects, attributes, or dimensions, just as all stimuli are themselves multidimensional. Although some of the attributes of sensation may correspond fairly closely to particular dimensions of the stimulus, nature has not in general decreed an exact correspondence between attribute and stimulus dimension. As a matter of fact, a one-to-one correspondence between sensation attribute and stimulus dimension occurs only rarely, even with very simple stimuli. Certain geometrical features of a stimulus, such as the length of a straight line, may elicit a perception of apparent length that is nicely proportional to the stimulus length. But, of course, any actual line has other dimensions besides length. It has color, slant, thickness, and so on, and those other dimensions may or may not elicit attributes that keep step with changes in the stimulus.

Some geometrical dimensions, such as the size of circles, have been studied intensively, and it has been found that their apparent size does not vary linearly with stimulus size (see, for example, Teghtsoonian 1965). Instead, apparent size increases approximately as the 0.7 power of the area of the stimulus. That power function relation turns out to have an important practical application in mapmaking, where the cartographer must select symbols to represent such things as the population of various cities. Many cartographers have seen that if they doubled the area of the symbol to represent a doubled population, the symbol would look too large. For example, in studies at the Yale Map Laboratory it was found that, in order to look right, a symbol designed to represent a doubled population should have an area not twice as large but only about 1.6 times as large. Of course, the mapmaker is also concerned with other dimensions of symbols, such as color and shape, for every symbol has several dimensions.

If no stimulus is one-dimensional, and if no sensation is limited to a single attribute, it becomes clear that acts of judgment demand some degree of selective abstraction. Attention must focus on one aspect or attribute, to the neglect of the many other aspects that could be attended to. In most psychophysical experiments the subject has the help of instructions designed to direct his attention to a single attribute of a stimulus, or to one or another of the interrelations among a series of stimuli. In some kinds of experiments, though, the subject may be asked merely to state which pair of stimuli is the most similar.

SIMILARITY

The world of perception presents varying degrees of similarity and dissimilarity. An ellipse looks more like a circle than like a triangle. A hiss sounds more like a whistle than like a roar. The ability of observers to make judgments of similarity leads to the use of such judgments to answer interesting scientific questions. Two types of questions have attracted the attention of psychophysicists. One concerns the configurations that form the basis of our similarity judgments. The other concerns the form of the function that governs similarity judgments made along a single perceptual continuum.

The first problem often goes by the name multidimensional scaling. The basic idea can be illustrated with colors. Given a set of differently colored stimuli, we can ask observers to judge degrees of similarity among the colors. One procedure is to present the colors, three at a time, and to ask which pair is the most similar—the method of triads. From judgments of that kind it may be possible by one or another mathematical technique to discover what basic attributes or dimensions underlie the judgments. Thus it has been shown by means of similarity judgments that perceived color has three attributes—hue, saturation, and lightness.

In multidimensional scaling experiments the word "similar" in the instructions is left vague. The observer is not told, similar with respect to what. The investigator usually assumes that the uninstructed observer will utilize all the basic attributes that govern his perception. In the experiment with colors the observer will presumably make use of hue, saturation, and lightness, and, it is hoped, with no bias toward one at the expense of another. Of course, if for some reason the observer decided to judge only in terms of one of the attributes, for example lightness, the purpose of multidimensional scaling would be defeated. By the same token, there remains a certain degree of uncertainty in such experiments regarding the way the observer did in fact weight the several basic attributes.

That type of ambiguity does not arise in the second type of study, the one concerned with similarity along a single perceptual continuum. When pairs of stimuli are presented and the observer is asked to estimate the degree of similarity in terms of a single specified attribute, a rather simple relation emerges. The perceived similarity varies as a power function of the ratio of the two perceived values presented. Here we have another instance of the similarity that emerges when quantities are measured in the proper units, in this case in subjective units.

The principle has been tested with four continua: the pitch of tones, the lightness of gray papers, the heaviness of lifted weights, and the apparent size of circles. In a first series of experiments the subjective magnitude scale for each continuum was determined. Judgments of similarity were then made along each continuum. Not only did the similarity estimations follow a simple power function of the subjective ratios presented but the exponents were all rather similar for the four continua tested. The observed exponents ranged from 0.7 to 0.9 (Künnapas and Künnapas 1971). The similarity of the exponents leads me to entertain the hypothesis that the similarity function may in fact be the same for all continua, provided the magnitudes are expressed in subjective units. There is even a possibility that if the regression bias could be removed from the experiments, the exponent might become 1.0 for all perceptual continua. Judged similarity would then be directly proportional to the ratio of the two subjective values. If future experiments confirm that hypothesis, psychophysics will have acquired one more simplifying invariance.

AUDITORY ATTRIBUTES

Under appropriate circumstances the mathematical procedures of multidimensional scaling may enable the experimenter to discover the attributes of a perceptual domain. Thus far, however, most of the known attributes of sensation have been discovered by the homely and mundane method of careful observation. The sensory scientist has tried to discern how sensations vary with stimulus changes.

In an experiment in 1933 some of my subjects made the kind of careful introspections that have led to the discovery of the subtle ways in which simple sensations can vary. In fact, those subjects made observations that led to the discovery of a previously unsuspected attribute of pure tones. I had asked the subjects to try to make two pure tones, each of a different frequency, sound equally large or voluminous by adjusting the intensity of one of the tones. That had turned out to be a straightforward task, rather easily accomplished. Although the low-frequency tone sounded more voluminous than the higher frequency, when the subjects made the higher frequency more intense, it grew more voluminous. Hence the subjects were able to equate the volume of the two tones by a simple matching procedure.

Because it is often instructive to ask subjects to try to describe what they are doing when they make sensory judgments, I asked the subjects to characterize their experiences in listening to the tones. The descriptions varied greatly, of course, but a recurrent theme in the subjects' introspections suggested that the higher tones are somehow harder, more compact, or denser than the lower tones.

With that cue to go on, another experiment was designed. This time I asked the subjects to try to make two pure tones appear equal in density.

That they did by reducing the higher frequency tone to a less intense level. Density, it seems, is an attribute of tone that increases with frequency and also increases with intensity (Stevens 1934a). Volume is an attribute that decreases with frequency and increases with intensity.

A pure tone has two additional attributes, of course, pitch and loudness. Pitch increases with frequency, and it also varies slightly with intensity. Loudness varies mainly with intensity, but a large change in frequency may produce a large effect on loudness. We find therefore that all four of the tonal attributes depend on both frequency and intensity. Question: are the four attributes related in any simple way?

That question was addressed some three decades later, after I had developed the method of magnitude estimation. A three-part experiment was designed around a set of ten sound stimuli that consisted of narrow bands of noise, each centered at a different intensity. Ten listeners took part in each part of the experiment, and in each part they heard all ten sounds presented twice each, in irregular orders. Except for one key word, the instructions were the same for all three parts of the experiment. The key word, loudness, volume, or density, was inserted into the blank space of the following instruction.

> I am going to present a series of noises. Your task is to judge the————of each noise. The————of the first noise will be called 10. Assign to each of the succeeding noises a number proportional to its apparent————; remember that the————of the first noise was called 10. For example, if the second noise sounds four times as————, call it 40; if half as————call it 5, and so forth.

Since most of the subjects were unfamiliar with the meanings of volume and density, it was explained that the word volume refers to the size of the sound, how large it appears to be, and that density refers to the compactness, concentration, or hardness of the sound.

Depending upon which of the three words appeared in the instructions, three very different sets of magnitude estimations were obtained. The subjects were able to make three different quantitative responses to the same array of elementary stimuli.

Moreover, there emerged a beautifully simple relation among the quantitative responses. A simple formula was found to relate the three sets of numerical estimates. When, for each stimulus, the number assigned under the volume instruction was multiplied by the number assigned under the density instruction, the resulting products turned out to be proportional to the numbers assigned for loudness. In other words, if we make the appropriate choice of units, we can say that loudness is equal to volume times density (Stevens, Guirao, and Slawson 1965).

The attribute pitch does not enter into the simple relation that binds loudness to volume and density. Pitch is a rather different type of attribute, a metathetic variable. Volume and density are prothetic. In fact, both volume and density grow as power functions of the stimulus intensity. For both attributes the exponents have been found to vary with the frequency of the stimulus.

An important principle finds itself exemplified in the research on the auditory attributes. The success of the schemapiric enterprise, in which we try to devise a schema to depict nature in a manner true to her empirical mold, depends critically on the discovery of the appropriate variables. If we try to describe the relations among the auditory attributes in terms of the stimulus variables, frequency and intensity, no simple relations emerge. On the other hand, when we use the subjective or sensation variables, we discover that loudness is simply the product of volume times density. The order and simplicity of nature often remain hidden until the scientist discovers the appropriate variables in which to cast his schemapiric account.

OBJECTIONS TO THE MEASUREMENT OF SENSATION

After experiments have been run—and indeed replicated—in which it has proved possible to measure some of the more subtle aspects of sound perception, it may seem curious that objections should persist regarding the possibility of measuring sensation and its many attributes. Yet objections do persist and polemics are written to condemn the claim that psychological magnitudes can be usefully assessed. One author contends that the proper action would be "to abandon the concept of psychological magnitude, thus abandoning both Stevens' law and Fechner's law, and any other law that is genuinely of the ψ-ϕ form" (Savage 1970, p. 408).

Such polemics concern meanings more than substance, however, and the scientist finds it thin to try to nourish his understanding by the ingestion of semantic disputation. More relevant to our present concern is the puzzle regarding measurement. Among those who have seemed freely to grant that there is indeed a ψ term (sensation) and a ϕ term (stimulus), why have so many insisted that the ψ term lies beyond the reach of measurement? One can only guess at the reasons for the persistent prejudice, but one factor may rest with the view that measurement is possible only if it can be done in imitation of the model provided by numerosity, length, and weight. We have already seen, for example, that both Fechner and Plateau denied that sensation could be measured except by indirect procedures that provided something that could be counted—JNDs for Fechner, contrast steps for Plateau. It seems that the absence of something to count was sufficient for William James to jettison the whole idea of sensation measurement. "The whole notion of measuring sensations numerically remains, in short, a mere mathematical speculation . . ." (James 1890, I, p. 539). But what precisely have others had to say? I have gathered a few examples that illustrate the range of views.

Ernst Mach was a physicist who thought deeply about psychophysical problems. Fechner's psychophysics stimulated him greatly, he tells us, although he came later to reject the logarithmic law. For purposes of description, however, he acknowledged that it may be useful to characterize and catalogue sensations by means of numbers determined psychophysically. Beyond that, according to Mach, we cannot go, "since there can be no question of an actual measurement of the sensations" (Mach 1906, p. 81).

Wilhelm Wundt, the founder of psychology's first important laboratory, conceded, as did most scholars, that we possess the ability to judge when one sensation makes a stronger or a fainter impression than another sensation. But, said Wundt, "How much stronger or weaker one sensation is than another, we are never able to say. Whether the sun is a hundred or a thousand times brighter than the moon, a cannon a hundred or a thousand times louder than a pistol, is beyond our power to estimate" (quoted in James 1890, I, p. 534). Admittedly the pairs of stimuli cited by Wundt do not lend themselves to ready incorporation in a psychophysical experiment; otherwise we could present the stimuli to subjects and ask for a judgment of the apparent ratio. Why did Wundt not try a simple experiment of that sort, the kind he pronounced impossible? After all, Wundt directed a busy and well organized laboratory, a laboratory founded in 1879.

Carl Stumpf, who differed with Wundt on many points, was in seeming agreement with Wundt's view that ratios of sensation have no meaning. "One sensation," he said, "cannot be a multiple of another. If it could," he continued, "we ought to be able to subtract the one from the other, and to feel the remainder by itself" (quoted in James 1890, I, p. 547). The second sentence there has the quality of a non sequitur, but the passage makes it clear that Stumpf would have no dealings with the notion that sensation ratios might be quantified.

E. B. Titchener was equally certain that the judgment of ratios was out of the question. He invited us to imagine two similar rooms, one lighted by five candlepower and the other by only two. "We can say, by eye," said Titchener, "that the illumination of the first room is greater than that of the second. How much greater, we cannot possibly say" (quoted in Herrnstein and Boring 1965, p. 86). That imaginary experiment happens to resemble an actual experiment carried out by one of my students. The total illumination of a room was varied over a range of 1000 to 1, or 30 decibels. At each level of illumination the subject, seated at an ordinary desk with a book in front of him, made a numerical estimate of the apparent brightness. Two groups of 14 observers served in two different experiments, with the results shown in Fig. 14. Contrary to Titchener's assumption, those subjects were able to make ratio judgments of the room illumination. And one group replicated the power function given by the other group.

Parry Moon, the author of a classic volume on illuminating engineering, would presumably have agreed with Titchener about judgments of apparent illumination, for he said, "We have no way of measuring sensation, in the sense that physical quantities are measured. We have no way of setting up a unit of sensation—a sensation meter stick. We have no way of applying this meter stick to determining how many times one sensation is greater than another. Consequently, there is no possibility of expressing sensation mathematically as a function of stimulus . . . Sensation does not reside in the world of physics and thus can never be treated as a physical quantity" (Moon 1961, p. 537).

When an otherwise careful and cautious scientist plunges into assertions regarding what measurements are possible and what are impossible, perhaps we should put it down to the very human tendency to believe that what science has failed to achieve lies somehow beyond its powers. Nevertheless, Moon is but one of many authors who have said that a sensation such as visual brightness cannot be measured.

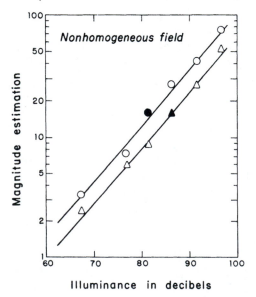

Fig. 14. Brightness functions obtained by varying the illumination falling on a desk top. In two different experiments the observers judged the apparent brightness of the total scene.

PARADIGMS, OLD AND NEW

The sample of citations given above contains only a few of the many that could be assembled to document the same theme. The two concepts, sensation and measurement, have been thought by very many scientists to be forever disjoined. Why? Mainly because sensations cannot be manipulated like beans or measuring sticks, so that sensation measurement cannot satisfy the axioms of additivity. For all but a relatively few scientists the additivity conception has provided the paradigm—the pattern of thought—that has governed actions and attitudes throughout the scientific fraternity. That paradigm has determined not only what men have said about the measurement of sensation, but also, and of a more serious consequence, what kinds of experiments they have been willing to undertake. For nothing stops research more effectively than the belief that a kind of measurement is impossible.

A new paradigm seems now to be pressing forward. The new pattern provides a conception of measurement based on the operation of matching—the operation of equating, coupling, or conjoining. Some operations of matching, for example, when weights are balanced in the two pans of a balance, fit the older paradigm, including its demand for a demonstration of additivity. Numbers are assigned to the weights in accordance with the way the various weights, singly or in combination, match one another on the balance, and the resulting weight scale is a ratio scale. But the new paradigm admits matching operations that do not accord with the additivity model. The fact that a few things in this world can be measured by addition does not prove that everything must be.

As we have seen, subjects can match numbers to sensations in ways that also produce ratio scales. And as we shall see in the next chapter, subjects can match sensations directly to other sensations, thereby performing a matching operation that does not involve numbers or numerical estimation.

If the new pattern of thinking about measurement and about sensation promises more than esoteric amusement for a few psychophysicists, it will need to be demonstrated that the measurement of sensation is good for something. Can the power law be put to use? William James concluded his criticism of Fechner's logarithmic law by asserting that "no human being, in any investigation into which sensations entered, has ever used the numbers computed in this or any other way in order to test a theory or to reach a new result" (James 1890, I, p. 539). That indeed lays down the challenge, and we must face the question, does the psychophysical power law come off any better than the logarithmic law?

In the matching of sensations across modalities, psychophysics has accepted the James challenge: it has produced experiments in which numbers have been used "to test a theory" and "to reach a new result." Before we pursue that development further, though, let us turn to a closely related procedure that has led to important discoveries regarding the sensory systems.

CHAPTER 3

Intramodal Matching

Each of the sense modalities responds to a range of different stimuli, and it is frequently of interest to know how sensitive the system is to diverse kinds of stimulation. We may ask, for example, what amplitude of vibration applied to the fingertip feels as strong as a given vibration applied to the arm? Do all the colors of the rainbow look equally bright? When they are produced with equal intensity, do all the notes of an organ sound equally loud? What concentration of sucrose tastes as sweet as a given concentration of fructose? Those and a host of similar questions compose the queries to which intramodal matching gives answers.

As a tool of measurement intramodal matching has both assets and liabilities. Clearly it makes use of the basic operation of all measurement, the operation of matching, but the restriction of the matches to those within a single sense modality places limits on the usefulness of the outcome. Nevertheless, many scientific questions concerning the behavior of sense organs have been illuminated by intramodal matching, to say nothing about the use of a sense organ as a comparison device—a null instrument, so-called—in the study of other things. For example, some three centuries ago Christiaan Huygens tried to compare the light of the star Sirius to that of the sun. He reduced the sun's light by making it pass through a small hole in a diaphragm at the end of a long tube. That was but one of the many early attempts to measure light, efforts that were also indulged in by the early Greeks. The culmination of centuries of trials manifests itself today in the art and science of photometry.

Two general paradigms characterize most of the systematic efforts made to quantify with the aid of intramodal matching.

1. Some one stimulus is chosen to serve as a standard, and other stimuli are matched to it. Thus we still measure light sources by their

candlepower, referring thereby to a custom that originated long ago when the candle flame was taken as the standard source of light. In acoustics, where measurement can claim far less ancient lineage than in optics, it has been customary to designate a standard sound, usually a pure tone, to serve the role of the candle in optics.

2. Under the second paradigm, the experimenter employs a stimulus to produce a perceived change of some sort and then measures how much of another stimulus variable it takes to undo the perceived change. For example, a patch of light seems to grow dimmer when the surrounding brightness is increased. The experimenter might measure that contrast effect by determining how much light must be added to the patch to restore its original brightness.

In this chapter we shall examine the two modalities, vision and hearing, because they have been studied most thoroughly, and because they illustrate the nature of the central problem common to all the senses—the problem whose solution rests on intramodal matching. Moreover, in both optics and acoustics the determination of the relative sensitivity of the sense organ has proved to be an engineering necessity, an essential step in the development of meaningful measures of light and sound. For obvious reasons it proves desirable to try to measure light the way the eye measures it, so to speak, and to measure sound the way the ear measures it. As a first step we must learn how the sense organs respond to wavelength or frequency.

EQUAL BRIGHTNESS CONTOURS

One way to determine the relative sensitivity of the eye to different wavelengths is to measure, at each different wavelength, the smallest amount of light energy that produces a sensation. By that procedure of measuring the absolute threshold in the dark-adapted eye, it has been found that the visual system exhibits its greatest sensitivity when the light has a wavelength of about 505 nanometers. The absolute threshold then reaches its lowest value—a very low value indeed.

The light level under which most people find it comfortable to read a newspaper lies about a million times higher than the absolute threshold. When the light level is suitable for reading, the eye's greatest sensitivity no longer falls at 505 nanometers. Rather it shifts to about 555 nanometers. In other words, a comparison of light at different wavelengths shows that the wavelengths near 550 nanometers appear the brightest, even though the energy at the different wavelengths is kept constant.

The question can also be turned around to ask, not which wavelength appears the brightest, but which requires the least energy in order to produce a given brightness. When that question has been answered for the range of visible wavelengths, the data can be plotted as an equal brightness contour, also called a luminosity function. A set of brightness contours is shown in Fig. 15. Along a given contour the brightness remains constant, although the hue may change through all the colors of the rainbow. As is shown in Fig. 15, the uppermost contour dips to its lowest point at about 555 nanometers. There the hue appears yellowish green. The dashed line cutting across the contours is meant to show how the eye's maximum sensitivity shifts to a shorter wavelength as the luminance of the scene decreases. At the lower levels the greens and blues become relatively more visible than the yellows and reds.

At levels well above threshold, the mapping of an equal brightness contour requires that different hues be matched for brightness. It is relatively easy to judge when two surfaces are equally bright, provided the eye is not embarrassed by a difference in hue. The art of photometry can boast an ability to measure with considerable accuracy when the problem is to determine the equality of two white surfaces laid side by side. But if one

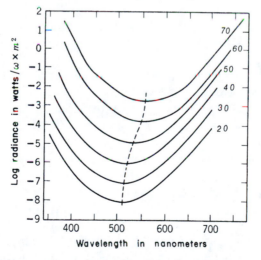

Fig. 15. Equal brightness contours showing how the radiant energy must change when wavelength changes in order to hold brightness constant. The contours are spaced at 10-decibel intervals in adapting luminance. The dotted line passing through the minima of the contours shows how the wavelength to which the eye is most sensitive changes with the luminance to which the observer is adapted (Purkinje effect). Zero on the decibel scale for luminance is 10^{-10} lambert (or π^{-1} microcandela per square meter), which is close to the absolute threshold. (After Judd 1951.)

surface is red and the other green, the two surfaces never look the same, no matter how their relative intensities are varied. Small wonder therefore that heterochromatic photometry, which undertakes to measure the relative brightness of different colors, suffers from many sources of uncertainty. As a matter of fact, the observer's judgments are about five times more variable when a red is matched in apparent brightness to a green than when one white is matched to another white (Walsh 1958).

Despite the great variability, heterochromatic brightness matches become unavoidable if crucial questions about the eye are to be answered. In making such judgments the human observer exhibits a most remarkable ability, i.e., the ability to separate out of a complex configuration one single aspect and to compare that aspect with the same aspect abstracted from another configuration. Thus he separates the brightness of the red from the hue aspect and he matches the brightness of the red to the brightness aspect of the green.

Actually, in all human judgment the observer abstracts or isolates one feature of the situation from those other features that he might have judged if the task had been a different one. There is always a selection process, even in the simplest sensory judgments. For there is no such thing as a one-dimensional stimulus—all stimuli are multidimensional. Thus a simple patch of light presents many aspects, any one of which the observer could be asked to judge or to match to some other stimulus. For example, a patch of light may have brightness, hue, saturation, duration, shape, and location. Each of those aspects has been studied at various times in one or another experiment.

In an experiment designed to determine an equal brightness contour for lights that differ in wavelength, provision may be made for the observer to see two patches or fields of light, each of a different wavelength. The observer may be allowed to control the luminance of one of the two fields so that he can make that field appear brighter or dimmer than the other. The aim, of course, is to make the brightness of the two fields equal, despite their obvious difference in hue. Since that judgment of equality is rather difficult to make, the observer is often instructed to turn up the luminance of one field until it is clearly brighter and then to turn the luminance down until the field is clearly dimmer than the other. In that way the observer is able to bracket the point of equality, which presumably lies somewhere between the value judged brighter and the value judged dimmer. The strategy of approaching the point of equality by bracketing has proved useful in many kinds of experiments.

One goal in heterochromatic photometry is to eliminate the need for that procedure. The visual scientist would like to be able to determine the brightness of any colored light without the necessity of asking observers to match each colored light to some standard stimulus such as a standard candle. In particular, he would like first to measure the physical spectrum of the light, determining thereby the energy (power) at each wavelength, and then by calculation determine what the brightness will appear to be. For that calculation procedure, however, he needs to know how effectively each wavelength produces brightness, which is precisely what the equal brightness contour tells him. So the scientist weights the spectrum of the colored light by values derived from the equal brightness contour and he then adds up the weighted radiant energy. The weighted sum predicts how bright the light will appear.

How well does the prediction work? Well enough, it seems, so that calculated brightness (luminance) has become a widely used measure for the specification of color in business and industry. It has the advantage of being a procedure based upon the visual response of an agreed-upon "standard observer." Whether the eye itself responds as though it were making a weighted energy summation is another question, however. Findings in several experimental studies suggest that equal values of calculated luminance may not, in fact, produce colors that appear equally bright.

An impressive demonstration of the brightness discrepancies was prepared by Chapanis and Halsey (1955). They erected a display board containing 171 differently colored filters, each of them illuminated from behind. It was a spectacular array of colors. The light through each filter could be made more or less intense, as desired, so that all the colors could be adjusted to appear equally bright. After the observers were satisfied that all the colors had been made equally bright, the spectrum of each color was measured, and the luminance was calculated by the standard procedure of summating the weighted energy. Among the equally bright colors the highest calculated luminance was 13 times as high as the lowest, even though in principle they should all have been the same. The standard deviation of the calculated luminances was about 40 per cent of the mean, or about 6 decibels.

The discrepancies were not random, though. Systematic trends were evident. In general, it was found that the more saturated colors tended to look brighter, except for those colors that are located near yellow. At the same calculated luminance, for example, a deep red looks brighter than a pale red (pink), and a deep green looks brighter than a pale or apple green. The experiment demonstrated that, although calculated luminance may serve many practical purposes, when it becomes a question of precisely how the visual system evaluates color, there is no substitute for the method of heterochromatic brightness matching. Calculated luminance gives approximate values only.

EQUAL LOUDNESS CONTOURS

Since the ear, like the eye, responds more readily to some frequencies than to others, we need to determine the form of the equal loudness contours. In hearing we encounter the same kinds of problems that arise in vision. Heterophonic matching, like heterochromatic matching, impresses the observer as a rather difficult exercise, although not an impossible one.

Early experiments concerned the relative sensitivity of the ear to pure tones, and four different investigations produced equal loudness contours based on loudness matches between a tone at one frequency and a tone at another frequency. Two methods of listening have been used, because the tones may be delivered either by a loudspeaker in an echofree anechoic chamber or by earphones worn by the listener. Equal loudness contours for pure tones obtained with earphone listening are shown in Fig. 16.

Since a pure tone is a rare event in the world of sound, scientists have been more interested in complex sounds—the sounds we usually call noise. Noises come in endless variety, but fortunately there exists one noise that is

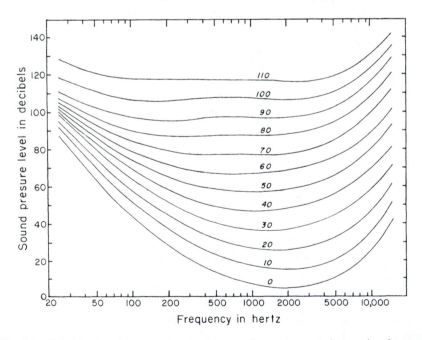

Fig. 16. Equal loudness contours showing how sound pressure must change when frequency changes in order to hold loudness constant. The contours are separated by 10 decibels at 1000 hertz. The zero contour is the curve for minimum audible pressure. The parameter is called loudness level. (After Stevens and Davis 1938.)

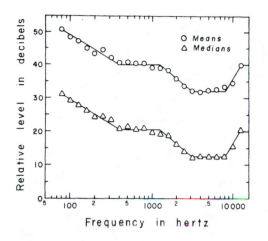

Fig. 17. Composite contours representing equal perceived magnitude for narrow bands of noise of medium loudness. Means and medians were calculated for data from 25 experimental determinations of equal apparent magnitude. The segmented line through each average shows the form of the contour used to fit the individual contours. The data show that the ear is most sensitive to a ⅓ octave band of noise when it is located at 3150 hertz. (From Stevens 1972a, *J. Acoust. Soc. Am.*, 51, 575-601. Reprinted by permission.)

the noisiest of them all—the most impure sound possible. We call it white noise. Whereas the pure tone has all its energy at one frequency, the white noise has equal amounts of energy at all frequencies. Thus a white noise is the antithesis of a pure tone; rather it is a pure noise. White noise sounds something like a sustained sh-h-h-h. By means of filters, white noise, like white light, can be divided into narrow bands. The narrow bands of noise can be used to explore the properties of the ear.

In eleven major studies carried out over a period of 25 years, bands of noise were matched to one another in loudness. Several different procedures were used in the various laboratories. Sometimes the observers were instructed to equate the noise bands for "annoyance," or "noisiness," as well as for loudness. The wording of the instructions appeared to make little difference, however, and the entire set of data, consisting of some 25 equal loudness contours, showed sufficient agreement to justify the taking of some kind of average (Stevens 1972a). Two kinds of average are shown in Fig. 17, where the triangles represent medians and the circles represent means of the decibel values. The points in Fig. 17 are spaced apart by a third of an octave, because ⅓ octave bands of noise were usually the narrowest bands used in any of the experiments.

The averaged data show that the sensitivity of the ear reaches its maximum for the ⅓ octave band of noise centered at a frequency of 3150 hertz. There the sound level required to produce a given loudness falls to its lowest value. Partly for that reason I have suggested that the ⅓ octave band at 3150 hertz could serve as a standard reference band, much as the candle (or the candela, as it is called) serves as a standard reference stimulus in visual science. The perceived level of a given noise, such as that of an airplane, could then be stated in decibels as the sound pressure level at which the reference band at 3150 hertz sounds as loud as the airplane noise. The standard reference band would serve as a yardstick, so to speak.

On the other hand, it is often not convenient, or even possible in some circumstances, to carry out the actual procedure of matching the standard reference band to each noise whose perceived level we would like to measure. Instead, we do what is done in the visual sciences, namely, we measure the physical spectrum. In the case of a noise we may use filters and sound level meters to determine the sound level in each of the ⅓ octave bands, obtaining thereby a ⅓ octave spectrum. If we then followed the procedure used in photometry we would weight each ⅓ octave band by a factor to reflect the ear's sensitivity to each band and then add the weighted bands.

Actually a comparable result can be achieved by adjusting the frequency response of the sound level meter so that it reflects the sensitivity of the ear to the different frequencies of sound. A suitable "ear weighting" for a sound level meter is shown in Fig. 18. That ear weighting curve is essentially the same as the equal loudness contours of Fig. 17 turned upside

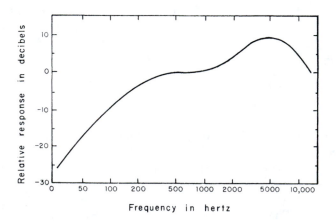

Fig. 18. The equal loudness contour of Fig. 17 has been turned upside down, so to speak, in order to show how a sound level meter should respond in order to mimic the response of the ear. The curve is the response of the electrical network in a meter designed to give an ear-weighted reading in decibels (E) or dB(E). (From Stevens 1972a, *J. Acoust. Soc. Am.*, 51, 575–601. Reprinted by permission.)

down. A meter with that frequency response measures sound more nearly the way the normal listener hears it than does the unweighted meter that responds equally to all frequencies.

Unfortunately loudness, like brightness, does not summate by a simple addition of energy. Neither the eye nor the ear responds precisely as though the task facing the sense organ was first to weight the spectrum by the sensitivity curve and then to add up the adjusted values. Although that simple summation procedure has much practical utility in both optics and acoustics, an effort has been made in acoustics to determine more exactly how the ear does in fact respond to a complex noise.

LOUDNESS SUMMATION

An alternative approach to the summation of weighted stimulus energy (power) is to consider how the auditory system sums sensations. For example, if two bands of energy sound equally loud when heard separately, do they sound twice as loud when presented simultaneously? In other words, do the two sensations add, so that two adjacent bands, each having a loudness of 10 sones, produce a loudness of 20 sones? In a scheme that was once proposed for measuring noise it was assumed that the answer was yes. By a straightforward loudness matching procedure, however, it was demonstrated that two equally loud bands do not sound twice as loud when they are sounded together. When frequency bands lie adjacent to each other they tend to mask or inhibit each other, with the result that two bands together sound much less loud than the sum of their separate loudnesses.

With that fact established, the question arose whether there is some simple rule by which loudnesses do in fact add. A theory based on the mutual inhibition of one band by another predicts that each successive band that is added to a group of equally loud bands brings with it only a fraction, F, of the loudness it would have if it stood alone (Stevens 1956b). Experiments undertaken to verify the theory and to find the value of the fraction F involved an extensive matching exercise. The listeners adjusted the level of a standard noise to make its loudness match the loudness of each of many different bands and combinations of various numbers of bands. The noise bands were mostly octave bands. The results of about 5000 loudness balances confirmed the rule of fractional addition. When the bands are an octave wide, the value of the fraction F is about 0.3. Consequently, if each of a set of octave bands has a loudness of 10 sones, two bands sounded together produce 13 sones. Three such octave bands produce 16 sones, and so on, each newly added band contributing three-tenths of its basic loudness. It has proved possible to make use of that principle of fractional addition in order to construct a procedure for calculating the perceived loudness level of an unknown sound. The calculated loudness level in hearing thus becomes the analogue of calculated luminance in vision, even though the two calculation procedures follow somewhat different rules.

By means of loudness matching procedures the equal loudness contours have been extended to other levels and other frequencies. The composite set of contours covering almost the entire auditory area is shown in Fig. 19. The spectrum is assumed to be divided into ⅓ octave bands. Thus the 1-sone contour shows that the reference band centered at the frequency 3150 hertz has the value 1.0 sones when the band pressure level is 32 decibels above the reference level of 20 micronewtons per square meter (μN/m²). The contours are so spaced that at 3150 hertz the loudness in sones doubles for each increase of 9 decibels in band pressure level. That rate of increase means that loudness increases as a power of the sound pressure, and that the exponent has the value two-thirds.

The contours in Fig. 19 have been extrapolated to very low frequencies. The data available at low frequencies suggest that the contours converge toward a common point located near 1 hertz at about 160 decibels. Actually no loudness matches have been carried out at such a low frequency, but some very remarkable experiments have managed to map the equal loudness contours down to a frequency as low as 3.15 hertz (Whittle, Collins, and Robinson 1972). Special procedures were needed to generate audible sounds at the very low frequencies. The listener was placed inside an airtight cabinet so that the alternating pressure of the sound wave could build up to the required amplitude. In order to reach a moderate loudness level, corresponding to about 70 decibels at 1000 hertz, the sound pressure at 3.15 hertz reaches a level of about 136 decibels.

The segmented form of the contours in Fig. 19 and the convergence to a point at the low-frequency end must both be regarded as graphical conveniences for the purposes of representation rather than as precise descriptions of the ear's performance. The equal loudness contours would probably turn out to be rather smooth if we could determine them with greater exactness. Available evidence suggests that, before they reach a frequency as low as 1 hertz, both the threshold of hearing and the equal loudness contours bend slightly downward, so that they do not in fact perform such a miraculous feat that they all end up at a common point. That, indeed, would be impossible.

The convergence of the equal loudness contours that seems to maintain itself down to the frequency 3.15 hertz was confirmed by the method of magnitude estimation. When the contours are becoming closer, it signifies that the exponent of the power function must be increasing. As would be predicted from the spacing of the equal loudness contours in Fig. 19, the exponent measured by magnitude estimation was found to be about three times as large at 3.15 hertz as at 50 hertz. In other words, the matching of numbers to sounds verified the results of matching sounds to sounds.

When listeners compare two sounds that differ in frequency or character, the task may prove easy or difficult, depending on the sounds. When the spectra of the two sounds do not differ greatly, the variability of the loudness matches made by a group of observers is usually quite small. Ob-

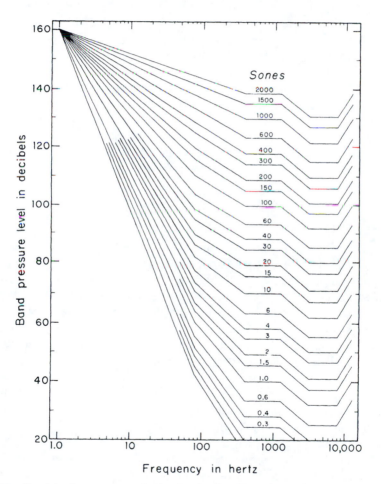

Fig. 19. Equal loudness contours for bands of noise. The contours have been extended to very low frequencies where they seem to converge toward a common point, 1.0 hertz at 160 decibels. Equal loudness measurements have been made at a frequency as low as 3.15 hertz. (After Stevens 1972a.)

servers show less agreement, however, when the sounds differ widely in frequency or in general quality. An instructive example was provided by the many loudness balances made by groups of observers, usually 12 to a group, in the experiments conducted to determine how loudness adds when different numbers of bands are combined. The comparison noise band that the observers adjusted to match the various combinations of other bands had a spectrum extending from 500 to 2000 hertz. When that comparison sound was matched to another spectrum that differed from it only slightly, the judgments of half the observers fell within 0.7 decibel of the average. That quartile deviation rose to 7.0 decibels—ten times as large—when the spectra differed greatly.

One of the most difficult tasks, and hence one that produces variable results, involves the matching of a pure tone to a broad-band noise such as a white noise. Individual listeners may occasionally differ by as much as 30 decibels when they adjust a pure tone to make it appear as loud as a given noise. Curiously enough, the average variability among observers turns out to be slightly smaller when the observers adjust the noise to match the tone. Why the difference? Observers often report that the noise has more definiteness about it, more body as it were. By contrast, a pure tone is a wispy, indefinite stimulus, hard to get hold of. The measured variabilities bear out those descriptions.

VIBRATION

The tips of the fingers are nicely tuned to the sensing of vibration, and numerous experiments have been carried out to relate sensed vibration to the frequency and amplitude of the vibrating stimulus. The first experiment designed to determine how the subjective magnitude of the vibration increases when the amplitude of the vibration is increased was carried out in 1957. As a stimulator I made use of an electromagnetic driving unit to which was attached a 4-inch length of metal rod, $\frac{1}{8}$ inch in diameter. The observer held the rod between the thumb and the fingertips and estimated the apparent intensity of various vibration amplitudes presented in 1-second bursts. The frequency of the vibration was 120 hertz. The geometric means of the magnitude estimations made by a dozen observers are shown by the circles in Fig. 20 (Stevens 1959b).

It later became clear that the exponent of the power function that governs vibration on the fingertips takes on different values for different frequencies of vibration. Thus the triangles and the squares in Fig. 20 show how the slope (exponent) changed when the rod was vibrated at 60 and at 240 hertz. The three slopes are 1.0, 0.81, and 0.62.

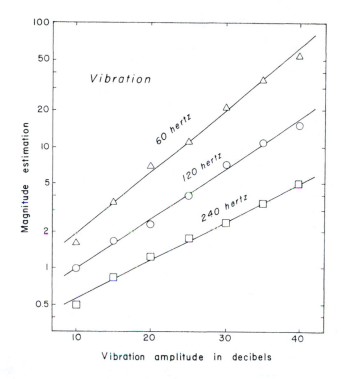

Fig. 20. Magnitude estimation of vibration intensity for three frequencies of vibration. The vibrating stimulus was a thin metal rod, ⅛ inch in diameter, held between the thumb and the fingers. Each point is the geometric mean of two judgments made by each of a group of observers. There were 12 observers for 120 hertz and 14 observers for the other two frequencies. The straight lines in the log-log coordinates indicate power functions. The exponents are 1.0, 0.81, and 0.62. The coordinate scales give relative values only.

Rather similar results are obtained when, instead of holding a vibrating rod, the observer places a fingertip on a small vibrating button. In an extensive series of such experiments, intramodal matches were made between vibrations at several different frequencies (Stevens 1968a). For example, the observer adjusted the amplitude of a 60-hertz vibration to match the apparent intensities of various amplitudes of vibration at other frequencies. The frequencies explored ranged from 15 to 320 hertz. As we should expect, the intramodal matches agreed with the implications of the magnitude estimations. Each intramodal matching function followed a power function, and the relative size of the exponent increased as the frequency decreased.

I have used those intramodal matching functions, together with the results of magnitude estimation, in order to construct a representative set

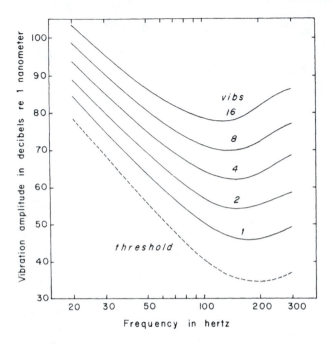

Fig. 21. Equal sensation contours for vibration on the fingertip. The approximate threshold is shown by the dashed line. The spacing of the contours reflects the power law growth of apparent intensity. Each contour is for a constant value of apparent intensity expressed in vibs. A vib is the vibration sensed on the middle finger when the stimulus is a sinusoidal vibration of 60 hertz at an amplitude of 1 micron.

of equal sensation contours for vibration, as shown in Fig. 21. I have called the subjective unit of vibration a *vib* and have defined it as the vibration felt on the tip of the middle finger when the stimulus is a 60-hertz vibration at an amplitude 60 decibels above a nanometer, or 1 micron. The vib value of each contour is indicated in Fig. 21. Note that the contours are close together at the lower frequencies where the exponent is larger, and farther apart at the higher frequencies where the exponent is smaller.

There seems to exist a curious and suggestive similarity between the exponents for vibration and those for the loudness of low-frequency tones. Below about 200 hertz the loudness exponent has approximately the same value as the vibration exponent. In other words, between about 20 and 200 hertz the change in spacing of the contours in Fig. 21 resembles the change in spacing of those in Fig. 19. That similarity leads to an interesting hypothesis. If an observer makes a direct cross-modality match between loudness and vibration at any one of the low frequencies, the matching function should be a power function with the exponent 1.0. An exploratory experiment has verified that prediction for frequencies lying between 60 and 200 hertz. Frequencies lower than 60 hertz have not yet been explored.

The similarity between the perception of vibration on the fingertip and the perception of low-frequency tones in the ear leads directly to the hypothesis that the two kinds of perception may be mediated by similar sensory processes. Over the low frequencies the ear responds to the sound stimulus much as a vibration sensor responds to vibration.

It is well known that the ear responds to low-frequency periodicities— temporal patterns that give rise to a kind of periodicity pitch, sometimes called the residue (Schouten 1970). For example, when a white noise is interrupted by being turned on and off 100 times per second, the listener detects a pitch that corresponds to the pitch of a 100-hertz tone (Miller and Taylor 1948). When the rate of interruption is increased beyond about 200 interruptions per second, however, the pitch quality becomes indistinct, and at higher rates the periodicity pitch becomes so uncertain that the listener is no longer able to adjust a pure tone to match the apparent pitch of the interruptions. The ability of the ear to perceive low-frequency periodicities in a sound signal composed of a broad band of high frequencies demonstrates that the ear, like the fingertip, is sensitive to a repetitive stimulus. Both ear and finger respond to periodicity over only a limited range of frequencies. Some of those general similarities between ear and fingertip remind us that, in its evolutionary and embryological development, the ear was derived from the skin.

ROLE OF INTRAMODAL MATCHING IN MEASUREMENT

One of the features that stands out when we consider the psychophysical import of intramodal matching concerns its role in measurement. If matching can claim to be the fundamental operation of measurement, then the matching of one light to another, or of one sound to another, must yield a form of measurement.

In photometry an orderly system of measurement is achieved by referring all other light stimuli to an arbitrary standard light. In early times the standard was the light from a candle of a particular construction. More recently the reference standard has come to be specified in terms of the light emitted by a black body when it is heated to the freezing temperature of molten platinum. Although the standard light is reproducible as regards both intensity and spectrum, it remains, nevertheless, an arbitrary yardstick for the evaluation of other lights.

Equally arbitrary, of course, is the use of a reference sound in acoustics. In acoustics, however, there was no noise source as available and convenient as a candle flame, so resort was had to pure tones. At different times the reference tone has been located at 700, 800, and 1000 hertz. As noted above, a ⅓ octave band of noise centered at 3150 hertz, where the ear reaches its greatest sensitivity, provides a more useful reference than a pure tone.

Much of the world's commerce, as it relates to light and sound, relies for its quantitative assessments on measures that in effect specify all stimuli in terms of the equivalent value on an arbitrary reference stimulus. Thus the luminance of a patch of light may be stated as the number of candles per square meter that would appear equally bright. Similarly, the perceived loudness level of a sound may be expressed as the sound pressure level in decibels at which the ⅓ octave band at 3150 hertz sounds equally loud. In other words, intramodal matching underlies both the visual and the auditory measures.

The practice of employing arbitrary yardsticks in the measurement of light and sound serves many good purposes, but it leaves unanswered a most basic question. Is the yardstick straight or bent? Otherwise said, do brightness and loudness grow in simple direct proportion to the values on the respective yardsticks, or does some other relation hold? The answer to that question does not lie in procedures based on intramodal matching. If the yardstick is curved—if, for example, 20 candles do not look twice as bright as 10 candles—the curvature implied by the discrepancy cannot be discovered by the procedure of matching one light to another. If the curvature is ever to be discovered and measured, at some stage in the experimental process lights must be matched to something besides other lights. In short, it is necessary to proceed beyond intramodal comparisons and perform some type of cross-modality matching. That requirement may be fulfilled in several ways, such as magnitude estimation, which can be regarded as a cross-modality procedure in which the observer matches numbers to lights that differ in luminance.

The requirement was also fulfilled in another type of experiment in which the observers adjusted the length of a line projected on the wall until it matched the brightness of a series of lights that differed in luminance (Stevens and Guirao 1963). If we assume that, from the observer's point of view, both line length and number represent linear continua, either continuum can serve as a criterion against which to gauge the straightness or curvature of the path along which brightness grows when the number of candles is increased. By both types of matching tests it turns out that brightness grows very nonlinearly, exhibiting in fact the curvature of a cube-root function. There is a similar curvature in the growth of loudness when sound energy is increased, and again the curvature has been confirmed by the cross-modality comparison of sound to both number and line length.

SENSORY INHIBITION

Some of the most dramatic sensory effects of all those we experience are produced by the interaction of two processes, excitation and inhibition. In describing the sensory systems we tend sometimes to stress excitation and to ignore inhibition. But our perception of the world about us would suffer impressive transformation if our sense organs were suddenly to lose their ability to inhibit. The sharp distinctness of a single pure tone would then become a blurred impression, and the black letters of the printed words in this book would lose some of their clarity. Those are but two of the many alterations that would overspread the perceptual domain.

The pure tone would become blurred because a pure tone stimulates a wide region on the basilar membrane. It is like touching your arm with a pillow. The sharp localization of the pure tone emerges from the wide pattern of stimulation because the excitation in the central region of the pattern inhibits the response of the neighboring regions (Békésy 1967a,b).

The print in this book looks black, but not because there is no light coming from the black area to your eye. Actually the black gives off so much light that, if we could remove all the white paper surrounding the black, the black standing by itself would seem to glow as brightly as a neon sign at night. That is because blackness results from inhibition—from the ability of the surrounding white to inhibit the region where the reflectance is less. When one area of the page reflects only about a tenth as much light as the surrounding part, that area tends to look black.

Perhaps a more striking example occurs with a television set (black and white). Before turning it on, note the color of the screen. It is a light gray. Now turn the set on and wait for the cowboy in the white hat to meet the bad man in the black hat. How can there be a black hat on a screen that was light gray to begin with? The electronic process in the television tube can only produce light—it cannot take away light—and the light that it produces is added to the gray of the tube face. There is no black paint to spread. But by adding light to the various parts of the screen, and by adding less light where the black is to appear, the television set causes your eye to see the hat as black. Inhibition makes the light gray turn black. Or, as I have often demonstrated to my students, black is white with a bright ring around it.

CONTRAST FUNCTIONS

If black can be produced by surrounding a white with a brighter surround, what quantitative rules does the process follow? Many investigators have carried out experiments to answer that question. A method they have often used is intramodal matching, which exploits the fact that the two eyes behave with almost perfect independence as regards the evaluation of brightness. That fact allows us to place a luminous disk or circle of light before each eye separately. Around one of the disks we then place a brighter annulus. Thereupon the apparent brightness of the disk surrounded by the annulus falls off. Now we have two interesting options, both involving intramodal matching. Either we can increase the intensity (luminance) of the surrounded disk until it again appears as bright as the disk in the other eye, or we can decrease the luminance of the other disk until it matches the brightness of the inhibited disk. Although both procedures have been used, the second has the greater utility, because that method uses the uninhibited disk to measure what happens to the inhibited disk.

The equal sensation functions obtained by a brightness match between

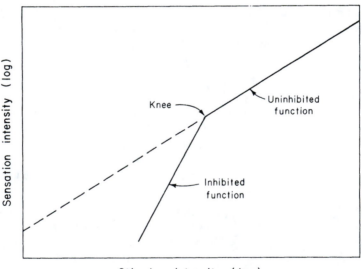

Fig. 22. Schematic diagram to illustrate how inhibition produced by masking or glare increases the slope (exponent) of the psychophysical function. The inhibiting stimulus is located at the knee. The overall psychophysical function then consists of two segments, both of which are power functions. The intersection of the two segments forms a knee at the critical level where inhibition ceases. With no inhibiting stimulus present, the growth of sensation would follow the dashed line. (From Stevens and Guirao 1967. Reprinted by permission.)

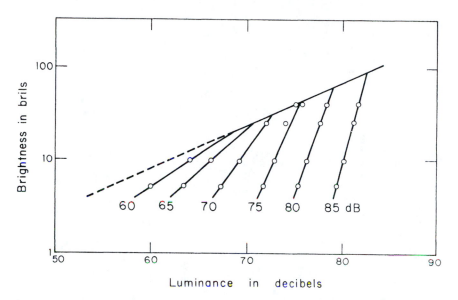

Fig. 23. Brightness functions for a target inhibited by a surrounding background annulus. The more intense the luminance or glare of the surround, the steeper is the inhibited function. Brightness contrast serves to lessen the apparent brightness of the target whenever it is dimmer than the surround. The dimmer stimulus does not affect the brightness of the brighter surround. (Data from Horeman 1965).

the uninhibited and the inhibited disks have been plotted in several different ways, but one of the most revealing configurations makes use of the fact that the brightness function for a single uninhibited disk is known. That knowledge makes it possible to add the subjective measure (in brils) to the stimulus measures and to plot the results of intramodal brightness matching in the manner shown by the diagram in Fig. 22.

If there were no surround present, then with increasing intensity the luminous disk would grow in brightness along the dashed line, for the function would be uninhibited. The presence of a surrounding annulus, whose intensity is located at the knee, causes the brightness function to bend down, because the inhibited function is steeper than the uninhibited function. How steep—how large the exponent of the inhibited function— depends on the intensity of the surround. The size and shape of the target and of the surround may also play a role, but with four different configurations it was found that the brighter the inhibiting fields, the steeper the inhibited function. Figure 23 shows six inhibited functions for a small target surrounded by an annulus (Horeman 1965). When the surround is 85 decibels above threshold, the exponent of the inhibited brightness function becomes quite large.

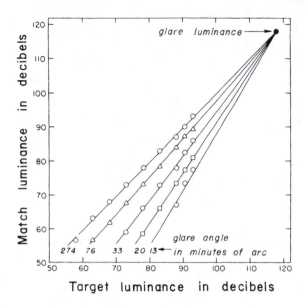

Fig. 24. When a small glare source is placed near a target, the brightness of the target is inhibited. The nearer the glare to the target, the steeper the inhibited function. Observers adjusted a glarefree field in the other eye to match the inhibited target. The functions project to a common point, which lies at the luminance of the glare. If the target had a luminance equal to or greater than the glare, the glare would have no inhibiting effect. (From Stevens and Diamond, "Effect of Glare Angle on the Brightness Function for a Small Target," Copyright 1965, Pergamon Press).

You experience the same phenomenon when the headlights of an oncoming automobile blind you to objects on the highway. The apparent brightness of the objects grows and declines along a steep power function, and the nearer the object is to the direction from your eyes to the headlights, the steeper is the power function.

In a laboratory experiment a tiny glare source having a luminance of 118 decibels simulated a headlight. It was placed near a small target whose luminance could be set to any desired level (Stevens and Diamond 1965). The glare inhibited the brightness of the target. The observer adjusted the luminance of a light source in his other eye to match the brightness of the inhibited target. The degree of the inhibition depended on both the luminance of the target and the glare angle separating the glare from the target source. The quantitative relations turned out to be beautifully simple and orderly, as illustrated in Fig. 24. At each glare angle the matching luminance increased as a power function of the luminance. In other words, when the location of the glare was changed it produced a power transformation, resulting in a new power function with a new exponent.

In Fig. 24 the lines converge to a point corresponding to 118 decibels—the level of the glare source. That point of convergence plays a role similar to that played by the knee in Fig. 22. The convergence accords with an important and fundamental principle: strong stimuli inhibit weaker stimuli, but weak stimuli do not inhibit stronger stimuli. Inhibition is a one-way street, so to speak.

In addition to the large and dramatic contrast effects that arise when a masking glare inhibits the brightness of an adjacent surface, there are interesting small scale effects near borders and transitions. The most celebrated of those effects is the one made famous by the physicist Ernst Mach, an effect now called the Mach band (Ratliff 1965). Whenever a gradual shading from light to dark changes from one gradient to another, a noticeable band appears. The band is presumably due to local inhibitory effects—a type of inhibition that seems also to occur in other sense organs and may serve to sharpen borders in the eye and pitch perception in the ear (Békésy 1972).

MASKED LOUDNESS FUNCTIONS

Whenever a circumstance alters the exponent of a sensory function, the result is a so-called power transformation. The dramatic power transformation caused by a bright annulus surrounding a visual target finds a parallel in hearing when a noise masks a signal. Since speech serves as our most useful signal, it is interesting to see what happens to the loudness of speech when it is masked or inhibited by a white noise. Two observers listened to recorded passages of speech alternately in the quiet and in the presence of a masking noise. The listener adjusted the level of the noisefree speech to make it appear equal in loudness to the masked speech. A wide range of speech and noise levels was used.

The results for each observer are plotted separately in Fig. 25. Two features are noteworthy. (1) The speech in the noise is an accurate power transformation of the speech in the quiet, because the coordinates are log-log and the lines through the data are straight. (2) The slope (exponent) of the masked or inhibited function increases with the level of the masking noise. Thus we see that noise masking in hearing behaves very much like glare in vision; they both produce a power transformation whose magnitude increases with the intensity of the inhibiting stimulus (Stevens 1966b).

In an ear suffering from Ménière's disease, loudness behaves much the way it does in an ear masked by white noise. The disease results in a power

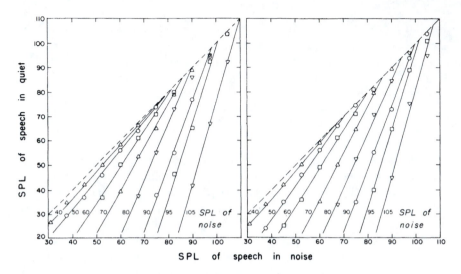

Fig. 25. Showing the effect of a white masking noise on the loudness of continuous speech. The ordinate shows the sound pressure level of the speech in the quiet, which was matched to the loudness of the speech masked by the noise. The level of the noise is the parameter. Each graph is for a single observer. The dashed lines at 45° show the locus of the loudness matching function in the absence of inhibition due to masking. Inhibition increases the exponent of the loudness function. (Data from Pollack 1949.)

transformation, so that loudness grows more steeply—by so-called recruitment—in the diseased ear than in a normal ear (Stevens and Guirao 1967).

POWER GROUP

It needs to be emphasized that the group of transformations produced by an inhibiting stimulus is a rather special group. Consider some of the alternative possibilities. Some investigators have suggested that when a masking noise is turned on, it may act to subtract a constant amount of loudness. Another possibility is that the masking noise may decrease the loudness by a constant percentage. Neither of those simple transformations, subtraction or division, describes what happens in hearing and vision when one stimulus is inhibited by another. Instead, the transformation belongs to what I have called the power group. A given value x is replaced by a new value x', such that

$$x' = ax^b$$

where a and b are positive constants. In terms of logarithms we can write

$$\log x' = b \log x + \log a$$

Thus the power transformation exhibits the very convenient property of becoming a linear function when expressed in logarithms. Consequently, in log-log coordinates a power transformation corresponds to a change in the slope and the intercept of a straight line. The fact that it becomes so simple in log-log coordinates should not be allowed to obscure the underlying nature of the rather complex power-group transformation.

ADAPTATION

The power group turns out to be one of the most common transformations in the sensory domain. Another everyday example occurs when you go from sunlight into a dimly lighted room. In the sunlight the eyes become light adapted to a high level, about 90 decibels above threshold, and in a dimly lighted room everything looks faint and obscure to a light-adapted eye. But after 10 or 15 minutes in the dimly lighted room, things will have brightened up so that objects previously invisible can be easily seen. When the eye is adapted to darkness, the exponent of the brightness function is 0.33. When the eye is adapted to a luminance of 100 decibels above the standard threshold level (10^{-10} lambert), its operating characteristic undergoes a power transformation that increases the exponent of the brightness function to approximately 0.44.

Both intramodal matching and magnitude estimation were used to determine the power transformation produced by adaptation in the eye (J. C. Stevens and Stevens 1963). The family of brightness functions for a wide range of adaptation states is shown in Fig. 26. For each state of adaptation the function takes on a different slope (exponent) and all the functions turn sharply downward when they approach the visual threshold. That fact is represented mathematically by a threshold constant ϕ_0 in the equation $\psi = k(\phi - \phi_0)^b$.

Although visual adaptation is often confused with contrast by both theorists and experimenters, the two phenomena are quite different. Contrast, also called masking, glare, and inhibition, occurs instantly. Adaptation takes time. For your eyes to become light adapted to the level of sunlight on snow takes 5 to 10 minutes, and for your eyes to return to a fully dark-adapted state may require as much as 40 minutes.

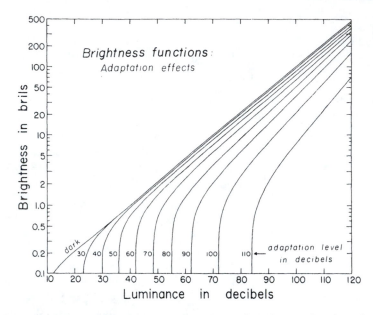

Fig. 26.   Brightness functions for various levels of visual adaptation. As the adaptation level increases, the slope (exponent) of the functions increases. The threshold also rises, as is shown by the bottom ends of the functions. (After J. C. Stevens and Stevens 1963.)

THE TONAL ATTRIBUTES

Although most experiments on intramodal matching have been concerned with the measurement of brightness and loudness, the procedure has also illuminated other interesting problems. For example, with the same experimental procedure—namely, with the observer allowed to adjust the stimulus level of a pure tone—the existence of four different subjective attributes has been demonstrated. The only difference in the four experimental procedures lies in a single word in the instructions. (See pp. 56-58).

In the experiments designed to map the equal loudness contours, pure tones at two different frequencies were presented alternately, and the observers were asked to adjust one of the tones to make it appear equal to the other tone in loudness. In place of the word loudness the instructions may employ the word pitch or volume or density. Depending on which word is used, the observer makes a completely different response. In other words, he can abstract from his perception of a pure tone at least four different attributes, and for each of the four attributes he can make intramodal matches. From a series of such matches we can then construct a contour, depending on the instructions, for equal loudness, equal pitch, equal volume, or equal density. Such contours are sometimes called isophonic contours.

PITCH

The pitch of a tone is closely related to the frequency of the tone, so much so, in fact, that pitch and frequency are sometimes thought to be synonymous. Consequently, in the course of carrying out other kinds of auditory experiments, I was greatly surprised to discover that the pitch of a tone seemed to change when the intensity was increased. Low-frequency tones seemed to become lower in pitch, and high-frequency tones seemed to become higher in pitch. Relatively little change took place for tones in the vicinity of 1000 to 1500 hertz. With the help of an observer who was especially precise in his judgments, I explored the effect of intensity on pitch for a wide range of frequencies (Stevens 1935). The observer adjusted the intensity of one tone until its pitch matched that of another tone having a slightly different frequency. The form of the equal pitch contours are shown in Fig. 27. The contours are placed so as to suggest the general principle that low tones become lower and high tones higher when the sound intensity is raised.

The effect of intensity on the pitch of a pure tone was named the Zurmühl-Stevens effect by Boring (1937), because Zurmühl (1930) had earlier explored the effect for frequencies below 3072 hertz. For those frequencies Zurmühl noted only a lowering of pitch with increased intensity. The increase in pitch at the higher frequencies may have been overlooked because the frequencies Zurmühl used were not sufficiently high.

Although the effect of intensity on the pitch of pure tones is definite and measurable, and enjoys a good measure of theoretical interest, it remains a relatively small effect. Like many sensory effects, the amount by which pitch seems to change with intensity varies from one person to another.

Many musicians have noted the change in pitch with intensity, but the phenomenon seems to exert little practical influence on music. Two reasons can be cited. In the first place, it requires a rather large change in the sound pressure level of a tone to produce a readily noticeable change in the apparent pitch. More important, perhaps, musical sounds are almost never pure tones. Rather, they consist of a rich harmonic structure, comprising, in effect, a whole bundle of pure tones. Some of the harmonics of a typical musical note will occur in the frequency region where there is little or no change in pitch with intensity. For example, middle C at a frequency of 256 hertz has a second harmonic at 512 hertz and a third harmonic at 1024 hertz. The higher harmonics occur in the frequency region where pitch rises

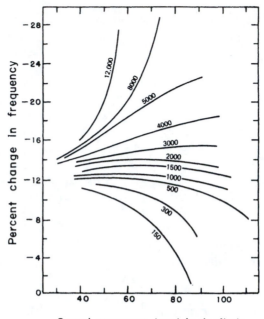

Sound pressure level in decibels

Fig. 27. Equal pitch contours. The contours are placed so as to show that when the intensity increases, low-frequency tones fall in pitch and high-frequency tones rise in pitch. For pure tones near 1000 hertz there is little change in the pitch with intensity. (After Stevens 1935.)

rather than falls with increasing intensity. Thus a single musical note may have harmonics that reside in the two regions of Fig. 27. the region where the contours fall and the region where they rise. It appears not unreasonable then that for many musical sounds the changes in pitch that are produced by intensity may offset or cancel one another, thereby stabilizing the listener's perception of the musical pitch.

VOLUME

Do pure tones have other attributes? That question agitated psychophysics for many decades. Those who trusted their phenomenal judgments felt sure that low tones seem large and voluminous; they seem to fill a lot of space. High tones, by contrast, seem sharp and small, occupying little space. Phenomenal introspection did not convince the skeptics, however, and experimental studies were attempted in the laboratory. For a time the approach followed the once popular notion that if volume was in fact a separate attribute, different from loudness and pitch, the just noticeable differences for the three attributes should be different in size. The results of experiments built on that conception seemed not, however, to resolve the issue. The results were so discordant that some authors were led to doubt the existence of volume as an independent attribute.

In a study undertaken for a doctoral dissertation, I was led to try a more simple-minded approach. I reasoned that if volume increased with intensity and decreased with frequency, it ought to be possible to balance one against the other. Accordingly, the observer was given two tones alternately, each at a different frequency, and he was told to adjust the intensity of one of the tones until the two tones seemed equal in volume. The task turned out to be straightforward (Stevens 1934b). Equal volume contours at three different intensities were determined in that first experiment. The general form of the contours is shown by one of the isophonic contours in Fig. 28. The volume contour shows that when I increased the frequency of the tone, the listener increased the intensity in order to keep the volume constant.

DENSITY

In the belief that it often pays to ask observers to try to describe what it is they think they are doing when they match disparate stimuli in terms of

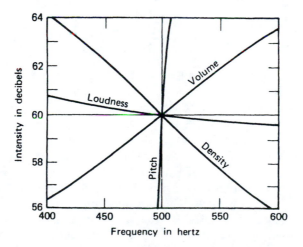

Fig. 28. Isophonic contours for pitch, loudness, volume, and density. Along each curve the attribute remains constant when frequency and intensity are varied in the right way. The contours are from a series of early studies (Stevens 1934c). Later studies extended the contours and produced scales to quantify each of the four attributes.

one of the more unfamiliar attributes, I noted the introspections offered by the observers. As they struggled to describe the phenomenal features of the tones they were listening to, certain words and phrases frequently reappeared. Some tones seemed hard, concentrated, and compact. They were the loud, high-pitched tones. Other tones seemed loose and diffuse, lacking in density. They were the faint, low-pitched tones. Those descriptive phrases led me to set for the observers the task of adjusting the intensity of one tone to make it appear equal to another tone in density. The form of an equal density contour, mapped by that intramodal matching procedure, is shown in Fig. 28 (Stevens 1934c).

While introspecting, after those first density judgments had been completed, one observer said, "The density of tones is not hard to judge. It is one of the most direct judgments I have made. Density is very much the same as the penetrating quality of the tone. The thing I am judging as density is right in the middle of the tone; it is the core of the tone, whereas what I was judging as volume was the limits of the tone—the outer edge."

Another observer said, "Some tones are thick—others are thin or diffuse. The high tones are solidly packed. They are solid all the way through. When one of the tones is weakened in intensity, it becomes more scattered. Then it is thinner and less dense."

Those introspections may help to picture the nature of the task as the observers experienced it. On the other hand, it was the observers' ability to make consistent intramodal matches that established density as an independent attribute of pure tones.

RELATION OF LOUDNESS TO VOLUME AND DENSITY

Although experiments based on the procedure of intramodal matching can be used to generate isophonic contours, including even extensive families of such contours, there remains open the question, how far apart do the contours stand? Thus the first three equal volume contours that I determined represented isophonic paths along which volume stood constant at a particular value—a different value of volume for each contour. The rank order of the contours was obvious if one listened to the tones, but whether the largest apparent volume was twice, ten, or a hundred times the volume represented by the lowest contour was a question whose mere formulation would have seemed too radical at that time to be seriously considered. Once the method of magnitude estimation had been developed, however, the tools became available to tackle such questions, and in due course the quantification of tonal volume was carried out (Terrace and Stevens 1962). Soon thereafter, magnitude estimation was also used to quantify tonal density (Guirao and Stevens 1964). Those studies made it possible to extend the isophonic contours for both volume and density and to assign to each contour the value determined by the consensus of observers' judgments under the number-matching procedure of magnitude estimation.

It is important to point out a basic asymmetry between the two different methods involved here. If observers have made magnitude estimations of tonal volume or density, we can use the results to construct equal volume or equal density contours. But the reverse is not possible. From intramodal matches of the kind used to map isophonic contours it is not possible to scale volume or density on a ratio scale and to assign to each contour a number proportional to the perceived value of the attribute.

When volume and density were scaled by magnitude estimation, several interesting relations emerged. For one thing, both volume and density increased as a power function of the sound pressure of the stimulus. Despite the fact that several dozen psychophysical power functions had been observed, it was not anticipated that volume and density could also provide examples of the power law. There was, however, an interesting relation among the exponents for the two attributes. The exponents for volume became larger as the frequency of the tones increased, whereas the exponents for density became smaller. There was, in fact, a suggestive relation between them, so that at a given frequency the two exponents added to an almost constant sum. The value of that sum was roughly the value of the exponent usually found when loudness is scaled by the same procedure of magnitude estimation. Now, if the exponents for volume and density add up to the exponent for loudness, an interesting hypothesis is suggested regarding the relations among the three attributes. Loudness may be the product of volume times density.

A decision was made to test that hypothesis by asking observers to make magnitude estimations for each of the three attributes on the same set of stimuli (Stevens, Guirao, and Slawson 1965). The stimuli were narrow bands of noise, about ¼ octave wide. Noise bands had been found to be easier for the observers to judge than pure tones. The bands used were centered at nine different frequencies ranging from 200 to 6000 hertz, and at sound pressure levels ranging from 42 to 100 decibels. In one part of the experiment the observers judged loudness, in another part volume, and in another part density. The geometric means were computed for each type of judgment and for each stimulus. Then for each stimulus the judgment made for volume was multiplied by the judgment made for density. Finally, the products, volume times density, were plotted against the loudness judgments. The graph in Fig. 29 shows that the hypothesis was confirmed to a rather remarkable extent. If the hypothesis were exactly correct and if there were no variability in the various experiments, the points in Fig. 29 would

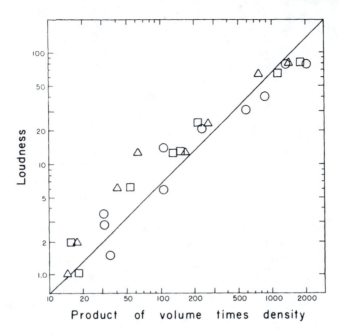

Fig. 29. Approximate proportionality between loudness and the product of volume times density. Each point represents a different product of volume times density, but the squares and triangles represent the same set of loudness values. Exact proportionality would be indicated if the points fell exactly on the diagonal line. (From Stevens, Guirao, and Slawson 1965, *J. Exp. Psychol.*, 69, 503–510. Copyright 1965 by the American Psychological Association. Reprinted by permission.)

lie along the line, which has a slope equal to 1.0. Despite the variability, in three different experiments, each represented by a different symbol in Fig. 29, there was an obvious tendency for the data to conform to the hypothesis that loudness is proportional to volume times density.

The validity of that hypothesis was further reinforced by an additional experiment in which observers were instructed to judge the inverse of each attribute. In other words, they made magnitude estimations not of loudness, volume, and density, but of softness, smallness, and diffuseness. Since other experiments had already proved that observers could judge the inverse aspects of several other perceptual continua, it was not surprising that the observers succeeded with little difficulty in judging the inverse aspects of the three attributes. Each of the inverse scales turned out to approximate a reciprocal function of the original scale. The hypothesis predicts that, if the reciprocal relation holds, then softness should be proportional to smallness times diffuseness. With the three inverse aspects the hypothesis was confirmed with somewhat less scatter than is shown by some of the points in Fig. 29.

HUE

When the direct light of the sun strikes a cloud of raindrops, the different wavelengths are reflected back at different angles. We then see the wavelengths spread out in space, as it were, giving us the spectacle of the rainbow. Each wavelength produces a characteristic hue. The association of hue with wavelength has been likened to the association of pitch with frequency. In both instances it turns out that the association is not a tight one-to-one relation. We have already seen in Fig. 27 that pitch changes with intensity—the Zurmühl-Stevens effect. The analogous phenomenon in vision is called the Bezold-Brücke effect.

The change of hue with intensity was investigated in an often-cited thesis study by Purdy (1929, 1937), who used intramodal hue matching to map the contours of constant hue. The observer looked at a 3-degree target, half of which was illuminated by a constant wavelength of light at a fixed intensity. The other half of the target was illuminated at a lower intensity. The observer could vary the wavelength of the low-intensity field until the two fields appeared to have the same hue. In that way Purdy determined pairs of equal hue points, and from about 70 such pairs he constructed the equal hue contours shown in Fig. 30.

Three of the wavelengths appear to be unaffected by intensity. They are called the invariant hues: blue (478 nanometers), green (503 nanometers), and yellow (572 nanometers). For those hues the contours representing constant hue are straight vertical lines, indicating the same hue at all intensities.

The contours that Purdy constructed represent extensive and careful measurements on a single observer. The general features of the contours have been confirmed in other studies, however, and the locations of the invariant hues have turned out to be approximately the same for other observers.

Like the equal pitch contours, the equal hue contours enjoy great theoretical importance, because they serve to correct the long-standing misconception that each perceptual attribute reflects a physical dimension of the stimulus. Although hue and wavelength exhibit a close dependence, the curved lines in Fig. 30 show that wavelength can be changed without changing hue. For example, we can change the wavelength from 540 to 510 nanometers without changing the apparent hue, provided we increase the intensity by about 23 decibels. Clearly, then, the eye does not provide a ve-

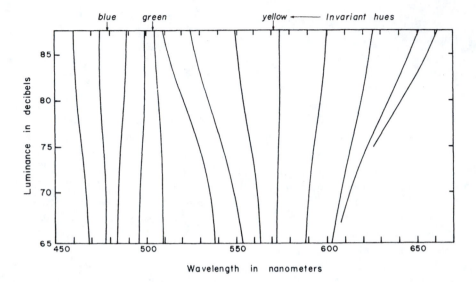

Fig. 30. Equal hue contours. In order to maintain a constant hue, wavelength must be changed when luminance is changed. The effect is called the Bezold-Brücke phenomenon. Changes in luminance do not affect the hue at certain invariant wavelengths: 478 (blue), 503 (green), and 572 (yellow). Note that the contours spread in a direction opposite to the change in hue. Thus with increasing luminance the appearance of wavelengths near 580 nanometers becomes more yellow, which can be compensated by increasing the wavelength. (After Purdy 1937.)

ridical indication of wavelength, even when the stimulus is a single wavelength, or, as is the case in most actual experiments, a narrow band of wavelengths. Hue, like each of the other attributes of "pure," single-wavelength stimuli, is a function of both wavelength and intensity.

Of course, most of the colors we see in everyday life are produced by impure stimuli, stimuli that involve a rich spectrum consisting of many wavelengths. The perceived hue then becomes not only a joint function of the spectrum and the intensity of the target stimulus, but a function of the surrounding stimuli as well. So rich and intricate are the interactions within the visual field among the three variables—location, wavelength, and intensity—that astonishing and colorful effects can be produced by stimulating the eye with a complex scene illuminated by only two wavelengths. Land (1964) has devised what he calls Retinex theory to explain how each of the three independent color systems, or retinexes, interacts with the others to give us the world of color.

SATURATION

In addition to brightness and hue, a light stimulus exhibits a third attribute called saturation. It refers to the depth or strength or vividness of a color. No one word quite covers the meaning. The largest and most obvious differences in saturation occur with complex stimuli. Thus white light, which has all wavelengths present in approximately equal amounts, appears very low in saturation, whereas a band of wavelengths near 630 nanometers appears high in saturation, giving a deep red. By mixing white light with the red light we can change the saturation through a wide range. By magnitude estimation it has been found that saturation grows as a power function of the percentage of red in the mixture (colorimetric purity). The exponent is about 1.7 (Panek and Stevens 1966). For other hues the exponent takes on different values (Indow and Stevens 1966; Onley et al. 1963).

Less dramatic but quite perceptible differences in saturation occur among the pure colors generated by single wavelengths of light. Thus the reds and the blues in the rainbow appear more saturated than the yellows. Not only does saturation vary with wavelength, but, like the other attributes, saturation also varies with intensity. The manner of the variation seems to be unique, however, for saturation may claim the distinction of being the only attribute that passes through a maximum at moderate stimulus levels and then declines. Consider, for example, the following sequence in which the intensity of a pure color is increased, beginning with a value below threshold. When the threshold is crossed the observer first sees a grayish patch of light that seems to possess no apparent hue. With a further increase in intensity the hue becomes detectable, but it appears very low in saturation. With increasing intensity the saturation grows and eventually reaches its maximum. Thereafter, as the intensity continues to increase, the patch of light takes on a whitish glare and the saturation falls off.

Curiously enough, no very thorough effort has been made to map the equal saturation contours, but their general form can be deduced from various investigations. A possible saturation contour based on Purdy's work was proposed by Boring (1937). An improved contour based on the additional data of Indow and Stevens (1966) is shown in Fig. 31. The dashed line shows the approximate location of the maximum saturation that can be obtained at a given wavelength. The path along which saturation remains constant appears to form a closed loop, like an equal elevation contour on a topographical map. As with a closed contour, if we follow the equal saturation path around the diagram we return to the starting point.

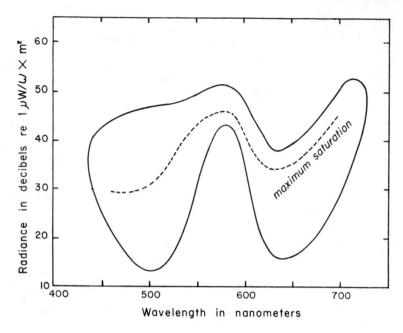

Fig. 31. Equal saturation contour. Unlike most sensory contours this contour forms a closed loop. When the intensity of a given wavelength is increased, saturation rises to a maximum and then declines. The dashed line marks the location of the maximum saturation.

Actually, at higher values of saturation, the single closed contour in Fig. 31 breaks up into two closed curves, one surrounding the high peak of saturation in the reds at the long-wave end of the spectrum, and the other surrounding the peak in the blue-violet region. The yellows never reach the elevations in saturation attained by the blues and the reds. In other words, the saturation hill is a kind of saddleback, lower in the central yellow-green region than at either the red or the blue-violet end. Of those two end humps, the red appears to lie somewhat lower than the violet. At wavelengths longer than about 700 nanometers the red hump slopes off with increasing wavelength, and the appearance becomes yellowish (Brindley 1955, cited in Wyszecki and Stiles 1967). Brindley found, for example, that the hue at 641 matched the hue at 887 nanometers.

FROM CONTOURS TO 3-D

As we have seen, one of the chief uses of intramodal matching lies in its ability to determine contours—paths along which the value of one or another sensory attribute remains constant. If we limit ourselves to the simple stimuli, pure tones and single wavelengths, we find that there are four families of isophonic contours and three families of isochromatic contours. Each family represents a slope or a hill, so that four hills are needed to represent the auditory attributes and three hills to represent the visual attributes. The hills have a variety of different shapes, as we can deduce from a study of the contours.

It is an interesting exercise to construct the various hills and slopes in three dimensions. It can be done with paper, clay, or other materials. With loudness, for example, we begin with a flat base, with frequency marked off along one side and intensity marked off along the other side. The problem then is to plot loudness vertically. One possible procedure is to erect a vertical rod of some sort projecting above each combination of frequency and intensity. The length of the rod represents loudness. With enough such rods, the form of the loudness surface becomes evident. In a similar manner the form of the surfaces for all the other attributes can be modeled.

When we face the task of erecting the three-dimensional model of an attribute surface, it becomes plain that we need measurements in the third di-

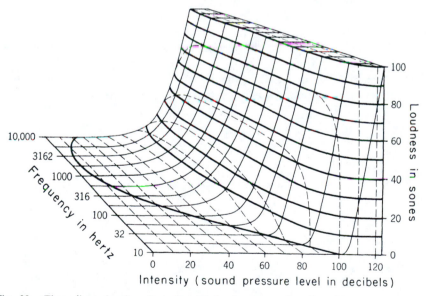

Fig. 32. Three-dimensional surface showing loudness as a function of intensity and frequency. Subjective loudness in sones is represented vertically above the intensity-frequency plane. The heavy curves coursing from front to rear in the diagram are equal loudness contours for pure tones, similar to the contours shown in Fig. 16. Note that the loudness scale is a linear scale, the other scales are logarithmic. (From Licklider 1951. Reprinted by permission of John Wiley & Sons, Inc.)

mension. Limited solely to intramodal matches, with the resulting equal sensation contours, we have no measure to tell how far apart the contours lie. It is like a topographic map on which the hills and valleys are represented by equal elevation contours spaced at unknown separations. The surveyor must tell us the elevation of each contour before we can construct a faithful three-dimensional representation of the landscape.

With few exceptions, before the 1950's the study of the sensory systems found itself confined to the flat plane of two dimensions, so to speak, with no attempt to scale values in the third dimension. One of the exceptions concerned loudness, for which a subjective unit, the sone, has been widely used ever since I proposed it in 1936. A drawing representing the loudness surface is shown in Fig. 32. Loudness in sones is plotted vertically above the frequency-intensity plane. The heavy lines running horizontally around the surface are the equal loudness contours. Thus we see how an equal loudness contour of the kind shown in Fig. 16 is in principle produced. We first cut the surface horizontally (parallel to the base plane) and we then project the cut surface straight downward onto the frequency-intensity plane. In the same way, each isophonic or isochromatic contour represents the cut edge of a surface projected down onto the base plane.

Once we have determined the entire attribute surface, other cuts can be made. For example, a cut along a constant frequency line in Fig. 32 shows how loudness grows as a function of intensity when frequency is held constant. Families of such equal frequency contours have sometimes been plotted.

The dashed lines in Fig. 32 show cuts along a constant intensity line. They illustrate how loudness varies when only the frequency of the tone is changed.

CHAPTER 4

Cross-Modality
Matching

Once we have established that several of the perceptual continua can be
scaled by the method of magnitude estimation, as well as by other ratio-
scaling procedures, an insistent question arises. Can the scales obtained by
number matching be used to predict how subjects will perform when they
are asked to make a direct comparison between two different sensory continua? Concretely, let us design an experiment in which your task is to
match the apparent loudness of a sound to the apparent strength of a vibration on your fingertip. Suppose I ask you to place your finger on a vibrating button, and at the same time to listen to a sound delivered to your
ears through earphones. I then ask you to adjust the level of the sound until
its apparent loudness seems as great as the strength of the vibration on
your finger. Now if I set the amplitude of the vibration at various levels,
can you adjust the sound to create an apparent match? And would results
obtained previously by magnitude estimation predict the levels at which
you set the sounds?

That type of experiment provides a critical test of the kind of prediction
that James prescribed, and a stringent probing into the validity of psychophysical scales.

Since an *experimentum crucis* seemed to be involved, it was not without
a certain trepidation that I set up the equipment for that test in the spring
of 1958. In addition to the presentation of sound and vibration, the apparatus made it possible to pass various amounts of electric current
through the subject's fingers. Thus three different modalities could be
stimulated, and the subject could adjust the stimulus in each modality so
that the intensity experienced could be matched to each of the other two,
making six experiments in all—any one of which could turn sour.

Actually, all six experiments met the test. The average response was
close to that predicted by the power functions previously determined by

magnitude estimation. The outcome was so nearly on target that cross-modality matching seemed clearly to offer a fruitful approach, and perhaps even a practical method of scaling.

PREDICTIONS

The basis for predicting the observer's behavior in a cross-modality matching experiment runs as follows. If the numerical estimations that a person makes when he is asked to judge the magnitude of his sensation reflects a fundamental property of the sensory system, then that same property should guide his behavior when he matches one sensation to another. We have seen that when the observer makes numerical magnitude estimations, the strength of his reported sensation grows as a power function of the stimulus intensity. We have also seen that the power functions in the different sense modalities tend to have different exponents. The question then is, when sensations in one sense modality are matched to those in another modality, what is the expected form of the matching function? The answer turns out to be simple: the expected matching function should be another power function. In other words, in log-log coordinates the matching function should be a straight line, and the slope (exponent) of the matching function should be equal to the ratio of the two original exponents.

The problem can be stated very simply with the help of equations. We assume that in the first sense modality the sensation ψ is related to its stimulus ϕ by a power function with the exponent m

$$\psi_1 = \phi_1{}^m$$

Likewise, in the second sense modality, we assume a similar equation, but with a different exponent n

$$\psi_2 = \phi_2{}^n$$

Now if ψ_1 is matched to ψ_2 at several different values over a range of stimuli, then for the equated values ψ_1 and ψ_2 we can substitute the stimulus values, so that

$$\phi_1{}^m = \phi_2{}^n$$

Then by taking the logarithm of each side of the equation we can write

$$m \log \phi_1 = n \log \phi_2$$

or

$$\log \phi_1 = \frac{n}{m} \log \phi_2$$

This last equation represents a straight line, provided the values are plotted in log-log coordinates. The slope of the line is n/m, the ratio of the two original exponents.

In the event that one of the original functions departs from a proper power function, its curvature in a log-log plot should be reflected by a related curvature in the matching function. In short, strong inferences could be drawn from the ability of cross-modality matches to produce a matching function of the predicted form. The test, if successful, would provide a powerful tool for validation.

LOUDNESS, VIBRATION, AND SHOCK

I had three principal reasons for choosing the three modalities, loudness, vibration, and electric shock, for the first test of the power-law predictions.

1.   The stimuli for all three modalities can be controlled by simple electrical circuits. Consequently, it becomes possible for the subject as well as the experimenter to adjust any one of the stimuli, allowing matches to be made in both directions, so to speak.

2.   The exponents of the three modalities vary considerably in size, with the consequence that the three predicted matching functions should have slopes that differ enough to forestall any possibility of confusing one with another.

3.   The typical observer's familiarity with the three sense modalities varies widely. Loudness is quite familiar, vibration less so, and a steady 60-hertz electric current through the fingers produces a strange sensation that the typical observer rarely if ever experiences. The sensation produced electrically is called shock for short, but the current through the fingers was always kept below the level of pain or discomfort. Some subjects expressed concern about the prospect of being "shocked," but none in fact was.

An occasional author has argued that the success of the method of magnitude estimation is based on the subject's extensive familiarity with the stimulus, so that he commits a kind of stimulus error. Instead of judging the magnitude of his sensation, the argument runs, the subject uses his knowledge of the stimulus in order to estimate the stimulus magnitude. That tactic on the part of the observer may of course prove possible when he is asked to judge the apparent length of lines, for the yardstick provides a familiar guide to the stimulus for length, but the argument loses its force when the task is to judge an unfamiliar stimulus like electric current. It is also interesting to note that even with very familiar stimuli, such as squares or circles of different sizes, the subjects can in fact judge the appearance as opposed to estimating the dimensions of the stimulus. Thus when subjects judge apparent length the exponent falls close to the value one, but when they judge the apparent size of squares the exponent differs significantly from one, falling to about 0.7. Yet when the observers undertake to judge the area by attending to one side of the square—and thereby estimate the area by squaring the length—the exponent increases to about one.

An instructive application of the psychophysical law governing apparent size can be found in the example from mapmaking discussed in Chapter 2. Experimental trial and error led some mapmakers to find a satisfactory relation between size of symbol and the populations of cities, and the relation that they settled on turns out to be a power function with the exponent 0.7.

In the cross-modality experiment, electric current was administered through salt solutions. The observer placed his first and third fingers in small glass cups, leaving his middle finger free to rest on the vibrator button. At the same time he wore earphones, through which a low-frequency band of noise could be delivered. With his right hand he could turn one or another of the three controls used to adjust the various stimuli. Other details are given elsewhere (Stevens 1959b).

The first task was to determine by magnitude estimation the exponents for the three sense modalities. With the apparatus as described, the exponent for the 60-hertz vibration on the middle finger was close to 1.0. For electric current the exponent was between four and five times larger, but, as was true in earlier experiments, the geometric means of the data for 10 observers did not correspond to a good power function. In log-log coordinates the judgments of electric current followed a line that was slightly concave downward. The exponent for loudness was taken to be 0.6, the approximate value previously obtained in numerous experiments. The question then becomes, will the matching functions accord with the ratios of those three exponents?

The matching of the apparent or subjective intensities of loudness and vibration was carried out in two complementary experiments. In one experiment the observer adjusted the loudness of the sound to match the perceived vibration. In the other experiment he adjusted the vibration to match the loudness. In this and the other matching experiments each of ten observers made two adjustments of each stimulus at each level, so that each measured value is based on the decibel average of 20 adjustments.

The results are shown in Fig. 33, where we see that the data determine two equal sensation functions, each with a slightly different slope. The slope depends on which stimulus the observer adjusts, symbolized by circles when the sound was adjusted and by squares when the vibration was adjusted. The two slightly different slopes provide an example of the im-

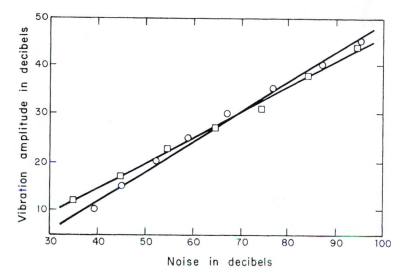

Fig. 33. Equal sensation function for vibration and loudness. The squares show the results when the vibration on the finger was adjusted to match the loudness. The circles show the result when the loudness was adjusted to match the vibration. Both sets of results approximate straight lines, representing power functions in the logarithmic (decibel) coordinates. The slope (exponent) is slightly different, depending on which stimulus the observer adjusts. The slope difference illustrates the ever-present regression effect.

portant and ever-present regression effect. The regression or centering tendency seems to characterize the subject's adjustments, whatever the kind of stimulus, so that the regression effect shows up in many kinds of matching experiments. The effect points up the desirability of a balanced design in which each stimulus is made to serve at one time as the standard and at another time as the variable or adjustable stimulus.

The two regression lines in Fig. 33 can be averaged by taking the geometric mean of the two slopes. The average function presumably lies closer to the true matching function than does either of the two individual lines. The interesting point to note is that the slope of the average line is 0.6, which is almost exactly the slope that is called for by the ratio of the exponents of the two functions previously obtained by magnitude estimation.

Not only did the results turn out as predicted, but the matching of loudness to vibration, and vice versa, also proved astonishingly easy from the observer's point of view. Some of the observers who served in experiments involving the intramodal matching of loudness expressed the opinion that the cross-modality matching between loudness and vibration was in some ways easier than matching the loudness of two sounds that differ widely in pitch or quality. The consistency of the judgments seemed to bear out that impression.

LOUDNESS VERSUS SHOCK

In matching loudness to shock and shock to loudness, each of ten observers made two adjustments at each stimulus level. A major difficulty with the use of electric current as a stimulus arises from the rather considerable adaptation that takes place. The effect of the current seems to diminish with time. For that reason the shock and sound were presented alternately for about one second each. Even so, the effects of adaptation can be detected when we single out the results of the first series of stimulations. Thus

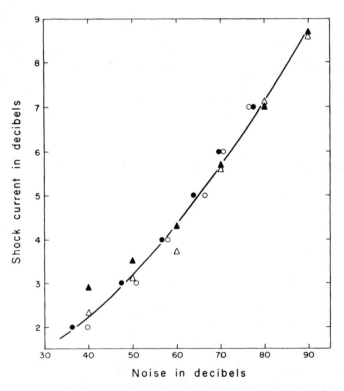

Fig. 34. Equal sensation function for shock and loudness. Triangles mean that shock was adjusted to match loudness; circles mean that loudness was adjusted to match shock. Unfilled symbols represent the means of the first adjustments; filled symbols represent the means of all adjustments. Some adaptation to shock is evident at low levels.

the unfilled symbols in Fig. 34 lie either slightly to the right of the filled symbols, or below them, especially at the low levels.

Despite the adaptation to the electric current, the overall picture portrayed by the data in Fig. 34 accords with the predicted outcome. Thus a curvature is present just as it was when shock was scaled by magnitude estimation. Furthermore, the overall slope of the line is about right. For example, when the current was changed by about 6 decibels, the observers changed the level of the noise by about 50 decibels in order to preserve the sensory match. In other words, they showed by their direct matching behavior that the exponent for shock is about eight times larger than the exponent for loudness.

Although no attempt was made to draw the two regression lines in Fig. 34, a slight regression effect can be detected in the data. The slope was a little steeper when loudness was adjusted than when shock was adjusted.

SHOCK VERSUS VIBRATION

In the exercise designed to equate the sensations of shock and vibration, two different counterbalanced experiments were run. In the first experiment the subject held his middle finger approximately horizontal, with the finger pad resting on the button of the vibrator. In the second experiment the middle finger was held nearly vertically downward, with the fingertip resting on the button of the vibrator. In the second position the finger usually shows slightly greater sensitivity to the vibration, perhaps because the axis of the finger is in line with that of the vibration.

As shown in Fig. 35, the two experiments gave rather similar results. The position of the finger made little difference. More important, though, both the slope and curvature agree closely with the expected outcome. Thus when the shock current was changed by 5 decibels, the observers changed the vibration amplitude by roughly 25 decibels, showing that the ratio of the two exponents must be about 5 to 1. That ratio, in fact, was the value indicated by the results of magnitude estimation.

As in other other cross-modality experiments, a slight regression effect can be detected in the data shown in Fig. 35.

TRANSITIVITY

The foregoing experiments calling for cross-modality matching among sound, vibration, and electric current have closed a circle of great importance for the validation of psychophysical procedures. For one thing,

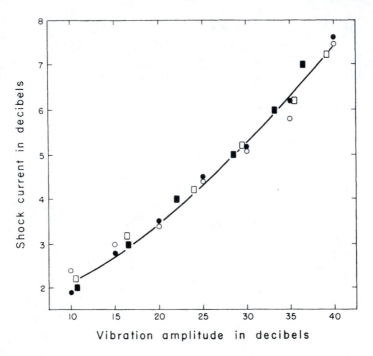

Fig. 35. Equal sensation function for shock and vibration. Circles mean that shock was adjusted; squares mean that vibration was adjusted. Unfilled symbols represent an experiment in which the middle finger was at right angles to the direction of the vibration. Filled symbols represent an experiment in which the middle finger was held parallel to the direction of the vibration. The parallel position allowed the vibrator to activate the end of the finger and gave what seemed to be slightly better results.

the outcome shows that we can use the results of magnitude estimation to predict what observers will do when they make direct matches among three different sense modalities. Magnitude estimation appears, therefore, to be a more powerful procedure than some of its critics have supposed.

But another basic principle emerges in the results of the foregoing experiments. There is a transitive relation among the power function exponents, in the sense that any two dictate a third. That relation is shown in the equal sensation functions in Figs. 33 to 35. Having matched loudness with vibration in Fig. 33, and loudness with shock in Fig. 34, we can predict the result of matching vibration with shock in Fig. 35. Or we could travel around the circle in another direction. Having matched loudness with shock and shock with vibration, we can predict the behavior of the observers when asked to match loudness with vibration. Two matching functions, with one sense modality in common, are sufficient to predict a third matching function. Otherwise said, the very important principle of transitivity holds among the matching functions.

ABSOLUTE SCALES AND THE REFERENCE CONTINUUM

The results in Figs. 33 to 35 tell us at a glance the relative sizes of the exponents that govern the three sensory continua. In Fig. 33, for example, we see that the apparent intensity of a 60-hertz vibration grows with an exponent approximately 1.5 times as large as the loudness exponent. Of course if we knew the value of either of the two exponents we could calculate the value of the other, for we know their ratio. But a knowledge of relative values does not tell us absolute values. Why not? What is missing?

The answer, in brief, is that nothing is missing except a decision concerning which continuum we should take as the reference continuum. Relative values become absolute values as soon as they can be related to a reference continuum. On the reference continuum the exponent, by definition, equals one.

What has actually happened in the matter of choosing a reference continuum is a kind of decision by default. Implicitly, if not explicitly, the number continuum has been accepted as the reference continuum. And the number continuum, as we learned in Chapter 2, goes back to man's early efforts to scale the numerosity of objects of one kind or another. In accepting number as the reference continuum with an exponent of unity, we are saying in effect that the subjective magnitude of number grows in direct proportion to number. We make that assumption whenever we take at its face value an exponent derived from the results of magnitude estimation— or better, the combined results of magnitude estimation and magnitude production. By averaging the two kinds of measurements, estimation and production, we cancel or at least diminish the bias caused by the regression effect.

There would in principle be nothing to prevent the choice of a different reference continuum. We could choose loudness, for example. If we chose that continuum, what would follow? First of all, it would be important to match each of the numerous perceptual continua to loudness. Actually, more than 20 continua have already been matched to loudness, so that part of the task is well under way. If loudness were to be considered the reference continuum, its exponent, instead of being ⅔ (its value when number is the reference continuum), would become exactly one. Then, of course, the exponent of the number continuum would cease to be one, but would move to the higher value 3/2. In addition, the exponents of all the other continua, such as those listed in Table 1, would, if measured relative to loudness, move upward by the same factor $\frac{3}{2}$. And since all the exponents move by the same factor, their ratios to one another remain unchanged. Those invariant ratios ensure that the transitivity among the cross-modality matching functions will continue to hold, so that predictions can still be made and tested as before.

The possibility of scaling all other continua relative to loudness, instead of relative to number, stands then as a straightforward option. If we do not avail ourselves of the option, it is perhaps for reasons related more to practice than to principle. An important practical fact is that many of the most basic scales of physics—numerosity, length, weight, and so forth—are linear (exponent = 1.0) against number. That being so, it becomes convenient to refer each perceptual continuum to number so that its relation to the physical family of linear functions becomes at once apparent as soon as we know its exponent.

OBJECTIONS

Until they have persuaded themselves by carrying out their own experiments, many scientists have rejected psychophysical measurement out of hand. A large variety of objections have been expressed, and the listing of all of them would make an extensive catalogue. Two objections prove of special interest, though, because one of them denies that the observer can associate numbers with sensations and the other argues that cross-modality matching is possible only because the observer can assign a number to each modality and then compare the numbers. Those two views seem to stand at opposite poles, yet they both raise interesting issues.

One of my early brushes with the issues raised by the first view occurred after a lecture I gave at Clark University in 1935. A distinguished psychophysicist, C. H. Graham, raised the question whether some of our early attempts at loudness scaling could really be called measurement. The most popular procedure in those days was to ask the observer to adjust one sound so that it seemed half as loud as a given standard sound. But the particular procedure used did not constitute the issue—the issue was whether the association of numbers with sensations provided true measurement in any sense. Professor Graham and I were destined to debate that question off and on for the next 35 years without coming to full agreement. Like many scientific discussions, that debate had the positive effect of stimulating several kinds of experiments that might not otherwise have been performed.

One of those experiments grew out of Professor Graham's objection to treating the observer's numerical estimates as though they were genuine numerical data. The observer may respond to a stimulus by emitting the name of a number, but is it really a number, the kind that can properly be averaged? Professor Graham thought not, which left us at an impasse. A way around, it seemed to me, might be to arrange for the observer to emit something other than numbers, but something closely related, such as line length. So an apparatus was constructed to project a thin line of light on a large screen in such a way that the observer, by merely turning a knob, could make the line any desired length (Stevens and Guirao 1963).

In the first experiment with that apparatus the observer was asked to adjust the line to match a series of numbers spoken in irregular order by the experimenter. The results of that magnitude production procedure demonstrated clearly that the exponent for line length is very close to 1.0. In other words, the relation is linear. Hence, from the subject's point of view (or, as we say, subjectively), number and line length are directly proportional.

The next step was to test the observer's ability to match line length to other modalities, such as loudness and brightness. Groups of 10 observers carried out the two experiments with the results shown in Fig. 36. Each observer made three matches to each of five stimulus levels for white light and for a band of white noise. Geometric means of the 30 matching judgments are shown by the symbols. The lines through the data do not represent the best fitting lines; rather they show the slopes (exponents) for loudness and brightness as determined by the consensus of numerous other experiments. Thus both lines have the slope $\frac{1}{3}$, which is the exponent for the two modalities when the stimuli for both are measured in terms of energy flow. (In terms of sound pressure the exponent for loudness becomes $\frac{2}{3}$.)

The data in Fig. 36 fall sufficiently close to the two lines to make it appear probable that line length could serve in place of number as the reference continuum. If the exponent for apparent length is indeed 1.0, then we could scale all the modalities against length without having to change any of the exponents, such as those listed in Table 1.

If the speaking of numbers, as in magnitude estimation, is objected to because no measurement is involved, perhaps that objection can be met by allowing the observer to emit lines, so to speak, lines that can then be measured in the conventional manner. With line lengths it could hardly be argued that the resulting numbers did not represent measurement.

Of course, there are practical limitations to the use of line length as the reference continuum. Special apparatus is required, but more important is the limited range available. One ordinarily thinks of length as unlimited,

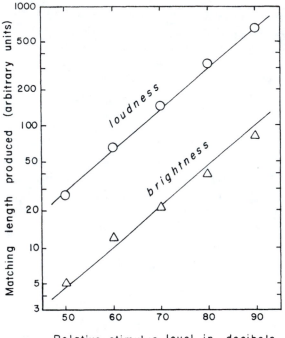

Fig. 36. Matching of line length to various magnitudes of loudness and brightness. The observers adjusted the length of a thin line of light projected on a screen in order to make its apparent length match the apparent loudness of a white noise at various levels and, in another experiment, the apparent brightness of a white light at various levels. The lines through the data represent power functions with the exponent ⅓. (After Stevens and Guirao 1963.)

but in the laboratory severe limits impose themselves, so that a range of stimuli greater than about 200 to 1 becomes difficult to achieve. The observer's visual acuity sets limits at one end and the finite size of indoor spaces sets limits at the other end. In practice the observer's adjustments of the line length must not take him too close to either limit. Consequently, when line length was matched to brightness and loudness, stimulus ranges of about 40 decibels were all that could be used. With number matching to loudness, on the other hand, I have used stimulus ranges as great as 90 decibels (see Fig. 9).

How does the observer go about making cross-modality matches? Is it true, as some theorists have surmised, that the observer makes a numerical estimate for each modality and then compares the numbers? In other words, is cross-modality matching mediated by magnitude estimation? In a conceptual or abstract sense, it may indeed be conceivable that observers turn sensations into numbers and then compare the numbers, but in my own experience with cross-modality experiments no evidence for such a number-mediated process has shown itself. It has seemed to me, and to other observers whom I have asked about the matter, that the matching of vibration to loudness, for example, is a direct and immediate judgment in which numbers play no part whatever. Furthermore, naive observers who have never made magnitude estimations match vibration to loudness quickly and directly. Indeed, it is noteworthy that in certain hearing clinics the matching of vibration to loudness has been used to diagnose the nature and degree of hearing impairments.

The history of psychophysics has been laced with obstructions created by those who refuse to credit the observer with the capacity to perform feats that turn out to be easy and straightforward. Thus Fechner, Plateau, and other eminent historical figures stated flatly that observers have no ability to judge the ratio of two sensations. Perhaps the decision on the part of a few modern theorists to explain cross-modality matching as a kind of numbers game provides another of those obstructions that the accumulation of experimental evidence may eventually overcome. In the meantime it appears that observers possess vast if unsuspected abilities to perform matching operations. And since matching is the basis of all measurement, it turns out that many things can be measured that were once thought impossible.

HANDGRIP

When you squeeze a hand dynamometer you feel a sense of strain that can vary in degree from weak to very intense. You yourself can regulate the intensity of the sensation. Suppose then that you also hear a noise of a certain loudness, can you squeeze the dynamometer with such a force that the sensation of strain appears as intense as the sensation of loudness? When that experiment was tried with a group of observers the response was immediate and satisfactory. It was plain that the observer can match across modalities by the simple process of emitting squeezes instead of numbers. That fact opens the possibility of scaling the other perceptual continua with the aid of a calibrated hand dynamometer. A dynamometer sold commercially is pictured in Fig. 37.

The results of matching force of handgrip to nine different continua are shown in Fig. 38. What we see there is quite a splendid family of power functions. On each of the nine continua, as the intensity of the criterion stimulus was changed by the experimenter, the observer squeezed a precision dynamometer with a force that he judged appropriate to indicate

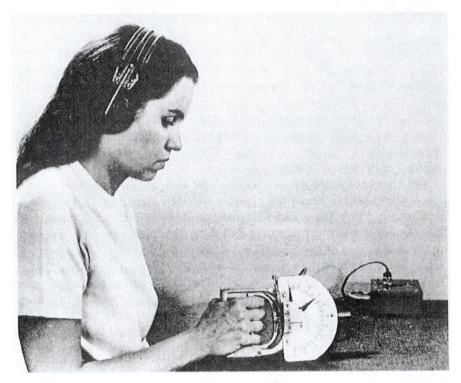

Fig. 37. A precision hand dynamometer. The subject is matching apparent force of handgrip to the apparent loudness of a sound produced in a pair of earphones.

the perceived magnitude. The remarkable fact is that the force of handgrip increased along a straight line when the data were plotted in log-log coordinates. Equally remarkable are the slopes of the lines. Their order from steepest to flattest accords with the order of the values listed in Table 1 for the exponents of the various continua. Thus it appears that not only does scaling by squeezing produce power functions, but the exponents of the functions line up in the same order as when the method of magnitude estimation is used.

For those who feel uneasy about using the method of magnitude estimation, then, handgrip matching may recommend itself as a substitute. Its dynamic range is rather limited, to be sure, but, for demonstrating the pervasive character of the power law, the handgrip procedure has proved itself quite adequate.

There remains the question, what is the value of the exponent for handgrip? If we decided to use handgrip as the reference continuum, then its value would, of course, be taken as equal to one. In that event the other nine continua portrayed in Fig. 38 would have the exponents equal to the slopes of the lines. Those values are listed in the first column of Table 3.

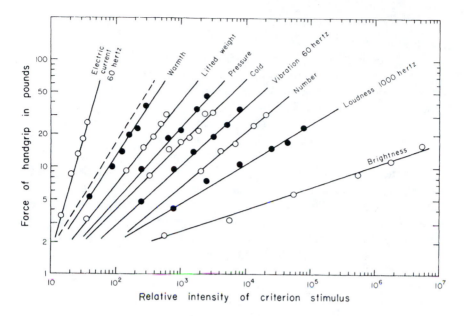

Fig. 38. Equal sensation functions obtained by matching force of handgrip to various criterion stimuli. Each point stands for the median force exerted by 10 or more observers to match the apparent intensity of a criterion stimulus. The relative position of a function along the abscissa is arbitrary. The dashed line shows a slope of 1.0 in these coordinates. (After J. C. Stevens, Mack, and Stevens 1960.)

Table 3. Comparison of obtained and predicted exponents for the matching of force of handgrip to other continua. The predicted value is based on the assumption that the exponent for handgrip itself is 1.7.

	Exponent obtained by handgrip	Predicted value	Difference in decilogs
Electric shock	2.13	2.06	0.14
Warmth on arm	0.96	0.94	0.09
Heaviness of lifted weights	0.79	0.85	0.32
Pressure on palm	0.67	0.65	0.13
Cold on arm	0.60	0.59	0.07
Vibration, 60 hertz	0.56	0.56	0.00
Loudness of white noise	0.41	0.39	0.22
Loudness of 1000-hertz tone	0.35	0.39	0.47
Brightness of white light	0.21	0.20	0.21
Average			0.18 = 4.4%

If, on the other hand, we want to continue to use number as the reference continuum, there remains another cross-modality experiment to be performed. We must match handgrip to number.

Interestingly enough, a tentative start on that project was made in the last century by Fullerton and Cattell (1892). They asked each of two observers to pull with a force of 300 grams on a special dynamometer and then to pull with twice the force. They also asked the observer to pull first with a force of 1200 grams and then with half that force. That procedure of ratio production could have carried those investigators a long way, perhaps even to the discovery of the power law for muscular efforts. Curiously, though, Fullerton and Cattell seemed more impressed with the negative aspects of the experiments than with the positive possibilities. They seemed puzzled, for example, by the fact that, when the observer judged his pull to be twice as great, the actual physical force exerted was less than twice the starting force. With halving also, the force applied to the dynamometer failed to keep pace with the observer's impression. What that meant, of course, was that the exponent for muscular effort has a value greater than one. But Fullerton and Cattell stated quite explicitly that the estimation of sensation is not possible, only the judgment of stimuli is possible. That seems to be the basis for their expectation that when the observer doubled his sense of strain he would in fact double the stimulus, meaning the force on the dynamometer.

Well, hindsight makes it all rather clear, but there in 1892 we have the remarkable spectacle of two distinguished psychologists being diverted from a scientific breakthrough by their belief that something that was in fact possible had to be impossible. Mired in their misconception, they were unprepared to heed the message of their own data. Instead, they commented on the disagreement between the results of the two observers, considering it "of interest in showing how difficult it is to make quantitative estimates of sensation." They then went on to say, "We, ourselves, think that such estimates depend on association with known quantitative relations of the stimuli . . ." (Fullerton and Cattell 1892, p. 100).

Their belief that the observer's estimates depend on his intimate acquaintance with a stimulus correlate of the sensation has proved popular through the years. For example, another eminent psychologist, H. Ebbinghaus (1890) said that we can estimate brightness only because we have seen a room lit by one candle, and by two candles (see Boring 1921). Of course, if that were in fact the basis of brightness estimates, the exponent would turn out to be 1.0 instead of 0.33. A more recent hypothesis places the burden on a more recondite variable, namely, our supposed intimate acquaintance with the inverse square law. That hypothesis would call for the exponent 0.5, which is still far from the observed value 0.33. Thus far, explanations that depend on the observer's knowing facts about the stimulus have not illuminated the problem.

It remained for J. C. Stevens and Mack (1959) to show how widely muscular effort departs from the linear relation that Fullerton and Cattell took for granted and that adherents to the stimulus-correlate notion would predict. When observers matched handgrip effort to numbers, the exponent, instead of being 1.0, was 1.7.

With that exponent determined, we are now equipped to predict the slopes in Fig. 38. We simply divide the value of the exponent listed in Table 1 by 1.7. The result of dividing the exponent by 1.7 gives the value listed in the second column of Table 3. It will be noted that the predicted exponent in column 2 agrees fairly well with the obtained exponent in column 1. That agreement assures us that the exponent for handgrip has a value close to 1.7, and it also gives us added confidence in the values of the exponents for the other nine continua.

LOUDNESS MATCHING

Another interesting family of equal sensation functions can be assembled from the many experiments in which loudness has been matched to a continuum in some other sense modality (Stevens 1966c). Ten such matching functions are described in Fig. 39 and in Table 4. Although differing in detail, the family of functions for loudness matching resembles in many respects the family of functions for handgrip matching. Actually, the loudness-matching functions were put together after the fact, as it were, with no attempt made to create a homogeneous set of experiments. In fact, the sound stimulus was sometimes a pure tone and sometimes a band of noise of one bandwidth or another. In most of the experiments the observers varied the loudness to match the sensation created by the criterion stimulus in the other modality. But in three instances (handgrip, vocal effort, and length) the fixed sound pressures were set by the experimenter and the observer varied the other stimulus to match the loudnesses. Consequently, in those three instances we are concerned with a different regression line, which makes the functions in Fig. 39 slightly less comparable than they would otherwise be.

Nevertheless, there is reasonably good agreement between the slope of each line and the slope that is predicted when the exponent in Table 1 is divided by the loudness exponent $\frac{2}{3}$. The largest discrepancy between obtained and predicted slope occurred in an experiment in which observers matched loudness to the apparent hardness of various rubber samples, ranging from a very soft sponge rubber to a hard sample that could barely

Table 4. Ten loudness-matching functions. The first column shows the exponents determined by numerical estimation (matching to number). The second column shows the slopes of the functions in Fig. 39. The ratio of the values in the first two columns predicts an exponent for the loudness function, as listed in the fourth column. The exponent for brightness is stated as 0.66 instead of the usual 0.33 in order to make it comparable to the loudness exponent, which is here given in terms of an amplitude rather than an energy measure.

	Exponent re number	Match slope	Predicted slope	Predicted exponent for loudness	Difference in decilog	Band-width for sound in hertz	Reference
Electric current (60 Hz through fingers)	4.5	7.5	6.8	0.60	0.42	100–500	Stevens 1959b
Force of handgrip	1.7	2.5	2.6	0.68	0.17	100–6600	J. C. Stevens, Mack, and Stevens 1960
Redness (saturation)	1.7	2.6	2.6	0.65	0	100–3000	Panek and Stevens 1966

Continuum						Range	Reference
Tactile roughness of emery cloth	1.5	2.6	2.3	0.58	0.53	500–5000	Stevens and Harris 1962
Vocal effort	1.1	2.0	1.7	0.55	0.70	100–2000	Lane, Catania, and Stevens 1961
Vibration on finger	0.96	1.6	1.5	0.60	0.28	100–500	Stevens 1959d
Number	1.0	1.45	1.5	0.69	0.15	1000-Hz tone	Stevens and Guirao 1962
Length of line	1.0	1.45	1.5	0.69	0.15	500–5000	Stevens and Guirao 1963
Visual brightness	0.66	0.88	0.99	0.75	0.51	75–4800	J. C. Stevens and Marks 1965
Hardness of rubber by squeezing	0.8	0.81	1.2	0.99	1.71	500–5000	Harper and Stevens 1964
Average					0.46 = 11.1%		

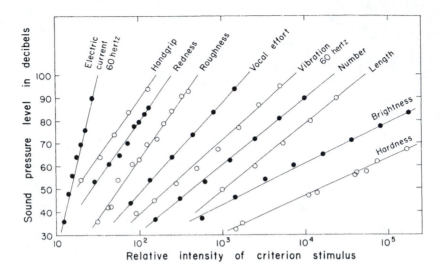

Fig. 39. Equal sensation functions obtained by matches between loudness and various criterion stimuli. The relative positions of the functions are arbitrary, but the slopes are those determined by the data. (From Stevens 1966c. Reprinted by permission.)

be dented by squeezing (Harper and Stevens 1964). The exponent obtained by two different experimenters using the method of magnitude estimation was 0.8. By loudness matching, therefore, the predicted slope (exponent) would become 1.2. The obtained slope in Fig. 39 is only 0.81. Thus far it seems that subjective hardness remains an exception to the general rule that two exponents can successfully predict a third.

It happened that my own interest in assembling the data in Fig. 39 grew out of a desire to learn more about the loudness exponent. Is its value 0.6, or would the value 0.67—or ⅔—be more representative? The slopes of the lines in Fig. 39 can be divided into the exponents listed in Table 1 in order to obtain a predicted loudness exponent. When that was done and the ten exponents were averaged, the geometric mean turned out to be 0.67. That outcome can be regarded as at least a partial confirmation of the value ⅔.

Another interesting confirmation of the ⅔ value of the loudness exponent was obtained in an extensive experiment on taste (Moskowitz 1968). In a grand total of 68 separate experiments, each involving 10 observers, taste intensity was scaled by each of two procedures, magnitude estimation and loudness matching. The stimuli included the four basic tastes—sweet, salt, sour, and bitter—plus various combinations in various concentrations. The observer sipped a solution of the taste substance and either assigned a number or, in another part of the experimental session, adjusted the level of a band of noise (500 to 5000 hertz) in order to produce a loudness that appeared to match the taste intensity.

The result then was 68 pairs of power functions, each pair involving the matching of number to taste and loudness to taste. Since both number and loudness were matched to the same continuum, we can compute the exponent that should have been obtained if number and loudness had been matched directly. The predicted exponent is the ratio of the two obtained exponents. The 68 ratios were computed and the distribution of exponents was displayed in a histogram, as shown in Fig. 40 (Stevens 1969). The geometric mean of the distribution is 0.676.

In some ways that determination of the loudness exponent stands as perhaps the most thorough determination yet made of an exponent. The determination has the important feature that, since the observers had adjusted both numbers and loudness to match the taste intensity, we are able to calculate the exponent for the number-loudness relation by making use of two comparable regression lines. For that reason the calculated loudness exponent is relatively uncontaminated by the regression effect. As a matter of fact, if it were true that the regression effects in the two parts of the taste

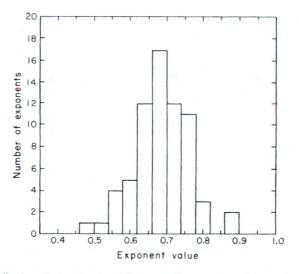

Fig. 40. Distribution of 68 estimates of the exponent of the loudness function, all based on experiments in which both number and loudness were matched to taste intensity. Both matches produced power functions. The ratio of the two exponents gave the values whose distribution is plotted. The geometric mean is 0.676, the standard deviation is 0.51 decilog, or 12.5 percent. (From Stevens 1969, based on data of Moskowitz 1968. Reprinted by permission.)

experiments were exactly equal, they would cancel out completely when we calculate the ratio of the two exponents.

The histogram in Fig. 40 gives us a realistic example of the amount of scatter that may occur in the value of an exponent determined with groups of 10 observers. The standard deviation of the distribution of the loudness exponents is 0.51 decilog, or 12.5 percent of the mean value. That value can be compared with the deviation of the observed from the predicted values when exponents are measured in other cross-modality comparisons. Thus a review of an extensive battery of cross-modality experiments conducted in Sweden led to a set of 14 obtained and predicted exponents. After correction for the regression effect, the average departure of the obtained from the predicted exponents was 0.52 decilog, or 12.7 percent (Stevens 1969). For comparison, the average departure of the obtained from the predicted exponent for the equal sensation functions in Fig. 39 is 0.46 decilog, or 11.1 percent (values shown in Table 4). For the more homogeneous set of experiments in which handgrip was matched to nine other continua (Fig. 38), the average departure of the obtained from the predicted exponent was only 0.18 decilog or 4.4 percent (values shown in Table 3). The close agreement between the predicted exponents and those obtained with handgrip matching is testimony mainly to the experimental skill of J. C. Stevens.

A word is in order concerning the general usefulness of loudness as a variable to be used in the measurement of other perceived magnitudes. It has been used to gauge more than a score of other subjective variables. Sometimes the problem has been purely practical. For example, in a study of automobile spring suspensions, observers turned the loudness in their earphones up and down to match the felt bumpiness of a ride on a stretch of rough road (Versace 1963). In the clinical study of a patient's pain or comfort, the usual query, "How do you feel?" has been replaced by some physicians with a request that the patient put on earphones and adjust a loudness to appear as strong as the discomfort felt. Such a "feeling meter," or thymometer as it is called in a commercial version, makes it possible to quantify the effectiveness of whatever medication may be used to alleviate the patient's distress (Peck 1966).

FIVE-YEAR-OLDS

Those who find themselves impelled to theorize about the basis of cross-modality matching—whether, for example, it requires prior acquaintance with the scales of the physical stimuli, or whether it is mediated by the observer's translating his impressions into numbers and then comparing the numbers—such theorists will surely want to temper their decision by considering a case of cross-modality matching by 5-year-old children (Bond and Stevens 1969).

The purpose was to push back to an early age and to see whether cross-modality matching between two sensory continua can be carried out by young children. In other words, could a game be contrived in which young children would report their sensory impressions, and would their reports agree with those of adult subjects playing the same game? The game: to make the light as strong as the sound.

The light was a circular patch produced by a 150-watt lamp behind a translucent screen. The brightness was controlled by a Variac voltage control that was very easy to turn. The experimenter controlled the loudness of a 500-hertz tone produced in earphones worn by the subject. The five children tested ranged in age from 4 years 2 months to 5 years 8 months, with an average of 5.0 years. The control group of five adults were students who had not previously tried to match brightness to loudness. Each child

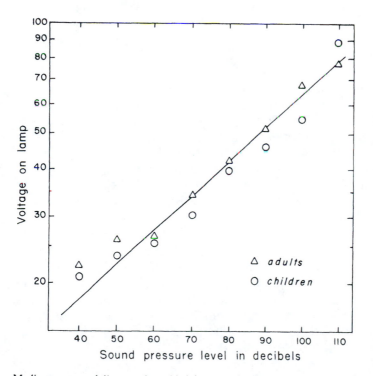

Fig. 41. Median cross-modality matches of brightness to loudness of 5-year-old children and adults. The voltage on a 150-watt lamp was varied to produce brightnesses that appeared as intense as the loudnesses of a 500-hertz tone heard through earphones. (From Bond and Stevens 1969. Reprinted by permission.)

was tested separately. Each was first given an opportunity to turn the Variac dial and to listen to some of the tones. The nature of the task was explained as turning the light up or down to make it as bright as the sound was loud.

As soon as the child seemed to grasp the nature of the task, the tones were presented at eight different levels (40 to 110 decibels), twice each in irregular order. The children performed astonishingly well. Some of them simply whipped through the series, setting the light level as fast as the experimenter could provide the criterion loudnesses. To some the game was fun.

The median results are shown in Fig. 41. For several technical reasons the results give only a fair power function, but the main point stands out clearly. The children (circles) performed almost precisely as did the adults (triangles). A performance of that sort seems hard to attribute to prior learning or to an ability to translate sensory impressions into numerical relations. A more plausible theory suggests that the strength of our sensory impressions depends on the transducer properties of the sense organs and that the eyes and ears of children perform like those of adults.

CLASS DEMONSTRATION

Lecture demonstrations sometimes succeed and sometimes fail. My first attempt to demonstrate cross-modality matching before about 200 students came close to disappointment. I projected a patch of light on a white screen and invited a student to put on a pair of earphones and to adjust a noise to make its loudness match the brightness. I also sent the sound to a loudspeaker system so that the entire class could hear the sound as well as see the light. In response to my changing the level of the light up and down irregularly over a total range of 40 decibels, the student turned the loudness up and down.

About halfway through the exercise the class began to hiss and boo—in customary Harvard irreverence. It appeared that they did not approve of the sound adjustments being made by the volunteer student. He was in fact acting as though seized by stage fright and was making only very small changes in the sound when I made large changes in the level of the light. After the trial was over, I said somewhat apologetically, "Well, at least that shows how cross-modality experiments are conducted."

Another student then volunteered. By the time he had made four adjustments a smattering of applause broke out, and, by the time he finished, the applause appeared to be almost unanimous. I had scarcely expected a large class to be so decisive about what constitutes acceptable (and unacceptable) cross-modality matches.

INVERTING THE CONTINUA

On some kinds of stimulus continua it may not be obvious just which end is up, so to say. When you rub your finger on a series of different grades of emery cloth or sandpaper, for example, do you experience roughness or smoothness? And when you squeeze a rubber sample, is it hardness or softness that commands attention? There are several such continua on which we may find it almost as natural to judge in terms of one attribute as its opposite. Judging the paleness of a color as opposed to its depth or saturation provides another common example.

Since observers have exhibited a remarkable ability to equate or match one sensory attribute to another, the question arises whether that ability extends to the matching of one attribute to the opposite of another attribute. Concretely, if the observer can match loudness to roughness, can he also match loudness to smoothness? And if so, what kind of quantitative relations will emerge?

Twelve grades or grits of emery cloth were presented in irregular order to each of ten observers who stroked each cloth twice with the middle finger and adjusted the level of a noise (500 to 5000 hertz) to make it appear as loud as the emery cloth was rough. Another group of ten observers adjusted the noise to appear as loud as the emery cloth was smooth (Stevens and Harris 1962). The geometric means (decibel averages) are plotted in Fig. 42.

There we see that both of the cross-modality matching functions approximate power functions, because the lines are straight in log-log coordinates. Equally notable, the line for the matching of loudness to smoothness (circles) slopes downward to the right with a negative slope. The actual value of the negative slope for smoothness is −2.6. The positive slope for roughness (triangles) is +2.6. Thus the two slopes (exponents) are equal but opposite in sign. That relation means that smoothness is the reciprocal of roughness. In other words, the cross-modality matches of the observers tell us that when a stimulus is twice as rough, it is also half as smooth.

It is important to distinguish between the reciprocal relation demonstrated in Fig. 42 and a complementary relation of the kind that would obtain if the roughness scale was merely turned upside down. The scale of smoothness is not the scale of roughness turned backward—it is not the reverse, it is the inverse. The same can be said for the other inverse scales, such as the softness of rubber and the paleness of a color. As a matter of fact, the inverse scale has been determined for more than a dozen different attributes. Most of the inverse scales have been obtained with the method of magnitude estimation. The success of those experiments may help to counter the argument sometimes put forth that numerical estimates

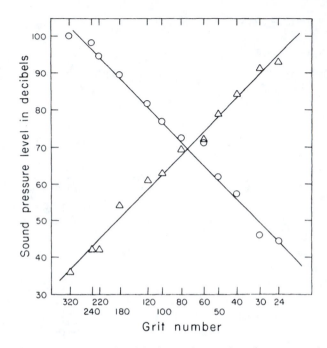

Fig. 42. Sound pressure levels produced in the earphones when observers matched the loudness of a noise to the roughness (triangles) and the smoothness (circles) of 12 grades of emery cloth. Both coordinates are logarithmic. Grit number refers to the number of holes per inch through which grit is strained. (From Stevens and Harris 1962, *J. Exp. Psychol.,* 64, 489–494. Copyright 1962 by the American Psychological Association. Reprinted by permission.)

are possible only because observers have learned to associate large numbers with intense stimuli and small numbers with weak stimuli. On the contrary, when the observer judges softness, for example, he associates large numbers with faint sounds and small numbers with loud sounds. That kind of behavior appears to eliminate simple association as the explanation.

The procedure can be inverted, of course, so that the experimenter gives the numbers and the observer produces the loudness or the softness. In an experiment of that sort we also asked the observer to adjust the level of a tone (1000 hertz) so that it appeared to be at a distance that corresponded to the numbers spoken to him. Under those circumstances the observer's judgments of "distance" turned out to be essentially the same as his judgments of softness, and both of them were the inverse, or the reciprocal, of his judgments of loudness (Stevens and Guirao 1962). The full story is told by the functions in Fig. 43.

It should be mentioned that the results of the softness and "distance" judgments shown in Fig. 43 depart slightly from a power function. It is fairly common to find that the inverse function is slightly concave down-wa . That feature of the outcome suggests two things. One is that judging the inverse of an attribute is somewhat less easy and straightforward than judging the attribute itself. That fact is scarcely surprising. The astonishing fact is that the observers do as well as they do at scaling the inverse of a continuum.

The second indication suggested by the slight curvature in the inverse scales is a procedure for telling which end is up. Thus, although Fig. 42 does not show much curvature in the smoothness function (circles), other experiments make it evident that roughness is the primary attribute and smoothness is the inverse. Similarly, extensive research on tactual hardness shows clearly that, when the observer squeezes rubber samples, hardness is the primary attribute and softness is the inverse (Harper and Stevens 1964). Likewise, brightness and loudness are primary, dimness and softness (faintness) are inverses.

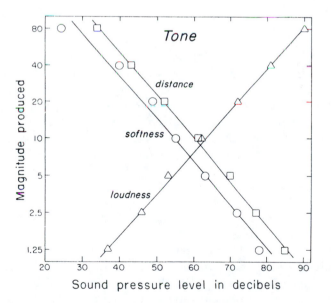

Fig. 43. Magnitude production of loudness, softness, and distance for a tone of 1000 hertz. The exponents for softness and distance are about −0.7. For loudness the exponent is about 0.7. Thus the judgments are reciprocally related. (From Stevens and Guirao 1962, *J. Acoust. Soc. Am.*, 34, 1466–1471. Reprinted by permission.)

The secondary, inverse nature of dimness and softness was evident in another experiment, whose results are shown in Fig. 36. In addition to matching length of lines to brightness and to loudness, the observers matched length to dimness and to softness. Overall the results showed that dimness is approximately the reciprocal of brightness, and softness is approximately the reciprocal of loudness. There was, however, the usual slight downward concavity in both inverse functions (Stevens and Guirao 1963). To the surprise of no one, then, it appears that brightness and loudness must qualify as the primary attributes. Dimness and softness are secondary.

RATIO MATCHING ACROSS MODALITIES

If the observer can match one perceptual continuum to a second continuum, or even to the inverse of the second continuum, it may be expected that the relation between two stimuli on one continuum can be matched by the relation between two stimuli on another continuum. That is indeed possible, but the outcome varies, depending on which relation is specified. The observer can be asked to match ratios or to match differences. Those are the two relations of most general interest. Curiously enough, observers perform well when they match ratios but not so well when they match differences.

An experiment on ratio matching was carried out in a thesis study by J. C. Stevens (1957). The observer adjusted a pair of loudnesses to match a ratio defined by a pair of brightnesses. Each of 15 observers adjusted the second of two noises presented through earphones in order to make the apparent ratio between the noises match the apparent ratio between two luminous targets seen against a dark surround. The median results are shown in Fig. 44 where the coordinates are logarithmic (decibel).

The data fall near the 45-degree diagonal, meaning that whatever ratio (number of decibels) the experimenter set between the two lights, the observer set approximately the same ratio (number of decibels) between the two sounds. The largest ratio set by the experimenter between the lights was 10,000 to 1, or 40 decibels.

An outcome such as the one shown in Fig. 44 coincides with the outcome predicted by the power law, provided both loudness and brightness have approximately the same exponent. For the exponents to be the same, both the light and the sound must be measured in comparable terms, namely, energy flow or power.

Additional evidence that loudness and brightness have similar exponents was obtained in a cross-modality matching experiment by J. C. Stevens and Marks (1965). They arranged a setup that permitted the observer to adjust

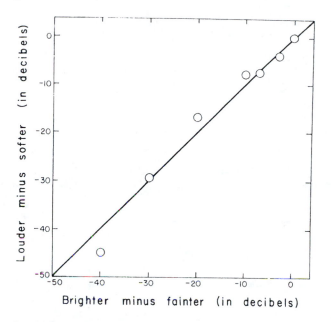

Fig. 44. Results of adjusting a loudness ratio to match an apparent brightness ratio defined by a pair of luminous circles. One of the circles was made dimmer than the other by the amount shown on the abscissa. The observer produced white noises by pressing one or the other of two keys, and he adjusted the level of one noise (ordinate) to make the loudness ratio seem equal to the brightness ratio. The brighter light was about 99 decibels above 10^{-10} lambert (or 0.3 μcd/m^2), and the louder noise was about 92 decibels above 10^{-6} W/m^2 (or 20 μN/m^2). (Data from J. C. Stevens 1957.)

both the loudness of a band of noise and the brightness of a luminous target of white light subtending a visual angle of 4 degrees. Both the sound and the light could be varied over a range as wide as 80 decibels. In a carefully counterbalanced procedure the observers matched sound to light and light to sound. There was, of course, the usual slight regression effect, but the average of the two regression lines was 1.0 in both of two separate experiments, each employing ten observers. One of the regression lines from one of the experiments is shown above in Fig. 39. It appears, therefore, that the results of ratio matching have been confirmed by direct matching and that the exponents of brightness and loudness have approximately the same value.

Ratio matching may also involve stimuli from the continuum of number. The experimenter can present two numbers, for example, 15 and 4, and ask the observer to adjust a pair of lights to stand in the same ratio. Or we can turn it about and present two loudnesses and ask for two numbers that stand in the same apparent ratio as the loudnesses. Of course, when we use numbers we are apt to indulge in verbal shortcuts and state the numerical value of the ratio directly. Thus we may present one loudness and ask the observer to produce a loudness that is twice as great. Conversely, in the method of ratio estimation we may present two loudnesses and ask the observer to estimate their ratio.

Historically, the method of ratio production holds claim to seniority over all other direct scaling procedures. It had its origin in Merkel's (1888) attempt to find what appeared to the observer to be the "doubled stimulus," as he phrased it. Unfortunately, nothing much came of that early effort, even though Merkel was on the right track, as was later demonstrated in the 1930's when ratio production served as one of the procedures that gave rise to the first loudness scale that gained serious attention. That was the scale for which I proposed the sone as the subjective unit, defined as the loudness of a 1000-hertz tone at 40 decibels sound pressure level (Stevens 1936).

The method of ratio estimation was later used extensively by Gösta Ekman in Sweden. He developed procedures for processing the data when estimates have been made among all possible pairs of a set of stimuli (Ekman 1958).

INTERVAL MATCHING ACROSS MODALITIES

When a pair of stimuli is presented in each of two modalities, instead of asking the observer to match ratios, we can ask him to match intervals. We can instruct him to make the apparent difference between the two stimuli of one pair seem equivalent to the apparent difference between the two stimuli of the other pair. Then by presenting differences of various sizes we can have the observer attempt to match the series of differences.

That procedure is especially straightforward when the stimuli for one continuum are beads on a wire or markers on a bar. The observer can slide the markers so as to make the distances between them appear to match the distances between, say, a series of lightnesses—stimuli representing shades of gray between white and black. An experiment incorporating cross-modal interval matching was used to test the spacing of the lightness values on the Munsell scale, which is a widely used standard series of grays. The interval-matching procedure confirmed the fact that the successive Munsell values represent approximately equal subjective intervals (Newhall 1950).

Shortly thereafter, working with tonal stimuli (1000 hertz), I presented a series of five loudnesses and asked the observer to space five markers along a steel bar in such a way that the apparent spacing among the markers matched the apparent spacing among the loudnesses. I also turned the procedure around. I set the markers to various irregular spacings and asked the observers to adjust the loudnesses so as to make the loudness spacing seem to match the marker spacing.

In one case I set the distances between successive markers exactly equal and asked the observers to adjust the loudnesses accordingly. In effect I was then instructing the observers to perform what is called an equisection, that is to say, to produce several equal intervals. When only three stimuli are involved, the procedure is usually called bisection. Bisection, of course, is the same as the procedure first used by Plateau when he asked eight artists to paint a middle gray halfway between black and white. The artists performed an interval production, producing two equal intervals.

Unfortunately, the usefulness of interval matching as a scaling procedure suffers severe limitations. Three main difficulties afflict the method when it is used to scale prothetic continua.

1. Hysteresis. Whenever stimuli are presented one after the other, as they must be when sounds are used, the order of presentation affects the apparent size of the successive intervals between the stimuli. For example, if three loudnesses are presented in an ascending order 1, 2, 3, the interval between 2 and 3 seems relatively larger. When the order is reversed, the interval between 2 and 1 seems relatively larger. Suppose we now ask the observer to adjust stimulus 2 so as to bisect the interval 1 to 3, or, in other words, to make the distance 1 to 2 equal the distance 2 to 3. In order to equate the apparent intervals in the ascending order, the observer must set stimulus 2 to a higher value than in the descending order. When the data are plotted, there results a kind of hysteresis loop, as illustrated by three examples in Fig. 45. The data show that hysteresis occurs in three different sense modalities when the stimuli are presented successively. If the stimuli were presented simultaneously, the hysteresis effect would presumably be averaged out. But with many kinds of stimuli subjective intervals cannot be marked off by stimuli presented simultaneously. With those kinds of stimuli there is no known way to avoid the biases of hysteresis.

2. Interval Measure. Even if all bias could be removed, the fact remains that interval matching would result at best in an interval scale, not a ratio scale. The measurement of temperature provides an instructive parallel, for the early inventors of thermometers tried to create devices to subdivide the interval between two arbitrary temperatures, say, the freezing point and the boiling point of water. Their success led to our currently used interval scales, Celsius and Fahrenheit, each with its own arbitrary zero point. The invention of a ratio operation later led to ratio scales, the Kelvin and Rankine scales, sometimes called absolute scales.

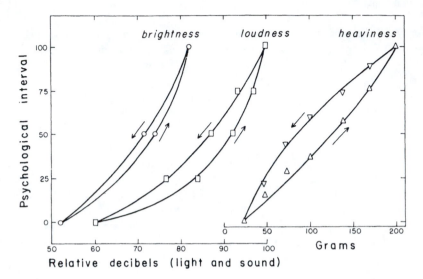

Fig. 45. Hysteresis effects in judgments of intervals on three sensory continua. The arrows indicate the order of stimulus presentation. For brightness and loudness the subject adjusted the middle stimuli to divide the range into two or four equal-appearing intervals. For heaviness the subject lifted three weights and indicated the relative apparent position of the middle weight by means of a slider between two markers on a bar. A different middle weight was used in each of five different experiments involving both ascending and descending order. (From Stevens 1957b, *Psychol. Rev.,* 64, 153–181. Copyright by the American Psychological Association. Reprinted by permission.)

3. Nonlinearity. In the measurement of temperature the Fahrenheit interval scale represents a linear segment of the Rankine ratio scale. But in psychophysics an interval scale generated by interval matching is not a linear segment of the psychophysical magnitude scale. The scale produced by interval matching is systematically curved relative to the scale created by ratio-matching procedures or by magnitude estimation and magnitude production. By whatever method the intervals are made to seem equal to the observer, it turns out that the curvature is always in the same direction. The curvature may vary greatly in amount, however, depending on the precision of the experiment. The persistent, pervasive nonlinear distortion in the interval scale created by partitioning a segment of a continuum is the main subject of the next chapter. Here it should be noted, however, that, despite all the handicaps that afflict interval scaling, the procedure can, if properly used, demonstrate that the psychophysical law is a power function. That demonstration is of capital importance, even though the estimate it gives of the exponent falls on the low side.

INTRAMODAL VERSUS CROSS-MODALITY MATCHING

Many scientists who readily admit the validity of intramodal matching have seemed reluctant to acknowledge that cross-modality matching may also produce valid results. Even though the change from intramodality to cross-modality may seem only a small step to some people, to others it looms as a leap across a chasm. Whether it amounts to a small step or a great leap depends, it seems to me, upon the kind of comparisons involved. Some kinds of intramodal matches present the observer with a difficult task, more difficult, in fact, than some kinds of cross-modality tasks. In an auditory experiment in which I asked observers to match the loudness of a high-pitched hiss to that of a low-pitched rumble, one observer made the match and then remarked afterward, "If you can match those two sounds, you can match anything to anything." That statement contains more truth than the observer realized.

Some cross-modality matches turn out to be much easier and less variable than some of the more difficult kinds of intramodal matches. Among the cross-modality matches that have proved relatively easy is the matching of the loudness of a low-frequency band of noise to the apparent intensity of a vibration applied to the fingertip. When the observer is allowed to turn the sound level up and down, he experiences little uncertainty about finding a level that appears to match a given amplitude of vibration on the fingertip. From the observer's point of view the match seems compelling, so to speak, and there seems to be no great range of uncertainty. On the other hand, when the observer matches line length to loudness, the same degree of compelling congruence does not attach to the point of subjective equality, and the range of uncertainty may become larger. Nevertheless, the typical observer does not match a short length of line to a very loud sound, nor does he match a long length of line to a very faint sound. Moreover, as the level of the sound is changed, the observer is quite able to adjust the line so that it remains proportional to the loudness.

As is the case with intramodal matching, then, the matching across modalities may impress the observer as easy or difficult, and the variability of the matches may vary accordingly. Variability need not defeat the scientist's purpose, however, provided the variability is properly random. By the strategy of taking larger samples of data, the experimenter can in effect reduce the ill effects of random variability through the simple process of averaging the data. There may, of course, remain systematic biases that cannot be removed by averaging. Those systematic effects must be controlled or evaluated in other ways.

Is it a fact, then, that anything can be matched to anything? That question may command no final answer, but, as we have seen, observers have managed to match a very wide variety of stimuli one to another. The inventory of cross-modality experiments has grown enormous. Out of the great variety of those experiments one general rule seems to emerge: any two stimuli can be equated by the procedure of cross-modality matching, provided they each have at least one aspect or attribute that varies in degree. Two continua that vary in degree can always be compared by one or another method of direct matching.

ABNORMAL SENSE ORGANS

It is especially instructive to examine the cross-modality matches made by a group of clinical patients with defective sense organs. From the population of a hearing clinic, the otologist Thalmann (1965) selected a group of ten patients, all of whom had normal hearing in one ear and a large hearing loss, equal to about 50 decibels, in the other ear. Five patients had a conductive hearing loss and five had a neural hearing loss. The experiment required that each patient adjust the amplitude of a vibration (150 hertz) applied to the finger in order to match the apparent loudness of a 1000-hertz tone delivered to one or the other of the patient's ears.

The median cross-modality matches are shown in Fig. 46. As we should expect, when the sound was delivered to the normal ear the patient produced matches that followed a power function, as shown by the circles. The five ears with conductive hearing loss yielded a similar matching function (squares), but the function was displaced about 50 decibels to the right. In other words, the conductive defect attenuated all sounds by 50 decibels, but it left the slope (exponent) of the matching function unaffected. A strikingly different matching function characterizes an ear that suffers from a deficiency in the sensorineural apparatus. As shown by the steep line through the triangles in Fig. 46, the matching function takes on a larger exponent, indicating that loudness grows abnormally rapidly when the sound stimulus is increased. At the level of 100 decibels the hard-of-hearing ear has caught up with the normal ear. The steep loudness function constitutes a phenomenon known as recruitment. A similar phenomenon can be created in a normal ear by masking with a white noise, as we saw in Fig. 25.

Although Fig. 46 presents the median results, the individual results showed that all the patients matched vibration to loudness in much the same way. The matches of each patient defined a power function for both the normal and the defective ear. Moreover, the relative slopes of the cross-modality functions were verified by direct matching—loudness in left ear matched to loudness in right ear. The patients were deliberately selected in

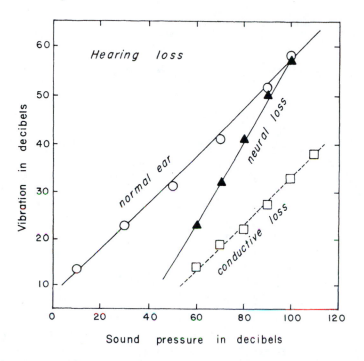

Fig. 46. Cross-modality matches performed by ten patients with abnormal sense organs. Five patients had a hearing loss in one ear due to a neural impairment; five other patients had a loss in one ear due to a conductive impairment. Each patient adjusted a vibration on his finger to match loudness in his normal ear and in his abnormal ear. The symbols show the median results. The conductive hearing loss shifted the function (squares) by about 50 decibels to the right of the normal function. The neural hearing loss transformed the slope (exponent) of the function, as shown by the triangles. The power-group transformation shown by the triangles is termed recruitment. (Data from Thalmann 1965.)

order to ensure that each patient would be able to carry out a loudness balance between his normal ear and his defective ear. The expected transitivity was obtained: the loudness balances of right ear against left ear were those predicted by the vibration matches. Conversely, the vibration matches were those predicted by the left-ear right-ear balances.

The cross-modality matches shown in Fig. 46 may have a special interest for those psychologists who have questioned whether such methods have the capacity to reveal the operating characteristics of the sensory transducers. Even though a sense organ may be defective, a well conducted experiment in cross-modality matching may still be able to reveal the nature of the defect. Dramatically different functions characterize two types of auditory defect.

CHAPTER 5

Partition Scales and Paradoxes

As we have seen, a straightforward procedure for dividing a continuum into equal-appearing intervals is to allow an observer to adjust a series of stimuli to match his conception of equal distances. That was Plateau's procedure when he asked eight artists to paint a middle gray between black and white. The result was a partition scale. But partition scales also come in other varieties. Some of them even turn up in experiments for which the investigator did not intend to produce partitionings. Yet regardless of their origin, all partition scales have one hallmark in common: compared to the magnitude scale, the partition scale is nonlinear. When the partition scale is plotted against the magnitude scale, the result is a curve that is concave downward.

The direction of the curvature of the partition scale is so constant and so independent of the procedures used that it stands as one of the basic invariances of psychophysics. Whenever, given a prothetic continuum, the matching procedure employed is such that the observer is forced out of ratioing and into differencing, so to speak, there results a distorted scale. The distorted scale can usually be described by a power function, so the power function again becomes a convenient descriptor of a stimulus-response relation. But with partition scales the power function has an exponent that is not the actual exponent of the continuum in question. Rather it is a kind of "as if" exponent, a virtual exponent. And as we shall see, the value of the virtual exponent lies below that of the actual exponent.

CATEGORY SCALE

Perhaps no scale is so well known, so often used, and so generally misunderstood as the ordinary category rating scale. A category scale is created when observers assign a category—such as large, medium, or small—to a series of stimuli. The categories may also be designated by a set of numbers, such as 1 to 7, or by letters of the alphabet, as is customary in the grading of college courses. Interestingly enough, the number of categories used makes relatively little difference to the form of the category scale. If the continuum is prothetic, the category scale exhibits a downward concavity when plotted against the magnitude scale. On metathetic continua, the pure category scale is linear. But since most perceptual continua are prothetic, most category scales share the defect of nonlinearity.

Why the nonlinearity? When he performs category estimation does the observer not assign numbers to stimuli, and is that not what he also does under the method of magnitude estimation? To be sure, the two methods exhibit a superficial resemblance, but they stand poles apart with respect to one crucial feature. Magnitude estimation permits the free assignment of numbers, so that magnitudes, as well as ratios among magnitudes, can be reflected in the numbers that the observer emits to depict his subjective impression. By contrast, category estimation sets a limit on the numbers, letters, or adjectives that the observer is allowed to use. As soon as that limit is set, the nature of the exercise changes and the game takes on a new character. No longer can the observer respond to relative magnitudes by placing them in their appropriate place on a ratio scale. He must instead try to spread the limited, finite set of numbers over whatever segment of the perceptual continuum is presented to him. In order to spread the numbers evenly, he tries in effect to subdivide the continuum into equal intervals. In other words, whenever the experimenter limits the numbers, the observer's response lapses perforce into a partitioning operation. A finite set of seven numbers, like a set of seven adjectives, can be used to mark off equal-appearing distances, but neither the numbers nor the adjectives can be used to express ratios.

It seems intuitively obvious that a series of adjectives do not lend themselves to the representation of ratios, for clearly there is no sense in which a ratio can be said to exist between the adjectives medium and small, or the adjectives large and small. But it may be objected that between two numbers there does exist a definite ratio. In what sense then is the ratio not useful? It is not useful for the same reason that ratios have no firm meaning on interval scales. The problem can be illustrated in this way. Suppose we add an arbitrary number, 100, let us say, to each of the numbers on a 5-point category scale. Instead of the numbers 1, 2, 3, 4, and 5, we then have 101, 102, 103, 104, and 105. For category scaling the second set of five numbers would serve quite as well as the first set. The smallest stimulus would be assigned 101, the largest 105, and the stimulus that seemed halfway between would be given the number 103. Clearly, however, the ratios among the numbers become very different after a constant such as 100 has been added to each of them. Nevertheless, although ratios have been altered, differences remain unaffected. Consequently, the middle number can still be assigned to the stimulus that appears to lie at the midpoint.

Many psychophysicists have been surprised to find that the category scale is curved in such a way that the midpoint determined by category estimation does not coincide with the midpoint determined by magnitude estimation. Around that issue there has swirled a series of controversies, usually oriented toward two questions: (1) whether it is in fact true that the observer's category judgment fails to hit the same midpoint as his magnitude judgment, and (2) whether, if the two midpoints do not coincide, there exists any basis for choosing one over the other. The first question can be settled directly by experiment, but the second question involves deeper considerations, such as the kind of measurement scale we may prefer to take as basic to the description of sensory functions, and the predictive power that we demand for the resulting system of measurement.

As we found in the previous chapter, the free cross-modality matching of numbers to sensory continua and the matching of one sensory continuum to another have met the severe test of transitivity. In particular, we have seen that the observer's responses in cross-modality matching can be predicted from the responses he makes in free magnitude estimation. Although the demonstration of cross-modal transitivity and its attendant predictive power has impressed many scientists as decisive evidence for the validity of the unconstrained use of numbers in magnitude estimation, not all investigators appear to have been convinced. An occasional author has preferred to believe that a better scale is obtained when the observer is denied the free use of numbers and is constrained to use a limited set of numbers. Thus one author has interpreted the nonlinear relation between the category and the magnitude scales as evidence that "magnitude estimation is biased." The author goes so far as to say that category ratings "constitute the true measure of sensation" (Anderson 1972). Such a boldly contrary view, if it were to prevail, would foreclose the measurement of sensation on a ratio scale and relegate sensation measurement to a mere interval scale. The greater power and utility of the ratio scale has been demonstrated in many different ways throughout the scientific enterprise. It seems unlikely that the science of psychophysics would be advanced by the deliberate choice of a weaker form of scale.

Many scientists have found it difficult to believe that the simple category scale can be as curved as actual measurement often shows it to be. My own first encounter with a curved category scale left me in a state of puzzled disbelief. The category scale in question was created in 1953 by a group of acoustical engineers who were concerned with the loudness of truck noise on the highway. A jury of listeners rated each passing truck on a 6-point scale. The noises were recorded and also converted into loudness in sones by means of an early version of the sone scale. The engineers seemed pleased with the results, because the two kinds of measures lined up fairly nicely on a graph. The point scattered rather closely about a straight line, with a correlation equal to 0.94. There was a catch, however, for the coordinates were semilogarithmic: the category ratings had been plotted against log sones. In linear coordinates, of course, the plot of category value versus sone value would follow a curve. Since the sone scale had been constructed to agree with people's judgments, I wondered what had gone awry.

Shortly after my encounter with that engineering study and the question it created about the sone scale, another study gave a similar result. People working in offices on a military air base were asked to express their opinions regarding the noisiness on a category rating scale. Again the category scale agreed better with the logarithm of the sone values than with the linear values.

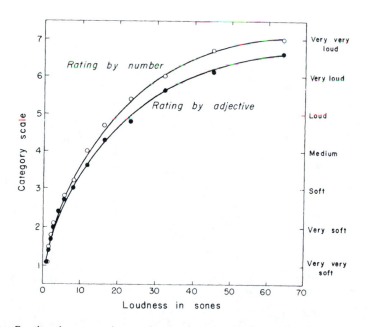

Fig. 47. Results of two experiments showing how the category scale produces a curvilinear plot against the ratio scale of loudness. The stimulus was a white noise that ranged from 40 to 100 decibels in steps of 5 decibels. The logarithmic stimulus spacing tends to increase the curvature. (From Stevens and Galanter 1957, *J. Exp. Psychol.*, 54, 377–411. Copyright 1957 by the American Psychological Association. Reprinted by permission.)

Soon thereafter a colleague and I brought the problem into the laboratory where we analyzed some 70 different category scales on a dozen different continua. On all the prothetic continua, the category scales were curved. On the metathetic continua, the category scales were straight (Stevens and Galanter 1957).

Figure 47 shows two category scales for loudness, both plotted against the sone scale of loudness. Twenty observers judged the loudness of white noise on a numerical scale from 1 to 7 and on a scale defined by seven adjectives. The faintest and the loudest stimuli were presented at the outset in order to define the two extreme categories. Then the stimuli, spaced at 5-decibel intervals from 40 to 100 decibels, were presented in irregular order, a different order for each observer. The points on the graph represent the mean category rating.

The two functions in Fig. 47 show that it makes little difference to the form of the function whether the observer uses adjectives or numbers. The tendency for the adjectival scale to fall below the numerical scale reflects a local artifact. It happened that some of the observers had been serving in other experiments where the sounds used were much more intense than any

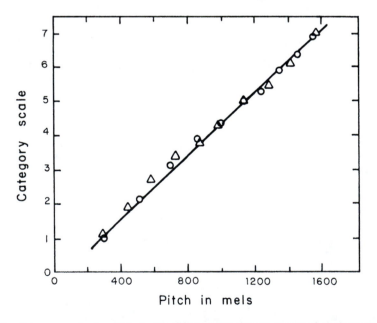

Fig. 48. Category scales for pitch. In two different experiments groups of 10 observers made category judgments of pitch on a 7-point scale. Stimuli were pure tones ranging from 200 to 2000 hertz. (From Stevens and Galanter 1957, *J. Exp. Psychol.*, 54, 377–411. Copyright 1957 by the American Psychological Association. Reprinted by permission.)

used for the category scaling. For those observers the modulus had so changed that the top stimulus did not meet their criterion of "very very loud."

The curvature of the prothetic category scale stands in striking contrast to the form of the category scale on a metathetic continuum such as pitch. Figure 48 shows the results of two experiments, in each of which groups of 10 observers made category judgments on a 7-point scale. The listeners judged pure tones ranging from 200 to 2000 hertz, or roughly from well below middle C to three octaves above middle C. The spacing of the tones differed slightly in the two experiments. The average category judgment was plotted against the mel scale of pitch—a ratio scale based on fractionation, equisection, and magnitude estimation. The data in Fig. 48 describe a rather straight line, suggesting that on a metathetic continuum the category scale is linearly related to the magnitude scale. Apparently, then, category scaling does not necessarily produce a biased, nonlinear outcome, provided its use is restricted to metathetic continua.

CATEGORY SCALES AND THE TIME ERROR

It turns out that certain factors in the experimental procedure can affect the form of a category scale, regardless of the kind of continuum under test. And still other factors that one might suppose would control the form of the category scale have relatively minor effects. Two factors whose effect on the form of the category scale is relatively unimportant are the range of the stimuli presented and the number of categories the observer is permitted to use. Those two factors can vary over rather wide limits without producing a large effect on the form of the category scale.

Since the older literature of psychophysics abounds with descriptions of lifted weight experiments, it is easy to find examples of category scales involving different numbers of categories, as well as stimulus ranges extending from the just discriminable to the widest practicable.

Three illustrative category scales for lifted weights are shown in Fig. 49. The category curves all have about the same form. They would all show slightly greater curvature if, instead of being plotted against the stimulus weight, they were plotted against the subjective weight scale in vegs. That follows because the exponent of the veg scale is about 1.5 and therefore concave upward.

Because the curves in Fig. 49 are plotted against grams, they also illustrate the interesting phenomenon known as the "time error," a constant error discovered long ago by Fechner. On the average, the second of two equal stimuli tends to be judged greater than the first. The time er-

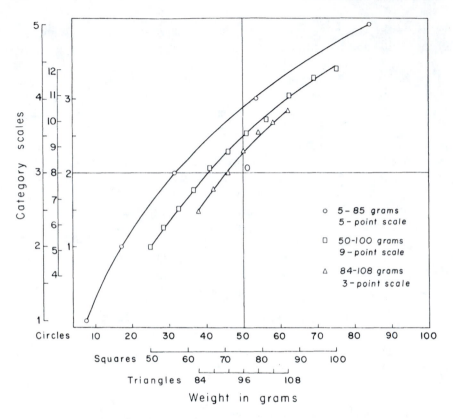

Fig. 49. Category scales for lifted weight, showing various stimulus ranges and numbers of categories. On the middle curve only every other point has been plotted. Note that the curves are all concave downward. The fact that they do not pass through the point 0 indicates a "time error." (From Stevens 1957b, *Psychol. Rev.*, 64, 153–181. Copyright by the American Psychological Association. Reprinted by permission.)

ror shows up especially clearly in experiments designed to measure a just noticeable difference on a prothetic continuum. The experiment that produced the triangles in Fig. 49 was such a study. The variable stimuli covered a very short range and the observer was asked to categorize the stimuli as light, intermediate, or heavy.

The so-called time error appears to have nothing to do with the passage of time; rather it has to do with the curvature of the category scale. The nonlinear asymmetry of the category curve causes it to pass to the left of the point labeled 0 in the center of Fig. 49. That is the point where the middle category would coincide with the middle stimulus. On prothetic continua, the middle category is assigned to a stimulus that is lower than the midpoint on the observer's subjective scale. By the same token, the stimulus at the midpoint is assigned a category value higher than the middle category value. In other words, the stimulus that equals the "standard" at the center of the series (whether that standard is presented or omitted) is, on the average, judged greater than the standard. Consequently, in the curvature of the category scale we encounter the simple relations needed to explain the long-debated mystery of Fechner's time error. A corollary, of course, is that no time error shows itself on metathetic continua. There the category scale is straight, and in experiments designed to measure the just noticeable difference, the observer assigns the middle category to the middle stimulus (Stevens and Galanter 1957).

Actually, in the experiment that produced the triangles in Fig. 49 no standard was used, because, curious as it may seem, the standard had been demonstrated to be superfluous (Wever and Zener 1928). How superfluous? Completely, it seems. As a matter of fact, when the standard is presented before every trial, a remarkable bit of involuntary behavior can be demonstrated. Each time one of the variable stimuli is presented for judgment, there is an attention response on the observer's part: his pupils open up in a momentary dilation. But, except on the first few trials, it has been found that no pupil dilation occurs when the standard is presented (Kahneman and Beatty 1967). Since the observer ceases to pay attention to the standard, it can be omitted entirely—with a great saving of time and effort, and at no cost to the experiment.

PURE CATEGORY SCALE BY ITERATION

In the rating procedure the principal factor that may alter the form of the category scale is the relative spacing among the stimuli. If the experimenter bunches the stimuli toward one end of the scale, he gets one result; if he bunches them toward the other end, he gets a very different result. Spreading the stimuli evenly over the range produces a third result. In short, each stimulus spacing produces a different category scale. How then do we determine the true form of the category scale, the so-called pure scale, unadulterated by the effects of an arbitrary stimulus spacing? That problem has often been addressed by psychometricians and psychophysicists. They have usually reached the conclusion that, as Titchener (1923) said, "The error cannot be eliminated." Thurstone (1929) also saw that the problem of stimulus spacing was a "serious limitation" for which, as he said, "I can offer no solution."

A more optimistic outlook is warranted, I think, provided the experimenter is prepared to perform more than one experiment and to let the outcome of one experiment serve as a guide to the procedure employed in the next experiment. That, of course, sounds like the kind of common sense rule that ought to apply to all experimental science. When the specific problem concerns the form of an unknown function, such as a category scale, the approach may be called experimental iteration. Iteration is a powerful procedure, which I have found useful in several contexts (Stevens 1955b). The iteration procedure can rectify the almost inevitable bias that results from the experimenter's necessarily arbitrary selection of stimulus values and other parameters at the outset of an investigation.

Experimental iteration can be applied to category scaling by carrying out a few simple steps. The first step is to choose an arbitrary stimulus spacing. For example, the spacing used to obtain the category scales in Fig. 47 was arbitrarily made logarithmic—5-decibel intervals from 40 to 100 decibels. (When the arbitrary spacing was made equal in sones rather than decibels, the curvature turned out to be quite different.) The second step is to use the category scale obtained with the initial arbitrary spacing to determine the spacing of the stimuli to be used in the second experiment. Thus if we decided to work with the category scale determined by adjectives in Fig. 47, we would first plot the category scale against the decibel stimulus scale. We would then use that curve to respace the 13 stimuli so as to reflect the category judgments. The middle stimulus, for example, would be moved from 70 decibels, where it was arbitrarily placed in the first experiment, to 78 decibels, which corresponds to the category judged medium. The other stimuli would also be moved to the new positions indicated by the category curve.

A second experiment would then be run and the results plotted. The stimuli would next be respaced to correspond to the second category curve. With that new spacing a third experiment would be run, and the process would be repeated. Iteration proceeds in that fashion until the results of an experiment show that no new spacing is called for; that is to say, until the category scale last obtained prescribes the same spacing as the spacing that was used to obtain it. At that point we have purified the scale of the spacing bias, and in that sense we have achieved a pure category scale.

Iteration provides a potent antidote to many kinds of bias that intrude because of the parameters and contexts that the experimenter must perforce start out with. Often only one or two iterations are required to reach a sufficiently unbiased endpoint. In a thorough study of many aspects and techniques of iteration Pollack (1965) observed, "At first, the several iterative techniques appear to act in a magical way to fashion stable rating scales. There is nothing magical about their action." He later concluded, "Rapid convergence upon an unbiased scale is achieved by a wide range of iterative techniques, for a wide range of stimulus variables, and for a wide range of psychophysical methods."

IS THE CATEGORY SCALE LOGARITHMIC?

Throughout the past century, there have been repeated claims that the category scale is logarithmic. The pure category scale is not logarithmic. If it were, it would appear as a straight line when plotted against the logarithm of the stimulus. (The power law entails that the category scale would also appear as a straight line when plotted against the logarithm of the subjective magnitude.) Instead, the pure category scale is concave upward when plotted against the logarithm of either the stimulus or the subjective magnitude. An example is shown in Fig. 50. The circles show the stimulus values that would be used if another iteration (the third) were to be undertaken, but that step did not seem to be called for.

Another procedure that produces a similar curve is the method of category production. The experimenter, instead of setting the stimuli, may present only the top and bottom stimuli at the outset and then name the

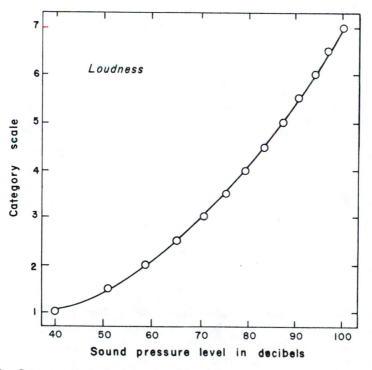

Fig. 50. Category scale for loudness plotted in semilogarithmic coordinates. The curve was obtained on the second iteration. The points represent the stimulus values that would be used if another iteration were undertaken. In semilogarithmic coordinates the category scale is concave upward.

categories in irregular order. The observer adjusts the stimulus to produce each category as it is named. Results obtained with the procedure of category production show a curvature very similar to that of the pure category scale in Fig. 50. To my knowledge, no instance of a category-production scale has been exhibited in which the form was demonstrably logarithmic.

Why then does the false notion that the category scale is logarithmic refuse to die? Several reasons can be named, ranging from wishful thinking by an author to experimental incompleteness. Fechner was one of those who looked for a logarithmic function wherever he could find it. He found a logarithmic relation, or thought he did, in that oldest category scale of all, the scale of stellar magnitude, in terms of which the early astronomers had judged the brightness of the stars (see Fig. 4). When it became possible to measure the light from the stars, and therefore to forego the procedure of subjective judgment that had produced the early category scale, the astronomers found that the measured values of the stars that had previously been categorized 1 to 6 coincided fairly well with a logarithmic function.

Why was the astronomer's category scale nearly logarithmic? (It was actually slightly more curved even than a logarithmic function.) The reason seems to rest with the tremendous skewness of the stimulus distribution. The faint stars outnumber the bright stars by many hundreds to one. As a distorted stimulus arrangement, the night sky shows a bunching near one end of the scale that far exceeds any spacing distortion that I have ever tried in the laboratory. It should be noted, however, that the excessive curvature of the category scale of stellar magnitude is precisely in the direction that laboratory experiments lead us to predict.

When we created in the laboratory a tiny source of light that resembled a star and asked observers to judge its brightness on a category scale, the result was a curve much like that in Fig. 50. Plotted against decibels of light intensity, the category scale was concave upward. By contrast, the 6-point category scale of the early astronomers was slightly concave downward when plotted against decibels (Stevens 1960). The difference between the two scales presumably results in large measure from the difference in stimulus spacing.

Thurstone (1929) undertook to test Fechner's logarithmic law by allowing 101 subjects to judge the numerousness of arrays of dots. He used a 10-point category scale. The 24 stimulus values were spaced in roughly equal logarithmic steps from 68 dots to 198 dots. Since the data appeared to follow a straight line in a semilogarithmic plot, Thurstone concluded that Fechner's law "has been verified." Actually, it seems to me that Thurstone's data show a slight upward concavity, the kind that shows up in dozens of other category scales. The curvature would presumably have been readily apparent had it not been for the shortness of the stimulus range. The largest stimulus was not quite three times the smallest stimulus.

As the stimulus range becomes shorter, the form of the function becomes more and more indeterminate. Over a very short range, the two functions, logarithmic and power, become indistinguishable. For example, a threefold stimulus range in sound pressure is equivalent to 10 decibels. Note how little curvature in Fig. 50 can be seen when you cover up all but a 10-decibel stimulus range. Unfortunately, Thurstone did not try longer ranges of stimulus values, nor did he try other relative spacings. If he had varied those parameters, it seems probable that he would have been less sure that he had verified Fechner's logarithmic law.

Other psychophysicists have clung to the notion that the category scale is a logarithmic function of the stimulus, not because they favor Fechner's law, but because they have found the logarithmic category scale congenial to their theorizing about what people do when they judge stimuli. Those with a theoretical bent sometimes enjoy a livelier concern with theory than with fact—with schematics than with empirics. If the schematizer can assume that the category scale is a logarithmic function and that the magnitude scale is a power function, then certain neat relations can be built into the schematic model. If, however, the theorist must contend with the empirical fact that the pure category scale is concave upward in a semilogarithmic plot (as illustrated in Fig. 50), the schematic model must be altered accordingly. Since that alteration may prove something of a nuisance, some theorists have preferred to go on assuming that the category scale is logarithmic.

APPARENT SIZE

In order to make the partition problem more concrete, let us consider some actual stimuli. Although it is impossible to conduct the experiment properly on the page of a book, I have attempted in Fig. 51 to picture some of the stimuli that are of special interest in experiments on apparent size. In a properly conducted experiment, each circle would ordinarily be drawn on a separate card, more circles of intermediate sizes would be added, and each circle would be presented separately for perhaps 1 second, to be followed by another circle chosen at random. Each observer would experience the stimuli in a different irregular order. If the task was magnitude estimation, the instructions would ask the observer to assign to each stimulus whatever number seemed appropriate to represent the apparent size. No standard stimulus is needed. If the task was category estimation, the smallest circle would be presented and called 1, and the largest would be presented and

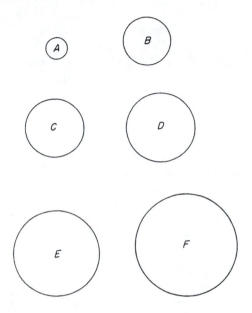

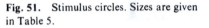

Fig. 51. Stimulus circles. Sizes are given in Table 5.

called 7, and the observer would be instructed to assign a number from 1 to 7 to each stimulus as it appeared. The stimuli would then be presented in irregular order, a different order for each observer.

The quantitative relations among the circles are shown in Table 5. If the exponent of the power function of the apparent magnitude scale is taken to be 0.7, then circle F would be judged to be 10 times larger than circle A. The area of F is actually 26.3 times larger than A. On the scale of apparent magnitude, circle D lies halfway between A and F. In category estimation

Table 5. Relative values relating to the six circles in Fig. 51. The subjective magnitude of apparent size is assumed to increase as the 0.7 power of the area.

Circles	Diameter ratios	Area ratios	Subjective magnitude
A	1.0	1.0	1.0
B	2.3	5.1	3.2
C	2.9	8.5	4.5
D	3.4	11.3	5.5
E	4.3	18.5	7.8
F	5.2	26.3	10.0

experiments, the consensus would place the midpoint closer to *C* than to *D*. The reader may or may not agree. When viewed simultaneously, the circles interact and affect one another's appearance by way of such factors as contrast effects, and it may not be obvious which circle, *C* or *D*, best marks the midpoint in apparent size between *A* and *F*.

Circle *B* represents the midpoint predicted by the logarithmic law. To most people *B* appears to lie well below the midpoint, seeming closer to *A* than to *F*. That judgment accords with the verdict of Fig. 50, which shows that the pure category scale is not a logarithmic function.

THE VIRTUAL EXPONENT

If the category scale is not a logarithmic function, the next question we might ask is whether it is a power function. The answer is yes. Most category scales can be described quite well by a power function, provided an appropriate constant is added to the category scale. We recall that a constant of any value whatever can be added to a category scale without impairing its ability to represent the observer's partitioning judgments. We are free, therefore, to add whatever constant will make the form of the category scale approach as close as possible to a power function.

We can see how the procedure works by examining Fig. 52, which is a log-log plot. The lower curve shows that the category scale, taken from Fig.

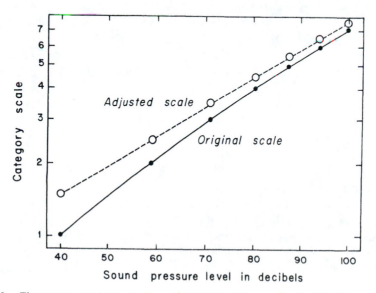

Fig. 52. The category scale for loudness plotted in log-log coordinates. The lower curve is from Figure 50. With the addition of the constant 0.5 to each of the categories the curve becomes straight, as shown by the dashed line whose slope (exponent) is 0.25.

50, does not give a straight-line power function in log-log coordinates. Rather it is decidedly concave downward. However, when we add a constant equal to 0.5 to each of the categories, the adjusted values describe a close approximation to a straight-line power function, as shown by the dashed line. Adding a constant in logarithmic coordinates changes the curvature because the constant has a larger effect at low values than at high values. Different constants may be tried until the maximum straightness is found.

Our next question concerns the exponent. The dashed line shows that the partition scale, adjusted by the addition of a constant, has a slope (exponent) of about 0.25. Clearly that exponent is not the actual exponent of the loudness continuum. The loudness exponent is near 0.67. The partition scale exponent can be regarded as a virtual rather than an actual exponent. In category scaling, and in other kinds of partitioning exercises, the observer behaves as though the virtual exponent were in charge of his behavior. His judgments accord with a virtual or "as if" exponent whose value is always lower than the value of the actual exponent of the continuum.

The first virtual exponent ever determined seems to have been the one calculated by Plateau, for whom the eight artists painted the middle gray. Plateau himself did not record the value of the exponent, but his friend Delboeuf reported it as ⅓. That value seems about right, because the standard Munsell gray scale, perhaps the most widely used partition scale in existence, has the same exponent ⅓. By contrast, the actual exponent of the black-gray-white series, as determined by magnitude estimation, is much larger, namely, about 1.2 (Stevens and Galanter 1957).

The virtual exponent serves to characterize category scales and equisection scales, as well as certain other types of partition judgments. Whenever the observer must in one way or another subdivide or partition a prothetic continuum, the outcome can usually be described by a formula relating partition scale values P to stimulus values ϕ

$$P + P_0 = k\phi^{\alpha}$$

The exponent α is the virtual exponent. The constant P_0 is the added value used to maximize the fit to a power function. When the partition equation has been applied to a wide variety of category and equisection scales, the fit of the power function has turned out to be quite good (Marks 1968).

The amount by which the virtual exponent α falls below the actual exponent β tells us how curved the partition scale will be when we plot it against the magnitude scale. If the exponents α and β were equal (as they may be on metathetic continua), the partition scale would constitute a linear segment of the magnitude scale. The relative curvature of the partition scale increases more and more as the value of α declines. When the value of the virtual exponent falls to close to zero, the curvature of the partition scale approaches that of a logarithmic function.

Conversely, we can consider what would happen if we assumed that in Fig. 52 the original category scale was as curved as a logarithmic function. Such a curve would pass through the two endpoints, but the midpoint would correspond to category 4 at the stimulus 70 decibels. Now, when we try to straighten that curve by adding larger and larger constants, the slope becomes more and more horizontal and the exponent approaches closer and closer to zero. Actually, except for an occasional idiosyncratic case, such as the astronomer's 6-point scale of stellar magnitude, the virtual exponent has always been found to lie above zero. Taking note of all the evidence now available, we can be quite certain that the pure category scale has a virtual exponent well above zero. The importance of a virtual exponent whose value differs decidedly from zero lies in the evidence it provides that the category scale is not a logarithmic function of the magnitude scale.

DIRECT ESTIMATION OF INTERVALS

The very useful concept of a virtual exponent with a value lying between zero and the value of the actual exponent stands ready to help in the description of many different kinds of partitioning judgments. It helps to make understandable some otherwise puzzling behavior. Consider an experiment in which the observer is presented with a variety of intervals and is asked to say how large they seem. The procedure involves magnitude estimation applied to intervals. For example, one of my students presented pairs of loudnesses and asked for a numerical estimate of the apparent difference between the members of each pair (Dawson 1968). It turned out that a constant loudness difference (in sones) is not judged to be constant. What happened instead was what the virtual exponent predicts: a given difference, for example, 30 sones, was judged relatively larger when the two stimuli marking the interval were faint sounds, and relatively smaller when the two stimuli were loud sounds. In other words, an interval of a fixed subjective size appeared to grow smaller as it moved upward along the continuum.

That statement has the ring of a contradiction, for we seem to be saying that intervals made subjectively equal do not appear subjectively equal. The paradox results, of course, from the nature of the procedure. The experimenter sets up the equal intervals by marking off equal distances or partitions on the sone scale, the scale determined by magnitude estimation, and he then asks the observer to judge how large the partitions appear to be. The sone scale is governed by the actual exponent, but it is the virtual exponent that governs the observer's assessment of the partitions. The difference between those two exponents resolves the paradox.

Let us examine some relevant experimental data from another investigation (Beck and Shaw 1967). Observers were asked to judge four loudness intervals, 5, 10, 15, and 20 sones in width. Each interval was located at four different stimulus levels. The median magnitude estimations for 28 subjects are shown in Fig. 53. In order to avoid too much crowding on the graph, I have omitted the points for the 15-sone intervals. All the data follow the

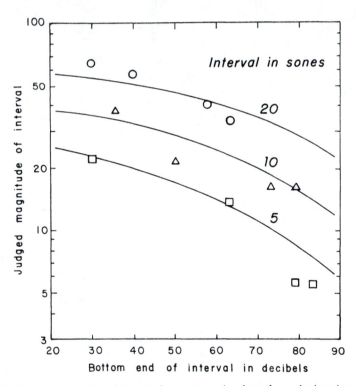

Fig. 53. The judgment of an interval of a constant size depends on the location of the interval. Observers made magnitude estimations of sets of intervals 5, 10, and 20 sones wide. The stimulus level at the bottom end of the interval is shown by the abscissa. The ordinate gives relative values only. As a constant interval moves upward in sound pressure level, the perceived size of the interval decreases. The family of three curves was generated by assuming that, instead of the actual exponent of the sone scale 0.6, the observers used a virtual or "as if" exponent equal to 0.3. (From Stevens 1971b, based on data of Beck and Shaw 1967, *Psychol. Rev.,* 78, 426–450. Copyright by the American Psychological Association. Reprinted by permission.)

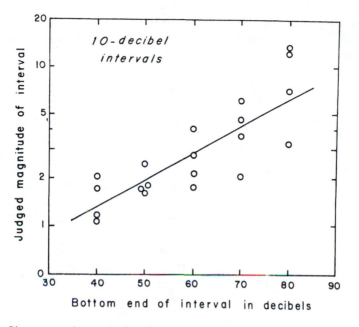

Fig. 54. Observers made magnitude estimations of the apparent size of intervals 10 decibels wide. The apparent size increases when the stimulus level is increased. Results from four separate experiments by Dawson (1968).

same general trend. The curved lines through the data show the predicted outcome. The prediction is based on the assumption that, when the subjects attempt to judge the size of loudness intervals, they perform as though they had adopted a virtual exponent about half as large as the actual exponent. The value assumed for the virtual exponent was 0.3. The scatter of the data about the predicted lines is fairly large, but the scatter appears to be more random than systematic. After all, the judgment called for—the quantitative assessment of the difference in loudness between two tones sounded in succession—places a heavy load on the listener. Under the circumstances, the data can be said to follow the curves well enough to confirm the basic principle, namely, that a given subjective difference appears smaller as it moves up the stimulus scale.

If the natural world were so constructed that equal prothetic intervals always appeared equal to the observer, the lines in Fig. 53 would be straight and horizontal. In fact, if the data points marched horizontally across the plot, we would be forced to conclude that the virtual exponent is equal to the actual exponent. In particular, if the observer's virtual exponent were 0.67 it would correspond to the actual exponent of the sone scale, and the predicted lines in Fig. 53 would become horizontal.

In the foregoing experiment the experimenter made the intervals equal in sones. Suppose instead he were to make the intervals equal in terms of a logarithmic measure such as decibels. What would the predicted function look like? If, as some authors have supposed, the partition scale is a logarithmic function, the equal-decibel intervals would be judged equal, and in a plot like that in Fig. 53 the outcome would follow a horizontal line. That is not what happens, however, as we can see in Fig. 54. There I have plotted the results for four experiments in which groups of observers judged an assortment of intervals 10 decibels wide, making magnitude estimations of the apparent size of the intervals (Dawson 1968). The 10-decibel intervals were incorporated in an experiment involving other sizes as well. Partly for that reason, plus the inherent difficulty of that type of interval judgment, the data show considerable scatter, but the general trend is far from horizontal. As a matter of fact, the general trend follows rather nicely the same trend that would be predicted if we assume that the observers make their judgments in terms of a virtual exponent equal to about half the value of the actual exponent. In order to illustrate the predicted slope, a line has been drawn in Fig. 54 with a slope equal to an assumed virtual exponent that is half the actual exponent. Here again we see how the concept of the virtual exponent gives a good account of the observer's behavior when he makes numerical judgments concerning the apparent size of prothetic partitions.

EQUISECTION AND THE PLATEAU PRINCIPLE

The most straightforward procedure for partitioning a continuum is to permit the observer to adjust the stimuli to produce two or more equal-appearing intervals. When two intervals are produced the method is usually called bisection. It is one of the oldest psychophysical procedures, having been invented by Plateau in the 1850's.

Although I once held firm expectations that the procedure of equisection would provide a tool with which I could examine the form of the magnitude functions for brightness and loudness in greater detail than other methods permitted, several difficulties arose to change my view. For one thing, I discovered the dramatic hysteresis effect that resulted when the stimulus order was changed. For another, I found that, try as I would through numerous procedural variations, I could not make the method of equisection yield an exponent equal to the actual exponent of the continuum. The equisection exponent was always too low. In other words, the observer bisected the interval by adjusting the stimulus to a value closer to the geometric mean than the actual exponent predicts that he should.

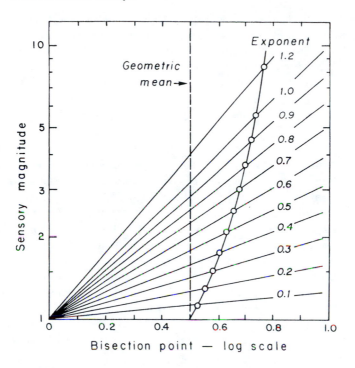

Fig. 55. Schematic diagram showing a family of power functions with exponents ranging from 0.1 to 1.2. The circles show the position of the bisection point, which moves upward along the stimulus scale (abscissa) as the exponent increases. Bisection at the geometric mean would correspond to a logarithmic function, or a vanishingly small exponent. (From Stevens 1971b, *Psychol. Rev.,* 78, 426–450. Copyright by the American Psychological Association. Reprinted by permission.)

The diagram in Fig. 55 is designed to illustrate some of the relevant facts and relations. In particular, it shows how the point of bisection depends on the exponent of the magnitude function. As the exponent (slope) increases, the bisection point moves farther up the stimulus continuum—farther to the right in the diagram, and farther away from the geometric mean. In the other direction, when the exponent becomes very low, the bisection point moves close to the geometric mean. If the bisection point falls precisely at the geometric mean, a logarithmic function is indicated. Thus we see how a logarithmic function behaves like a power function with a vanishingly small exponent.

Despite the failure of the method of equisection to answer the question concerning the exact value of the exponent on a prothetic continuum, the method has other assets. It is capable of providing a powerful demonstration that the psychophysical law is in fact a power function. The demonstration that a power function holds requires that the virtual exponent remain invariant when the experimenter changes the endpoints of the segment by a given factor. In other words, the relative position of the apparent bisection point must remain constant when all the stimuli are increased or decreased by the same factor, or, what amounts to the same thing, when all the stimuli are moved the same number of decibels up or down.

The invariance of the virtual exponent under that kind of stimulus transformation provides evidence for the power law in accordance with what I shall call the *Plateau principle*. It appears that Plateau was the first to invoke the principle. When his eight artist friends each painted a gray to bisect the distance between black and white, Plateau was struck by a remarkable fact. Since each painter went off to his own atelier, each must have worked under a different level of illumination. Nevertheless, the artists produced eight bisecting grays that, when viewed in the same setting, were *"presque identiques."* In order for the same bisection point to be reached despite wide variation in the illumination, the sensory magnitude must follow one of two laws, either a power law or a logarithmic law. The logarithmic law can be eliminated, however, if the bisection point falls above the geometric mean. If that happens, the power law becomes the sole contender.

The Plateau principle can also be applied to bisections and equisections even though the experimental results show the hysteresis effect. Presumably Plateau's artists looked back and forth and canceled or averaged out the hysteresis effect. As we shall see, when the stimulus order is controlled, the hysteresis effect shows up in brightness bisections.

BRIGHTNESS BISECTION

Although the program of brightness bisection that I began in 1953 was designed to study the hysteresis effect, the main rewards of the investigation must be ascribed to serendipity; the agreeable discoveries were not sought for. The first unexpected revelation was a striking similarity between the results for vision and hearing, together with a fairly clear indication that both brightness and loudness are governed by a cube-root law—a suggestion I published that same year (Stevens 1953). There were anomalies, however, and they seemed so puzzling that the complete study was never published. The hysteresis effect still remains baffling, but the discrepancy between the results of bisection and fractionation seem now to fit nicely with the conception of the virtual exponent.

In the bisection experiment, the observer sat in a dark room about 2 feet in front of a black screen with a 1.5-inch stimulus hole at approximately his eye level. There were three finger keys in front of him which he could press in sequence. The left key turned on a dim luminous stimulus, the middle key turned on a stimulus that the observer could adjust, and the right key turned on a bright stimulus. The objective was to adjust the middle stimulus so that it seemed to bisect the distance between the other two brightnesses. The two end stimuli were usually separated by 31 decibels. The observer adjusted the middle stimulus by controlling the voltage on a lamp by means of a Variac autotransformer. The slight color changes that occurred with that procedure did not prove in the least troublesome, partly because the changes were relatively minor, but mainly because the stimuli appeared only successively. Under simultaneous viewing, such color changes may prove quite disturbing.

Groups of 14 to 19 observers adjusted the middle stimulus three times for each stimulus interval presented for bisection. The results are listed in Table 6 and are plotted in Fig. 56. The total stimulus range covered 80 decibels—a range of 100 million to one. The small arrows in Fig. 56 indicate the direction of the stimulus sequence—ascending or descending. As can be plainly seen, the apparent midpoint was adjusted to a higher level when the stimulus order proceeded upward from dim to medium to bright than when the order was reversed.

Table 6. Brightness bisections for six different stimulus ranges. The first two columns show the range in decibels above 10^{-10} lambert (0.32 μcd/m^2). Each of 14 to 19 observers made three bisections of each range. The virtual exponent α in the last column was calculated from the average of the ascending and descending bisections.

Bottom	Top	Ascending bisection	Descending bisection	Virtual exponent for mean bisection
80	107	98.9	97.3	0.23
67	98	90.4	87.9	0.27
57	88	79.8	77.7	0.25
47	78	69.8	67.0	0.22
37	68	59.8	58.0	0.26
27	58	50.6	49.5	0.33
Average				0.26

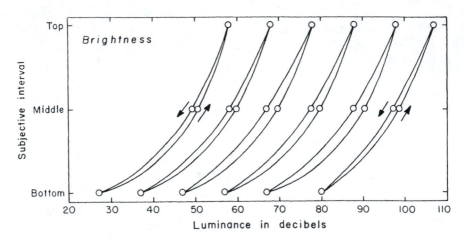

Fig. 56. Bisections of brightness intervals, showing the hysteresis effect produced by the order of stimulus presentation. The abscissa shows the luminances in decibels, relative to 10^{-10} lambert. The apparent midpoint is at a higher luminance when the luminances are viewed in ascending order. Each bisection was made by from 14 to 19 observers, each of whom repeated the task three times, in both ascending and descending order. Thus each point is based on from 45 to 57 bisections. The bisection values obtained by averaging the ascending and descending series are consistent with a power function having an exponent of 0.26. (From Stevens 1961b, *Science*, 133, 80–86. Copyright 1961 by the American Association for the Advancement of Science. Reprinted by permission.)

A striking feature of Fig. 56 shows up in the approximate similarity of the curves drawn to connect the midpoints with the top and bottom levels. That feature of approximate similarity is precisely what the Plateau principle calls for and, to that extent, the data in Fig. 56 provide a rather powerful demonstration that subjective brightness is governed by a power law. The logarithmic law is ruled out as a possibility, because the lines are curved rather than straight.

But what about the exponent? If we do away with the hysteresis by averaging the midpoint values for the ascending and descending bisections, we obtain a single bisection point. I have calculated the virtual exponent of the power function that corresponds to each of the average bisection points. The procedure used was graphical, based on the principles illustrated in Fig. 55.

A formula can also be written for the virtual power function in terms of the three stimuli ϕ_1, ϕ_2, and ϕ_3. If we assume that the observer has set ϕ_2 to appear equidistant from ϕ_1 and ϕ_3, we can write

$$\phi_3{}^\alpha - \phi_2{}^\alpha = \phi_2{}^\alpha - \phi_1{}^\alpha$$

The value of the exponent α in that equation can be found by iteration with the aid of an appropriate computer program.

By my graphical calculations, the average value of the virtual exponent α turned out to be 0.26, a value that falls below that of the actual exponent 0.33, which is the value based on the consensus of many experiments.

BRIGHTNESS FRACTIONATION

Using the same apparatus that was employed for bisection, I also determined a brightness function by the method of fractionation to half brightness—a form of ratio production. I merely turned off the bottom stimulus and asked the observer to adjust the middle, or variable, stimulus so that it appeared half as bright as the top, or standard, stimulus. The observer was permitted to turn on alternately the standard and the variable stimulus as often as desired while adjusting the variable to the apparent half value. Under those circumstances the results, shown in Table 7, led to an average exponent equal to 0.37, a value slightly higher than the consensus value for brightness.

In those two experiments, bisection and fractionation, we encounter a curious paradox. When I turned off the bottom stimulus, instead of lowering the level of the middle or halfway stimulus, the observer raised the level of

Table 7. Brightness fractionation (ratio production). Each of 13 to 15 observers adjusted a variable brightness three times to make it appear half as bright as a top or standard stimulus. The average of the fractionation values corresponds to the exponent 0.37.

Top	½	Difference in decibels
107	98.1	8.9
98	89.7	8.3
88	78.9	9.1
78	69.5	8.5
68	60.4	7.6
58	50.9	7.1
48	40.8	7.2
38	31.0	7.0
Average		8.0

```
Interval              Ratio
bisection             production

top ─────             top ─────



                      half ─────
middle─

                                    Fig. 57.  The midpoint obtained in the bisection of an in-
bottom─                             terval is generally lower than the value obtained when the
                                    observer adjusts the stimulus to appear half as bright as the
                      "zero"        top stimulus.
```

the halfway stimulus. It is as though halfway from the top stimulus to "zero" were somehow less than halfway from the top to a value well above zero. Figure 57 is a diagram illustrating that paradoxical state of affairs. We must bear in mind, however, that, in the method of fractionation, the observer "bisects" between the top standard and "zero" only in a purely figurative sense. Zero is only an abstraction; it is not a stimulus. What the observer does, in fact, is to produce ratios. In the present instance his 2-to-1 ratio productions gave the exponent 0.37, but when he tried to bisect the distance between two brightnesses, his partition response corresponded to the virtual exponent 0.26.

LOUDNESS EQUISECTION

When observers divide a segment of the loudness continuum into equal-appearing intervals, we see the same general features that are exhibited when brightness is partitioned. The hysteresis effect is actually more prominent in hearing than in vision, and the virtual exponent appears to be generally somewhat smaller.

In one part of my series of loudness experiments the observer pressed five keys, one after the other, to produce five stimulus levels of a 1000-hertz tone. The top and bottom levels were fixed and the three intermediate levels could be adjusted to divide the loudness range into four equal-appearing intervals. A similar experiment had been performed by Garner (1954) and I had alerted him to the hysteresis effect—an effect that he proceeded to verify. In an effort to cancel the hysteresis effect, I asked the listener to press the keys in both ascending and descending order. An occasional observer objected that, when the intervals sounded equal in the ascending order, they did not sound equal in the descending order. He would be asked, nevertheless, to try to compromise by finding the best intermediate value. The stimulus levels in decibels set by the listeners are listed in Table 8. A virtual exponent was calculated from the bisection setting for each stimulus range, and that exponent is also listed in Table 8. The average virtual exponent is approximately 0.4, which compares with the value 0.67 for the actual exponent when the stimulus is measured in terms of sound pressure. The virtual exponents calculated for Garner's equisection experiment averaged about 0.2.

The effect illustrated in Fig. 57 was especially striking with loudness. When I made the bottom stimulus very faint, so that it was barely audible, the observer set the bisection point to a particular value. I then made the bottom stimulus too faint to be heard. Thereupon the observer revised the setting and adjusted the middle stimulus to a higher level. In other words, he switched from partitioning to fractionating (ratio production). The phenomenon seemed quite baffling when I first encountered that paradox, but it now appears more understandable. The phenomenon can be described in terms of a change from the virtual to the actual exponent.

I also explored other procedures in an effort to counter the hysteresis effect and to try to make equisection agree with fractionation. One procedure

Table 8. Loudness equisections for 1000-hertz tones. Each of 9 to 16 observers adjusted three loudnesses to create four equal-appearing intervals between fixed top and bottom levels. The stimulus levels were heard in both ascending and descending order. The observer adjusted each stimulus three times. Tabled values are in decibels above 20 μN/m².

Bottom	¼	½	¾	Top	Virtual exponent
16	32.9	42.5	50.3	56	0.30
16	47.8	61.4	69.9	76	0.33
26	52.0	63.0	70.2	76	0.40
36	56.3	65.3	71.1	76	0.48
56	76.4	85.4	91.5	96	0.49
90	101.6	109.6	115.3	120	0.38
101	111.8	119.3	125.0	130	0.35
111	123.6	130.6	136.0	140	0.48
Average					0.40

was to take the control of the stimulus levels out of the hands of the listener. Accordingly I set five stimulus levels and asked the listener to adjust the spacing of five sliding markers along a steel bar so that the spacing of the markers represented his perception of the relative spacing of the five loudnesses. Various stimulus spacings were presented to 25 observers who listened to the stimuli in both ascending and descending order. The results are shown in Fig. 58, where they can be compared with a curve drawn to represent the locus predicted by the two-thirds power law.

In some ways the experiment was fairly successful. The observers found the task straightforward, and the adjustment of the sliding markers proved a satisfactory way of indicating the distances separating the perceived loudnesses. Like all experiments, however, that one had its own set of biases. The most obvious was the well-known centering tendency that afflicts all rating scales on which the subject indicates his judgment by marking a position along a line between two endpoints or categories. People tend to mark the more central positions and to avoid the extremes. That tendency is clearly evident in Fig. 58. Near the bottom the points are elevated; near

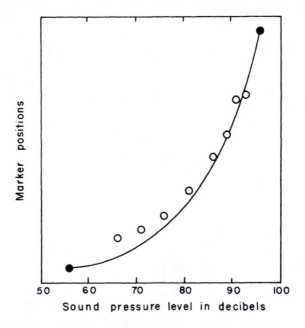

Fig. 58. Results of matching the position of markers on a steel bar to apparent spacing among loudnesses. In each session each of 25 observers listened to five loudnesses in both ascending and descending order. The end markers were fixed and the observer could slide the three intermediate sliders. The curve is drawn according to a power function with the exponent $\frac{2}{3}$.

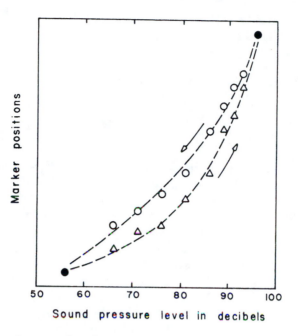

Fig. 59. Fifteen observers adjusted marker positions to match apparent spacing among five loudnesses. In a given session the loudnesses were either ascending or descending. The marker positions demonstrate the hysteresis effect.

the top the points are depressed. As a result of the centering tendency the points do not follow the course of a power function such as the one illustrated by the continuous curve, which represents a power function with the exponent ⅔.

An automatic timer was then introduced to present the stimuli in fixed sequences. A group of 15 observers adjusted the markers to reflect the spacing of the loudnesses presented in ascending order and, in separate trials, in descending order. The observer's use of the markers did not abolish the hysteresis effect, as can be seen in Fig. 59. The centering tendency is also evident in Fig. 59. As regards the virtual exponent, if we average out the hysteresis and look only at the middle or bisection point, it appears that the virtual exponent is about 0.5, which is slightly higher than the average in Table 8.

It is also possible, of course, to turn the marker procedure around and do the interval matching in the opposite direction. Using that procedure I set the markers to various spacings and asked the observers to adjust the loudnesses to match the apparent spacings of the markers. An appropriate name for that method is multisection—a partitioning into unequal intervals. The method of multisection did not appear to give results that differed from the special case of equisection—a partitioning into equal intervals.

LOUDNESS AND THE PLATEAU PRINCIPLE

Despite the many disappointing features that seemed to afflict the experiments on the partitioning of loudness, I was impressed with the fact that the relative position of the bisection point did not change in any systematic way when I changed the stimulus intensities over an enormously wide range. The stability of the bisection point is reflected in the approximate constancy of the virtual exponents listed in Table 8. Those virtual exponents suggest two things: first, that the underlying loudness function must approximate either a logarithmic or a power function, and second, that, since the virtual exponents differ significantly from zero, the power function emerges as the only real possibility.

Another way of eliminating the logarithmic function is by appeal to the form of the curves in Figs. 58 and 59. In those semilogarithmic coordinates the graph would result in a straight line if the function were logarithmic. The observers signaled very clearly, by their placement of the sliding markers, that the partition function is curved in a semilogarithmic plot. Moreover, the curvature departs from the logarithmic function in the direction of a power function.

UPPER LIMIT OF LOUDNESS FUNCTION

A question of special importance concerns the range over which the power function holds. In attempting to answer that question I persuaded a dozen listeners to subject themselves to stimulus levels so intense that the sound produces a sharp pain in the ear. The task was to make equisections of the interval between 111 and 140 decibels. Other listeners had already made equisections of the interval between 101 and 130 decibels, which most listeners find definitely painful. To my surprise, the equisections gave no evidence of any change in the loudness function at those very high intensities. The evidence is contained in Table 8, where we see that the virtual exponent for the interval 111 to 140 decibels is 0.48, a value that is not out of line with the other values in the table.

It is often assumed, of course, that, beyond some level of stimulus intensity, loudness must stop growing, or at least slow its rate of growth. That may indeed be true, but the solid evidence from the equisection experiment suggests that, at 140 decibels, loudness is still growing in accordance with the same power function that governs the growth of loudness at moderate intensities. As one of the listeners in the experiment, I can testify that a 1000-hertz tone at 140 decibels sounds about twice as loud as the same tone at 130 decibels. Both levels of tone produce other sensations in addition to loudness, namely, a kind of pricking or burning pain. The discomfort dictated that each listener should be asked to make only one equisection at the highest intensity, 111 to 140 decibels. Three repetitions had been made at all the other levels. Also, listening was monaural at the highest level, whereas it had been binaural at the lower levels. The purpose was simply to confine any possible hearing damage to only one ear. Without that concession it proved difficult to find willing listeners.

In an earlier research program concerned with deafness and hearing aids, we showed that speech could be fully understood even when the peak sound pressure of the sound waves reached 142 decibels (Davis, Stevens, et al. 1947). In the speech intelligibility test at that level, each test word produced a piercing pain, but the ability to understand the speech was not impaired.

How loud is a tone of 1000 hertz at a sound pressure level of 140 decibels? Louder than any sustained (nonexplosive) sound that most people have ever experienced. In order to find a comparable sound pressure level we must look to such noisemakers as the jet engine of a fighter plane operating with its afterburner turned on. On an aircraft carrier deck, within 50 feet of such a machine, the noise level may reach 140 decibels. For comparison, conversational speech averages about 60 or 70 decibels. Very loud talking may reach 80 decibels. For the average listener genuine discomfort begins at about 120 decibels (see Fig. 13).

Additional evidence for the continuing growth of loudness at high levels was obtained by the method of ratio production. A group of 22 observers adjusted a variable loudness to sound half as loud as a standard. They also adjusted the variable to sound twice as loud (Stevens 1957a). The standard was set at a sound pressure level of 30, 60, 90, and 120 decibels. Overall, the ratio productions confirmed the power law as the approximate form of the growth function for a tone of 1000 hertz. What is especially interesting is the fact that when the observers undertook to double the apparent loudness of a tone of 120 decibels, they adjusted the level upward by the appropriate number of decibels. The median upward adjustment was close to 9 decibels. In other words, 129 decibels was judged to be twice as loud as 120 decibels. That result accords with the prediction of a power function with the exponent $\frac{2}{3}$.

EQUISECTION AND THE PITCH SCALE

One situation in which the method of equisection proved well adapted to the scaling task was in the construction of a scale of apparent or subjective pitch. The scale of apparent pitch must be distinguished from the musical scale, which is really a scale of frequency. The notes on the musical staff signify the stimulus frequency that the performer is to produce. By apparent pitch is meant the subjective height of a tone as it sounds to the listener. In other words, it is based on human judgment. Stated in terms of operations, we use subjects to determine subjective pitch, but we use either mechanical or electronic instruments to determine frequency. The musical scale is essentially a logarithmic scale of frequency. Apparent pitch is not a simple function of the stimulus frequency, and it bears no simple relation to the musical scale.

The bisection of pitch distances has had a long and curious history. It was, in fact, the subject of a classic controversy in which two giants of early experimental psychology, Wilhelm Wundt and Carl Stumpf, generated a parade of polemics. The question at issue was simple. Where does the observer set the frequency when he bisects the apparent distance between two fixed frequencies? Wundt appealed to some experimental measurements made by one of his students and said that the bisection point was near the arithmetic mean of the two fixed frequencies. Stumpf, who was himself an accomplished musician, undertook to reanalyze the experimental results and to interpret them quite differently. Stumpf believed the bisection should fall at the geometric mean, which would correspond to the midpoint in terms of the musical scale. The dispute began calmly enough, but when rejoinder followed rejoinder the argument became more strident and more personal until at last, several rejoinders later, the debaters were writing more about each other than about the bisection of tonal intervals (Boring 1929). What we now know about the pitch scale suggests that both polemicists were correct, provided we are free to choose the particular frequency interval to be bisected, but neither was correct if his claim was supposed to hold for all intervals.

The first attempt to create a ratio scale of apparent pitch employed the method of fractionation (Stevens, Volkmann, and Newman 1937). A standard and a variable tone were presented alternately, and the observer adjusted the frequency of the variable to make it sound half as high in pitch as the standard. Three years later a second experiment was undertaken with improved apparatus and provision for the use of two experimental procedures, fractionation and equisection (Stevens and Volkmann 1940a). For the second experiment we constructed an electronic piano that produced pure tones. The frequency of each tone could be adjusted by means of a knob located directly above the piano key, as illustrated in Fig. 60. For the second experiment we also made it possible for the observers to experience very low frequencies, as low as 25 hertz in one part of the experiment. That frequency was near the lower limit imposed by the loudspeakers, and it sounded like a very low pitch indeed.

The data obtained by fractionation agreed rather precisely with the data obtained by equisection. In fractionation the observers set one tone to appear half as high in pitch as a standard tone. In equisection the observers divided various frequency intervals into four equal-appearing pitch distances. The combined results are shown in Fig. 61. The unit of the pitch scale, called a mel, is defined so that 1000 mels corresponds to the pitch of a 1000-hertz tone. A table relating pitch in mels to frequency in hertz is presented in Appendix B.

The pitch scale has both theoretical and practical importance. In addition to providing us with a prime example of a metathetic continuum, the pitch scale bears important relations to several other quantitative aspects of hearing. Three of those relations are the following.

1.   Map of the Cochlea.   Many attempts have been made to determine the place along the basilar membrane where each tonal frequency does its stimulating. The various maps show generally good agreement with one

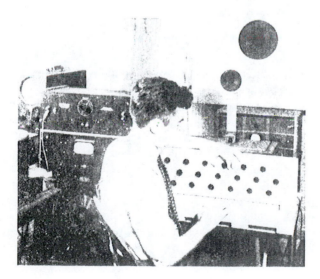

Fig. 60.   Showing an observer adjusting the frequency of one of the keys of the electronic piano. (From Stevens and Volkmann 1940a. Reprinted by permission.)

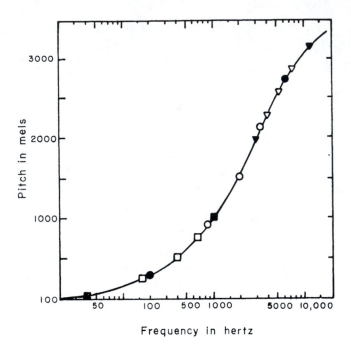

Fig. 61. The curve shows how pitch, scaled in subjective units (ordinate), varies with frequency. The circles, squares, and triangles represent data obtained in the experiment using equisection. The filled symbols mark the ends of three frequency ranges, and the empty symbols show the points arrived at when the observers divided the ranges into four equal intervals of pitch. (From Stevens and Volkmann 1940a. Reprinted by permission.)

another. One of the earliest and most complete maps was determined for the guinea pig by procedures described in Chapter 7 (Stevens, Davis, and Lurie 1935). There appears to be a remarkable coincidence between two functions—equal distances along the basilar membrane and equal pitch differences in mels. In other words, the pitch function provides a linear map of the basilar membrane, which means that when the observer produces equal pitch extents by equisection, he sets the stimuli so that their positions of stimulation are equally separated along the length of the inner ear.

2. Resolving Power. The smallest change in frequency that the ear can detect varies with frequency. The just noticeable difference serves as a measure of the ear's resolving power. The important point for our present concern is that the just noticeable difference varies with frequency in the same way that pitch varies. It turns out, in fact, that the smallest resolvable difference corresponds to about one mel (Stevens 1954).

Looked at from another point of view, if we do what Fechner proposed and count off the just noticeable differences, we obtain the mel scale of pitch. Thus we find that Fechner's procedure, which fails so completely on prothetic continua, leads to a useful result when applied to the metathetic continuum of pitch.

3. Critical Band. Several kinds of experiments have shown that one rule holds when stimulus events are widely separated on the basilar membrane and that a different rule holds when the stimulus events occur within close proximity to one another. The boundaries that define those two regions or proximities are said to mark the critical bandwidth. The concept was invented by Harvey Fletcher (1940), who discussed it mainly in terms of the spread of the masking effect of one stimulus on another, but the concept has proved useful in other contexts as well (Zwicker, Flottorp, and Stevens 1957). For example, when two equally loud tones, spaced far apart in frequency, are turned on simultaneously, they sound about twice as loud as one tone alone. But when both tones lie within the same critical band, their loudnesses no longer add up to twice the separate loudnesses. Rather, within the critical band, according to Fletcher (1953), it is not the loudnesses but the energies that summate. It follows that two equally loud tones lying within a critical band sound as loud as one of the tones increased by 3 decibels. By contrast, it takes about 9 decibels to double the loudness of a tone.

We find a remarkably close relation between the critical band measured in various ways and the pitch scale. All critical bands turn out to be approximately the same width in mels. On the basis of the evidence currently available, I have proposed that the critical bandwidth may be defined as 100 mels.

To sum up, four quantitative features of the auditory system exhibit interesting similarities as regards their relation to stimulus frequency. The four are: equal mel intervals, just noticeable differences, critical bands, and distance along the basilar membrane. The conclusion seems compelling that the pitch scale reflects a fundamental feature of both the anatomy and the behavior of the inner ear.

MUSICAL INTERVALS

If the pitch scale is not the same as the musical scale, we can ask how they are related. In particular, can the mel scale be used to measure the size of musical intervals? For example, when a musical fifth—the frequency ratio 2 to 3—is produced by two notes sounded in succession, is it the same in subjective size, regardless of whether the notes are sounded in a low or a high register? Musicians are often surprised to be told that the apparent size of a fifth expands to sound about seven times larger when it is moved from a low-frequency interval, 64 to 96 hertz, to a higher-frequency interval, 2048 to 3072 hertz. Those intervals both sound like musical fifths—the frequencies are in the ratio 2 to 3—but as Stumpf and other observant and psychologically oriented musicians have noted, a fifth in an upper register seems perceptually larger than a fifth in a lower register. This is also true with octaves. The higher octaves seem wider than the lower octaves.

The subjective size of other musical intervals at various locations on the frequency scale can be determined with the aid of the table in Appendix B. All musical intervals grow subjectively larger as frequency increases up to about four octaves above middle C. In other words, throughout the whole of what is usually called the musical range, intervals made up of equal frequency ratios (i.e., musical intervals) increase in perceived pitch extent with increasing stimulus frequency.

Those facts contradict the widely held notion that equal intervals of frequency give rise to equal intervals of pitch. The misconception arises, of course, because it is often thought that the musical scale based on frequency ratios is somehow a subjective scale. It is not. True, the violinist tunes his strings to equal musical intervals by ear and not by actually measuring frequency. But he tunes his strings to certain ratios of frequencies—he tunes to the musical scale, not to the scale of subjective pitch. The musican's "equal interval" generally means equal in frequency ratio, and equal frequency ratios do not in general produce equal intervals in subjective pitch.

THE PARADOX

Let us return now to the puzzle that has run through much of this chapter. Why, when subjects do so well in partitioning a metathetic continuum like pitch, do they show such a stubborn systematic error when they try to partition prothetic continua like brightness and loudness? It seems obvious that the explanation does not lie with the procedure, for similar procedures have been used with both types of continua. There must be something about the prothetic continuum that differentiates it from the metathetic continuum and that makes the partition paradox more understandable. Actually, several features can be cited to differentiate prothetic from metathetic continua. If we take loudness and pitch as illustrative prototypes of the two kinds of continua, we can list the distinguishing features in the manner shown in Table 9.

Table 9. Characteristic properties of prothetic and metathetic continua.

	Prothetic	Metathetic
Prototype	Loudness	Pitch
Main concerns	Quantity or degree—how much	Quality or location—what or where
Error behavior	Relative error approximately constant—hence the JND measured in sones grows larger when stimulus intensity increases	Absolute error approximately constant—hence the JND measured in mels remains constant when stimulus frequency increases
Variability distribution	Approximately log normal	Approximately normal
Time error	Present: stimulus equal to standard is judged greater	Absent: stimulus equal to standard is judged equal
Hysteresis effect	Strong	Little or none
Partition judgments	Disagree with ratio judgments; hence partition scales are nonlinear	Agree with ratio judgments; hence partition scales are linear
Physiological mechanism	Additive: loudness increases when new excitation is added to old excitation	Substitutive: pitch increases when new excitation is substituted for old (locus of excitation moves)

Seen in terms of Table 9, the partition paradox—the failure of partition judgments to agree with ratio judgments—takes its place among several interesting features that create the contrast between the two kinds of continua. Perhaps what I have called the partition paradox is no more paradoxical than some of the other distinguishing features. Is it not strange, for example, that the JND for pitch stays constant in mels as frequency increases, but for loudness the JND grows enormously larger in sones as intensity increases? In particular, the JND measures about 0.1 sone at 40 decibels, but grows to about 8 sones at 100 decibels. In other words, a 60-decibel increase in the stimulus causes the JND for loudness to increase in subjective size by eightyfold. Yet no such change takes place with the JND for pitch.

If there were no relativity of error on the prothetic continuum, or if the error remained nearly constant, judgments of intervals could conceivably agree with judgments of ratios. As it is, however, our expectation that judgments of intervals and ratios will agree runs head on into a contradiction.

Let me illustrate with an example. From the sone table in Appendix C, we can determine that the interval from 41 to 50 decibels has a width of 2 sones. If we ask an observer to judge the apparent size of the 2-sone interval, he will be able to do so with no difficulty. Now suppose we set up another 2-sone interval farther up the intensity scale near 100 decibels. We find that the interval from 100 to 100.1 decibels corresponds to 2 sones. Should the observer judge this new interval to have the same width as the first interval? Since the JND has a value of approximately half a decibel, it seems clear that when two sounds differ by only 0.1 decibel they will prove almost indistinguishable. How then can we expect the observer to judge the apparent size of an interval that falls below his resolving power? In the extreme case, then, it becomes obvious that observers cannot be expected to assess all loudness intervals the same, even though the intervals measure a constant number of sones.

Another example to illustrate the problem that arises in the judgment of differences on a prothetic continuum is shown in Fig. 62. Let us suppose that we are concerned with the judgment of apparent length. If I present each of the lines in Fig. 62, plus a few others, briefly, one at a time, in random positions, and ask you to assign numbers to reflect the apparent length, you will assign numbers that on the average are approximately proportional to the physical length (exponent equal to 1.0). If I ask you for some kind of partition judgment, however, a nonlinearity will set in. Perhaps you can see why that is true if you try to judge the difference between the pair of lines on the left and to compare that difference with the apparent difference between the pair on the right. Which difference seems the more obvious? Probably the one on the left. Which difference seems the larger? The answer to that question may seem less clear. Actually, both dif-

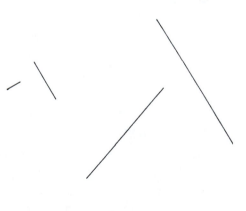

A   B   **Fig. 62.**   Four line lengths.

ferences are the same. The lines were drawn with 1, 3, 8, and 10 units of length. If the paper were larger, I could have drawn another pair with, say, 50 and 52 units of length. It would be difficult to tell those two lengths apart, much less to make a consistent judgment of their apparent difference. Thus the obvious difference seen in the left-hand pair of Fig. 62 transforms itself into an undetectable difference when we keep the difference the same but merely lengthen the lines.

Another way to describe what the observer does when he tries to judge intervals or differences is to say that he confuses differences with ratios. Thus the ratio between the two shorter lines in Fig. 62 seems clearly greater than the ratio between the two longer lines. In the face of the obviously larger ratio, do you tend to perceive the difference also as relatively larger? In other words, is the partition paradox nothing but a kind of illusion, involving perhaps a compromise between a pure interval judgment and a pure ratio judgment? I invoked that type of "explanation" when I first encountered the nonlinearity of the category scale based on loudness judgments, but I am not wholly convinced that it explains the partition effect under all the different circumstances and procedures that have been used to exhibit the effect. I also appealed to the difference-ratio confusion in an attempt to explain our difficulties with the bisection experiment (Stevens and Davis 1938).

If the observer does in effect allow his interval judgments to be swayed and contaminated by a compromise with ratio judgments, we can ask what would happen if the contamination were complete, so to speak, so that when we asked for interval judgments the observer gave us ratio judgments. In that event the virtual exponent would fall to a value near zero, because the partition scale would become a logarithmic function (cf. Torgerson 1961). Since the virtual exponents for the pure category scale and for the equisection scale stand quite far from zero, we can say that if the observer's judgments of intervals are swayed by his being confronted also with ratios, the contamination is seldom complete, but only partial.

Regardless of how we choose to interpret the possible reasons for the partition paradox, the hard fact remains that none of the many procedures of partitioning seem able to provide us with a linear segment of a prothetic continuum. Category scaling, the most widely used method of partitioning, ought especially to be avoided in serious psychophysical measurement. The proper place for the use of category procedures is in the measurement of thresholds. All threshold measures rely on category methods.

CHAPTER 6

Thresholds
and the
Neural Quantum

One of the most remarkable properties of the sensory systems is their extreme sensitivity as measured by the absolute threshold. The ability to tell one intensity from another—the just noticeable difference or differential threshold—is also very good, but not nearly so astonishing as the fine ability to tell whether a faint stimulus is present or absent. The minute amount of stimulation needed to initiate a sensation makes it appear that nature has pushed close to the theoretical limits in providing us with receptors to detect chemical, mechanical, and electromagnetic events in the environment. Such acute sensitivity no doubt has served a decisive role in evolution and has made it possible for complex, mobile animals to survive in ecological competition. The study of sensory thresholds has become a central concern of psychophysics.

We think of a threshold as an all-or-none affair. If I turn on a faint sound you either hear it or you do not. If I start with a sound so faint that you cannot hear it and proceed to turn up the intensity, eventually the sound will cross your threshold and you will hear it. Conceptually, then, the sensory threshold resembles the threshold of a house; the stimulus must rise above the threshold before it can enter. That straightforward conception runs into difficulty, however, as soon as we repeat the procedure. On the next try the location of the threshold will probably have moved up or down, so that the stimulus that crossed it before may or may not be sufficient to cross the threshold again. Although at any given instant the threshold value may be fixed and definite, on two different occasions it may exhibit two different values. Since the sensitivity of the organism bobs up and down from moment to moment, when we want to measure a threshold we are forced to make repeated trials and to strike some kind of average to represent the result. For that reason it is commonly stated that the threshold is a statistical concept.

THE POIKILITIC FUNCTION

The absolute threshold of hearing is probably measured more often on more people than any other absolute threshold. Visual acuity is often measured too, but the absolute threshold of the eye is rather seldom measured. When you have your hearing tested you are asked to place an earphone on your ear and to press a button whenever you hear a tone. The audiologist turns the intensity of the tone up and down and tries to locate the intensity that makes you hear the tone about half the time. The audiologist's procedure is a kind of short-cut statistical procedure.

A more elaborate procedure can be illustrated by a test that we used in an aural rehabilitation project following World War II (Davis, Stevens et al. 1947). A set of carefully chosen words was recorded in such a way that the words could be reproduced at the patient's ear at any desired intensity. The goal was twofold: (1) to determine the faintest intensity at which the patient could hear the speech, and (2) to compare that intensity with the intensity at which a normal ear responds to speech. The difference in decibels between the patient and the normal represents the patient's hearing loss.

First let us consider the threshold of the normal listener. At a given faint intensity he may hear some of the words but not others. If we raise the intensity slightly, he hears a larger percentage of the words, and if we make the speech loud enough he hears all the words. When we plot the percentage heard against the stimulus intensity, we obtain an S-shaped curve like the one on the left in Fig. 63. The curve resembles what is called the ogive of the normal probability distribution. It is not in itself a distribution, but it represents the cumulative form of a distribution. It starts at the low end where none of the stimuli are effective and rises toward 100 percent where all the stimuli become effective. The curve shows the scatter and variability that emerge when we attempt to measure a precise threshold. Historically the curve has often been called the psychometric function, but it has little or nothing to do with psychometrics, which is a discipline concerned with the testing and measurement of intelligence and other traits. In order to distinguish it from psychometrics I have called it the poikilitic function, a term that refers to scatter or variability.

Having determined a poikilitic function, we must decide what to take as the threshold. It seems sensible to define the threshold as the stimulus value at which the listener hears half the words correctly. In terms of the un-

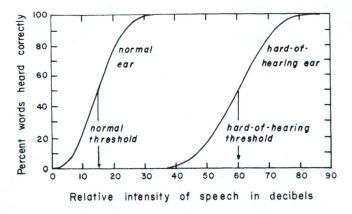

Fig. 63. Poikilitic functions for absolute thresholds. The two poikilitic functions show how the percentage of words heard correctly increases as the intensity of the speech is raised. The intensity at which half the words are heard correctly is defined as the absolute threshold. The amount of hearing loss is the difference between the threshold of the patient and the threshold of a normal ear. In this case the hearing loss is 45 decibels.

derlying frequency distribution, of which the poikilitic function is the ogive, the 50-percent point corresponds to the median value.

For a patient with a hearing loss we carry out the same procedure and determine his 50-percent point. For the example shown in Fig. 63 the patient's hearing loss for speech would be recorded as 45 decibels. Compared to the normal listener, the patient's threshold is elevated by 45 decibels, a fairly severe loss that would require a hearing aid if the patient were to understand ordinary conversational speech.

Another feature characterizes the patient's poikilitic function. The curve rises less steeply than the curve for the normal ear. That means, of course, that the underlying distribution spreads more widely—indicating greater scatter and variability in the response of the patient's ear. That greater scatter becomes understandable when we remember that speech is a very complex type of signal. Since a hearing loss impairs the reception of some combinations of sounds more than others, a greater spread of intensity is needed to bring into perception both the easiest and the most difficult combinations.

It should again be pointed out that when we undertake to measure thresholds we use category methods—those same methods that were shown in Chapter 5 to be so unsatisfactory for scaling. We change our attitude toward the category methods because the problem has changed, and we fit the procedure to the problem. The question at issue in threshold measurement is the location of a boundary between two categories, such as heard and not heard. For that determination the subject uses, in effect, a 2-point category scale. In other contexts more categories may be called for. For example, in a community noise survey people might be asked to use the categories, quiet, noisy, very noisy, and unacceptable. The main purpose of the survey would be to try to find the noise levels that characterize the boundaries between the categories. It might be asked, at what noise level, on the average, do we cross the threshold from noisy to unacceptable? In order to answer that question we could plot a poikilitic function showing how the number of people that found the noise unacceptable increases with noise level. Although the use of a rating scale in such a noise survey may look superficially like category scaling, if the purpose is to locate one or more category boundaries, the procedure may be classed as a type of threshold measurement. In that procedure and in all the many other forms of threshold measurement, the observer is required to match stimulus to category or category to stimulus.

TRACKING

An interesting instance of automation was introduced into threshold measurement by Georg von Békésy (1947). He automated the procedure by making the patient's response button drive the stimulus level up and down. The patient presses a button as long as the sound is not heard and releases the button when the sound is audible. Whenever the button is pressed the stimulus level moves gradually upward, and when the button is released the level moves gradually downward. The stimulus level is recorded by a pen on a moving chart. Sample records are shown in Fig. 64 for two different tonal frequencies tracked for rather long periods of time.

Several important features may be noted in those two attempts to follow the threshold continuously over a 15-minute period. Both records show that the threshold wavers up and down, usually at a slow rate. Thus if we were to draw a line through the middle of each track in order to average the pen excursions, the line would rise and fall irregularly with a maximum swing of about 5 decibels. That variation provides a rough indication of how the overall sensitivity of the auditory system fluctuates in time.

Although the wavering line recorded on a Békésy audiometer seems to bear no obvious relation to the poikilitic function, both types of graph contain similar information. They both show that what we take to be the threshold must be conceived as a statistical value. The median location of the midline through the tracings of Fig. 64 would correspond to the 50-percent point on the poikilitic function. The steepness or flatness of the poikilitic function is reflected in the extent of the pen excursions in Fig. 64.

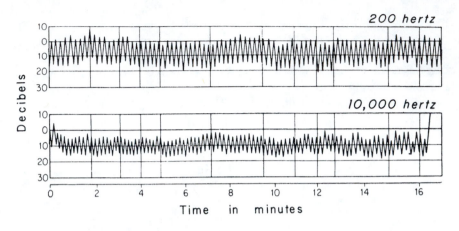

Fig. 64. Records made with a Békésy audiometer. The observer tracked his threshold over a period of about 15 minutes. The stimulus for the upper record was 200 hertz, for the lower record 10,000 hertz. (From Békésy 1947, 1960. Reprinted by permission.)

Thus we see that the height of the excursions is about 15 decibels for the low tone (200 hertz) and about 10 decibels for the high tone (10,000 hertz). Those values suggest that the poikilitic function for 10,000 hertz would be steeper than the poikilitic function for 200 hertz.

Does the Békésy audiometer employ a category procedure? Since the subject votes yes or no with his finger, it seems clear that he is using a 2-point category scale. Automation does not change the basic nature of threshold determination. The observer still matches category to perception.

The Békésy procedure is often classed as a tracking procedure, because the observer in effect follows his threshold up and down. On some audiometers the change of threshold with the frequency of the tone can be tracked. The tone is made to vary slowly from very low to very high, and the observer tracks his threshold throughout the range of audible frequencies. The tracking procedure has also been used with visual as well as other kinds of stimuli.

THEORY OF SIGNAL DETECTION

In many ways the task of an observer trying to hear a faint tone or see a faint light resembles the tasks encountered in sonar and radar. The radar system sends a radiowave signal to the moon, for example, and then tries to detect the returning echo as the wave is bounced back off the moon's surface. The echo is so faint that only the most sensitive radar systems can detect it. Why is it so hard to detect? Mainly because of what is called "noise." All systems in nature generate one or another form of noise or variability. At all ordinary temperatures, atoms, electrons, and molecules move about and create minute disturbances. Consequently, when the engineer undertakes to construct a very sensitive amplifier, he runs into electrical noise as the limiting factor in the amplifier's operation. You can sample some of that kind of noise if you tune your radio or television off the station and turn the sound control up. You will then be amplifying some of nature's electrical noise and turning it into audible noise.

The effective sensitivity of the radar receiver can be improved by a variety of engineering tricks, one of which is to reduce the internal noise of the receiver by cooling the receiver to a very low temperature. Regardless of any ingenious techniques, however, noise sets the ultimate limit on the detection of faint signals. It has become necessary, therefore, for the scientist to try to understand exactly what is involved in the detection of a signal immersed in a noise. What can in theory be achieved? What factors set limits on the correctness of the decision that a suspected signal was indeed a signal and not just a bit of noise? Phrased in that way, the question moves us into the realm of statistics—the testing of statistical hypotheses. Given the burgeoning development of statistics, we are not surprised that the mathematical theory of signal detection has become a well developed tool in the service of the engineer. (For a textbook treatment, see Whalen 1971.)

Since the human observer may also serve as a signal detector, it was only natural that certain features of statistical detection theory should be applied to the human detection process. Our ability to hear a tone is limited by noise. It has been calculated that the motion of the molecules at body temperature generates a noise that is not far below the level of the faintest sound the ear can hear under quiet conditions. If in addition we add an external noise, then the detection of a signal becomes a problem that resembles even more closely the radar problem. As a matter of fact, the addition of external noise has become a popular experimental paradigm among those who have oriented their investigations around signal detection (Green and Swets 1966). By controlling both the noise and the signal, the psychophysicist creates a situation that calls on the extensive mathematical apparatus of decision theory. The task then is to explore the factors that influence the observer's decision processes. In particular, the performance of the real live observer can be compared to that of the ideal observer—a mathematical conception that tells how an optimal decision among alternatives depends on the several parameters of signal, noise, and situation. For a given situation the ideal observer serves as a baseline for the evaluation of human observers, whose performance, as we might expect, seems always to fall short of the mathematical ideal.

By casting the theory in the mold of statistical decision—was it signal or was it noise?—some students of detection theory have been led to postulate that there is no genuine threshold in the classical sense. To be sure, signal detection theory has no need for the concept of a steplike threshold that the stimulus must rise above in order to step over. On the other hand, the fact that it may not be needed in a particular theory does not rule out the existence of a threshold step function. As we shall see later, other ways of examining the fine structure of threshold phenomena make it clear that step-function thresholds cannot be ruled out. It appears that a first requirement, if one is to find evidence for a step function, is to turn off the external noise.

The many investigations conducted thus far under the banner of signal detection theory have served to keep alive a tradition that has been both a strength and a weakness in psychophysics. In 1938 Woodworth expressed the then-current view by saying, "The task of psychophysics calls for measurement of thresholds and variabilities. . . . The preliminary task of devising adequate methods has proved so fascinating as to absorb a surprisingly large fraction of the energies of the psychophysicists from Fechner down to the present" (p. 395).

Thresholds and variabilities were indeed the main task of psychophysics before the advent of the so-called new psychophysics, which concerns itself more with magnitude functions than with thresholds. Yet the earlier fascination with methods for threshold measurement has flared anew as interest has focused on the niceties of the mathematical models that relate to signal detection and on experimental investigations that fit the mold of statistical decision. Like the fascination that engaged the psychophysicists of an earlier century, the concern of the investigators who follow the statistical approach is often more methodological than substantive. There is much honing of the tool's edge, but little cutting.

Thurstone once complained that psychophysics had degenerated into hairsplitting exercises concerning the best way to measure a JND, or a difference limen as it is sometimes called. "Now, it seems strange," he said, "that I have never seen a psychologist who really cared much about any particular person's limen for anything" (1959, p. 287). Perhaps the same thing can be said about the measurement of signal detectability. Although several man-years of effort have gone into refining a decision-type measure of detectability, and to explore its relation to numerous experimental procedures, the question presents itself, would Thurstone be able to find anybody who cared about any particular person's detection performance?

MASKED THRESHOLDS

When a signal is immersed in a noise, interesting substantive problems arise to command our attention. How does the threshold for a pure tone, or for speech, vary with the level of the masking noise? And how does an ideal white noise affect the threshold of tones at different frequencies? Those are two of the questions posed in a study undertaken near the end of World War II (Hawkins and Stevens 1950). In the Psycho-Acoustic Laboratory we had the good fortune to have a full-time crew of observers whose skill was sufficient to enable them to make reliable threshold settings by adjusting a stimulus so that it appeared barely audible. Four members of the crew determined threshold levels for sixteen different frequencies, each in the presence of a masking noise at one or another of eight different levels. Two basic principles were established by the threshold settings.

1. Critical Ratio

When a pure tone is just strong enough to be heard in the presence of a white noise—a noise made up of the whole spectrum of audible frequencies, all at the same intensity—we may assume that those noise frequencies that lie close to the frequency of the tone do more of the masking than the noise frequencies far removed from the tone. How far, in a white noise, does the effective masking spread? That question is easy to ask but difficult to answer. We can, however, replace it with a more tractable question. The alternative question can be phrased thus: how wide a range of frequencies must the noise band encompass in order for the imaginary noise band to be as strong as the tone when the tone stands at its masked threshold? I call the band imaginary because it has no independent existence, being only a part of the wider white noise. What we find is that the required bandwidth varies with the frequency of the tone. At 1000 hertz, for example, the tone at its masked threshold has the same energy as a band of the noise about 63 hertz wide. At 9000 hertz the imaginary noise band must be about 700 hertz wide in order to encompass as much energy as is contained in the tone at its masked threshold.

When we compare how the width of the imaginary band must vary with frequency in order to keep its energy at a constant ratio to the energy of the masked tone, we discover a most interesting fact. The bandwidth varies with frequency in such a way that the width remains approximately constant in terms of the pitch scale. The critical ratio, as I have proposed to call it, represents a pitch width of about 50 mels.

Since the pitch scale provides a linear map of the basilar membrane (Chapter 5), it appears that the bandwidth required to keep the masked tone and the imaginary band of noise equal in energy is such that the imaginary band always spreads the same distance along the basilar membrane.

The bandwidth corresponding to a critical ratio of 1.0 (tone energy equal to band energy) has sometimes been called the critical band. Actually, our arbitrary decision that the ratio should be 1.0 results in an imaginary bandwidth that is about half as wide as the critical band determined by other procedures. By choosing a different ratio we could, of course, make the two kinds of bandwidth measures agree more closely. For example, we could decide that the effective imaginary band that does the masking in a white noise is wide enough to have twice the energy of the masked tone. In that event, the critical ratio would be 2.0, and the imaginary band would be about 100 mels wide, which is approximately the value of the critical band.

The important point in all this rests with our ability to tie the various facts together. We can explain how the masked threshold varies with frequency by appealing directly to the function that relates frequency to its place of excitation along the basilar membrane. Thus we can add the masked threshold to the list of quantitative relations that accord with the pitch scale and that have their basis in the anatomy and functioning of the inner ear.

2. Signal-to-Noise Ratio

Here we turn to another important aspect of the masked threshold. We can pose the question in this way: when a tone is at its masked threshold, what happens if we raise the level of the masking noise? If the noise is increased by 10 decibels, for example, by how many decibels must we increase the tone in order for it once again to reach audibility? The answer turns out to be beautifully simple. We must raise the tone by however many decibels we raise the noise. For a tone at its masked threshold in a white noise, there is, then, a basic invariance: the signal-to-noise ratio stays constant. The ratio of the energy in the tone to that in the noise stays the same, regardless of the level of the noise.

It was especially important to establish that invariance, because in the 1940's the suggestion had been made that the masking noise grows more and more effective, the higher its level. The finding that the ratio of signal to noise remains constant at all levels does much to simplify our conception of the auditory system and its manner of functioning.

The concept of signal-to-noise ratio also provides an important measure for other types of signals, such as speech. In order to provide a good stimulus with which to investigate speech, we made recordings of speech delivered in a carefully controlled voice. The speaker read aloud some dull and polysyllabic passages from *The Wealth of Nations* by Adam Smith. The masked threshold for continuous discourse was measured in two ways. The listener adjusted the level of the speech to the point where he could just detect the presence of speech, but without any of it being intelligible. On another occasion he adjusted the speech to the level of bare intelligibility. The threshold of intelligibility was defined as the level at which the listener was just able to perceive the meaning of almost all sentences and phrases in the connected discourse.

The two thresholds are depicted in Fig. 65, where we see that both thresholds keep step with increases in the level of the white masking noise. The two signal-to-noise ratios remain constant, as shown by the straight portions of the functions, which have a slope of 1.0.

Except for the lowest levels of the masking noise, the threshold of intelligibility stands approximately 9 decibels above the threshold of detectability. That difference is a fairly large one. For most auditory stimuli

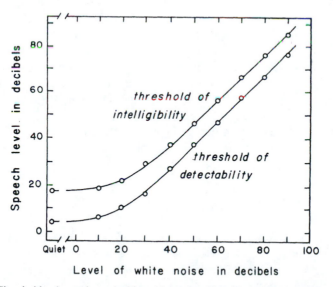

Fig. 65. Thresholds of speech masked by white noise. The threshold of intelligibility is about 9 decibels higher than the threshold at which speech can just be detected. The straight parts of the two functions have a slope of 1.0, which means that for both kinds of thresholds the signal-to-noise ratio stays constant as the noise level changes. (After Hawkins and Stevens 1950.)

an increase of 9 decibels results in a doubling of the apparent loudness. In the presence of a masking noise, however, a 9-decibel increase in the signal may represent much more than a doubling of loudness. See, for example, the steep functions of Fig. 25 in Chapter 3.

WEBER'S LAW

The signal-to-noise ratio tends to remain constant, not only for speech thresholds in noise, but under many other circumstances as well. The same kind of basic invariance shows itself in the principle known as Weber's law. In the 1830's Weber noted that, in order for the observer to perceive one stimulus as greater than another, the greater stimulus had to be increased by a certain ratio. Furthermore, the just detectable ratio remained approximately constant even though the absolute values of the stimuli were varied. We are dealing here with a principle of relativity that pervades all of psychophysics: the just perceptible increase in a stimulus is a relative matter; it depends on the stimulus that was there to begin with.

Although Weber stressed the just detectable ratios of various kinds of stimuli, we more commonly speak of just noticeable differences, JND. Unlike the ratio, the difference does not remain constant. Instead, the JND grows in proportion to the stimulus to which the difference is added. For example, in order to make a weight feel just noticeably heavier, we must add 10 grams to a 50-gram weight, 20 grams to a 100-gram weight, and 100 grams to a 500-gram weight. Thus the JND requires a 20-percent increase in weight. Actually, the percentage required is usually found to be larger for stimuli close to threshold. We see a similar effect in Fig. 65, where the straight lines depart from the slope of 1.0 near their bottom ends. In order to widen its application, Weber's law can be revised slightly by the addition to the stimulus S of a small constant S_0. We then write

$$\text{JND} = k(S + S_0)$$

That formula is sometimes called the general form of Weber's law. By adding the constant S_0 we make allowance for the inevitable noise that remains in the perceptual system, while at the same time we preserve the basic principle that resolving power is essentially relative.

In writing the formula for Weber's law I have deliberately avoided using the customary notation ΔS in place of JND. The symbol Δ has misled many scientists into thinking that the formula can be used in a manner analogous to the way a differential equation is used in physics. The JND is not the derivative of the magnitude function for loudness, brightness, or any other attribute. The JND, as we shall see, is actually a measure of error or variability.

CLASSICAL METHODS

When Fechner decided that the sensation increment corresponding to a stimulus JND could be made to serve as a unit for the sensation scale, he set about to perfect procedures for measuring thresholds, both absolute and differential. We will examine two of those methods, in order to see in what sense the JND is a measure of variability or noise.

1. Method of Average Error

The observer is required to adjust one stimulus to make it appear equal to another. The observer is given a target, so to speak, and he tries to hit the bull's eye. His adjustments scatter about the mark, and, with a sufficiently large number of trials, his settings of the variable stimulus may be plotted as a bell-shaped distribution resembling the normal distribution. Fechner proposed that the scatter of the observer's settings could be used to measure the JND. The observer's settings miss the mark more widely if his sensitivity to small differences is poor, and the settings scatter less widely if his sensitivity is good.

On that basis, then, we take as the JND one or another measure of dispersion. The average deviation about the mean was formerly a widely used measure of dispersion. But the choice of which measure to use is essentially arbitrary. Modern usage might favor the standard deviation. Less important than the particular measure used is the principle involved. Since the definition rests on a statistical distribution, the JND emerges as a measure of dispersion or, as it is often called, noise.

As an example of the use of the method of average error, an experiment on the vibrato can be cited (Youtz and Stevens 1938). A musical vibrato is produced when a violinist wiggles his finger back and forth on a string of the violin and thereby changes the frequency of the tone up and down. How does the extent or range of the frequency change affect the definiteness of the pitch? Youtz and I simulated a musical vibrato by modulating the frequency of a pure tone up and down eight times per second, and we asked observers to adjust a steady tone to appear equal in pitch to the modulated tone. The results are shown in Fig. 66.

It appears that the vibrato makes the tone into a fuzzy, indefinite target, and the indefiniteness becomes more pronounced when the extent of the

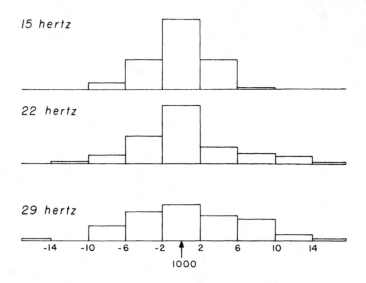

Fig. 66. Histograms showing distributions of settings when observers adjusted a 1000-hertz tone to match the pitch of a tone with vibrato. Three extents of the vibrato were used, 15, 22, and 29 hertz. The narrowest vibrato gave the narrowest distribution—top histogram. Each histogram represents 90 settings. (After Youtz and Stevens 1938.)

modulation is increased. Thus the narrow distribution shown in the top histogram of Fig. 66 is for a modulation range of 15 hertz, whereas the broad distribution shown in the bottom histogram is for a range of 29 hertz. The middle histogram is for a range of 22 hertz. If we were to compute the standard deviations and use them as the JND, we would find that doubling the range of modulation in the vibrato produces an approximate doubling of the size of the JND. The data suggest that the musician with a strong vibrato can be farther off tune without its becoming noticeable than if he produces only a narrow vibrato.

2. Method of Constant Stimuli

This method removes the stimuli from the observer's control and sets them at predetermined constant values. The observer's task is to categorize the stimuli as greater or less than some criterion or standard stimulus. Each stimulus is paired with the standard in random order until enough category judgments have been obtained to plot a poikilitic function.

An example of a poikilitic function obtained by the method of constant stimuli is shown in Fig. 67. The experiment was concerned with the saturation of the color red (Panek and Stevens 1966). A gray and a red were mixed in various proportions by means of a rotating color mixer. A standard stimulus, 80 percent red and 20 percent gray, was presented first and was followed by various other mixtures. On each presentation, the subject judged the second stimulus as more red or less red. The circles in Fig. 67 show the percentage of the presentations on which the second stimulus was judged more red than the standard.

As was noted in Chapter 5, the use of a standard with the method of constant stimuli turns out to be a waste of time and effort. Since the observer's task is simply to categorize the comparison stimuli, he very quickly ceases to pay attention to the standard. As noted earlier, his pupils cease to expand when the standard is presented (p. 141). Like many experimenters, my collaborator was skeptical when I told him that we did not need to use a standard stimulus, and so we ran the experiment both with and without a standard. The triangles in Fig. 67 show the results obtained with no standard. The results obtained with and without the presentation of a standard can be described by similar poikilitic functions. Some measure of the slope of the function is defined as the JND, for example, the difference between the stimuli corresponding to 50 and 75 percent.

The poikilitic curve in Fig. 67 has a form that approximates the cumulative ogive of the normal distribution. It also resembles the form that

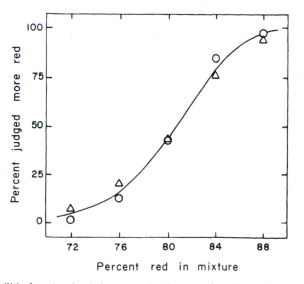

Fig. 67. Poikilitic function for judgments of redness produced by mixing red and gray. In one experiment (circles) a standard (80 percent red) was presented before each comparison stimulus. In the other experiment (triangles) no standard was presented. The observers categorized the stimuli as more red or less red. (Based on data of Panek and Stevens 1966.)

we would obtain if we plotted the cumulated curves for the histograms shown in Fig. 66. In other words, the poikilitic function and the histogram can be regarded as two sides of the same coin—two representations of the underlying variability, error, or noise in the system.

A fundamental principle emerges from the foregoing considerations: the JND is a statistical measure of variability or noise. It is a measure of the spread or scatter of a distribution. Two statistics often used to measure scatter are the standard deviation and the quartile deviation. On the ogival form of the poikilitic function the quartile deviation is the distance between the 50- and the 75-percent points. Other conventions for measuring the JND are sometimes encountered, but the point needs to be stressed that, under most experimental procedures, the JND turns out to be a measure of something that goes by many names, among them scatter, variability, dispersion, error, and noise. Under the classical experimental procedures the poikilitic functions resemble normal ogives, and they exhibit little or no evidence of a step that could properly be called a threshold.

THE NEURAL QUANTUM

Yet there must be a threshold. The physiologists have demonstrated all-or-none conduction in nerve fibers and across synaptic junctures. It would be strange if the well-documented threshold effects that appear in the behavior of nerves and synapses had no counterpart in any kind of psychophysical effect. Boring had that thought in mind in 1926 when he hypothesized that "sensory quanta" may manifest themselves in perception as critical points where a smooth function is broken by a discontinuity. "It should be perfectly feasible experimentally," he wrote, "to determine the presence or absence of critical points."

It remained for Békésy, who later won a Nobel Prize, to demonstrate the existence of critical points. Curiously enough, what appears to have motivated Békésy's experiment was the search for a basis for Fechner's logarithmic law. Fechner had made two assumptions: (1) that the JND is a constant proportion of the stimulus—Weber's law—and (2) that each just noticeable increase in the stimulus corresponds to a constant increment in sensation. The second assumption, we now know, is quite erroneous. Nevertheless, Békésy translated those two assumptions into neural terms. He proposed that the total magnitude of a sensation such as loudness depends on the number of cells excited, and that the JND corresponds to the addition or subtraction of one excited cell. "Since the cells of the nervous system are very much alike," he wrote, "it seems anatomically plausible that the excitation of each new cell entails the same sensation increase, regardless of how many cells are already active" (Békésy 1930, 1960).

Although that simple neural conception, which would lead to a logarithmic law rather than a power law, now needs revision, it served as the rationale for an experiment that led eventually to the demonstration of step-function thresholds. Békésy first tried to find evidence for the addition or subtraction of an excited cell by employing the method of constant stimuli. A brief standard tone of 300 hertz was presented first and was followed 2 seconds later by either a stronger or a weaker tone. The observer judged in terms of two categories, same or different. As with other experiments of that type, the results can be described by an S-shaped poikilitic function, with no evidence of a critical discontinuity where the activity of a new cell may have been added.

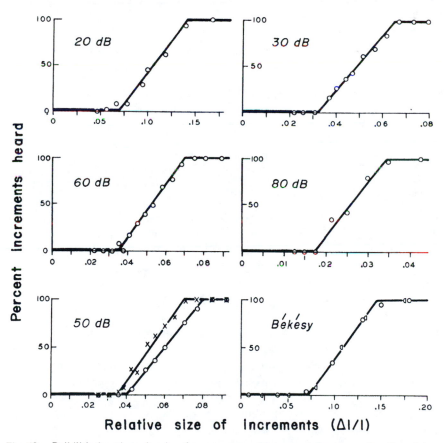

Fig. 68. Poikilitic functions showing the percentage of increments heard as a function of the intensity of the increment added to a steady 1000-hertz tone. The level of the steady tone is indicated on each plot. Békésy obtained his data by the method of constant stimuli. The circles are for positive and the half circles for negative increments. (From Stevens and Volkmann 1940b, *Science*, 92, 583–585. Reprinted by permission.)

Békésy then hit upon a crucial idea. Perhaps, he reasoned, the 2-second time interval between the standard and comparison tones was long enough for random variability to enter and to obscure the discontinuity. He therefore arranged for the comparison tone to follow directly after the standard with no intervening time interval. Békésy then obtained a new kind of poikilitic function—a function that suggested the existence of a steplike threshold. Sample data are shown in one of the plots in Fig. 68.

The new poikilitic function is a straight line between two critical points. Along the abscissa the second critical point occurs at exactly twice the stimulus value of the first critical point. Why that is so I will try to explain later. First let me tell about the other functions in Fig. 68, for they were discovered accidentally by a method rather different from that used by Békésy.

INCREMENTS ADDED TO A STEADY TONE

In 1940 John Volkmann and I were trying to replicate a Russian experiment in which the fluctuations of the absolute threshold had been measured. The observer was given a brief series of faint tone pulses very close to the absolute threshold, and he was asked to report how many pulses he heard. We found the procedure frustrating and difficult, mainly because our sound room was too noisy. Finally we decided to introduce a 1000-hertz tone to provide a steady background that would mask the faint room noises. We then added brief incremental pulses to the steady tone, and the observer pressed a key each time he heard the increment in loudness. A block of 25 increments, one increment every 3 seconds, was presented before the size of the increments was changed to another value.

After Volkmann had made several hundred judgments, I told him to rest while I plotted the number heard against the size of the increment. What emerged was a remarkably straight line. We promptly forgot about the Russian experiment and proceeded to exploit our new procedure. Before long, we had obtained the poikilitic functions shown in Fig. 68. Each point is based on from 50 to 100 judgments (Stevens and Volkmann 1940b). The two functions in one plot represent two runs in the same experiment. The crosses were obtained after a rest period during which Volkmann drank a cup of coffee. It is clear that if we had added or averaged the two sets of data, the resulting function would have become S-shaped and the critical points would have been obscured.

Our discovery of a new procedure for demonstrating the action of the neural quantum was a happy bit of serendipity. Other experimenters have used the procedure with equally good results. The functions obtained exhibit four features: (1) increments below a critical size produce no responses; (2) above that critical size the number of increments perceived increases linearly with the size of the increment; (3) all the increments are heard when the increment exceeds a second critical size; and (4) the second critical size is twice the first.

THE NQ MODEL

The four features of the poikilitic function suggest that somewhere in the sensory system there exist neural quanta (NQ) that behave as functional gates and that operate in all-or-none fashion once a threshold is crossed. The gating mechanism probably resides in the central rather than in the peripheral nervous system. It is probably not the afferent nerve fiber that Békésy seemed to identify with Fechner's JND. How the NQ model operates may be visualized with the aid of the diagram in Fig. 69.

The steady background tone (the standard) activates all the shaded neural units and does so with a little to spare. When a stimulus increment

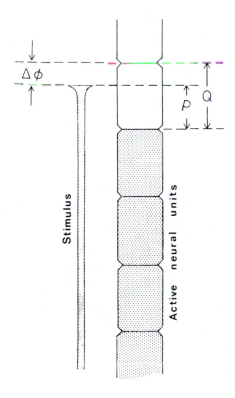

Fig. 69. The neural quantum schema. The stimulus pictured on the left is strong enough to activate several neural units, but it leaves a leftover surplus p, which remains insufficient to activate the next unit unless an increment $\Delta\phi$ is added. The symbol Q represents the size of the neural quantum measured in terms of the stimulus. When the addition of two neural quanta is needed to produce a response, the requisite stimulus increment becomes $\Delta\phi + Q$. (After Békésy 1930, 1960. Reprinted by permission.)

occurs, the leftover surplus gets added to the stimulus increment, and, if the two together add up to a neural unit, then the unit next in line will be activated by that increment. At any moment one value of the surplus is as likely as any other. The rectangular distribution of the surplus is what produces the rising straight line in the poikilitic function.

Now we must make another assumption. When the increment is added to a steady tone, the observer is not able to report when a single NQ is activated. Why? Because the overall fluctuation in the observer's sensitivity causes a "steady" stimulus to wax and wane—a process that would produce up-and-down quantal jumps. Against the fluctuating, steplike background, the observer must adopt a 2-quantum criterion for reporting the occurrence of an increment. The one-quantum jump is indistinguishable from the background.

Assuming that two added NQ are required to produce a response, we can write an equation for the percentage R of the increments that will be detected by the observer

$$R = 100\left(\frac{\Delta\phi}{Q} - 1\right)$$

A graphical representation of that equation is shown in Fig. 70. I have extended the straight poikilitic line to its intercept at -100 in order to illustrate a convenient feature of the NQ model. The projection point at -100 provides a useful aid when NQ functions are fitted to data by eye. I have laid a straight edge on that projection point in fitting NQ functions to about 200 sets of results from several different laboratories (Stevens

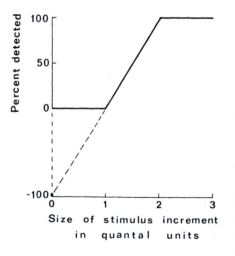

Fig. 70. Form of the poikilitic function predicted for a 2-quantum criterion. Stimulus increments produce no response (zero detections) unless the size of the increment exceeds one neural quantum. With further increase in the size of the increment the percentage detected grows linearly and reaches 100 percent at the point where the increment equals 2 quanta. The downward projection of the line passes through a point that corresponds to the ordinate value -100 percent. (From Stevens 1972b, *Science*, 177, 749-762. Copyright 1972 by the American Association for the Advancement of Science. Reprinted by permission.)

1972b). Over a span of 40 years evidence has accumulated to a sufficient depth to lend strong support to the NQ model.

Are so many experimental examples needed? Some years ago when the NQ theory was being widely disparaged, I asked my colleague Békésy what he thought of the attacks on the theory. He shrugged and said, "You only have to prove it once." That may be true in a sense, but other questions pose themselves. Can the NQ theory be demonstrated with other sensory attributes and in other sense modalities? And can the NQ function be obtained with different kinds of procedures? It is important that experiments give positive answers to those questions.

Large numbers of studies have another justification. The problem we are trying to solve requires that we record samples of the observer's responses. But sampling is inherently a noisy and variable process. Hence no single set of data for a poikilitic function matches precisely any other set of data. Therefore multiple samples are needed if we are to assure ourselves that we know the form of the underlying distribution. One of our problems is to decide whether the underlying distribution is more like a rectangular distribution or a normal distribution.

Space does not permit a display of all the poikilitic functions that satisfy the requirements of the NQ model, but a few representative functions will be presented—enough, I hope, to dispel the view that only one kind of experiment has confirmed what Luce (1963) called the Békésy-Stevens model of the neural quantum. It will be recalled that the procedure devised by Békésy was quite different from that invented accidentally by Stevens and Volkmann. Still more variations in procedure have been made by various investigators in subsequent studies.

NEURAL QUANTUM FOR PITCH

Since the attribute pitch is mediated by a physiological mechanism that relies on place of stimulation rather than amount, it seemed important to determine whether pitch discrimination exhibits a quantal threshold. With the apparatus rearranged to produce brief frequency increments in the steady 1000-hertz tone, we obtained NQ functions similar to those we had obtained with intensity increments. Results for six different observers are shown in Fig. 71.

The various observers show rather large differences in the measured values of the NQ. Thus the NQ for observer RR was 2.8 hertz and for MJ only 1.1 hertz (Stevens, Morgan, and Volkmann 1941).

Sets of NQ functions for two of the experimenters are shown in Fig. 72. The level of the steady tone was set to various numbers of decibels above

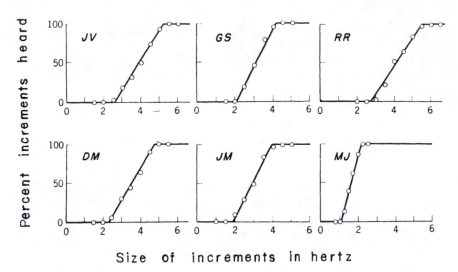

Size of increments in hertz

Fig. 71. Poikilitic functions relating percentage of pitch increments heard to the size of the increment in frequency for six different observers. To a steady, continuous reference stimulus (1000 hertz) an increment lasting 0.3 second was added every 3 seconds. Each point is the average of 100 judgments. The lines were drawn to fit the points and at the same time to satisfy the slope requirement that the intercepts at 100 and 0 percent should stand in the ratio of 2 to 1. The size of the NQ, measured in stimulus terms, differs almost threefold between observers RR and MJ. (From Stevens, Morgan, and Volkmann 1941. Reprinted by permission.)

the absolute threshold, as indicated on each plot. It can be seen that the NQ for pitch decreases with increasing stimulus level. At a given level Morgan's NQ was smaller than mine, and the difference between us remained remarkably constant over a wide range of stimulus levels. The stability of that difference suggests that the measure called the NQ may constitute a basic feature of the sensory system.

Evidence that the mechanism of the NQ for pitch may be central rather than peripheral was obtained in an experiment comparing the effect of listening with two ears instead of only one ear. The foregoing data were obtained with monaural listening. Binaural listening was then tried with four observers. Three of them gave results like those in Fig. 73. The left and right ears were nearly equally sensitive, but the sensitivity increased dramatically when listening was binaural. The NQ then fell to about two-thirds of its monaural value.

In my own case, however, I could find no difference in the NQ when I listened with both ears. In order to make certain of that fact, I judged more than 2500 increments in a single sitting that lasted between 2 and 3 hours.

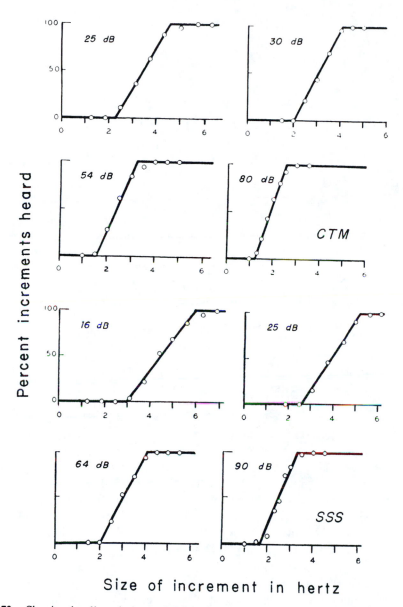

Fig. 72. Showing the effect of stimulus level on the measured size of the NQ for pitch. The upper four functions are for observer CTM, the lower four curves for observer SSS. The size of the NQ decreases with increasing stimulus level. (After Stevens, Morgan, and Volkmann 1941. Reprinted by permission.)

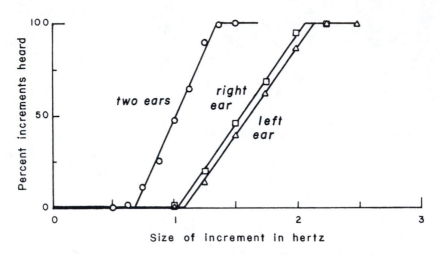

Fig. 73. Monaural and binaural NQ functions for pitch. The NQ was smaller when the tone was delivered to both ears. (From Stevens, Morgan, and Volkmann 1941. Reprinted by permission.)

The increments were delivered to right ear, left ear, and both ears in random order, but the three poikilitic functions coincided almost exactly.

VISUAL STUDIES

Both the eye and the ear are so sensitive to their respective stimuli that under optimal circumstances the nature of the physical stimulus is thought to set limits on the sense organ's performance. In visual studies especially, there has long been concern whether the quantal nature of the photon of light may affect the form of some of the visual poikilitic functions.

When the number of photons becomes sufficiently small, they make up a stream that patters irregularly, like rain on the roof, and some authors have proposed that the statistical properties of the photon bombardment may determine the distribution of the observer's visual responses. On the other hand, it seems unlikely that all the variability resides in the photon stream, and that the observer in fact contributes no noise or variability. More probably, the warm-bodied human observer provides most of the variability—the controlling share of the noise. In that case, we might expect discrimination experiments to give evidence, not for bombardment by discrete photons, but for the operation of a quantal gate within the observer—the same effect that reveals itself in the NQ for pitch and loudness.

As it turns out, most of the evidence for a neural step function in vision has been gathered by investigators who apparently had no interest in the NQ. Nevertheless, their measurements produced poikilitic functions having the predicted form and slope, but only as a by-product of their main concern. In some ways the data carry considerable conviction when they serve to verify a theory that the experimenter does not believe in. The following are two samples of visual experiments.

While exploring various procedures for measuring visual thresholds, Blackwell (1953) obtained data that bear upon the NQ—in his opinion negatively, in my opinion quite positively. The observer viewed a screen illuminated at about 76 decibels above the absolute visual threshold. At intervals of about 12 seconds, a small spot was flashed on the screen. The increment spot subtended 18.5 minutes of arc and was placed 7 degrees to the right of the central fixation point. It lasted 60 milliseconds. In some series the increment spots were presented at 14 contrast levels and in blocks of 20 increments of the same size. In other series the size of the increment was randomized. With both the block and the random presentations, catch trials involving the omission of the increment were also used.

Examples of data obtained from one subject are shown in Fig. 74. The evidence for a quantal effect looks fairly impressive. Certain features of the data command particular interest.

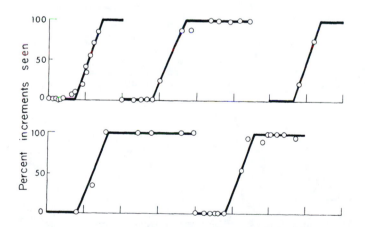

Fig. 74. Brightness increments were presented as brief flashes of a small target 7 degrees to the right of the center of a large screen. The background luminance was 76 decibels re 10^{-10} lambert. All the NQ functions are for the same observer. For the top three functions the increments were randomized. For the two lower functions the increments were presented in blocks of 20. Catch trials were used in all the experiments. The NQ remained fairly constant under several variations in procedure. (Data from Blackwell 1953.)

The top three poikilitic functions in Fig. 74 were obtained with randomized increments. For the first function on the left, the incremental stimuli produced a contrast so faint that most of the increment spots were seen less than half the time. For the next function the increments were spread out over a rather wide range, so that most increments were either always seen or never seen. For the third function, only two sizes of increments, plus catch trials, were used. It is especially interesting to note that the straight line through the two points turns out to have the slope predicted by the NQ theory.

The two lower functions in Fig. 74 were obtained with blocks of increments—20 similar increments in a row before a different size was presented. That procedure is modeled on the method developed by Stevens and Volkmann for loudness increments. The catch trails were also in blocks. All in all, the five experiments depicted in Fig. 74 show that the observer was able to produce rather good NQ functions under a remarkably wide variety of stimulus spacings and presentation procedures.

A quite different type of incremental target was employed in a study by investigators interested in pattern perception. The target was a square, 2.25 degrees on a side, and made up of light and dark vertical stripes whose brightness could be controlled. The stripes could be made to appear for a brief period (760 milliseconds) on the face of the cathode-ray tube whose

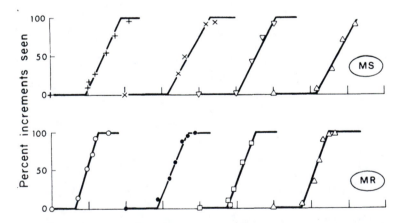

Fig. 75. The increment was a striped pattern that appeared for 0.76 second on the face of a cathode-ray tube whose normal luminance was 83 decibels re 10^{-10} lambert. The pattern of vertical stripes contained 14 stripes per degree. Data for two observers are shown. Each NQ function was determined on a different day. Increment size (contrast) was varied randomly from trial to trial and catch trials were included. (Data from Sachs, Nachmias, and Robson 1971.)

background luminance was approximately 83 decibels above threshold. The observer pressed a switch to initiate a trial, and he said yes if he saw a change from the constant luminance display and no if he did not. The size of the increments was randomized, and catch trials were used (Sachs, Nachmias, and Robson 1971).

The examples of data shown in Fig. 75 were obtained from two observers. Each point is based on 100 judgments and each function was determined on a different day. The NQ varied by a very slight amount from day to day. The NQ was consistently smaller for observer MR than for observer MS. The authors drew S-shaped curves through their data, but straight-line poikilitic functions with critical points in the ratio 2-to-1 seem to provide a better description of the experimental results.

STATISTICAL TEST

Can we not run a curve-fitting test to help us decide whether the straight line fits the data better than the normal ogive? One of my collaborators once ran such a test, but I now believe that a curve-fitting comparison is not appropriate. Why? Mainly because the two alternatives have different degrees of freedom. The theory behind the normal ogive assumes that the observer's judgment is subject to an assortment of random errors. That assumption holds great appeal, but it does not tell us how the standard deviation of the error distribution is related to the mean. The mean and the standard deviation may vary quite independently. Translated into the poikilitic ogive, the random-error theory specifies no exact relation between the slope of the ogive and the location of the midpoint of the curve. Hence the ogive enjoys two degrees of freedom. It can be given any steepness at any location.

By contrast, the NQ function has only one degree of freedom—for a given midpoint there is only one slope. As graphed in Fig. 70, we can see how the one degree of freedom reduces to the angle between the two dashed lines that intersect at −100. Only that angle can vary. It seems quite inappropriate, therefore, to try to decide, by curve fitting, the relative merits of two such different models.

The model with the fewer degrees of freedom is the more powerful model on that account because it predicts more. Given the midpoint, the NQ model predicts the slope. Given the midpoint, the error model predicts nothing further. Consequently, even if a test by curve fitting should show no advantage for the NQ model, its greater power would still recommend it.

REQUIRED PROCEDURES

What can be said about the kind of experiment that will ensure the production of good NQ functions? The success of an experiment can never be
guaranteed, of course, but a few of the necessary, if not sufficient, conditions may now be discerned. So far as I can determine, the main conditions
are these.

    1.   Standard or reference stimulus. An ongoing steady tone or a steadily
illuminated visual field has worked well as a reference background. On the
other hand, the reference stimulus can be as brief as 0.3 second, as it was in
Békésy's experiment. What seems to be contraindicated is an unsteady
reference standard, such as a noise. The NQ becomes obscured when the
background is made to jitter irregularly.
    2.   Transition. The increment must be added and removed abruptly,
with a negligible time interval between the standard and the comparison
increment. Instantaneous transitions create no problems with visual
stimuli, but with pure tones an abrupt transition scatters energy into other
frequency regions. In some experiments the scattered energy has been
removed by filtering.
    3.   Duration of the increment. The comparison stimulus (increment or
decrement) should presumably not last so long that the observer's
sensitivity could change during the presentation. Increments as brief as 0.02
second and as long as 0.75 second have been used. The size of the NQ
increases as the duration of the increment is shortened (Garner and Miller
1944).
    4.   Stimulus level. When the standard reference stimulus is reduced in
level, the size of the NQ for loudness, pitch, and brightness increases. There
is some evidence that at low levels the poikilitic function tends to become
noisier and less clearly rectilinear. If the reference standard is reduced
below threshold, the comparison stimuli may then be judged in the same
way we determine an absolute threshold. If the assumptions of the NQ
theory are correct, there should be no evidence of critical points or
threshold steps in measurements of the absolute threshold.
    5.   The observer. The ability to maintain concentration appears to differ
among observers. Some of the poikilitic functions presented above were
based on as many as 1500 judgments made in a single session, although approximately half that number is normally sufficient to determine a good
NQ function. Even with only a few hundred judgments, the requirement of
sustained attention is rather severe (for examples showing an occasional
"noisy" observer, see Stevens 1972b). Of course, the failure of any

particular observer to give a clean, rectilinear function does not constitute evidence against the NQ theory, because too many other observers have shown that good NQ functions can be produced. In reviewing the published literature I counted a total of 31 observers whose NQ functions can be classed as excellent.

LOCUS OF THE NQ MECHANISM

Where do we look for the neural response that operates like a gating device, storing excitation and then opening the gate to fire off in quantal fashion? The holding action entailed by the concept of quantal action means that, over a finite range below the threshold level, increments to the stimulus can be added with no effect, no response by the observer. The increment must rise to a critical level before it triggers a reaction. Actually, gating mechanisms are a familar feature of many parts of the nervous system. Indeed, quantal action is so widespread in nerve fibers and synapses that the all-or-none response does not by itself provide a guide to the identification of the specific neural mechanism that mediates the NQ in sensory discrimination.

The foregoing pages have presented examples from three different sensory continua. Not only has the evidence for a neural quantum been demonstrated in two different sense modalities, vision and hearing, but in the auditory modality the evidence has appeared equally clear cut for the metathetic attribute of pitch and for the prothetic attribute of loudness. Pitch depends on the locus of stimulation along the basilar membrane, whereas loudness depends on the amount of excitation at whatever locus is activated. Pitch is based on a substitutive physiological mechanism, loudness on an additive mechanism. Pitch changes when new stimulation is substituted for old. Loudness changes when new stimulation is added to old.

It now seems probable, therefore, that the mechanism of the neural quantum may need to be sought in a gating action that is sufficiently general to apply to more than a single sense modality and to accommodate at least two different modes of action in the peripheral machinery of the auditory system.

Another fact that may bear on the problem of the physiological mechanism is the change in the size of the NQ for pitch when listening changes from monaural to binaural. The change in the NQ when two ears instead of one are used makes it appear likely that the neural quantum for pitch probably does not reside in the sense organ or in the peripheral nervous system. Instead, a more central mechanism seems indicated.

THE NQ AND FECHNER'S LAW

Does the demonstration of the existence of an all-or-none threshold in sensory discrimination mean that we can now salvage the principle underlying Fechner's law? Fechner postulated that with each added JND there goes a constant increment to sensation. It has been argued that a JND is merely a measure of variability or error, and that Fechner was in effect turning a measure of dispersion into a scale unit. If, instead of using a JND based on a statistical measure, we use the NQ, do we then have a valid scale unit? In other words, can we count off the neural quanta and arrive at the loudness scale or the brightness scale? The answer appears to be no. On the other hand, we could presumably arrive at the pitch scale by counting off the neural quanta for pitch. On the prothetic continuum of loudness or brightness, the size of the NQ—in keeping with the general principle of Weber's law—grows larger when the stimulus increases. Measured in subjective units, sones or brils, the NQ grows larger with increasing loudness or brightness. On the metathetic continuum of pitch the size of the NQ has not been measured for different frequencies, but it would presumably vary in such a way that each NQ would correspond to a constant number of mels.

Generally speaking, the basic factors that affect the size of the ordinary JND, measured, for example, by the method of average error or the method of constant stimuli, affect also the measured size of the NQ. Thus the NQ for brightness was found to approximate the general form of Weber's law, at least as a first approximation, when the stimulus luminance was varied over a range of almost a million to one (Mueller 1951; see also Stevens 1972b). In other words, when the stimulus increases, the NQ varies in approximately the same way that the JND varies. The NQ is not a fixed value independent of the level of the stimulus. Nor is it independent of a host of other parameters.

Then is the NQ also a measure of noise or variability? I think the answer to that question must be yes, in the sense that, if it were possible to eliminate all noise and fluctuations, the response would go from zero to 100 percent instantaneously, so to speak. The poikilitic function would rise vertically as soon as the threshold was crossed. It is the presence of noise or variability that causes the poikilitic function to rise linearly along a gradual slope. The linearity signifies that the underlying distribution is rectangular rather than bell-shaped.

Another question is whether the JND bears some fixed relation to the NQ. No simple answer is possible, because several different procedures may be used to gather the data, and different statistical measures may be used to define the JND. For any given method, however, we have reason to suppose that, when the stimulus level is varied, the JND and the NQ keep roughly in step.

Unfortunately, the procedures that give rise to NQ functions cannot be easily applied in all sense modalities. Where they can be applied, the Békésy-Stevens model of the NQ appears to offer a useful approach to the study of the basic sensitivity of the organism.

CHAPTER 7

Neural
Correlates

How does the outside world make itself known to us through the miraculous system of detectors called sense organs? For thousands of years that question has caused men to speculate, but only in recent centuries have facts begun to replace fanciful surmise. Foremost among such facts is the so-called "specific energies" of the nerves: no matter how you stimulate a nerve, the sensation produced belongs to the modality normally served by that particular nerve.

In the year 1800 Volta assembled a large battery of the electric cells that he had recently invented, and he connected the total array to a pair of metal rods inserted in his ears. Then he closed the switch. He felt a jolt in the head, he tells us, followed by a noise like the boiling of thick soup. It seems that he decided not to repeat the experiment.

Goaded by a similar curiosity some years later, E. H. Weber persuaded his brother to submit to electrodes in the ears. When the switch was closed, brother Weber heard nothing, but he saw a light that seemed to pass right across his head. Electrical stimulation can apparently cause seeing as well as hearing.

Since those heroic days, many experimenters have confirmed the specificity of the sensory systems: however we excite them, they respond in their separate ways. Sensory quality depends, it seems, on which nerve is activated and where in the brain it leads. But there the problem rests, for we still have nothing better than location in the brain to explain why taste and smell and touch and sight and sound create superbly different sensory qualities.

The brain, however, can distinguish quantity as well as quality. What about the magnitude of the sensation? The noise of the approaching airplane grows from a gentle rumble to a thunderous roar, all the while firing messages through the same sense organ and along the same auditory nerve.

How does the system manage the processing of such vast differences in stimulus intensity?

ALL-OR-NONE IMPULSES

That question became a genuine scientific question only in the 1920's when the neural code was broken and it was disclosed that nerve impulses behave as all-or-none events. Prior to that discovery, the physiologist felt free to assume that an increase in stimulus intensity would cause the nerves to do more of whatever it was they were doing in the first place. But once the deciphering of the neural code had shown how each nerve fiber carries a train of impulses, and how all the impulses are built on a similar design, the problem acquired a new perplexity. After an impulse has passed along it, the fiber must rest for a brief period. Consequently, the impulse train must space itself out to a limit of a few hundred impulses per second. How then can a sound intensity seem to vary continuously over a stimulus range of several millionfold? The mediation of sensory intensity by all-or-none impulses ranks among the major puzzles of physiology.

Actually the initial impact of the all-or-none law was softened by the misconception then current regarding the form of the psychophysical law. Fechner had convinced most of the scientific public that sensation grows as the logarithm of the stimulus. As a consequence, little consternation was generated by the constraints inherent in the all-or-none principle, even though a ceiling on the rate of neural firing imposed an obligation to rethink the problem. If perceived magnitude was indeed subject to a range reduction as severe as the logarithmic compression that Fechner claimed, then perhaps there was no great cause to worry. Perhaps changes in the stimulus intensity could be mediated by changes in the frequency of the nerve impulses. As a matter of fact, some of the earliest studies of nerve impulses in Lord Adrian's laboratory at Cambridge, England, had displayed a slow and approximately logarithmic growth of firing rate when the stimulus was increased.

That appeared to settle the matter. Vindication, it seemed, had arrived at last for Fechner, the father of psychophysics and a principal progenitor of experimental psychology. And many subsequent studies showed, or seemed to show, that nerve activity grows approximately as the logarithm of the stimulus intensity, so that a belief took hold and grew widespread that electrophysiology had confirmed the Fechner law. We will return to that problem later, but first let us look at the pitch continuum, an aspect of sensory function where psychophysics and physiology stand in happy accord.

MAPPING THE BASILAR MEMBRANE

Pitch, as an attribute of sound, belongs among the metathetic continua, the qualitative kind that are concerned with *what* and *where*, as opposed to the prothetic continua concerned with *how much*. As we might expect, then, our attempt to understand the physiological basis of pitch does not land us in the difficulties created by the all-or-none law, but instead directs our attention to the anatomy of the ear. We need to ask especially about the structure of the inner ear—inside the cochlea—where the sensitive receptors reside. There we find an arrangement of special significance. Some 30,000 hair-cell receptors line themselves up in neat rows along the basilar membrane, a membrane that stretches the full length of the inner ear, about 3.5 centimeters.

One of the triumphs of modern science has been to explicate the delicate motions of the inner ear—the only really complex mechanical system in the human body. In 1928 Békésy showed how a sound, relayed by the eardrum and the ossicles, reaches the fluid-filled inner ear and there launches a traveling wave that sweeps along the length of the basilar membrane. A crucial feature of the traveling wave lies in its propensity to build up to a maximum height and then die down as it moves along. Where does the wave reach its greatest height? That depends on the frequency of the sound. For high frequencies the maximum is near the oval window, where the sound first enters the inner ear. As the frequency is made lower, the maximum moves farther and farther toward the helicotrema at the other end of the basilar membrane. By careful dissection of the tiny auditory mechanism, Békésy succeeded in viewing some of those microscopic events under stroboscopic illumination.

Years later, while a member of the Harvard Psychophysics Laboratory, Békésy received the Nobel Prize for his discoveries in hearing. He had showed how the frequency of a sound wave gets itself transformed into a specific locus of stimulation on the basilar membrane. Different frequencies touch the membrane, so to speak, at different places, much the way the skin of your hand may be touched at different places. Just as you can tell one spot from another on the skin, you can tell one frequency from another by where it touches the hair cells on the basilar membrane. Each different membrane location produces the sensation of a different pitch.

The hair cells are spaced so evenly along the membrane that a close relation exists between the scale of apparent pitch, measured in mels, and the place of excitation along the membrane. The exact place of excitation on the membrane cannot be determined with high precision, but different experimenters have produced maps that agree in their general outline.

In 1935 with two colleagues at the Harvard Medical School I produced a cochlear map that disclosed several important relationships. First we drilled tiny holes into the cochleas of guinea pigs in order to damage the hair cells at various locations along the basilar membrane. We then determined at which frequencies there was an alteration in the normal electrical response of the cochlea. A plot could then be made to relate the position of the damaged hair cells to the frequency of the sound for which the electrical response was deficient. The plot of membrane location versus sound frequency provided a map that was later found to agree with the mel scale of pitch, when that scale was determined in 1940. Both the mel scale of pitch, showing the relation of pitch to frequency, and the cochlear map determined by the damaged hair cells are shown in Fig. 76. The curve of the pitch scale passes close to the map determined by localized damage to the basilar membrane.

The prime fact is that the pitch scale in mels conforms to the layout of the sensitive hair cells, so that equal separations in pitch correspond to equal distances along the basilar membrane. The pitch scale also exhibits other significant relations. The most noteworthy, perhaps, concerns the

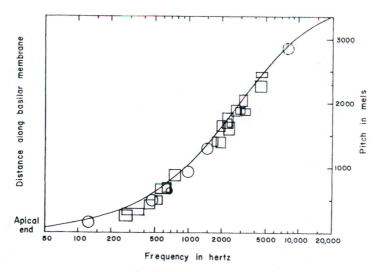

Fig. 76. Comparison of the human pitch function with guinea pig data locating the positions on the basilar membrane that are stimulated by tones of various frequencies. The linear extent of the basilar membrane is represented by the ordinate (left), and along the same axis is laid the pitch scale (right). The curve represents the pitch function; the rectangles and circles show the locations of stimulation by various frequencies. (After Stevens, Davis, and Lurie 1935; and Stevens and Volkmann 1940a. Reprinted by permission.)

smallest change in the frequency of a tone that the ear can detect, the just noticeable difference for pitch. It turns out that the size of the JND is approximately constant when measured in mels. As a matter of fact, the JND is almost exactly equal to 1 mel all up and down the scale.

That feature, the constant size of the JND when measured in the subjective units called mels, provides the criterion that leads us to classify pitch as a metathetic continuum. If it were a prothetic continuum like loudness, the JND would not remain constant throughout the scale, but would grow enormously larger in subjective size at the upper end of the scale. Specifically, for a faint sound at 40 decibels, a JND for loudness amounts to about a tenth of a sone; whereas for a loud sound at 100 decibels, a JND amounts to about 8 sones, a value that is 80 times larger.

Because of the way it is usually determined, the JND is a statistical measure of scatter. It is an index telling how wide is the spread of the variability or error that occurs when the observer tries to tell the difference between stimuli that lie very close together. The physiological basis of pitch perception, depending as it does on orderly rows of receptors spaced evenly along the basilar membrane, provides a straightforward explanation for the tendency of the error in pitch discrimination, the JND, to remain constant. In order for you to tell that one pitch is higher than another on, say, 75 percent of the test trials, the two pitches must stimulate positions on the basilar membrane whose separation is comparable to the distance between adjacent hair cells. With loudness, however, there is no such tidy correlation with anatomy. The error in loudness discrimination is not constant but relative.

Let us turn then to the physiological mechanisms that underlie some of the prothetic continua. The question concerns the extent to which techniques of electrical recording have been able to produce evidence for the psychophysical power law. If in every sense modality the intensity of the sensation grows in proportion to the stimulus intensity raised to a power, some neural correlate of that principle ought to prove discernible.

TRANSDUCERS

One of the scientist's motivations in trying to discover the correct form of the psychophysical law is to learn as much as possible about the input-output characteristics of the sensory systems. In its many different forms and aspects, the energy of the outside world passes through the windows of the sense organs, thereby gaining access to the nervous system. Only within the neural nets can external reality make its configurations known in perception. Light, sound, heat, cold, odor, pressure, and many other stimulus energies affect us through the sense organs. Yet many forms of energy find no sensory window to enter. Radio waves, for example, pass through us constantly and we sense nothing at all. Suppose we could "see" radio waves, what then would the world look like?

For any stimulus to become effective it must strike a sense organ that is capable of changing or transducing the stimulus into some kind of neural effect. The scientist reasons that the sensory transducer must, in at least one fundamental respect, resemble the other transducers that he is familiar with. Between the input and the output there must exist some specifiable relation—a relation that is called the operating characteristic of the transducer. From the form of the input-output function, we can say, for example, what happens to the output when we double the input.

Although the sensory power law provides no automatic disclosure of the exact mechanism of sensory transduction, it may draw a helpful guideline for future research by instructing us to look for physiological processes that conform, not with logarithmic functions, but with power functions. When the human subject makes cross-modality matches, he is behaving as a comparator, and he tells us by his reactions just where the guideline must run. When, for example, the experimenter varies the luminance of a visual target and the subject varies the level of a noise in order to keep the apparent loudness in step with the apparent brightness, the subject is in effect comparing the operating characteristics of the visual and auditory transducers. And so also with the many other cross-modality comparisons that have been made among the different sense modalities. The resulting equal-sensation functions provide a quantitative model of the input-output relations of the sensory systems. It is a model that may help to point the direction for the development of transducer physiology.

"Sensory physiology in a broad sense," said Max Delbrück in 1969 when accepting a Nobel Prize, "contains hidden as its kernel an as yet totally undeveloped but absolutely central science: transducer physiology, the study of the conversion of the outside signal to its first 'interesting' output. I use the word 'interesting' advisedly because I wish to exclude . . . the primary photochemical reactions of the visual systems. . . . Transducer physiology proper comes after this first step, where we are dealing with devices of the cell unparalleled in anything the physicists have produced so far with respect to sensitivity, adaptability, and miniaturization" (Delbrück 1970).

Transducer physiology is indeed the "central science," as Delbrück said, and, strangely enough, we do not as yet know precisely how any sensory transducer works. The development of transducer physiology remains a challenge for the future, but one of its concerns will be to explicate the mechanisms that generate the psychophysical power functions. The power law tells us *what* the transducer does. We have yet to learn *how* it does it.

In the meantime, though, we may ask what happens when we record some of the many electrical potentials that occur after the transducer has done its work. Whenever we stimulate a sensory receptor, electrical potentials are generated both in the sense organ and in the nervous system. Do those neurelectric effects increase according to a power law? Some appear to do so, though others do not. Complexity and variability characterize our experiments in electrophysiology, but positive evidence for a power law has frequently been found (Stevens 1970, 1971a).

THE EYE

Many revealing studies have been made of the eye of the horseshoe crab *Limulus* because its individual elements happen to be readily accessible. In 1932 Hartline and Graham undertook the delicate task of teasing one single fiber out of the bundle of fibers that make up the optic nerve. They placed an electrode on the fiber and then stimulated the sense organ. The onset of the light produced a burst of electrical impulses in the single fiber. The frequency of the impulses declined after a second or two, and the response became a steady train of impulses. The frequency of the impulses in the train increased with the light intensity along the path shown by the stars in Fig. 77. Since both coordinates of Fig. 77 are logarithmic, the straight line through the stars represents a power function. The slope of the line defines the exponent, which here is equal to 0.29.

The improvement of amplifiers and the development of microelectrodes have enabled physiologists to record the electrical potential generated inside a single sensory cell of the *Limulus* eye. Inside the visual cell the light stimulus produces an electrical effect sometimes called the generator potential—a potential quite different from the impulses that flow along a single fiber of the optic nerve. The magnitude of the generator potential was found to increase with the intensity of the stimulating flash of light. The total response to each flash, which I determined by integrating the area under the oscilloscope records published by Fuortes and Hodgkin (1964), grew in the orderly manner shown by the triangles, squares, and circles in Fig. 77. There we see that in three different experiments the generator potential increased as a power function of the stimulus intensity. The slope (exponent) was close to $\frac{1}{3}$, which is the exponent we encounter in psychophysical experiments designed to measure the apparent brightness seen by human subjects.

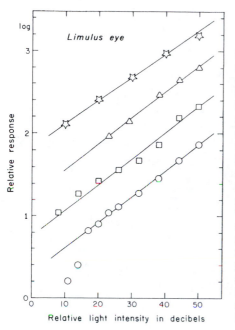

Fig. 77. Power function responses in the eye of the horseshoe crab *Limulus*. The stars represent frequencies of nerve impulses recorded by Hartline and Graham in 1932 from a single fiber of the optic nerve. Frequency was measured 3.5 seconds after the onset of the light. The lower three functions represent responses to 0.02-second flashes of light, recorded with intracellular electrodes in single ommatidia. The plotted points represent the areas under oscillographs published by Fuortes and Hodgkin in 1964. The straight lines in the log-log coordinates are power functions, whose slopes (exponents) are 0.29 for the stars and 0.32 for the other three functions. Both coordinates give relative values only. Eyes were dark adapted. (From Stevens 1970, *Science,* 170, 1043–1050. Copyright 1970 by the American Association for the Advancement of Science. Reprinted by permission.)

Neurelectric functions like those in Fig. 77 show that a visual system is capable of transductions having a power function form. It is noteworthy that the scientists who produced those interesting experiments seemed unaware that their data followed power functions. They were not looking for a power law, and it is hard to find what you are not looking for. By and large, before 1960 physiologists looked only for Fechner's logarithmic law, for that is the law the textbooks have expounded. Beginning in the 1960's, though, a few physiologists have begun to look for physiological correlates of the psychophysical power law.

AUDITORY SYSTEM

In 1936, long before the sensory power law had fully asserted itself, Hallowell Davis and I compared an early version of the loudness scale to measurements we had made of the cochlear microphonic—the electrical potential that can be picked up by an electrode placed in the middle ear of a cat or a guinea pig. The growth of the cochlear microphonic seemed to run parallel to the growth of loudness, at least over a good part of the intensity range. We concluded that the form of the loudness function is imposed by the behavior of the cochlear mechanism. That conclusion may still be essentially correct, but further research has suggested that the cochlear microphonic, which has the exponent 1.0, is probably not the direct instigator of the loudness response, which has the exponent ⅔.

When we inserted small concentric electrodes directly into the auditory nerve of a cat, we sometimes recorded an electrical response that also resembled the loudness function. Since the electrode recorded a partial summation of the all-or-none impulses in the nerve fibers, the congruence with the growth of loudness seemed to support the hypothesis that loudness depends on the total activity in the nerve.

That conception still serves as a good working hypothesis, but there has always remained a nagging difficulty. True enough, as the stimulus is increased, the cat's nerve response grows larger. But at a moderate stimulus level the nerve response reaches a maximum, and thereafter it ceases to grow and may even decline. Even in an individual nerve fiber, the impulse rate rises to only a few hundred per second and then often falls off. But when you listen to a sound whose intensity continues to increase, the loudness you hear grows on and on, up and up. How?

Why does the growth of loudness not reach a maximum and turn down at high stimulus levels? With the help of a dozen volunteers, I once suc-

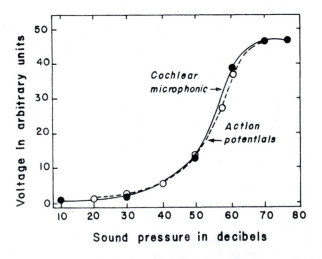

Fig. 78. The initial voltage of the action potentials of the auditory nerve (broken line) and the voltage of the corresponding cochlear microphonics (solid line) as functions of the intensity of a 500-hertz tone. The voltage scales are arbitrary and have been adjusted so that the two curves coincide at their maxima. The two amplitude functions ran a very similar course in this instance, but in other experiments they diverged significantly. (After Stevens and Davis 1938.)

ceeded in showing that the power function for loudness holds its course all the way up to at least 140 decibels—a painful level indeed (see Chapter 5).

Figure 78 shows, in semilogarithmic units, an instance in which the voltage generated in the cochlea of a cat and the summated potentials in the auditory nerve followed rather similar paths. The stimulus was 500 hertz. As a function of the stimulus level, both the cochlear response and the nerve response grew to a maximum. Beyond a moderate stimulus level both the responses ceased to grow. Although the details may differ for other cats and for other kinds of stimuli, the ceiling effect can nearly always be counted on. Neurelectric responses refuse to keep pace when the stimulus is pushed to a high level.

Perhaps the electrode provides only a clumsy access to the mysteries of the sensory nervous system. Thus far, however, it is the best access we have. And there is an occasional glimpse of provocative clarity, as when, for example, Boudreau (1965) recorded potentials that followed a power function over a range of 60 decibels in a cat. But that, he said, was a "rare cat." Perhaps, but it is unlikely that the experimenter who pokes an electrode into a neural complex will record the maximum capability on every thrust.

The average response that Boudreau recorded in 25 cats with electrodes in a part of the auditory nerve tract (the superior olivary complex) exhibited an interesting relation to the level of the stimulus, which was an 800-hertz tone. Over a considerable range of stimulus intensities the response amplitude increased in accordance with a power function with an exponent of approximately $2/3$, the same value as the exponent of the human loudness function. Figure 79 shows how the potentials in the nerve tract of one cat increased as the stimulus level was raised. Over a range of about 50 decibels the voltage increased in accordance with a power function having an exponent of about 0.57. At about 55 decibels the response reached a ceiling and ceased to grow further.

If good fortune should favor us and we should find a point in the auditory system where the neural potentials keep exact pace with the loudness function, we would then enjoy the seductive prospect of an objective measure of the loudness exponent. Instead of our having to resort to magnitude estimation and the other cross-modality matching procedures of psychophysics, all of which exhibit considerable variability, the sensory response could be read directly by a meter. Unfortunately, however, the variability seen by electrodes is seldom smaller, and is sometimes greater, than the variability of cross-modality matches. Thus, for example, the exponent derived by electrical recording in Boudreau's 25 cats ranged from about 0.3 to 1.0, with a mean of 0.68 and a standard deviation of 0.16. A study of 11 human subjects who matched numbers to loudness by the method of magnitude estimation gave a mean exponent of 0.73, a range of 0.4 to 1.0, and a standard deviation of 0.19. The two sets of results show remarkable similarity, but the variability in the two kinds of experiments probably stems from quite different causes.

Many factors combine to create variability in the neurelectric response, and much ingenuity has been exercised in an effort to curb the sources of instability. Working with guinea pigs, Teas, Eldredge, and Davis (1962) attacked the problem with a delicate procedure that enabled them to place a pair of electrodes inside the cochlea itself, one electrode above and one below the basilar membrane, to which are attached the receptor hair cells. Several different potentials can be picked up by such electrodes, including the action potentials of the auditory nerve. Those potentials show up as a diphasic wave. In response to brief bursts of tone, the amplitude of the action-potential wave grows roughly as a power function of the stimulus intensity over a range that may reach 90 to 100 decibels. Certain irregularities are seen in the growth of the action potentials, however, and some of the irregularities can be traced to the successive recruitment of three different populations of neurons. The power functions described by the growth of the action-potential wave have exhibited exponents ranging from perhaps 0.2 to 0.5. An example is shown in Fig. 80. Seen by electrodes in the guinea pig cochlea, then, the growth of the summated nerve impulses proceeds at a slower pace, that is to say, with a lower exponent, than the growth of loudness in the human ear.

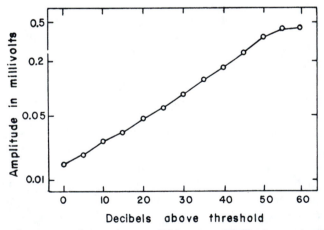

Fig. 79. Neural response to bursts of tone at 800 hertz, recorded in the superior olivary complex of a cat. The response grows as a power function with the exponent 0.57. (After Boudreau 1965, *J. Acoust. Soc. Am.*, 37, 779–785. Reprinted by permission.)

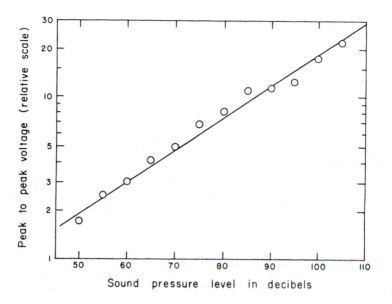

Fig. 80. Showing how the neural action potential grows in amplitude when a brief sound pulse is made stronger. The action potential wave was picked up by electrodes driven into the cochlea of a guinea pig. One electrode was in the scala vestibuli, the other in the scala tympani. Although the points fall approximately on a power function whose exponent (slope) is 0.42, the departures from the straight line may represent the involvement of different populations of nerve fibers. (Data from Teas, Eldredge, and Davis 1962.)

Why a power function with a lower exponent? As we wrestle with that problem, we must remember that the finding of a power function in a neurelectric recording does not prove that the electrical potentials picked up by the electrodes have anything to do with the loudness we hear. Conversely, our failure to find an expected neurelectric function does not prove that no such function exists. If we leap to hasty conclusions regarding the physiological basis of sensation, we risk entanglement in neuromythology. Yet the research goal seems now to be set, for at last we know what kind of function we are looking for. Patience and imagination may lead us to an understanding of the neural mechanisms that respond to stimuli by power transformations.

CORTICAL POTENTIALS

Electrodes on the human scalp normally pick up an assortment of brain waves, so-called, that tend to obscure the potentials evoked by a stimulus to a sense organ. But computer techniques have made it possible to average large numbers of cortical waves and thereby suppress or cancel most of the irregularities. In the averaged response we see only those features that repeat in a stable fashion. With the noise thus suppressed, the potential evoked by a repeated click delivered by an earphone becomes distinct and measurable. The click is repeated 100 times, say, and the click response is the only feature in the brain wave that recurs on each trial. Therefore, it alone remains visible in the averaged response. The development of aids to averaging led promptly to the remarkable demonstration that the evoked potential at the scalp of a normal conscious subject could be detected when the click stimulus was only a few decibels above the psychophysical threshold.

When the amplitude of the click was increased, the cortical potential became larger, sometimes conforming to a power law. But there were large individual differences among subjects and large changes due to experimental procedures, as well we might expect. The potential recorded at the scalp represents a summation of neurelectric potentials that may have such widely separated origins that it becomes far from obvious what aspect, if any, of the cortical potential should correlate with perceived magnitude. An example of an averaged response to 1-second bursts of tone repeated 100 times is shown in Fig. 81. The stimulus was 1000 hertz at about 65 decibels above threshold.

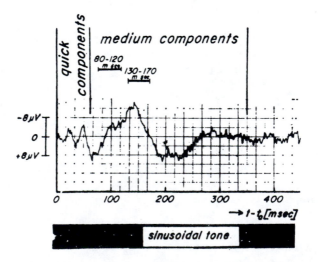

Fig. 81. Averaged cortical potentials in response to 1-second bursts of tone repeated 100 times. The tone frequency was 1000 hertz. The large upward excursion that occurs at about 150 milliseconds was found to be a feature that grew as a power function. (From Keidel and Spreng 1965, *J. Acoust. Soc. Am.*, 38, 191–195. Reprinted by permission.)

In an effort to discover some aspect of the cortical potential that might grow as a power function, Keidel and Spreng (1965) measured the amplitude of one of the slow components of the cortical wave, a part of the wave that follows about 130 to 170 milliseconds after the stimulus has occurred. Three kinds of stimuli—tone, electric current, and vibration—all produced power functions. All three exponents were smaller than the corresponding psychophysical values, but an interesting relation appeared to hold. The relative values of the three exponents were approximately the same as the relative values obtained in psychophysical experiments.

A further study of tactual vibration produced families of power functions relating averaged potentials to stimulus amplitude. Five different frequencies of vibration were tested and the exponent was found to be smallest at 200 hertz, where it was 0.52, and largest at 50 hertz, where it was 0.62. The change in the size of the exponent with frequency was not unlike the change in exponent found in psychophysical experiments (Stevens 1968a), but again the absolute values of the exponents for the cortical potentials were smaller than those obtained when a subject places his finger on a vibrating button and judges the stimuli by magnitude estimation.

Like other potentials recorded on the scalp, the cortical response to a flash of light is a complex wave that changes form and amplitude when the light intensity is altered. When the potential was measured at an appropriate latency (190 to 300 milliseconds), the response was found to grow as a power function of light intensity, with the exponent 0.21 (Loewenich and Finkenzeller 1966). The power function was shown to hold over a stimulus range as wide as 48 decibels, which is a range of about 65,000 to 1. The color of the light made little or no difference. Approximately the same exponent was obtained with red, blue, green, and white light. Here again, the exponent for the visual evoked potential was smaller than the psychophysical value, but it was consistent in relative size with the exponents determined by cortical potentials for sound, vibration, and electric shock obtained by Keidel and his collaborators.

It appears, then, that there are at least four sense modalities in which some particular aspect of the human cortical potential has been shown to follow a power function, and in which the four exponents exhibit the same relative values as those obtained in psychophysical experiments.

Numerous experiments have been carried out by Davis and his colleagues to determine the nature and properties of the so-called vertex or V potential—an evoked potential that seems to be generated rather diffusely in the cerebral cortex and is best recorded by an electrode on the top of the head, with a second electrode placed near the ear. When the stimuli consist of repeated bursts of tones, the V potential grows slowly with sound pressure. Power functions fitted to the data for five subjects gave exponents that ranged from 0.10 to 0.18 (Davis, Bowers, and Hirsh 1968). When power functions have low exponents, they can be distinguished from logarithmic functions only if the variability is small, because, as the exponent decreases, the power function comes more and more to resemble a logarithmic function.

The failure of the cortical vertex potentials to exhibit growth functions having the same exponents that govern perceived sensory magnitude does not, of course, rule out other interesting comparisons. We may ask, for example, whether stimuli that appear subjectively equal produce similar vertex potentials. Despite a considerable variability, it appears that when sounds of different spectra were equated for loudness they gave rise to approximately equal voltages at the cortex.

The same question can be extended to cross-modality comparisons. If stimuli in different modalities have been equated for apparent magnitude, do they produce similar cortical potentials? That a positive answer may prove possible was indicated by Davis, Bowers, and Hirsh, who said, "In a set of cross-modality comparisons of V potentials evoked by sounds, flashes of light, vibration, or electric shock . . . we found that stimuli that were adjusted to equal subjective magnitude evoked similar V potentials."

Thus there exists positive evidence that the cross-modality matching of certain kinds of sensory stimuli may be based on something more solid than a kind of computational exercise mediated by the subject's resort to magnitude estimation. Some critics have supposed that in cross-modality matching the subject merely estimates the numerical magnitude of each stimulus and then compares the numbers. But if each stimulus produces some form of electrical response whose magnitude reaches about the same level when the subject makes the two sensations appear equally intense, then it begins to appear that cross-modality matching may have an objective basis in physiology. The vertex potential offers a positive lead in that direction.

EVOKED RESPONSES FROM CUTANEOUS SENSES

Tactile pulses on the finger produce evoked cortical potentials that have been averaged and compared with psychophysical functions determined with the same subjects (Franzén and Offenloch 1969). The stimuli were produced by a moving-coil vibrator activated by a brief electrical pulse lasting 1.5 milliseconds. The subjects made magnitude estimations of the apparent intensity of the pulses. Then on the same day the potentials evoked by repeated pulses were recorded and averaged. It was found that the growth of the overall peak-to-peak amplitude of the evoked potentials as a function of stimulus amplitude could be described by power functions with exponents of approximately 0.5. The magnitude estimations gave exponents of approximately 0.6. In comparing those exponents we must remember that magnitude estimation underestimates the size of the exponent, owing to the ever-present regression effect (see Chapter 9). It appears rather certain, therefore, that the cortical potential grows with a lower exponent than the experienced intensity. In that respect the experiment confirms what has been found in other sense modalities.

A similar conclusion was reached by Beck and Rosner (1968) who applied pulses of electric current directly to the skin. The subjects made magnitude estimations of the apparent intensity of the shocks, and from eight of the subjects the cortical potentials were recorded and averaged. Although the exponents for the psychophysical data "were somewhat larger than those for evoked potentials," the authors noted that, of all the formulas they applied to the data, the power function emerged as the "most parsimonious description for results on scaling and on evoked potentials." Beck and Rosner also called attention to the fact that the difference in the values of the exponents suggests that "the electrophysiological and psychophysical responses to intensity of stimulation are nonlinearly related."

That outcome has thus far proved to be the most general finding with averaged evoked potentials: in those rather numerous instances in which the growth of a cortical response has seemed to follow a power function, the value of the exponent has fallen systematically below the corresponding value of the exponent obtained in psychophysical studies. When two power functions differ in exponent, they are nonlinearly related.

Let us consider one more instance. Electrical pulses applied to the tongue produce taste sensations, and at the same time the potentials evoked at the cortex may be recorded and averaged. By measuring appropriate features of the resulting evoked potentials, Plattig (1967) found that the amplitude grew as a power function with an exponent of 0.8. Although that exponent recorded at the cortex is quite large, it is smaller than the psychophysical exponents for either electric current or taste.

NEURAL RESPONSES TO LIGHT

Electrical recording directly from nerves and cells can be most easily accomplished with animals, but the implantation of electrodes for the stimulation and recording of neural activity in the human brain is a developing art. An example of the possibilities for sensory investigations with implanted electrodes was presented by Pinneo and Heath (1966), who recorded from stainless-steel electrodes located near the left optic tract.

The patient made judgments of the apparent brightness of a flickering field. The judgments reflected the well-known brightness enhancement that occurs when the frequency of the flicker lies in the vicinity of 10 per second.

Corresponding to the brightness enhancement there was a change in the average amount of electrical activity measured by means of a recording voltmeter. As the frequency of the flicker changed from 1.5 to 50 flashes per second, the recorded voltage passed through a maximum that corresponded approximately to a frequency of 10 flashes per second. Above about 35 flashes per second, the voltage was comparable to that produced by a steady light of the same average intensity—a direct neural verification of the basic principle known as the Talbot-Plateau law.

When we look for power functions among the neural potentials in the visual system, we encounter numerous curiosities. The single cells of the lateral geniculate of the monkey may respond to steady light with a steady rate of discharge. But, depending on the type of cell involved, an increment in the light intensity may cause either an increase or a decrease in the firing rate. A typical cell of the kind that slows its firing when the light increases was found to produce neural impulses in the manner shown in Fig. 82.

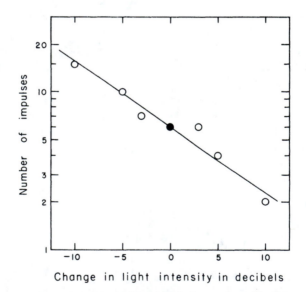

Fig. 82. Response of a single cell in the lateral geniculate nucleus. The firing rate of this cell decreased when the light intensity increased, and vice versa. The filled circle represents the steady response rate that occurred when the eye was stimulated at the level to which it had been adapted. The exponent for this cell is about −0.4. (Data from DeValois, Jacobs, and Jones 1962.)

There we see a kind of upside-down effect. A decrease in the light level produces more impulses per unit time; an increase produces fewer. The rate of discharge can be described quite well by a power function with an exponent of about -0.4 (DeValois, Jacobs, and Jones 1962).

A novel approach to the problem of the operating characteristic of the visual system was devised by Easter (1968) who recorded the neurelectric spikes produced by single ganglion cells in the goldfish retina. The stimuli were brief flashes of red light directed so as to fall on either one or two small retinal areas. The problem was to compare the responses to single-spot and double-spot stimuli. The question was, what intensity falling on a single spot is needed to produce a response as large as that produced by a given intensity falling on two spots? The two tiny spots, it should be said, were equally sensitive points within the same receptor field, in fact, within the same "critical area" as would be defined by Ricco's law. If it is assumed that the stimulation of two equally excited spots in the same receptor field produces twice the value of excitation, then it becomes possible to determine how the excitation varies with light intensity. Easter showed that the excitation function, thus defined, is a power function of intensity, with an exponent of about 0.5. That value is interesting, because, when the value of the exponent for a point source or a brief flash is determined in psychophysical experiments, the exponent turns out also to be about 0.5 (Stevens 1966a).

The temptation is great to conclude from the coincidence of those exponents that a powerful method for the analysis of the operating characteristic of the visual transducer has at last been formulated in the novel approach by Easter, and that the site of those events that determine the psychophysical power law has been shown to lie in the retina. That may well be the case, but proof is not easy to establish in these matters. At the present stage of knowledge, the variety and richness of physiological findings serve mostly to signal directions for future excursions.

It should be pointed out that Easter's approach to the operating characteristic of the visual system followed the same type of strategy that was devised by Fletcher and Munson (1933) for the purpose of measuring the loudness response of the auditory system. Instead of Easter's two tiny spots of light, Fletcher and Munson used the observer's two ears. They made the assumption that the stimulation of two ears produces twice the loudness produced by the stimulation of one ear. The experimental task was then to determine what intensity in two ears sounded as loud as a given intensity applied to only one ear. From such monaural-binaural loudness matches, Fletcher and Munson constructed a loudness scale that differed only slightly, but systematically, from the currently accepted power function. The assumption that loudness heard by one ear exactly doubles when two ears are stimulated may be almost but not quite correct. Instead of remaining constant at 2 to 1, the binaural-monaural ratio appears to be smaller at low stimulus levels and larger at high stimulus levels (Reynolds and Stevens 1960).

VISUAL REACTION TIME

How long it takes for the visual system to process an optical input has fascinated investigators for almost a century. As the light intensity increases, so does the speed of the visual reaction. In the Harvard Psychophysics Laboratory, Mansfield (1970), using a conventional reaction-time procedure, explored the problem, how quickly can the subject move his finger when the light comes on? The speed of the visual reaction can also be measured by electrical recording from various points in the visual system, including, of course, the back of the head. There appears to be a remarkably close agreement between the speed of reaction measured by electrical and by behavioral responses. First there occurs a small and irreducible latent period. Once that latent period is passed, the speed of the visual reaction increases as a power function of the light intensity, with an exponent equal to about $\frac{1}{3}$. Since that value coincides with the exponent that governs the growth of subjective brightness with intensity, it appears that the velocity of the visual reaction, measured either behaviorally or neurelectrically, is directly proportional to subjective brightness.

Where does the variable time delay take place? In the retina, it seems. Electrical recordings from the peripheral parts of the visual systems in various animals have exhibited rather similar exponents when speed of reaction is plotted against stimulus intensity. The power law with the exponent $\frac{1}{3}$ is the approximate rule at the periphery, at the level of the cortex, and in the behavioral response (Vaughan, Costa, and Gilden 1966).

An intense concern with the problem of latency was exhibited by the great French psychophysicist Piéron, who was perhaps the most erudite and distinguished of the modern defenders of the Fechnerian view. Piéron and a colleague measured the speed of reaction to visual stimuli and showed that the speed varies approximately as the $\frac{1}{3}$ power of the stimulus intensity. As a matter of fact, Piéron had earlier established the general principle that "the variable part of the reaction time is inversely proportional to the stimulus intensity raised to a certain power . . ." (Piéron 1955, p. 467). Now, the interesting thing is that Piéron occasionally entertained the idea that there may be an intimate connection between the speed of reaction and the subjective magnitude of the sensation. He even went so far as to say, "If . . . we admit a strict parallelism between the speed of reaction and the magnitude of the sensation, then we must admit that the law governing the changes in speed also governs the changes in perceived magnitude."

Although that sentence sounds as though Piéron stood ready to embrace the sensory power law, his later writings dispelled that prospect. After reviewing many of the results obtained by the direct scaling methods of the "nouvelle psychophysique," Piéron (1963) marshaled what appeared to him a convincing array of negative findings. "But Stevens," he wrote, "has remained impermeable to all the criticisms, and to all the research results that they have inspired." Actually, instead of remaining impermeable, I have probably reacted more strongly to the criticisms than wisdom might dictate that I should. It should be said, though, that the criticisms have served to inspire many new experiments that I might otherwise have overlooked. To me, the more puzzling and frustrating question is why I was never able to perform decisive enough experiments to attract Piéron to the psychophysical power law. Although he had at one time formulated his own power law of visual latency and seemed on the verge of abandoning the Fechner view, to the end of his life he held fast to Fechner's "fundamental postulate," according to which just noticeable differences are assumed to mark off equal units of sensation magnitude.

In 1960 Piéron undertook to review the notable impression that Fechner had made on modern science. The review closed with a short paragraph:

> Thus in our day the shadow of Fechner still hovers over many American laboratories—laboratories that had probably never heard so much talk about Fechner as when Stevens declared that nothing remains of his work.

I am happy to have had a hand in reviving an interest in Fechner, for no one can deny Fechner credit for having founded psychophysics and for propounding the right question—a quantitative question about stimulus and response. That question casts a long shadow, for it defines the central issue of psychophysics.

SOMATIC RESPONSES

Mountcastle and his co-workers have provided much insight into the kind of physiological mechanisms that may underlie the psychophysical power law. In numerous experiments on kinesthetic movement involving a monkey limb, the relation between stimulus magnitude and neural response has been traced in such a way that lawful and quantitative transformations have emerged. It was found, for example, that the relation between joint position and the activity of third-order neural elements can be usefully described by a power function. "What is of additional importance," wrote Mountcastle et al., "is that this transformation has occurred so early as the thalamocortical stage of the chain of sequential neural transformations leading to the behavioral response. What it may mean in terms of neural mechanism is that those neural transformations subsequent to the cortical input stage *may* occur along linear coordinates, so far as the value 'intensity' is concerned" (Mountcastle et al. 1962).

The same suggestion of linearity in the central transformations recurs in other contexts, for example, in the studies of the neural response to mechanical pressure on the glabrous skin of the monkey's hand (Mountcastle et al. 1966). The number of impulses in a myelinated axon of the monkey's median nerve was found to grow as a power function of stimulus magnitude, measured as amount of indentation of the skin. The exponent was close to 1.0, which is close to the exponent 1.1 obtained when human subjects judged the apparent intensity of pressures applied to the palm of the hand (J. C. Stevens and Mack 1959).

Interestingly, the exponent for pressure on human hairy skin does not indicate the nearly linear response exhibited by the glabrous skin. On the hairy skin of the forearm the response follows a power function, but the exponent drops to about half the value observed on the glabrous skin of the middle finger. A similar change in the exponent was evident in the neural responses in the monkey. Glabrous skin, as noted above, gave a linear response (exponent 1.0) to degree of indentation, whereas hairy skin gave a response characterized by an exponent that averaged about 0.5 (Harrington and Merzenich 1970).

THE TASTE NERVE

The sense of taste has provided a unique testing ground for the hypothesis that apparent sensory magnitude is mediated by the total activity in a nerve. By a curious quirk of anatomy, the taste nerve from the front part of the tongue passes through the cavity of the middle ear on its way to the brain. When the eardrum is removed in order to open the middle ear during certain types of surgery, that branch of the taste nerve, the chorda tympani, becomes exposed in a way that permits an electrode to be applied directly to it. An electrical recording can then be made of the neural potentials while the gustatory system responds to substances applied to the tongue of the patient. In fact, the summated neural responses can be compared directly with the quantitative estimates of taste intensity made by the patient for the same taste substances.

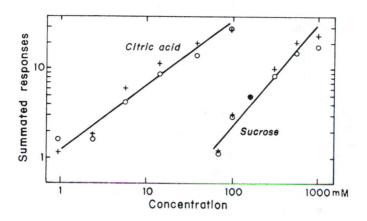

Fig. 83. Mean values of neural response (open circles) and of subjective responses (crosses) from two patients, plotted against the concentration (molarity) of taste solutions applied to the tongue. The exponents indicated by the slopes of the straight lines are about 0.77 for citric acid and 1.2 for sucrose. (From Borg et al. 1967. Reprinted by permission.)

A series of such experiments was performed with the taste substances, sucrose, sodium chloride, and citric acid. Figure 83 shows the averaged data from two patients for citric acid and sucrose. There we see that both the subjective estimates and the neural responses can be described by power functions—straight lines in log-log coordinates.

The authors summed up their work by saying, "Quite aside from the question whether the function describing the relation between the strength of a sapid solution and the summated electrical response satisfies a Stevens power function or a Fechnerian log function, it is apparent that there is fundamental congruity between neural activity and perceptual intensity" (Borg et al. 1967).

It would be interesting if other sense modalities could provide a demonstration as direct and dramatic as the data shown in Fig. 83, but nature has usually managed to hide the sensory nerves far from easy access.

Nevertheless, the foregoing examples of neurelectric functions recorded in the different sense modalities make it clear that the sensory systems can be probed with electrodes in such a way that they reveal a kind of behavior that accords with the psychophysical power law.

The evidence suggests that the transducer holds the key to the form of the psychophysical response to stimulus intensity. Apparently it is at the interface between the organism and its world—at the peripheral sense organ—that the input-output characteristic of the sensory system is imposed. In vision and hearing, for example, the transducer process uses a low exponent. A most fortunate circumstance, because the transducer's low

exponent enables it to bend the sensory function into a curve that is concave downward. In that way it permits the eye and the ear to respond to
enormous ranges of stimuli—ranges of energy that may exceed billions to
one. Perhaps, therefore, it is to transducer physiology, what Delbrück
called the "undeveloped but absolutely central science," that we must look
if we are to understand how equal stimulus ratios produce equal sensation
ratios—the ratio invariance that underlies the psychophysical power law.
The presence of power functions in the electrical recordings of neural
events seems to affirm the hypothesis that the transducer imposes the
power law in the sensory systems.

NEURAL MODELS

Man's chronic yearning for explanations leads him to invent models and
schemas with which to lessen the mystery of nature's ways. The need for a
plausible model grows especially acute when an apparent contradiction in-
trudes itself. When the power law was first invoked, it seemed at variance
with what was then regarded as established, namely, a logarithmic relation
between the stimulus and the resulting excitation at the level of the
receptor. The question was posed: if the transducer responds log-
arithmically, can the overall response, as evidenced by cross-modality
matching, follow a power law?

As a possible answer to that question an interesting model was formulated by MacKay (1963). His aim was to show that a power law is not pre-
cluded by a logarithmic transducer. Let us assume that the output of the
transducer goes to a comparator and is there opposed or balanced by a
signal generated centrally. Let us assume also that the central signal is itself a logarithmic function. We would then have two logarithmic functions
operating on the comparator, and the comparator output would be a power
function. According to the model, sensation intensity becomes not solely
the inward flow from the sense organ, but also the outward flow from a
central generator. The central generator produces a signal of the size
needed to match or counterbalance the inward flow. MacKay observed that
his model "requires nothing but approximately logarithmic . . . transformations . . . at receptors . . . yet leads directly . . . to a prediction of Stevens'
power law."

Whether the nervous system utilizes comparators analogous to those familiar to the electronic engineer is not yet known, of course. Nevertheless,
the virtue of MacKay's model lies in its demonstration that the experimenter has no guarantee that his electrode will necessarily record a power
function merely because cross-modality matching gives power functions in

psychophysical experiments. Within the nervous system many alternative modes of action are conceivable. Of course, if the electrode does record a response that follows a power function, the comparator model may not be needed. The transducer itself may supply the power-law characteristic.

The limitations imposed by the all-or-none action of the nerve fiber has also inspired efforts to understand how a system that operates on a kind of pulse code might manage the delivery of power-law responses. A train of nerve impulses sweeps along each nerve fiber. At some point the pulses must somehow add or cumulate. If the summation occurs by straight linear addition, then only linear transformations would take place in the central nervous system. Is it conceivable, though, that power-law transformations other than linear can be mediated by the addition of all-or-none impulses? An affirmative answer was made by Cohen and Little (1971) in what they called a "neural model for the Stevens power law." They appealed to a principle that is well known in the branch of mathematics called the calculus of finite differences. The principle can be illustrated by a simple example, a power function with the exponent 2—a square law. If we take the numbers 1, 2, 3, 4, . . . and square each one, we obtain the numbers 1, 4, 9, 16. . . . Now if we take the difference between each successive square, we obtain the first-order differences 3, 5, 7, 9. . . . Finally, if we take the second-order differences, we obtain 2, 2, 2, 2. Thus with two orders of differences we reach a fixed finite value. For power functions having other exponents, more orders of differences may be required, but for any power function there will be convergence toward a finite difference. Now the importance of the principle is this. The subtraction procedure that produced the differences can also be worked backwards, so that we can reconstruct a power function by sequences of simple addition.

Cohen and Little described an electronic model that would respond to input impulses in such a way that it produced a power-function output. By an analogous neural network, according to the authors, power functions could be produced by the nervous system despite the all-or-none action of the nerve fibers. The all-or-none impulses would need to impinge on neural gates that make the impulses add in appropriate sequences.

Whether actual neural gates behave in the required manner remains to be determined, but the conceptual model based on the summation of finite differences provides another conceivable way in which the sensory systems might operate to produce power-law responses.

Both the comparator model and the finite difference model provide possible mechanisms that might relieve the transducer of the burden of responding in accordance with a power law. It may turn out, however, that the transducer does not need that kind of assistance, for its input-output characteristic may follow a power function to begin with.

One final point. In thinking about these matters, it is well to remember that we need not take an either-or approach. It may be that no single mechanism is adequate to explain all the possible invariances that accord with a power law.

EVOLUTION

Whatever the physiological mechanism may prove to be, we can ask why nature seems to favor power-law responses. Is there some wider principle that makes it plausible that ratios in the world outside should map into ratios in the perceptual interior? In other words, does the power-law response provide some evolutionary advantage? First let us consider what kinds of functional principles it would be desirable to have in perceptual systems. For survival in a heterogeneous environment, the animal needs two basic features in its sensory processing. One is a feature that tells the animal approximately how things stand outside. The other is a feature that guarantees perceptual stability despite changes in the inputs to the sense organs. In other words, in order to promote survival, perception should be both functionally veridical and reasonably stable. The required stability means, for example, that, when the sun goes behind a cloud and the light intensity falls by a large factor, the perceived relations among objects remain essentially as they were.

From considerations such as those, the physicist Yilmaz (1967) formulated two postulates: (1) perceptual organizations tend to model the environment in a homological manner, and (2) percepts tend to remain invariant under environmental variations. From those two postulates Yilmaz showed how the power law can be deduced.

Such a theoretical deduction does not prove that nature is constrained to behave in precise accord with the theoretician's model. Nevertheless, the empirical scientist can take satisfaction in the fact that the observed power function does not appear to clash with a mathematical derivation from a pair of reasonable postulates.

CHAPTER 8

Scaling the Social Consensus

Although the new psychophysics set as its first priority the rewriting of the psychophysical law, the direct scaling procedures have produced dividends in other areas of behavioral science. The fallout from the development of the direct methods of cross-modality matching has introduced ratio-scale quantification into sociology, criminology, and political science. The procedures used to scale brightness and loudness have found immediate translation into the scaling of such variables as the perceived status of occupations, the seriousness of crimes, and the degree of national aggressiveness. Magnitude estimation has been the procedure most often employed in the new ventures into what might be called social psychophysics, but other cross-modality matches have occasionally been made. The widespread application of the direct scaling procedures in several different laboratories has established the usefulness and the validity of ratio scales of opinion created with several kinds of nonmetric stimuli.

When a subject is asked to judge the seriousness of various crimes, for example, we commonly class the stimuli as nonmetric, because the stimuli—statements describing acts of depredation—are not measurable on a metric scale analogous to the scales we use to measure the stimuli in vision, hearing, and most other sensory domains. It has sometimes been asserted that sensory psychophysics enjoys a distinct advantage over other behavioral sciences because it can measure its stimuli on ratio scales. Measurable stimuli provide benefits, to be sure, but the scale used to measure the stimuli does not determine the kind of scale of subjective magnitude that we can erect. A ratio scale of judged seriousness can be erected for crimes even though the stimuli are verbal statements depicting delinquent acts. As stimuli, such statements can be scaled only on a nominal scale, but for each statement the perceived degree of seriousness can be scaled on a ratio scale. The general principle is this: if we have some way of telling one stimulus from another—so that the stimuli can be placed on a nominal scale—we can proceed to scale whatever common attribute of the stimuli the subjects are able to perceive as existing in amount or degree. In other words, ratio scales of opinion require for their creation no underlying stimulus metric. A social psychophysics can therefore be made a reality.

The application of psychophysical methods in the area of opinion is nothing new. The methods of the older classical psychophysics also found their way into opinion scaling. As a matter of fact, Fechner himself worked for a decade on the problem of esthetics, publishing a dozen papers and laying the foundations of experimental esthetics. Among other innovations he obtained judgments of esthetic preference for two versions of Holbein's *Madonna*—paintings that had aroused a storm of controversy over which of them had been painted by Holbein.

It was Thurstone, though, who brought the Fechnerian psychophysics to bear on the scaling of attitudes and opinions. Thurstone tells us that his introduction to "the interesting problems of the subjective metric came in teaching the classical psychophysical methods." In the 1920's he decided to retain the "logic," as he called it, of Fechner's approach, but to liven up the content. He later wrote, "Instead of asking students to decide which of two weights seemed to be the heavier, it was more interesting to ask, for example, which of two nationalities they would generally prefer to associate with, or which they would prefer to have their sister marry, or which of two offenses seemed to them to be the more serious" (Thurstone 1959). By means of engaging questions like those, Thurstone managed to electrify a dull subject matter, even though he made no basic changes in method. For Thurstone, as for Fechner, a measure of variability became the unit of the psychophysical scale. Both men built their systems on what I have called poikilitic measures.

It is appropriate at this point for us to review the three kinds of measures that have been used for the scaling of nonmetric stimuli. As we shall see, the interrelations among the three kinds of measures remain the same, regardless of the kind of stimuli used.

THREE KINDS OF MEASURES

Although the century-long development of psychophysics has seemed to spawn a surfeit of methods and procedures, the scaling measures that have been produced fall into three major classes: magnitude, partition, and

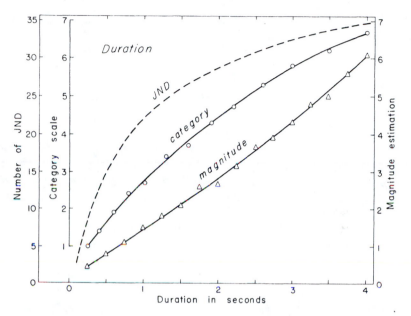

Fig. 84. Three basic scaling measures applied to the apparent duration of a noise stimulus. The JND scale, category scale, and magnitude scale are plotted in linear coordinates in order to show the relative curvatures of poikilitic, partition, and magnitude measures. The triangles are mean judgments of 12 observers who estimated the apparent duration of a white noise turned on and off by an automatic timer. The stimuli were presented in a different irregular order to each observer. The circles are mean category judgments made by 16 observers on a scale from 1 to 7. The shortest and longest stimuli were presented at the outset to indicate the range. The dashed curve is the function, approximately logarithmic, obtained by summation of the just noticeable differences. (From Stevens 1957b, *Psychol. Rev.*, 64, 153–181. Copyright by the American Psychological Association. Reprinted by permission.)

poikilitic. Some of the main features and interrelations of the three classes will be discussed. Figure 84 shows examples of the three measures applied to the scaling of apparent duration, which is a rather simple perceptual continuum and one that proves relatively easy to judge. The coordinates of Fig. 84 have been made linear in order to portray the relations more clearly.

1.   Magnitude Measures

The direct measures of subjective magnitude were historically the last to be developed, but they now stand first in importance for they lead to ratio scales. Magnitude measures become possible because people have a remarkable ability to match one thing to another. They can match numbers to apparent loudness or apparent loudness to numbers. They can match loudness to the strength of a vibration on the fingertip, and vice versa. And they can match numbers or items from any other continuum to a nonsensory variable such as prestige of occupations.

As we have seen, direct scaling procedures based on a free and unconstrained matching of one continuum to another have shown that the magnitude of a sensation grows as a power function of the stimulus. With nonmetric stimuli, where we have only a nominal stimulus scale, the power law principle cannot be tested, but other interesting comparisons can be made, provided poikilitic (JND) or partition (category) scales have also been erected. The type of relations exhibited in Fig. 84 should then make themselves apparent.

The matching operation, as we have seen, is basic not only to magnitude measures, but to other measures as well, for matching stands as the basic operation in all psychophysics. The differences among the three classes of measures arise because stimuli have many different aspects, and the question becomes: what aspect is matched to what? Magnitude measures derive from direct cross-modality matching of magnitude or degree on one continuum to the same aspect on another. One of the continua may be the number continuum. The ability of the typical observer to make such direct matches has become the well-documented theme of the new psychophysics. The typical observer's capacity for magnitude matching is generally far greater than some experimenters have seemed willing to believe.

2.   Partition Measures

All procedures that require the observer to match apparent differences or intervals produce partition measures. We meet an early example of a partition scale in the productions of Plateau's eight artists who painted samples of a middle gray that appeared to bisect the distance from black to white.

The most common form of the partition measure is the category rating scale described in Chapter 5. The procedure may require the observer to assign each stimulus to a category such as strong, medium, or weak. Or the categories may be designated by numbers, as Hipparchus did when he used the numbers 1 to 6 to rate the brightness of stars.

Like all partition scales, the category scale is nonlinear relative to the magnitude scale. In the example shown in Fig. 84, we see that the form of the category scale does not parallel the curvature of the magnitude scale. In fact, relative to the scale of judged magnitude, the partition scale is quite curved. Yet it is less curved than the poikilitic measure based on a summation of JNDs.

As was shown in Chapter 5, the relations among the three types of measures can be conveniently expressed by the exponents of the various scales, for the exponents provide an index to the curvature. The exponent of the partition scale—the virtual exponent—falls intermediate between the other two exponents. The virtual exponent of the partition scale is always smaller than the actual exponent of the magnitude scale, but it is greater than the very low, near-zero, exponent of the poikilitic scale.

Applied to social variables about which the scientist may seek to quantify a social consensus, the category scaling procedure seems seductively simple. As a consequence, unfortunately, the procedure enjoys unmerited popularity. Category procedures result at best in interval scales, not in ratio scales. In most cases only a slight rewording of the instructions would allow the observer to employ, not a restricted set of category numbers, but any numbers he thinks appropriate to express the apparent magnitude of the stimulus. It would then be possible for the observer to generate a ratio scale.

3. Poikilitic Measures

The first poikilitic scales were those created by Fechner when he counted off the just noticeable differences and obtained a scale similar to the JND scale in Fig. 84. The JND is called a poikilitic measure because its determination requires the application of one or another statistical measure to the scatter of responses obtained when an observer judges small stimulus differences. The observer is confronted with a succession of small differences and is asked to categorize them in some way. He may be asked, for example, to categorize them as greater or smaller than some standard, as in the method of constant stimuli.

When we sum or count off JNDs we in effect mark off steps of equal variability or equal confusion along the stimulus scale. As a general rule the resulting scale resembles a logarithmic function—not exactly, but approximately. So the poikilitic scale on a prothetic continuum approximates a logarithmic function of the magnitude scale.

Thurstone had the insight to perceive that, if equal amounts of variability or confusion can be used to create a scale in sensory psychophysics, it can also be used to create scales in other areas such as attitudes. Variability and confusion can be found in all human judgments. Thurstone extended Fechner's mathematical apparatus to make it applicable to nonmetric stimuli. In his "equation for comparative judgment," as he sometimes called it, he provided a technique for transforming measures of dispersion or variability into units of poikilitic scale. In order to make the procedure work on real data, an assumption has to be made. Although several assumptions have been explored, the assumption most commonly invoked (called Case V) is that equal dispersions in judgment represent equal distances along the subjective continuum. The assumption is sometimes set forth in the phrase "equally often noticed differences are equal"—a false but appealing notion. Fechner had made an equivalent assumption to the effect that equal increments in sensation go with successive JNDs. Curiously enough, neither Fechner nor Thurstone explored the assumption that equal units of dispersion represent not equal distances but equal ratios along the subjective continuum. Since the equal-ratios assumption has seemed to me important enough to deserve a designation, I have called it Case VI (Stevens 1959c). That assumption accords better with reality than any of the assumptions—Cases I to V—that Thurstone explored. It should be noted, however, that even if the demands of Case VI were fulfilled exactly, the resulting scale would not constitute a ratio scale, but only what I have named a logarithmic interval scale—a fifth kind of scale to be added to the four scale types described in Chapter 2. It would be a logarithmic interval scale because equal units of dispersion would mark off equal ratios rather than equal intervals. The defining invariance of the logarithmic interval scale is called the power group, for the permissible transformations of the scale include raising all values to a power (Stevens 1957b). The logarithmic interval scale appears to be a type of scale with few practical uses.

The experimental scatter or dispersion that Thurstone utilized for the scaling of attitudes and opinions came from several procedures, foremost among them the method of paired comparisons. Under that method each stimulus is paired with every other stimulus and the observer is asked to say which member of each pair has more of some attribute. The inconsistencies among the observer's choices provide the data needed to create a poikilitic scale. Thurstone also transformed the data of category scaling into a poikilitic scale. The procedure there is to ignore the mean category assignment and to process instead the confusions or overlap among the category judgments. The resulting scale is not the simple category scale that Hipparchus devised. Rather it should be called a poikilitic category scale.

Beginning with the research of Thurstone, several of the methods of psychophysics have been applied to the scaling of an interesting variety of nonmetric stimuli. We will next review a few of those studies and we will find that all three of the basic measures—magnitude, partition, and poikilitic—have been used with nonmetric stimuli. As a fortunate consequence we are able to decide whether certain of the nonmetric continua belong to the prothetic class. Mostly they do. And by and large the same interrelations that we found among the three basic measures in sensory psychophysics have also been found among the three comparable types of measures in social scaling (Stevens 1966d, 1968b).

ATTITUDE SCALE

In 1929 Thurstone and Chave used a version of category or partition scaling in order to scale the strength of the attitude expressed by each of 130 statements concerning one or another aspect of religion. The resulting strength scale, based on the responses of 300 subjects, achieved a well-deserved fame, for it represented a serious and effective effort to introduce a metric where none had existed before.

In 1959 at Harvard, Finnie and Luce undertook to apply a larger battery of scaling devices to some of the same attitude statements. When they used

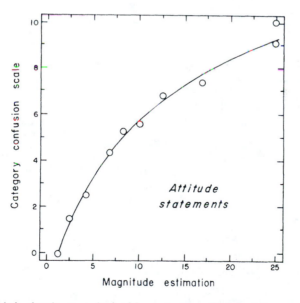

Fig. 85. Two kinds of scales were obtained from observers who judged the strength of the attitude expressed by various statements concerning the church. The ordinate scale is a poikilitic measure based on the confusions among the observers' category judgments. When plotted against the scale obtained by magnitude estimation, the poikilitic category scale is concave downward. (From Stevens 1968b, *Science*, 151, 530-541, based on unpublished data from Finnie and Luce 1960. Copyright 1968 by the American Association for the Advancement of Science. Reprinted by permission.)

Thurstone's method of sorting the statements into 11 categories the resulting partition scale correlated highly with the original partition scale of Thurstone and Chave. The passage of 30 years and the use of a new sample of subjects apparently made little difference.

A large change in the form of the scale resulted, however, when the subjects made a magnitude estimation of the strength of the attitude expressed by each of the statements. When the magnitude estimation scale was compared with the poikilitic category scale for the same set of statements, the relation turned out to be highly nonlinear, as shown in Fig. 85. The curve of Fig. 85 shows that the relation between the poikilitic measure and the scale obtained by direct magnitude estimation is approximately logarithmic. That indeed is the relation we should predict if the perception of apparent strength of attitude constitutes a prothetic continuum.

Once a scale has been created, it can be put to account. Thurstone and Chave went on to use their attitude scale to measure the attitudes of individuals drawn from various classes of people—college freshmen, graduate students, divinity students, and so on. An individual's position on the attitude scale was determined by the statements he was willing to endorse. As expected, the divinity students endorsed only certain statements about the church. The attitudes of the graduate students, on the other hand, spread over a wider range.

EKMAN'S LAW

At about the same time that Finnie and Luce were scaling attitude statements at Harvard University, experiments were under way at the University of Stockholm designed to show the relation between the Thurstonian indirect methods of scaling and the direct procedures of ratio and magnitude estimation. On seven different nonmetric continua thus far studied in Stockholm, the Thurstonian poikilitic scale has been shown to be a logarithmic function of the magnitude scale. Since that effort, led by Gösta Ekman, is perhaps the most extensive yet undertaken, the case for use of the direct scaling methods in all areas involving human judgment receives much of its support from the Stockholm studies. Some of the studies will be reviewed below, but first let me call attention to the basic, underlying principle.

In several studies Ekman (1956, 1959) took pains to establish the generality of a principle that was conjectured in 1874 by Brentano and that has been demonstrated occasionally by others in various contexts (see, for example, Harper and Stevens 1948). The principle states that, when variability is measured in subjective units, it is linearly related to psychological magnitude measured in the same units. That relation is the analogue of

Weber's law, which concerns the linear growth of variability among human judgments as a function of the stimulus measure. Both Fechner (in deriving his law) and Thurstone (in his Case V) proposed a different assumption, namely, that variability in psychological units is constant along the psychological continuum. The Fechner-Thurstone assumption has been found to be adequate for metathetic continua, but not for prothetic continua. As Ekman and his collaborators (Ekman and Künnapas 1957; Björkman 1958, 1960; Eisler 1962) have repeatedly demonstrated, on prothetic continua the variability in subjective units tends to grow as a linear function of the subjective magnitude. Assuming that both Weber's law and the power law hold, a derivation can be made to show that Ekman's finding constitutes the predicted outcome (Stevens 1957b).

Since it seems more important to have established the empirical generality of a principle than merely to have conjectured it, as Brentano did in 1874, or to have derived it, as I did in 1957, I have proposed that the principle of the linear growth of subjective variability be called Ekman's law— the subjective counterpart of Weber's law.

When we measure perceptual magnitudes in subjective units like sones and brils, certain quantitative relations take on a simpler form. There exists evidence, for example, that the slope constant in Ekman's law has the same value, 0.03, for several different sensory continua (R. Teghtsoonian 1971). In other words, expressed in subjective units, the size of all JNDs may turn out to be approximately 3 percent.

The importance of Ekman's law in the present context is clear. Although the principle was developed and tested with metric stimuli in the area of perceptual psychophysics, there is reason to believe that the same principle applies when the stimuli are describable only in terms of a nominal scale. Indeed, the repeated finding that Thurstone's poikilitic scale for nonmetric stimuli is related to the scale of magnitude in a logarithmic manner constitutes direct evidence for Ekman's law.

Thurstonian scales are usually erected on the assumption (Case V) that subjective variability is constant all up and down the continuum. If Thurstone had gone on to what I have called Case VI, he would in effect have adopted Ekman's principle. Under Case VI the Thurstonian scale would tend to be a power function of the magnitude scale, but the exponent would be arbitrary.

PREFERENCE FOR WRIST WATCHES

Before turning to the Stockholm studies, we may note how busily the Zeitgeist works to produce similar experiments in different places. In that same year, 1959, Indow (1961) was presenting pictures and descriptions of wrist watches to 127 university students in Japan and asking for paired comparisons and ratio judgments. The student was asked to say which of each pair of watches he preferred, and also to indicate by marking a position on an 8-centimeter line what the relative strength of his preference was. The subjects, in effect, matched length of line to subjective value, a kind of cross-modality procedure. By comparing the ratio scale determined with the aid of the 8-centimeter line to the Thurstonian scale (Case V) derived from the "noise" or confusions in the pair comparisons, Indow was able to demonstrate an approximately logarithmic relation between the two kinds of scales. That nonlinear relation is shown in Fig. 86.

In another part of Indow's experiment the students were asked to state what they would regard as a fair price for each of the wrist watches, given that the price of a particular watch was a stated number of yen. For each of three different groups of students a different standard (watch and price) was designated. The interesting aspect of the outcome concerns the relation of the averages of the price estimates to the ratio scale of desirability previously established. That relation is shown in log-log coordinates in Fig.87. The fact that the data approximate a straight line suggests that fair price is judged to be a power function of degree of desirability. The low value of the exponent, 0.32, indicates that the relation between judged price and judged desirability is rather far from linear. It would be interesting to know whether a power function with a similar exponent would be obtained in other circumstances where preferences are measured.

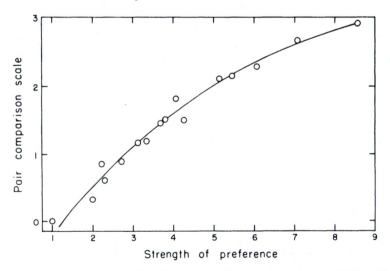

Fig. 86. Plot showing the curved relation between the pair comparison scale (Case V) and the scale of preference for different kinds of wrist watches, derived from ratio judgments made by marking distances along a line. (Data from Indow 1961.)

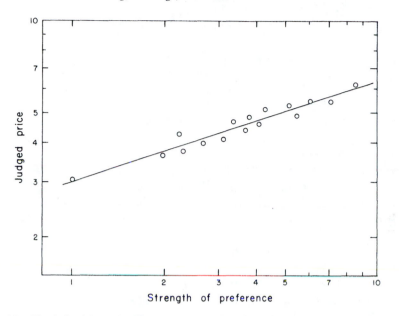

Fig. 87. The judged fair price (in yen × 10³) for various wrist watches plotted against the judged strength of preference. The coordinates are logarithmic. The line through the data points determines a power function with an exponent of 0.32. (Data from Indow 1961.)

ESTHETIC VALUE OF HANDWRITING, DRAWINGS, AND MUSIC

Two separate studies of the esthetic value of handwriting were carried out by Ekman and Künnapas (1960, 1962a). In both studies, samples of handwriting were scaled by Thurstone's method of pair comparisons and by a variant of the method of ratio estimation (Ekman 1958). The first study, which used seven samples of handwriting, is especially instructive because it seemed not to show the expected logarithmic relation between the scale by paired comparisons and the scale by ratio estimation. The second study used 18 samples of handwriting covering a wider range of quality. The second experiment demonstrated that the approximately linear relation of the first experiment became an obviously logarithmic relation when the wider stimulus range made the form of the function easier to determine. The form of the function is often obscure when the range is short.

A related study by similar methods was carried out on 17 drawings of a tree. The samples were selected from some 200 drawings produced by sixth grade students (Ekman and Künnapas 1962b). Again it was found that the confusion scale derived from paired comparisons was quite precisely proportional to the logarithm of the magnitude scale derived from ratio estimations.

Esthetic judgment in the musical sphere was investigated by Koh (1965), who played 51 vocal selections and 60 piano pieces to various populations of subjects, including college students and patients in the alcoholic ward of a hospital in North Dakota. Each musical excerpt lasted from about 15 seconds for the piano pieces to about 60 seconds for the vocal pieces. The total population of subjects, numbering 330, was divided into six groups, two groups each of college males, college females, and alcoholics. Half of the groups, one of each kind, heard vocal selections, the other half heard piano selections. The subjects in each group made magnitude estimations of the affective value of each selection and also judged each selection on a category scale expressed in terms of nine adjectives ranging from "most pleasant" through "indifferent" to "most unpleasant." The category values were treated as a 9-point numerical scale, and the ratings of each piece of music were averaged.

For each of the six groups, the average rating scale value was plotted against the logarithm of the geometric means of the magnitude estimations. In those semilogarithmic coordinates the product-moment correlations between the category and the magnitude values ranged from 0.90 to 0.96. The variability tended to obscure the upward concavity that usually occurs when category scales are plotted against the logarithm of the magnitude scale: Nevertheless, for one group the upward curvature was quite clear.

As Koh remarked, the relation between the category and the magnitude scales was strikingly invariant under differences in the age, sex, education, occupation, and pathology of the subjects. "These empirical invariances," he concluded, "strongly suggest the usefulness of magnitude estimation for complex judgmental processes."

IMPORTANCE OF SWEDISH MONARCHS

The direct method of ratio estimation and the indirect method of paired comparisons were used by Ekman and Künnapas (1963a) to construct scales of the political importance of eleven Swedish monarchs who lived between 1550 and 1850. Eighty-three students of psychology at the University of Stockholm made the judgments. The scale, derived from paired comparisons based on the assumption of Thurstone's Case V, was a logarithmic function of the magnitude scale derived from direct ratio estimation. The scale of magnitude shows that, on the average, the students considered the leading monarch to be about four times more important than the one who was least well regarded. Whether it is useful to determine ratios among items of that kind remains to be seen. The point here is to note that ratio determinations of student consensus have been achieved.

PLEASANTNESS OF ODORS

The scaling of odors presents an especially instructive example of the potentialities of the ratio scaling methods. From experiments with those methods we learn that apparent pleasantness and apparent intensity follow different rules. The apparent intensity of each of a variety of odors has been scaled by magnitude estimation, always with approximately the same results. The apparent intensity of the odor grows according to a power function of the concentration, and the exponent is less than 1.0, usually of the order of 0.5 or 0.6. Furthermore, the range from the faintest to the strongest perceptible odor is relatively small—nothing like the enormous dynamic range of loudness or brightness.

The subjective range for odors was increased more than a hundredfold when, instead of the intensity of a single odor, the pleasantness of 18 different odors became the attribute that the observers were asked to estimate (Engen and McBurney 1964). The hedonic aspect of odor exhibits a wider dynamic range than the intensity aspect. With smell it is quality, not quantity, that carries the message.

When the pleasantness of the odors was judged on a 9-point category scale, the result was typical of category judgments on other prothetic continua. Plotted against the scale produced by magnitude estimation, the category scale of pleasantness became concave downward. Plotted against the logarithm of the magnitude scale, the category scale became concave upward. The upward curvature in a semilogarithmic plot demonstrates the principle that the curvature of the category scale is generally intermediate between a linear and a logarithmic function of the magnitude scale.

LIBERAL—CONSERVATIVE

Thus far there appears to be one possible exception to the rule that a scale based on the unitizing of variability approximates a logarithmic function of the magnitude scale generated by a procedure of direct estimation. Ekman and Künnapas (1963b) assembled a set of 17 statements designed to sample the liberal-conservative continuum and asked 82 subjects to assess the degree of conservatism expressed by each statement. As it turned out, the scale defined by ratio estimations was roughly linearly related to the scale defined by the procedure of paired comparisons (Case V). That unusual result was further examined in a series of experiments by Künnapas and Sillén (1964) who used as stimuli the same 17 statements. In the second study, judgments were also made of the degree of liberalism expressed by the statements. Only in one part of the second study was there evidence for the expected logarithmic relation between the poikilitic Thurstonian scale and the magnitude scales.

The authors entertained the hypothesis that degree of liberalism represents a continuum that is qualitative or metathetic, which, if true, would account for the general nature of the results. An alternative hypothesis is that the heterogeneity of content among the statements made it too difficult for the observers to assess the degree or intensity of one particular attribute. The statements concerned such diverse matters as world government, church and state, sex education, movie censors, school prayers, abortion, capital punishment, and so forth. The problem is analogous to the task of judging loudness when every tone presented has a different pitch. With loudness such judgments have proved possible, but they have also proved to be much more variable than those obtained when only the intensity of the tones is varied (Stevens, Guirao, and Slawson 1965). It seems likely that the 17 statements used in the foregoing experiments did not elicit judgments related to the same subjective continuum for all the subjects. By contrast, the attitude statements scaled by Finnie and Luce all contained explicit reference to the church. Perhaps a chief problem in these areas of research is to refine the statements until a sufficient homogeneity is achieved to make it easy for the subjects to judge degree or intensity. Thurstone and Chave gave many helpful rules for the elimination of ambiguous and irrelevant statements and for the refinement of scale items.

With simpler materials, such as single adjectives describing personality traits, it proved quite possible for people to abstract an attribute and judge its intensity. Ekman and Künnapas (1963c) asked 95 subjects to judge the degree of masculinity expressed by each of eleven personality adjectives. The subjects also judged the degree of femininity expressed. In both instances the scale derived from paired comparisons (Case V) approximated a logarithmic function of the scale derived from direct ratio estimation.

POLITICAL DISSATISFACTION

The ability of magnitude estimation to produce a useful scale of a complex political attitude was demonstrated in a study by Welch (1971). The author took pains, first of all, to sample a wide range of attitudes, and second, to refine the scale items by subjecting them to appropriate tests and criteria of relevance. Statements covering a wide spectrum of attitudes were generated by asking over 500 college students, "In one or two sentences, what is your opinion of the American political system?" The statements were edited and reduced to a pool of 45 items which were then presented to 81 judges with instruction to estimate the degree of dissatisfaction expressed by each statement.

The judgments were made relative to a reference standard, called 100, which was the statement: "The American political system is far from perfect, but it is also far ahead of whatever system is in second place."

The 20 items that behaved best under magnitude estimation and in other tests were retained for the final attitude scale. The scale was then administered to various campus groups at the University of Texas. The students checked those statements that they agreed with. On the average, the dissatisfaction scores were about three times higher for those who classified themselves as political activists than for those who claimed to be apolitical.

PRESTIGE OF OCCUPATIONS

Several studies have been made of opinions related to the standing of different occupations. Since some of the studies used more than one scaling method, we are able to compare the kinds of scales obtained. A logarithmic relation between the poikilitic scale and the magnitude scale tells us that strength of preference for different occupations behaves like a prothetic continuum. And the partition (category) scale has a curvature that is intermediate between the other two.

Figure 88 shows the magnitude scale preference for different occupations expressed by 74 students at the University of Stockholm. In the Stockholm study two different procedures—ratio estimation and magnitude estimation—were used to scale occupational preference, and a third procedure—paired comparisons processed according to the assumption of Case V—was used to produce a Thurstonian scale. The two magnitude scales were found to be linearly related, as would be expected. The poikilitic scale derived from paired comparisons approximated a logarithmic function of both magnitude scales.

For the 74 students in the Stockholm study, the occupation of physician surpassed all others in prestige. Opinions about such matters vary from person to person, as well as from nation to nation, but among the students in Stockholm the consensus was sufficiently close to establish a scale representative of the group. Since the procedure allowed the students to make magnitude estimations, the scale in Fig. 88 is one on which ratios

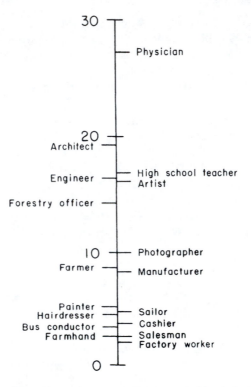

Fig. 88. Degree of preference for various occupations expressed by students at the University of Stockholm. (Data from Künnapas and Wikström 1963.)

have a meaning. We can say, for example, that the architect enjoys about twice the prestige of the photographer.

A few years later the same list of occupations, with a few changes and additions, was presented to 24 men at the University of Notre Dame. That time, however, the procedure was different. For each of the occupations, which were presented to the student in irregular order, the student squeezed a hand dynamometer to indicate by the force of his handgrip how desirable he thought the occupation to be. In still another part of the experiment the student adjusted the intensity of a sound in a pair of earphones to make the apparent loudness seem as strong as his appraisal of the occupation.

Interesting questions are raised by those studies. First, we may ask whether the handgrip squeezes produced the same rank order as the loudness adjustments. The rank-order correlation, 0.94, was satisfactorily high, especially when we note that some of the occupations differ very little in prestige or desirability.

Another question concerns the form of the actual magnitude scale of desirability when it is determined by the matching of sound intensity to occupation. Does the scale determined by loudness matching agree with the scale determined by number matching, as represented by the magnitude estimations made in Stockholm? In order to answer that question, I converted the median sound levels produced by 24 students into units of subjective loudness in sones. The sone value obtained for each occupation is listed in Table 10 alongside the magnitude estimations obtained in Stockholm.

The table shows that there is considerable agreement between Swedish and American students on the desirability or prestige of the various occu-

Table 10. Prestige of occupations. The magnitude estimations were made by 74 students at the University of Stockholm. The loudness matches (sones) were made by 24 men at the University of Notre Dame. They adjusted the level of a tone (1000 hertz) to produce a loudness that appeared to match the desirability of each occupation. (Data from Künnapas and Wikström 1963, and Dawson and Brinker 1971.)

	Matching loudness in sones	Magnitude estimates
Physician	28.3	28.0
College professor	25.3	
High school teacher	22.0	16.9
Business executive	18.7	
Architect	18.3	19.4
Engineer	16.2	16.6
Photographer	13.0	10.0
Salesman	12.2	2.6
Artist	12.0	16.3
Forestry officer	11.0	14.4
Farmer	8.9	8.7
Manufacturer		8.3
Painter		5.2
Cashier	8.9	3.7
Sailor	6.6	4.7
Farmhand	6.2	2.6
Bus driver	5.0	
Bus conductor		3.3
Factory worker	4.8	2.1
Hairdresser	2.4	4.5

pations. It is also clear that a person can express his opinion about occupations either by numerical judgment, as in magnitude estimation, or by producing a subjective loudness that matches his opinion in strength or degree.

The major disagreement in Table 10 occurs in the judgments concerning salesman. Students at Stockholm placed that occupation near the bottom of the list, whereas the students at Notre Dame placed it near the middle. That and other discrepancies between the two studies may reflect a genuine difference in personal values. On the other hand, some of the discrepancies may reside in differences in meaning or in ambiguity in the names used to designate the occupations in different countries. For instance, does salesman mean a grocery clerk or an engineering sales representative? There can be large differences in prestige among people who sell things.

As a general principle, loudness matching can be used to measure a subjective attribute of any stimulus that can be presented at different levels or degrees to an observer. Loudness matching has also proved useful in the hospital setting as a procedure to determine the degree of a patient's suffering, or the changes produced by medication. The patient indicates his condition by adjusting the noise in his ear until it seems as strong as his pain or distress.

SOCIAL STATUS

The social status enjoyed by a person has been thought by many scholars to be composed of several attributes, among them occupation, income, education, race, religion, and so forth. We have just seen how the prestige of occupations has been measured on a ratio scale by several different procedures. A person's status, of course, is an attribution that other people, by the consensus of their subjective appraisal, confer upon a person. A man stands in social esteem only where others think he stands.

The question arises whether some of the other component variables that contribute to status can be scaled in a similar way. What about income? How does status vary with income? Several experimenters, following Robert L. Hamblin, have conducted studies to determine the effect of income and other variables on status. The methods used include magnitude estimation, ratio estimation, and a cross-modality matching procedure in which the subjects drew a line whose length served to indicate the amount or degree of status conferred by a given income.

All three methods produced fairly good power functions relating status to income, and as a rough average the exponents were similar. They fell in the vicinity of 0.6 or 0.7. In other words, a person's status grows with his income, but it does not double when his income doubles. Rather the consensus expressed by the subjects' responses indicates that an increase of 100 percent in income confers an increase in status of only 50 or 60 percent.

An example showing how status increases with income is presented in Fig. 89. The data represent the pooled results (geometric means) from several subsamples of randomly selected subjects who were interviewed in Boston and its environs. Toward the end of an hour's interview, which was related to other topics, the respondent was given brief instructions about how to make quantitative estimates. The interviewer then asked for some magnitude estimations of the apparent sizes of circles drawn on a card. After performing that task the subject was asked to make magnitude estimations of various status variables, including income.

The line drawn through the data in Fig. 89 has a slope equal to 0.73. Since the coordinates are logarithmic, the slope is equivalent to the exponent of the power function relating status to income. In linear coordinates, the data would appear as a curve concave downward. Actually, it

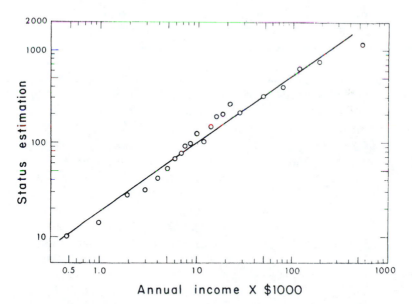

Annual income X $1000

Fig. 89. Subjects attributed higher social status to people with higher incomes. Respondents chosen at random in an opinion survey were asked to judge the general standing of people whose annual income was stated by the interviewer. The magnitude estimations of status are described fairly well by the straight line whose slope defines a power function with the exponent 0.73. Each respondent judged a subset of the income levels. Each point represents the geometric mean of the judgments of approximately 45 respondents. (Data from Rainwater 1971.)

may turn out that two power functions are involved, one for incomes below the median and another for incomes above the median. In any case, the form of the function must be decided by future research.

We are reminded that a power function relation is exhibited by other aspects of money, in particular its perceived subjective value, or "utility," as the economists call it. The value of money, when viewed as a potential acquisition, is judged by the typical subject to grow approximately in proportion to a power function with an exponent of about 0.5. In other words, the marginal utility—the subjective value added by one more dollar—grows less and less as the amount increases. A similar decreasing marginal utility appears to be reflected in judgments concerning the contribution of income to status.

The same respondents who gave estimates of status as it depends on income also estimated the status they would ascribe to a person whose educational level was specified by the interviewer. Eighteen different amounts of schooling were specified, ranging from second grade to Ph.D. degree. The status estimates are plotted in linear coordinates in Fig. 90. It appears that advanced degrees confer large increments in status on the recipient.

When the data were plotted in log-log coordinates, the curve rose quite steeply, so that the best fitting power function had the exponent 2.6. But a straight line did not fit the data very well. Other studies have also suggested that social status may not be a power function of educational level when the level is expressed as years of schooling. Instead of a power function, the relation may be closer to an exponential function. The difference is this: the power function has a constant exponent; the exponential function has a variable exponent. In actual fact, however, the data in Fig. 90 curve upward even more sharply than an exponential function. Another possibility was explored by Hamblin (1971). To the years of education he added a constant representing the preschool span. The additive constant made his data fit a power function quite closely.

Whatever may prove to be the best mathematical description, it may be relevant to ask whether duration of schooling is more than a superficial indicant of some more basic variable, or set of variables. For example, the intelligence of the person may be an important determinant of his status, and educational level may provide an approximate but nonlinear measure of intelligence. Interesting problems remain to be sorted out in that area.

Jones and Shorter (1972) made the point that simple power functions are not especially likely when respondents make quantitative judgments of complex matters like social status—judgments that depend on past experience with social determinants. Since the subject's response "is learned," they said, "there is no a priori reason for expecting the relationship to follow Stevens' power law." That is indeed correct; the kind of rela-

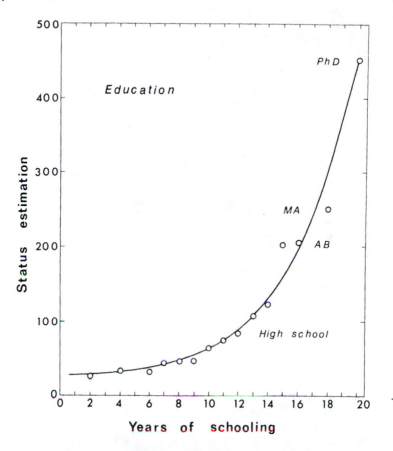

Fig. 90. Social status grows more and more rapidly as educational level increases. Respondents were asked to judge the general standing of persons whose education was described by the interviewer. Note that the status conferred by college graduation was judged to be slightly more than twice that conferred by high school graduation. The Ph.D. counted more than twice as much as the A.B. (Data from Rainwater 1971.)

tionship involved is an empirical question, not to be decided a priori. The remarkable thing though is that quantitative judgments of such matters as social status are possible, and that different investigators obtain rather similar functions.

PERCEPTIONS OF NATIONAL POWER

Another interesting study in social scaling was carried out by Shinn (1969). He quantified the opinions of 25 subjects regarding the power status of various fictional nations. Each nation was described in terms of three attributes: population, per capita gross national product (GNP), and percentage of GNP devoted to its military establishment. The subjects, all of whom were students in advanced courses in international politics, were given various combinations of the three national attributes and asked to make a magnitude estimation of each nation's power.

The results showed that all three attributes contributed to apparent national power, but the growth of national power followed a somewhat different path for increasing amounts of each of the three attributes. It was found that the data could be described very closely by three power functions, a different one for each attribute.

The next question we must ask is how the three national attributes combine to create the total perceived power of the nation. Two possible answers were examined. One model assumed that the three attributes combined by simple addition. The other model assumed that the attributes combined by multiplication. The multiplicative model proved far superior. The perceptions of the 25 subjects could be described by an equation multiplying three terms, thus

$$\text{National power} = k(\text{Pop})^{0.4} \times (\text{GNP})^{0.6} \times (\text{Mil})^{0.3}$$

where k is a constant that depends on the units employed.

Whether that formula controls power relations among nations in the real world may be open to question, of course. Nevertheless, the results of the experiment make rather good intuitive sense. The exponent for GNP is the largest, the exponent for population is about two-thirds as large, and the exponent for military development is only about half as large. In other words, perceived national power grows most rapidly when overall productivity increases.

NATIONAL CONFLICT AND COOPERATION

Throughout history nations have plunged from time to time into conflict, and there has been no supernational police force capable of ensuring international tranquillity. Inevitably, therefore, nations expend great effort in trying to assess the friendliness or hostility of other nations. There have been few attempts to apply quantitative methods to the assessment problem, but the beginning of a quantitative endeavor aimed at the ratio scaling of national behavior was carried out quite successfully at Harvard in a study by Corson (1970).

The first task was to assemble a large list of statements defining different kinds of national actions, both cooperative actions and actions indicative of conflict. The lists of actions used in the experiments contained 54 that could be classed as conflictive and 38 as cooperative. A brief statement of each action was typed on a separate card, and the set of cards was presented to academic, governmental, and military experts in international affairs. The respondents were asked to arrange the 54 cards describing conflictive actions in a rank order from least to most serious or offensive. They also rank-ordered the 38 cooperative actions. Thus the first phase of the project provided two ordinal scales, one for conflict, the other for cooperation.

For the next phase of the project, 14 actions, covering the full range of the ordinal scales, were selected from each of the two rank orders. Both sets of 14 actions were typed with each action on a separate sheet and assembled in irregular orders in booklets. Each respondent was then asked to proceed page by page through a booklet and to assign a number to each action to indicate its intensity as he perceived it. The geometric mean of the magnitude estimations was then computed for each action. In that way, two ratio scales of intensity or degree were obtained, one for conflict and one for cooperation.

The two sets of actions and their intensity scale values, as determined by magnitude estimation, are shown in Tables 11 and 12. The intensity values are the geometric means of the estimates of 16 respondents.

The specific instructions to the respondents contained the following statement.

> This booklet presents, in irregular order, a series of *conflict actions*—that is, unfriendly or hostile actions that one nation (nation A) might direct at another nation (nation X).
>
> You are asked to indicate how intense the actions seem by assigning numbers to them. To the first action in the booklet, assign any number that seems appropriate. Then assign successive numbers to the remaining actions in such a way that the numbers reflect your subjective impression of the intensity of conflict that the actions represent. For example, if the second action seems 20 times as intense as the first, assign it a number 20 times as large as that assigned the first. If it seems one-fifth as intense, assign it a number one-fifth as large, and so forth. Use fractions, whole numbers, or decimals, but make each number assigned proportional to the conflict intensity as you perceive it. Please do not assign zero or negative numbers. Write the number in the space marked "conflict intensity" on each page.

For the statements involving cooperation, the instructions were the same, except for appropriate changes in wording.

Table 11. International Conflict. Nation A acts in a hostile manner toward nation X. The nature of the action and its judged intensity are presented. (After Corson 1970.)

Brief title	Statement describing action by nation A	Intensity
Protest arrest for espionage	Nation A protests to nation X concerning X's arrest of a citizen of A for alleged espionage.	2.1
Reject protest of arrest for espionage	Nation A rejects a protest from nation X concerning A's arrest of a citizen of X for alleged espionage.	3.3
Break cultural exchange agreement	Nation A breaks an agreement with nation X providing for the exchange of technical delegations, exhibitions, and performing artists.	3.4
Reduce trade	Nation A reduces its trade with nation X by 10 percent.	4.2
Increase military budget	Nation A increases its military budget by 10 percent following similar action by nation X.	11
Join military alliance	Nation A joins a military alliance for mutual defense against nation X. Nation A's territory does not border on X, but touches a third nation that borders on X.	14
Offensive weapon development	Nation A announces development of an offensive weapon capable of reaching nation X.	18
Military maneuver	In the context of a developing conflict with nation X, nation A holds large-scale troop maneuvers.	51
Military mobilization	In the context of a rapidly developing crisis with nation X, nation A mobilizes a large number of military reserve forces.	75
Troop movement	In the context of a rapidly developing crisis with nation X, nation A moves a large number of troops closer to troops of X.	78
Specific threat of attack	Nation A threatens to attack nation X if X does not meet A's demands. Nation A sets no time limit for X's compliance.	127
Military clash	Troops of nation A and nation X engage in limited fighting. Action lasts less than 24 hours, and involves only troops stationed in a limited geographic area.	225
Ultimatum: attack	Nation A threatens to attack nation X if X does not meet A's demands within 24 hours.	235
War	Nation A attacks nation X. Attack lasts more than 24 hours, and actively involves 0.1 percent of A's population. Nuclear weapons are not used.	514

Table 12. International Cooperation. Nation A acts in a friendly or cooperative manner toward nation X. The nature of the cooperative action and its judged intensity are presented. (After Corson 1970.)

Brief title	Statement describing action by nation A	Intensity
Declare possibility of ending attack	Nation A makes verbal reference to the possibility of ending its attacks against nation X.	1.0
End attack: unilateral	Without prior negotiations or agreement with nation X, nation A ends its attacks against X.	2.4
Negotiation on prisoner exchange	Two nations negotiate on the exchange of prisoners.	4.6
Prisoner exchange	Two nations carry out an agreement to exchange prisoners.	5.6
End trade ban	Nation A ends its action prohibiting trade with nation X.	10
Exchange ambassadors	Two nations carry out an agreement to exchange ambassadors.	14
Negotiations on trade	Two nations negotiate on increasing trade with each other.	19
Increase trade	Two nations carry out an agreement to increase trade with each other by 10 percent.	27
Negotiations on arms control	Two nations hold formal arms-control negotiations on the limitation of weapon levels.	42
Arms control	Two nations carry out an arms-control agreement limiting weapon levels.	64
Military alliance	Two nations establish a military alliance for their mutual defense in case of attack or threat of attack.	95
Economic community	Two nations establish an economic common market in which they share control.	208
Joint military command	Two nations establish a joint military command in which they share control.	290
Political federation	Two nations form a political federation by establishing joint sovereignty.	580

It may be noted that the instructions parallel closely those often used in sensory psychophysics. In recommending that those simple instructions be tried for the scaling of national behavior, I could not, of course, be sure that they would prove effective with stimuli consisting of verbal statements. The results, however, seem to settle the question. No standard was designated to provide the respondent with a modulus. Instead the respondent was left free to assign a number to each statement, including the first statement, with no constraints imposed by the experimenter. In this and other experiments, free number matching with no designated standard has proved to be a simple and effective way to elicit an unconstrained quantitative judgment from a subject. Subjects appear to like the procedure. In my own experience, the difficulty is less with subjects than with experimenters. Some experimenters find it hard to believe that such a simple procedure can produce the desired results.

Let me digress briefly to discuss that problem. There seem to arise two blocks that dissuade experimenters from seizing the positive advantages that can be gained by allowing the subject to choose his own modulus. One lies in the experimenter's natural and commendable desire to be helpful. Help in the form of an assigned standard or modulus turns out, however, to constrain the subject and to interfere with his freedom to assign numbers. If the experimenter cannot resist his urge to be helpful, he should divide the subjects into subgroups and designate a different standard for each subgroup. That would tend to distribute the distorting effects of such factors as the round-number tendency and allow the distortions more nearly to cancel one another. The other block seems to arise from a misconception about averaging. To be sure, if the arithmetic mean is to be computed, all subjects should be made to use the same unit or modulus. But the geometric mean obviates that necessity. The form of the function determined by the geometric means is not altered when each subject's judgments are based on a different subjective unit.

What can the political scientist do with ratio scales like those in Tables 11 and 12? He may want first, of course, to assure himself through replications of the study that the consensus expressed by the magnitude scales is adequately representative. With the consensus established, he can then begin to keep quantitative score on the behavior of actual nations. It becomes possible, for example, to measure the build-up and subsidence of international crises in quantitative form, rather than at the level of verbal description. Indeed many hypotheses regarding the interactions of nations may be formulated in the more testable form of quantitative measurement.

SERIOUSNESS OF OFFENSES

In another study carried out in Stockholm brief descriptions of 17 actions, each more-or-less immoral, were used for a study of moral judgment, as it was called (Ekman 1962). The actions ranged from hit-and-run by a drunken driver to stopping in a no-parking zone to mail a letter. Eighty subjects made judgments concerning the seriousness of the actions. They judged the actions, pair by pair, first saying which action in each pair was the more serious, and then estimating the seriousness of the less offensive action as a percentage of the more offensive one. The poikilitic measure, based on the disagreements among the paired comparisons, was found to be a logarithmic function of the scale based on the direct ratio estimations, which were made in terms of percentage. The logarithmic relation accords precisely with what we expect when poikilitic scaling and ratio scaling are both used on the same prothetic continuum.

A decade after Ekman pioneered in the scaling of immoral actions, Raffel (1972) undertook, as part of an undergraduate thesis study, a cross-modality matching of loudness and brightness to the degree of morality or immorality implied by 13 different actions. Brief descriptions of the actions were printed on cards and presented in irregular order. The actions ranged from "helping an old lady across the street" to "dealing in heroin." In order to match auditory and visual stimuli to such a wide range on the scale of morality, special apparatus was needed. The intensity of the light from a 300-watt projector lamp was controlled by two circular light attenuators (neutral filters) rotating in opposite directions, giving a total adjustable range of about 80 decibels. The auditory stimulus, a broad band of noise, was controlled by a standard 100-decibel attenuator. Sixteen subjects made the cross-modality matches, half adjusting the light first, half adjusting the sound first. The average decibel settings are plotted in Fig. 91, where each point represents a different immoral action.

Two features command our interest. One is the remarkably high correlation between the judgments of immorality expressed by brightness matches and those expressed by loudness matches. The points lie close to a common straight line. The other feature concerns the slope of the line, which is about 0.9. Since loudness and brightness both have exponents equal to approximately one-third, provided both kinds of stimuli are measured in terms of energy flow, the expected value of the slope in Fig. 91 is 1.0. The obtained value is about 10 percent off, which can be considered reasonably good. Within that difference of about 10 percent, then, the two scales expressing degree of immorality, the one scale obtained by loudness matching, the other by brightness matching, tell the same quantitative story. Translating from decibels into subjective values we find, for example, that selling heroin was judged about 20 times as immoral as selling marijuana, and about 100 times as immoral as going to jail rather than submit to military service.

The two foregoing studies, like most studies carried out in university laboratories, were methodological in intent: the object of interest was method and procedure, not the achievement of a useful, substantive outcome. An investigation of another sort, in which method was the means

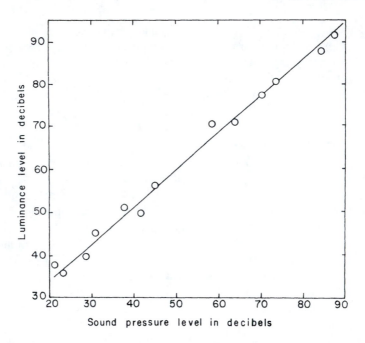

Fig. 91. Cross-modality matching of both brightness and loudness to the degree of immorality involved in various actions. Each point represents a different immoral action. Half of the 16 subjects matched first loudness and then brightness to degree of immorality, and the other half made the matches in the other order. The line has a slope of about 0.9, which confirms the approximate equality of the exponents for brightness and loudness when the stimuli are measured in terms of energy flow. (Data from Raffel 1972.)

rather than the end, was carried out by Sellin and Wolfgang (1964). The chief aim of the study, reported in their 423-page book, was the improvement of the methods used to compile police and court statistics for the purpose of measuring the burden that society bears because of crime and delinquency. The research design placed major emphasis on delinquency events, not on delinquent persons, for the purpose was to measure the amount and type of harm that the community suffers because of antisocial acts.

The general strategy of the three-year study was as follows. First, a representative set of delinquency events was selected by random sampling from the universe of all such events that took place in Philadelphia, Pennsylvania, in the year 1960. Scaling procedures were then applied to a set of events chosen from the larger sample in order to convert the seriousness of the events into numerical scores. A final combination of all the information produced a delinquency index—a numerical device that may be used to gauge the total incidence of delinquency and the effectiveness of whatever preventive measures may be brought to bear on the problem of antisocial behavior.

It is the second stage of the study that most concerns us here, the quantification of the gravity of delinquent acts—a quantification that must rest ultimately on the judgment of the members of society. In brief outline, the study proceeded as follows: a list of 141 offenses was first compiled, and a briefly phrased statement was made of each offense. Those statements, typed on cards, were submitted to 17 raters, mostly college students, who rated the seriousness of each offense on a 7-point category scale. Three representative offenses were then selected from each of the seven categories for use in further testing. The 21 offenses, presented in randomized orders, were judged by 569 people—comprising 38 juvenile court judges, 286 police officers, and 245 students from two universities. About half of each class of raters made magnitude estimations of the seriousness of the offenses; the other half rated the offenses on an 11-point category scale.

The next question of interest concerns the relation between the two kinds of judgments, category (partition) and magnitude. Figure 92 shows a direct comparison between the results obtained from the 38 juvenile court judges, 20 of whom used the 11-point category scale and 18 of whom made direct magnitude estimations. The two types of judgments behave in the way that is characteristic of prothetic continua. When the partition (category) scale of degree of delinquency is plotted against the magnitude scale, the curve is concave downward (Fig. 92a). When the same category ratings are plotted against the logarithm of the magnitude scale, the resulting curve is concave upward (Fig. 92b).

An important feature of Fig. 92 is the demonstration that the partition scale is not a logarithmic function of the magnitude scale. If it were logarithmic, the line in Fig. 92b would be straight. The curved line accords with the principle noted earlier, namely, that the partition (category) scale can be described by a power function with a virtual exponent having a value smaller than the value of the actual exponent but significantly greater than zero. It is interesting that those basic facts and relations of psychophysics show themselves in people's judgments when they quantify degrees of delinquency.

Finally, a poikilitic scale was created by processing the variability or confusion among the category assignments. When that procedure was used, the resulting scale became logarithmic, like a Fechnerian scale. A plot of the poikilitic category scale against the logarithm of the magnitude estimations then produced a line that is approximately straight (Fig. 92c). The several features and relations exhibited in the three parts of Fig. 92 occur

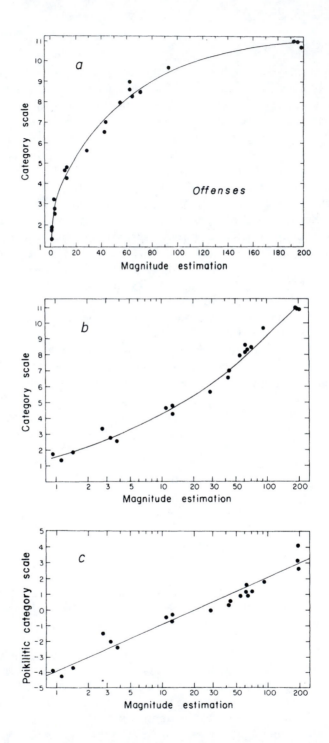

throughout all of psychophysics, regardless of what type of stimulus a person is asked to judge, provided only that the perceptual continuum is prothetic.

For different subgroups of those who judged delinquency, the age of the offender was specified as 13, 17, or 27 years, or it was left unspecified. Ten different plots like the plot in Fig. 92c were made from the judgments of the ten subgroups of raters. The impressive feature of the ten plots was their invariant form. They all looked much alike. And quite surprisingly, no significant difference attached to the age specified for the offender. It was the offense itself that seemed to determine the judgment of seriousness. Apparently a given depredation is judged serious to a specific degree, regardless of whether the perpetrator is juvenile or adult.

Equally important, there was also impressive agreement among the different classes of raters. Juvenile court judges produced scales that were closely comparable to those produced by police officers and college students. It may seem surprising that all three classes of raters agreed, for example, that stealing and abandoning an automobile is only about one-tenth as serious as robbing a man of five dollars and wounding him in the process. Also, according to the consensus, robbing and wounding becomes about two-and-a half times more serious if the victim dies. Out of the magnitude estimations, the authors say, "a pervasive social agreement about what is serious and what is not appears to emerge, and this agreement transcends simple qualitative concordance; it extends to the estimated degree of seriousness of those offenses."

The next major step in the study was an item analysis designed to refine the statements used to define the offenses. It is not always easy to describe a delinquent act briefly and unambiguously and in such a way that a rater feels no uncertainty about what is meant. Statements that had proved unsatisfactory were revised or eliminated, and the revised statements were then used in a retest with a new population, a group of 195 students from still another university. That final testing gave results that correlated highly with the earlier data and thereby provided added justification for the construction of an index of delinquency on a representative ratio scale of seriousness.

Fig. 92. (*a*) Relation between the means of the category judgments and the geometric means of the magnitude judgments for seriousness of offenses, as rated by juvenile court judges. The coordinates are linear. Like all partition scales on prothetic continua, the category scale is concave downward when plotted against the magnitude scale. (*b*) Plotted against the logarithm of the magnitude scale, the category scale is concave upward. (*c*) The poikilitic measure derived from the confusions among the categories is linear in semilogarithmic coordinates. (From Stevens 1968b, based on data from Sellin and Wolfgang 1964, *Science*, 151, 530–541. Copyright 1968 by the American Association for the Advancement of Science. Reprinted by permission.)

An advantageous feature of the final index resides in its provision for the additivity of offenses. That crucial feature finds its justification in the outcome of the magnitude estimations of seriousness. For example, the stealing of five dollars or less was arbitrarily assigned a unit value of 1. Trespassing in a locked building was found to have a similar value. Trespassing *and* stealing five dollars was given the value 2, because the magnitude estimation score for the seriousness of the combined act was approximately double the score for each act separately. As another example, forcible rape has the value 11, a value made up of 8 for the forced sex act, 2 for the intimidation of the victim, and 1 for the inflicting of minor injury.

The extraction of the additive components of the complex delinquent acts was achieved, of course, through the process of analyzing the results of the magnitude estimations. It is doubtful that any of the raters were conscious of the underlying additivity in any explicit way, and some of them would probably be offended by the thought that one forcible rape can be equated to some number of money thefts. Nevertheless, both the quantitative estimates of large numbers of raters and the gradations in the punishments prescribed by the law make a strong argument for equatability and additivity among offenses.

THEFTS OF MONEY

Among the offenses rated by magnitude estimations there were a few that dealt with the stealing of money. Statements naming stolen amounts of 5, 20, 50, 1000, and 5000 dollars had been scattered at random among the other statements describing offenses. Figure 93 shows how the judged magnitude of the seriousness of the thefts increased as a power function of the amount of money stolen. The value of the exponent, 0.17, suggests that, in order for one crime to be considered twice as serious as another, the amount stolen must be about 60 times as large. Although it is worse to steal two dollars than one dollar, it does not appear to be twice as bad.

The exponent in Fig. 93 is lower than the exponent 0.5 conjectured in 1728 by Gabriel Cramer for the subjective value of money, the so-called utility. The difference in those two values is not surprising. For one thing, there is probably a considerable degree of regression taking place to lower the exponent in the crime study. For another thing, the money amounts in the crime study were embedded in a context that required the raters to assess factors other than the subjective value of money as such.

It should be mentioned that in subsequent replications of the crime study the seriousness of money thefts continued to grow as a power function of the amount stolen, with exponents in the vicinity of 0.2. In an extensive Ca-

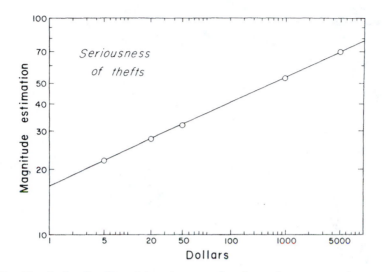

Fig. 93. Magnitude estimations of the seriousness of stealing various amounts of money. The values on the ordinate are the geometric means of estimates made by 105 university students. The line defines a power function with the exponent 0.17. (From Stevens 1968b, based on data from Sellin and Wolfgang 1964, *Science*, 151, 530–541. Copyright 1968 by the American Association for the Advancement of Science. Reprinted by permission.)

nadian study involving more than 2000 students from both French and English universities, the exponent for money thefts was 0.25 (Akman and Normandeau 1967). In all major respects the Canadian study confirmed the general findings of the Philadelphia study. It is of interest to note that cultural differences among the Canadian raters—some French, some English—made no difference in the judged seriousness of delinquent acts.

PUNISHMENT

How well does society's accumulated wisdom, or lack thereof, in legislating punishment accord with the judged gravity of offenses? In particular, what does the Pennsylvania Penal Code say about penalties for the 21 offenses scaled in the main study? The answer is both interesting and encouraging. The product-moment correlation between seriousness of offense as judged by university students and maximum penalty stated in terms of time in prison was 0.88. (A death sentence was interpreted as a prison term equal to the life expectancy of the median perpetrator of homicide.) The correlation was even higher, 0.94, for the judgments by police officers. Both sets of results are shown in logarithmic coordinates in Fig. 94. As Sellin

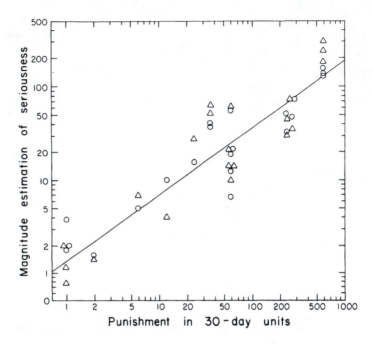

Fig. 94. Relation between the geometric means of the judged seriousness of 21 offenses and the maximum penalty prescribed by the Pennsylvania Penal Code. The raters were police officers (circles) and university students (triangles). The line shows the approximate trend of the data. (From Stevens 1968b, based on data from Sellin and Wolfgang 1964, *Science,* 151, 530–541. Copyright 1968 by the American Association for the Advancement of Science. Reprinted by permission.)

and Wolfgang expressed it, "These correlations are surprisingly high considering . . . that the Penal Code provides no variation in the maximum penalty for amounts of money stolen and relatively few intervals between thirty days' imprisonment and death." Note also that the punishment scale is truncated at its lower end, because the smallest stated value for a maximum penalty is 30 days in jail.

The high correlation between the magnitude estimation of seriousness and the maximum penalties prescribed by law can be viewed as a measure of the agreement between two groups of people—the raters in the present study and the legislators who, some time in the past, set forth a schedule of penalties. Both groups made quantitative estimates. One group made numerical magnitude estimates, the other group named what they judged to be an appropriate number of days in jail. That the decisions of the two groups exhibit a remarkable agreement demonstrates that a quantitative consensus can be achieved by human judgment, even when the judges perform in rather different roles.

The study of delinquency has been able to attack an urgent social problem with methods that were developed in psychophysics for the study of human sensory systems. The methods borrowed seem to have produced useful results. It is a large task to develop and refine by repeated revisions a scale with useful properties in an area as complex as delinquent behavior. The one-shot experiment, so typical of the academic investigator, does not suffice when the goal is to provide a scientific basis for serious social action. In the 3-year study of delinquency, the extension of the ratio-scaling methods to social variables proved successful, perhaps because the caliber of the problem justified the investment needed to track down and eliminate needless sources of variability and error. Scientists often do their best work when they face a problem worth solving.

A LOCAL REPLICATION AND A RESIDUAL PROBLEM

Like a skeptical scientist, I initially entertained reservations about the scaling of delinquent acts. The remedy for such doubts was to replicate the scaling here at Harvard University. During the summer of 1966 an opportunity arose to administer the scaling exercise to a group of 53 students. The 14 delinquent acts listed in Table 13 were arranged in booklets, one action to a page, and the sequence of the acts was randomized. The subject wrote a number on each page expressing his opinion of the seriousness of the act. The geometric means of the magnitude estimations are shown in Table 13.

The same 14 offenses had been judged by 2616 students in 13 Canadian universities and I wanted to see how well the relatively small local group agreed with the extensive Canadian assessments. In order to test the agreement I plotted the Harvard scores against the Canadian scores in log-log coordinates, as shown in Fig. 95. The correlation is obviously very high, and the few inversions that occurred in the rank order of judgments of seriousness involve only small numerical differences. All in all, it appears that the social consensus regarding the quantitative seriousness of offenses extends at least across national and cultural frontiers.

Despite the quantitative agreement exhibited in the foregoing studies, an important question remains open. To what extent did the regression effect compress the range of the responses when the subjects assigned numbers to the various offenses? In order to compensate for the regression effect, how much should the seriousness scales be stretched out? That problem was not faced when the original studies were carried out, because no obvious experimental solution had as yet been discovered. Now, however, we know how to remove a major component of the regression effect. That component is the order bias, an effect that can be measured directly by means of an appropriate experimental design. The procedure is outlined in Chapter 9.

If correction were made for the order bias, there would result a sizable increase in the ratio between the numbers assigned to the least and the

Table 13. Delinquent acts and magnitude estimation scores for 53 Harvard students.

Description of delinquent action	Geo-metric mean
1. Without breaking into or entering a building and with no one else present, an offender takes property worth $5.	7.0
2. An offender breaks into a building and without anyone else present, takes property worth $5.	9.0
3. Without breaking into or entering a building and with no one else present, an offender takes property worth $20.	9.6
4. Without breaking into or entering a building and with no one else present, an offender takes property worth $50.	10.7
5. An offender takes an automobile which is recovered undamaged.	11.9
6. An offender knocks a victim down. The victim does not require any medical treatment.	17.5
7. An offender without a weapon threatens to harm a victim unless the victim gives him money. The offender takes the victim's money ($5) and leaves without harming the victim.	19.5
8. Without breaking into or entering a building and with no one else present, an offender takes property worth $1000.	20.8
9. An offender with a weapon threatens to harm a victim unless the victim gives him money. The offender takes the victim's money ($5) and leaves without harming the victim.	26.6
10. Without breaking into or entering a building and with no one else present, an offender takes property worth $5000.	31.7
11. An offender inflicts injury on a victim. The victim is treated by a physician but his injuries do not require him to be hospitalized.	38.6
12. An offender inflicts injury on a victim. The victim is treated by a physician and his injuries require him to be hospitalized.	56.4
13. An offender forces a female to submit to sexual intercourse. No other physical injury is inflicted.	72.2
14. An offender inflicts injury on a victim. The victim dies from the injury.	164.2

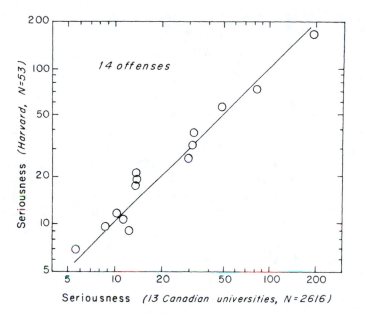

Fig. 95. Magnitude estimations were made of the seriousness of 14 offenses by 53 Harvard students and by 2616 Canadian students from 13 universities. Each point represents one of the offenses listed in Table 13. The straight line with the slope 1.0 would represent perfect agreement between Canadian and Harvard students.

most serious offenses listed in Table 13. Exactly how much the magnitude estimation scale would be stretched remains for a definitive experiment to decide.

WORD FREQUENCY

Professor B. J. Underwood wrote to me in 1964 expressing pleasure and surprise at the outcome of a simple experiment. He presented a list of short three-letter words to 78 students and asked them to judge the relative frequency with which each word occurs in print. The instructions included the statement:

> Your task is to assign a number to each word, such that the number you assign represents your judgment of the frequency of that word relative to the other words.

Underwood then plotted the judged frequency against the "objective" frequency as measured by a large-sample word count (Thorndike-Lorge).

In a log-log plot the subjective estimates of relative frequency described a remarkably straight line—a power function with the exponent 0.35 (Underwood 1966).

Shortly thereafter, in the Harvard School of Education, a thesis (Shapiro 1967) was designed to explore the subjective scaling of word frequency in relation to "the Fechnerian and the Stevens psychophysical theories." Another goal was to test the performance of various subject populations, ranging from sixth-grade children to a group of industrial chemists. A total of 184 subjects participated. Instructions to judge in terms of spoken as opposed to written language made no significant differences in the responses.

Two kinds of scaling were tried: magnitude estimation and a special variety of a Thurstonian pair-comparison scale. For all groups tested, the results of magnitude estimation followed a power function of the objective frequency derived from word counts. The Thurstonian procedure gave results that followed a logarithmic function, as such procedures usually do.

Shapiro resisted the common impulse of the experimenter to assign a standard. The instructions for magnitude estimation read in part as follows:

> In this form you are presented with a series of words. Your job is to tell with numbers how frequently these words occur in written English. Give one of the words any number that seems appropriate to you. Then give numbers to the other words so that these numbers give your own impression of the relative frequency of these words in written English.

The pooled results for 120 adults on one of the two 60-word lists used could be described by a power function having the exponent 0.60. For the other list of 60 words (including 31 from the first list) the exponent was 0.66. Among the adult subgroups, the industrial chemists gave the largest exponent and the college sophomores the lowest.

Sixty of the words used by Shapiro were later studied by Carroll (1971). Using essentially the same instructions and procedure, Carroll obtained magnitude estimations from 15 experienced lexicographers who were members of the staff of a dictionary publisher. The exponents for the individual lexicographers ranged from 0.36 to 1.95. The median exponent was 0.87. As shown in Fig. 96, the line of best fit to the pooled data represented the exponent 0.83. If we allow for the inevitable regression effect, which tends to make the exponent fall below its true value, it appears that the expert lexicographers were giving estimates that fell fairly close to the objective frequency values. Agreement with the objective frequencies would call for an exponent of 1.0.

Carroll raised the interesting question whether the subjective estimates of lexicographers constitute a more valid measure of relative word frequency

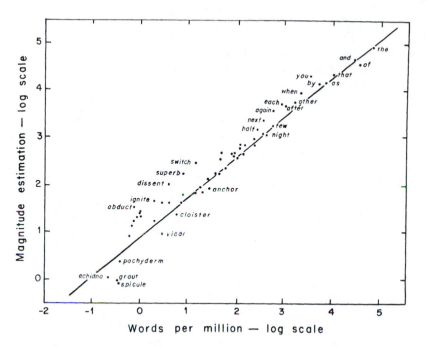

Fig. 96. Magnitude estimations of relative word frequency made by 15 persons expert in lexicography. A few of the 60 words are identified, including some of those that departed farthest from the straight line. The line represents a power function with the exponent 0.83. The product-moment correlation between the geometric means of the magnitude estimations and the objective frequency count is 0.97. (Data from Carroll 1971.)

than objective counts made on large but arbitrary samplings from arbitrarily selected sources. Objective frequency counts are especially subject to bias for words that occur only rarely. "Thus," said Carroll, "the argument that subjective estimates are more valid than objective data tends to be stronger in the case of low-frequency words."

In Fig. 96, as well as in Shapiro's study, the scatter of the points is greatest for the relatively rare words. We are led to ask which measure contributes most of that validity and noise, the subjective estimates or the sampling involved in word counts? Consider some examples from Fig. 96. According to the word count, *cloister* is more frequent than *dissent*. The expert lexicographers said that *dissent* is more than four times as frequent (0.64 log unit). The word count made *vicar* more frequent than *ignite*, whereas the experts judged *ignite* to be more than five times as frequent (0.73 log unit). Which estimates are the more nearly correct? We are left here with an interesting question. Is the consensus of the magnitude estimations the best estimate of relative word frequency? For some purposes magnitude estimations by highly literate subjects may well be superior to samples of objective word counts.

Whatever the usefulness of estimated frequency may turn out to be, from the foregoing studies we now possess replicated evidence that the method of magnitude estimation produces consistent power functions when applied to the relative frequencies with which people experience words. It is also noteworthy that some of the experiments employed enormous ranges of stimuli (rarity of words), which elicited enormous ranges in the subjects' estimates of relative frequency. The responses (ordinate) in Fig. 96 covered a range of about 100,000 to 1.

THE INVARIANCES

What are the invariances in the manifold experiments involving human judgment? A convergence of evidence from fields as disparate as sensory psychophysics and criminology has pointed to stable and constant relations. One such relation states that subjective magnitude is a power function of stimulus magnitude. The underlying invariance then becomes the simple principle that equal stimulus ratios produce equal subjective ratios.

The state of psychophysics was reviewed in 1965 by Ekman and Sjöberg who summed it up as follows, "After a hundred years of almost general acceptance and practically no experimentation, Fechner's logarithmic law was replaced by the power law. The amount of experimental work performed in the 1950's on this problem by Stevens and other research workers was enormous. . . . The power law was verified again and again, in literally hundreds of experiments. As an experimental fact, the power law is established beyond any reasonable doubt, possibly more firmly established than anything else in psychology."

On many of the continua investigated, the stimuli can be measured only on a nominal scale, for the stimuli are verbal statements, occupations, crimes, and other nonmetric items. On those continua the power law cannot be confirmed directly, but there emerges another notable invariance.

For both kinds of continua—those based on metric stimuli and those based on nonmetric stimuli—we find a constant relation between the scale erected by direct judgment and the poikilitic scale derived from a unitizing of variability or confusion. Whether the stimuli themselves are measurable on ratio scales or only on nominal scales, the judgmental scale based on units of variability is approximately proportional to the logarithm of the scale constructed by one or another of the direct scaling methods, such as magnitude estimation. The extensive invariance of that logarithmic relation attests to a principle known throughout all of science—namely, that error or variability tends to be *relative*: the size of the error grows with the magnitude of the thing measured. The principle finds expression under many phrasings: the standard deviation increases in proportion to the mean; the coefficient of variation (percent variability) remains constant; accuracies are statable as one part in so many. The emergence of a similar rule in the subjective domain—a rule that variability tends to increase in proportion to the apparent magnitude—suggests an essential unity among the principles that govern quantitative relations in widely diverse endeavors.

When nonmetric stimuli are scaled by a partition procedure, such as category scaling, the results show the same disagreement with magnitude estimation that has been demonstrated scores of times with metric stimuli. With both kinds of stimuli the category scale is nonlinear relative to the magnitude scale. Hence category scaling does not recommend itself as a procedure for the quantification of social variables. Category methods have a justification only for determining one or another type of threshold, such as the category boundary between acceptable and unacceptable.

For those who must build their science on a consensus based on one or another expression of human judgment, the way stands open for an effective ratio-scale quantification, provided the experimental subjects are given unconstrained freedom to match numbers, loudness, length of line, or some other variable, directly to the items of interest. By means of such direct matching operations the foundations of social psychophysics have been set in place.

CHAPTER 9

Hazards and Remedies

When we try to discover the quantitative rules that govern the human perceptual systems, we find ourselves faced with many-faceted problems of practical measurement. If the task of quantification in psychophysics impresses us as overly complicated, perhaps it is because we have not sampled the frustrations of scientists in other fields. Whenever a scientist refuses to settle for rough approximations and pushes instead toward exactitude, he is apt to find himself thwarted by those twin goblins, systematic errors and random errors. No scientist ever entirely escapes their jinx—provided he strives for the ultimate in accuracy.

Scientists must learn to put up with whatever accuracy the state of the art provides. When psychophysical power functions agree within about 5 or 10 percent we are apt to find ourselves reasonably satisfied. And we look with envy at those who can measure with vastly greater certainty, as when the physicist measures distance to a minute fraction of 1 percent. But accuracy is a relative matter. Distance measurement has its own limitations, and the uncertainties of measured distances become a frustration to the geologist when he tries to measure the exact velocity of the drifting continents.

What strikes the scientist as a reasonable degree of accuracy varies widely from field to field, and even from problem to problem. Approximations become the rule at the forward edge of any advancing science, and the accepted notion of what degree of accuracy will qualify as reasonable may alter as the art of measurement evolves. The history of astronomy provides a fascinating procession of changing views on what constitutes reasonable agreement between theory and measurement. Slight discrepancies in the reasonable agreement achieved by Ptolemy's theory became proof for Copernicus that a radically new theory was in order.

During a quarter-century period in psychophysics, different laboratories achieved reasonable agreement in the measurement of loudness ratios. The consensus showed that a change of 2 to 1 in loudness requires an energy change of about 10 decibels (Stevens 1955c). In the 1950's that 10-decibel rule was adopted for acoustical engineering purposes by the International Standards Organization. But some of the more recent cross-modality experiments have seemed to show that 9 decibels rather than 10 may correspond more closely to a 2-to-1 loudness ratio. The exponent $\frac{1}{3}$ corresponds to 9 decibels for doubling. And there is yet another change that may come about because of increases in accuracy. The standard reference frequency, which has long been 1000 hertz, has lately become a candidate for replacement, because the growth of loudness at 1000 hertz departs slightly but detectably from a power function. A narrow band of noise centered at the frequency 3150 hertz has been proposed as a better reference frequency (Stevens 1972a). Changes of that kind provide examples of progress based on the increasing certainty that has been achieved in psychophysical measurements.

Much uncertainty remains, however, as it probably always will. I should like to describe a few of the pitfalls that have afflicted experiments and to discuss some of the potential remedies. No exhaustive catalogue is possible, because error, like its cognate namesake, the errant knight, roams about in ever novel and unpredictable meanders. There is no limit to the number of ways an experiment can go wrong.

AVERAGING

The pooling of observations provides an effective weapon to subdue random error, but it often leaves systematic error unaffected. A scientist needs to be cautious about pooling data. In my own experience with psychophysical functions it has proved helpful to plot the data distributions in order to inspect them before I undertake to describe them by one or another kind of average. In that way I discovered, for example, that the arithmetic mean of magnitude estimations was not a good choice of an average. With the arithmetic mean the outcome was too much determined by the particular observer who happened to use the largest numbers. In order to protect against that source of bias I used the median—a kind of average that is safer than the mean, but somewhat less efficient. A frequently quoted rule is, when in doubt use the median.

After experiments with large groups of subjects had supplied sufficient data, J. C. Stevens (1957) determined in his thesis study that the distribution of the logarithms of the magnitude estimations is approximately normal. The efficient average for a log-normal distribution is the geometric mean. Consequently it has become customary to use geometric averaging with magnitude estimation. Caution is still in order, however, for outlandish values can turn up to distort the picture. The experimenter may then want to resort to the less efficient but less vulnerable median.

When should the arithmetic mean be used? I think the proper answer is practically never. The reason lies in the nearly universal tendency of error to be relative, not absolute. On most physical as well as subjective continua on which there is variation in intensity or amount, the error grows larger when the magnitude grows larger. For example, an error of a millimeter in the measurement of a meter may become an error of a meter in the measurement of a kilometer. The psychophysicist recognizes that principle as Weber's law—the JND grows larger in direct proportion to the stimulus magnitude. A similar rule is approximated throughout much if not most of science. Then why does the physicist not make greater use of the geometric mean, as the relativity of error would dictate proper? I think the reason is a practical one. When errors are very small, the difference between the arithmetic and the geometric mean becomes negligible. In psychophysics, though, the error often distributes itself extensively enough to make the choice of an average an important matter.

When the observer's responses have been artificially restricted, as in category scaling, the arithmetic mean may prove an appropriate average. The geometric mean is not appropriate for a category scale, because a category·scale is not a ratio scale.

An interesting problem arose in an experiment on loudness equisection. The observers adjusted three attenuators in order to divide a larger loudness interval into four smaller equal-appearing intervals. The observers' settings were recorded in terms of decibel values, and the question arose, how should the decibels be averaged? The settings could equally well have been recorded in terms of voltages across the observers' earphones. The decibel mean would differ from the voltage mean. Which, if either, of those arbitrary stimulus measures should the experimenter average? A study of the distributions of the data suggested that the best average was not the arithmetic mean of a stimulus measure; rather it was the mean of the subjective loudness, for which the unit is the sone. When the stimulus values were converted into sones, the skewness of the error distributions decreased and the distributions became more symmetrical (Stevens 1955b). A table relating decibels to sones is given in Appendix C.

An additional problem arises in the equisection experiment when the subjective value that we would like to average is some unknown function of the arbitrary meter readings used to record the data. How can we proceed if the function is unknown? It appears that the best option is to fall back on the powerful method of iteration and proceed step by step to a solution. We first average the meter readings and use the mean results to determine a first approximation to the unknown function governing subjective magnitude. The meter readings are then converted into subjective values on that approximate function, and the resulting subjective values are averaged. The new mean values determine a new function, and the meter readings are then converted into values on the new function. That process can be repeated until no significant change results from a further step in the iteration.

REGRESSION EFFECT

We have seen that cross-modality matching exhibits a stubborn bias called the regression effect. For examples see Figs. 12 and 33. The regression effect also afflicts intramodal matches, as is shown in Fig. 97. There the observer adjusted the loudness of a white noise so that it sounded the same in one as it did in two ears. The slope of the matching function depended on whether the observer adjusted the monaural stimulus or the binaural stimulus. After the student who ran that experiment in 1955 had obtained one of the two matching functions, I suggested that he should interchange the fixed and adjustable stimuli. He objected that the observers had just completed the loudness equation. But a week or so later, when he carried out the complementary experiment, he was surprised to obtain a different regression line. (For more on the problem of binaural versus monaural loudness, see Reynolds and Stevens 1960.)

The regression effect is pervasive in all kinds of matching experiments. Another example is shown in Fig. 98. The inverse continuum, softness instead of loudness, was scaled by magnitude estimation and magnitude production. Scaling the inverse of a continuum produces a negative slope, but the steepness of the negative slope is greater for magnitude production than for magnitude estimation. Here as elsewhere, interchanging the continua controlled by the observer produced a power group transformation of the kind discussed in Chapter 3.

With continua like loudness, which can be put under the control of the observer, it is possible to evaluate the magnitude of the regression effect. It is also possible to combine the data from balanced complementary procedures in order to reduce the bias in the resulting function (Hellman and Zwislocki 1968). If the two slopes (exponents) are combined by averaging, the geometric mean should probably be used, because that is the average that remains invariant under an interchange of the two coordinates (Indow and Stevens 1966). Whether or not to average the two slopes may remain a problem, however, for the question arises whether the error sources in magnitude estimation are exactly balanced by the error sources

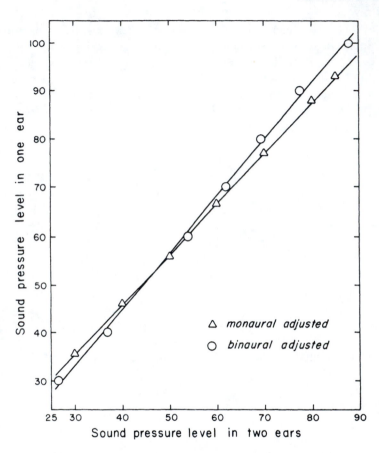

Fig. 97. Monaural-binaural loudness matching. The stimulus was a white noise heard alternately in one ear and in both ears. Seventeen observers adjusted the binaural sound to match the monaural sound. Fifteen observers did the reverse. (From Stevens and Greenbaum 1966, based on data of E. Tulving. Reprinted by permission.)

in magnitude production. Although exact balance may be possible, it seems hardly inevitable. One ought not to count too much on symmetry.

Unless the continuum can be placed under the control of the observer as well as the experimenter, we ordinarily see only one of the regression lines, and we must inquire further, therefore, into the cause of the regression effect and its possible remedies. At least four different factors have been identified as possible contributors to the regression effect. I shall call them noise, comfort, caution, and order.

1. Noise. Some matching exercises are more variable and noisy than others. In the task of matching two tones for loudness, the variability is small when the two tones have the same frequency. When the two tones have different frequencies, the difficulty increases and the variability mounts. Along with the increased noise and variability there emerges an increased regression effect. As a general rule the angle between the two regression lines tends to increase as the noise load grows heavier.

2. *Comfort.* The observer favors the more comfortable stimulus level. For example, when he tries to match one sound to another at a very high level, the errors in his adjustments tend to fall more toward the lower than toward the higher levels. The observer seldom sets the painful stimulus too high.

At the other extreme, when he must strain to perceive a stimulus, he does not tend to set the matching stimulus too low. The asymmetry caused by a preference for the more comfortable level was shown especially clearly in an experiment in which observers doubled and halved the apparent loudness of an uncomfortable stimulus at 120 decibels and also a faint stimulus at 30

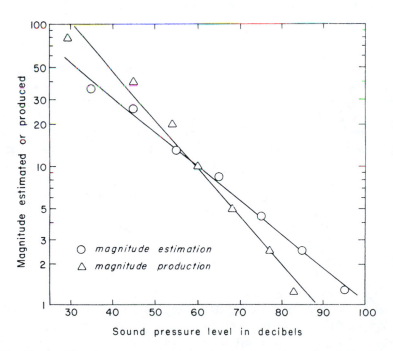

Fig. 98. Matching functions between number and an inverse attribute, the softness of a tone of 1000 hertz. Each point is a geometric mean of 20 judgments, two by each of 10 observers. (From Stevens and Greenbaum 1966, based on data of Stevens and Guirao 1962. Reprinted by permission.)

decibels (Stevens 1957a). Of course, the factor of comfort does not apply to most experiments, but only to those that try to explore extreme stimulus ranges.

3. Caution.   Observers differ in the degree to which they seem willing to explore wide ranges of the variable that is placed under their control. I have already described the constricted reactions of an inhibited student who matched loudness to brightness in a class demonstration (Chapter 4). When the adjusted and criterion variables can be interchanged, some observers produce a dramatic difference between the slopes of the two regression lines. It seems to be the overly cautious or constrained observers who show the largest regression angles. Two examples are shown in Fig. 99. Observer K gave the most extreme example that occurred in a series of experiments on loudness (Stevens and Guirao 1962). Observer J was slightly less extreme, especially if the line for magnitude estimation is fitted so as to include the bottom point, which I have purposely ignored. That point, located at the round number one, provides a striking example of the so-called round-number tendency—a tendency to favor such numbers as one, ten, and the like.

Some investigators have seemed ready to take at face value the different exponents obtained from different observers in magnitude estimation and to argue that the different observers have different auditory power functions. Jones and Marcus suggested (1961) that "the power law must be modified to include a constant characteristic of the individual subject." Thus there would be a "personal exponent" attached to each of us. Jones and Marcus used only magnitude estimation, however, and Fig. 99 suggests, that a one-variable matching exercise may be quite misleading with regard to personal exponents. Thus, for observer K the exponent by magnitude estimation was 0.4, but by magnitude production it was 0.9. Interestingly enough, the geometric mean between those two values is 0.6, a value close to the accepted value for the loudness exponent. In other words, before too much is made of differences among exponents obtained by one particular method, the experiment needs to be counterbalanced. Individual differences tend to diminish when counterbalanced procedures are used (Stevens 1971b).

Of course, an experimenter seriously interested in the power function exponent for a particular person will not stop with magnitude estimation and production, but will pursue the results of a balanced array of additional cross-modality matching experiments. The evaluation of personal exponents, if there are such, is not a task that can be mastered by means of a one-shot experiment.

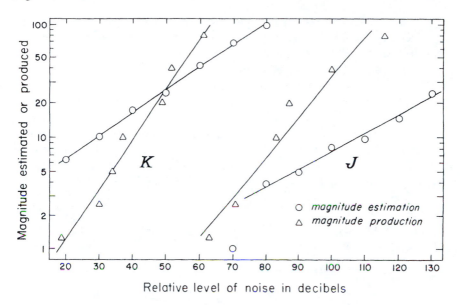

Fig. 99. Matching functions between number and loudness for two individual observers. Each point is the geometric mean of two estimations or productions. The stimulus was a band of noise 500 to 5000 hertz wide. (From Stevens and Greenbaum 1966, based on data of Stevens and Guirao 1962. Reprinted by permission.)

4. Order. In matching procedures like that involved in the method of magnitude estimation, the observer's judgment of a particular stimulus seems to depend to some extent on the stimulus that preceded it. For that reason it is advisable to present the stimuli in a different irregular order to each observer. That strategy tends to spread the order bias more evenly over the stimulus ensemble. On the other hand, it does not free the experiment of the order bias. In order to see that some degree of order bias must still remain, we need only consider the top and bottom stimuli. The top stimulus cannot be preceded by any higher stimulus, and the bottom stimulus cannot be preceded by any lower stimulus. By similar reasoning we see that, in general, higher stimuli must on the average be preceded by lower stimuli, and lower stimuli must on the average be preceded by higher stimuli.

Now, the effect of the order bias is regressive. By that I mean that a stimulus tends to be judged lower when preceded by a lower stimulus than when preceded by a higher stimulus, and vice versa. Thus the observer's estimate of a given stimulus, say, the middle stimulus in the series, is biased upward if a high stimulus precedes it and downward if a low stimulus precedes it. Stated another way, as the experimenter presents each successive stimulus the observer does not move his number as far as the experimenter moves the stimulus. The observer seems to move his number only some part of the expected distance.

D. V. Cross (1973) has described an interesting experiment on the order bias in loudness estimation. It was carried out with 18 observers here in the Laboratory of Psychophysics. Each stimulus was a half-second burst of a standard (so-called USASI) noise presented 7.5 seconds after the preceding stimulus. Care was taken to have each stimulus precede each other stimulus, including itself, an equal number of times. In that experiment the order effect made itself evident in such a methodical fashion that Cross was able to evaluate its magnitude and thereby eliminate its contribution to the regression effect.

Figure 100 tells the story. The large unfilled circles show the geometric means of the magnitude estimations averaged over 18 subjects and six

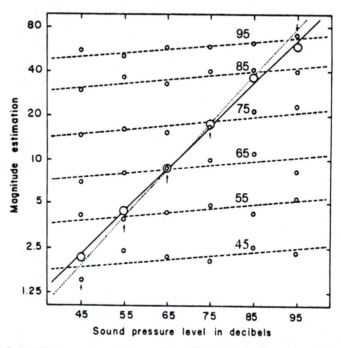

Fig. 100. Order bias in cross-modality matching. The large circles represent the geometric means of the magnitude estimations of 18 observers who judged half-second bursts of a-standard noise (USASI). Each stimulus level was made to follow each other level (including itself) an equal number of times. Each small circle is the geometric mean of the judgments made when the noise was at the level shown as the parameter on the dashed curves and when the preceding stimulus was at the level shown on the abscissa. Thus the dashed lines with the low slope 0.055 show how the observers' judgments increased when the preceding stimulus was at a higher level. (After Cross 1973.)

stimuli. The straight line through the large circles shows that the pooled magnitude estimations fall fairly close to a power function. The design of the experiment permitted an additional breakdown in the analysis of the data. The small circles show the magnitude estimations as a function of the preceding stimulus. Hence the dashed lines show how the observer's estimate increases as the preceding stimulus increases. For example, the points along the lowest dashed line show the judgments of the 45-decibel noise when it was preceded by itself, by 55 decibels, by 65 decibels, and so on. Each large circle represents the average of the corresponding small circles, and we see that the upper large circles are biased downward whereas the lower large circles are biased upward.

Now the problem we face is how to find the power function that would be free of the order bias. Presumably that function would be the function determined by the magnitude estimation of stimuli that were preceded only by themselves. We cannot carry out such an experiment, of course, for we would be limited to only one stimulus value. As soon as we used a second stimulus value the order bias would set in. On the other hand, we can look at those stimuli in the Cross experiment that were preceded by themselves. I have indicated each of those stimuli by a small arrow in Fig. 100. It appears plain that if a line were fitted to the judgments of those stimuli, the slope would be steeper than the slope of the line determined by the large circles. It would be wasteful, however, to base the function solely on the points indicated by the arrows, for we would then be discarding the information represented by the other points in the graph.

Instead, we can make use of the dashed lines that have been fitted to each row of points. In particular, we can ask where the dashed lines in Fig. 100 intersect the ordinates erected above each stimulus level. That intersection represents the value at which the order effect has been neutralized. The dotted line represents the power function determined by those neutral intersections.

The analysis by Cross displays in clear relief the manner in which the order bias produces a systematic error in the measured exponent of a power function. The solid line in Fig. 100 has a slope (exponent) equal to 0.585. By the elimination of the order bias the exponent increases to 0.64, as represented by the dotted line. The difference between those two exponents is 0.055, which corresponds to the slope (exponent) of the dashed lines. In other words, the order bias is itself a power function of the stimulus, and the exponent of the order bias provides a component that can be added to the exponent of the matching function determined by the large circles in Fig. 100. Otherwise said, the observer's judgment behaves as though composed of two component power functions—one for the stimulus presented and one for the stimulus immediately preceding. Although stimuli more remote than the preceding stimulus may need to be considered, the present discussion will consider only the immediately preceding stimulus.

Let us express the relations in terms of an equation. The observer's judgment J becomes a power product involving the currently presented stimulus C and the preceding stimulus P. We can write the equation

$$J = C^a P^b$$

The power function C^a is the function usually computed in magnitude estimation—the solid curve in Fig. 100 representing the geometric means over all observers and stimuli. The power function P^b represents the bias function—the dashed lines in Fig. 100. Now let us consider what happens when the intensity of the preceding stimulus P approaches nearer and nearer to that of the current stimulus C. In the limit when the two stimuli coincide, we have to deal with only one stimulus, which we will call ϕ. Then, if we consider our familar equation for the power law $\psi = \phi^\beta$, we can see that the exponent β becomes the sum of the two exponents, a plus b. In the present example, $a = 0.585$, $b = 0.055$, and $\beta = 0.64$.

Although the foregoing treatment has considered an example that employed magnitude estimation, we must remember that magnitude estimation constitutes only a special case of cross-modality matching. There is no reason to suppose that the analysis does not apply also to other forms of cross-modality matching. Since the order bias appears to be a major component of the regression effect, it may prove to be as ubiquitous as the regression effect itself.

The order bias also emerged when observers were asked to sort loudnesses into 20 categories which the observers had been taught in advance to recognize (Garner 1953). The errors made by the observers were regressive. On the average, a stimulus was placed in a higher category when the preceding stimulus had been higher, and vice versa. In that respect, category recognition behaves like magnitude estimation.

Garner noted that the resulting centering tendency or regression effect goes quite contrary to the so-called adaptation level theory (Helson 1964). According to Helson's AL theory, a high preceding stimulus ought to raise the adaptation level, which in turn ought to lower the number that the observer assigns to the stimulus presented. What actually happens is the opposite. Perhaps that fact ought to dispose of the AL notion, but the AL conception has been woven into such a loose and pliable pillow of a theory that no mere contrary fact, such as the order bias underlying the regression effect, can hope to impose a permanent dent. What the AL theory seems to concern is merely the modulus of the observer's category scale (Stevens 1958). The observer adjusts his modulus—what he will call medium, for example—to fit whatever assortment of stimuli he is asked to categorize.

Under most of its applications AL theory has nothing to do with the adaptation of a sense organ, a process that can produce dramatic effects of the kind shown in Fig. 26 of Chapter 3.

Another point relating to the order bias concerns its role in the scaling of nonmetric stimuli, such as the seriousness of offenses. The effect of the order bias is to shorten the range of the scale obtained by magnitude estimation. As a matter of fact, it may be assumed that the various scales discussed in Chapter 8 are shorter than they would be if the order bias could have been eliminated. At first sight, it might seem that, with no stimulus metric available, we could not use Cross's approach as illustrated in Fig. 100. Fortunately, however, that approach is quite possible, because the outcome of a scaling by magnitude estimation places each nonmetric stimulus on a ratio scale. Therefore, the scaled values of the stimuli can be used as though they were the metric stimulus measures, and an analysis of the order bias can proceed in the manner outlined above.

In order to visualize the procedure, imagine that the decibel stimulus values on the abscissa of Fig. 100 were not known. Only the ordinate values, the magnitude estimations, would be known. We could then construct an abscissa scale by simply using as the abscissa the logarithmic ordinate scale, giving us the same logarithmic scale on both coordinates. On the new plot the large circles would lie on the 45-degree diagonal, but the small circles would describe gently sloping lines, much as they do in Fig. 100. The slope (exponent) of those lines would provide a correction to be added to the exponent 1.0 represented by the 45-degree diagonal. The new larger exponent would determine a steeper function, which would in effect stretch the range of the magnitude estimation scale represented by the ordinate. The stretched scale would be free of the regression effect caused by the order bias. One of the very attractive features of the model developed by Cross to describe the order bias lies in its potential application to nonmetric as well as to metric stimuli.

REGRESSION REMEDIES

The goal of achieving a psychophysical power function free of the regression effect can be approached in three ways. Two of those approaches have already been discussed, but I will list them here along with a third possibility.

1.   Balance one regression against another by interchanging the fixed and adjustable stimuli. If the two regression effects happen to be equal,

regardless of which continuum the observer adjusts, then the two obtained exponents may be combined by taking their geometric mean.

2.   Design the experiment in such a way that the magnitude of the order bias can be evaluated in accordance with a model like that worked out by Cross.

3.   Evaluate the magnitude of the regression by way of a third continuum.

For the approach through a third continuum, two principal strategies can be distinguished. I will describe them in terms of three continua, A, B, and C.

First strategy.   Let us assume that we want to know the exponent relating B and C. We allow the observer to adjust continuum A to match B and also to match C, and we determine the two exponents. The ratio of those two exponents determines the exponent of the function relating B to C. When the B-to-C exponent is derived in that way it presumably bypasses the regression effect. As an example, the ratio of the two exponents obtained by the matching of number to loudness and to vibration on the finger gave a regression-free estimate of the exponent relating loudness and vibration. That estimate was confirmed, as is shown in Chapter 4, Fig. 33.

Second strategy.   The other procedure for balancing out the regression effect is to adjust both A and B in order to match a common continuum C. The two matching functions then provide exponents whose ratio gives the exponent for the power function relating A to B. As a concrete instance, in a thesis study by Moskowitz (1968), the observers matched both loudness and number to the apparent intensity of various tastes and combinations of tastes, a total of 68 two-part experiments. Although the taste study was initiated with no thought of investigating the loudness exponent, it was possible after the fact to derive 68 regression-free exponents relating number to loudness. The distribution of those exponents can be seen in Fig. 40 in Chapter 4.

In both of the foregoing strategies involving a third continuum, we have assumed that two different regression effects would turn out to be so nearly equal that they could be balanced against each other. Equality in the regression effect may or may not obtain in actual experiments.

Needless to say, the elimination of all or part of the regression bias does not necessarily free the exponent of other kinds and sources of bias. I once read a paper by an author who claimed to have eliminated all known biases from an experiment on the estimation of loudness ratios. Such a claim strains the reader's credulity. Biases often have a kind of complementarity about them. The principle of complementarity suggests that biases can perhaps be eliminated singly, one at a time, but their elimination all at once in the same experiment probably lies beyond possibility. In order to locate and assess the systematic errors, multiple experiments are often needed in physics when serious measurements are undertaken. In psychophysics the need for the multiple experiment approach is even more acute.

RANGE EFFECTS

Whenever an observer matches one continuum to another, the outcome depends to some extent on the stimulus range involved. By range I mean the ratio—the spread measured in logarithmic units. If the experimenter presents only a small range of the target stimuli, the exponent of the matching function tends to be larger, and if he presents a large range the exponent tends to be smaller. The question immediately suggests itself: can we find an optimal range for which the exponent is neither too large nor too small? In other words, can we neutralize the range bias? With the aid of counterbalanced experiments, neutralization may prove possible, as we shall see. But I would like first to comment on a misunderstanding.

Some commentators have alleged that the exponents of the various sense modalities (Table 1) are in reality merely the products of various procedural artifacts, among them the range effect. Poulton (1968) wrote that the stimulus range "accounts for about ⅓ of the variance in S. S. Stevens' table of exponents." That kind of statistical jargon leaves the reader to wonder whether the phrase "accounts for" implies cause and effect, and if so which came first, the range or the exponent? Actually a further examination of some of the Stevens exponents has found that Poulton's estimate was low, and that 87 percent of the variance in the exponents is "accounted for" by variation in the stimulus range (Teghtsoonian 1971). How did such a close relation come about?

In arranging experiments to explore the various perceptual continua I have usually tried to present a range of stimuli that seemed comfortably large. Admittedly, in the first experiment with magnitude estimation, I presented as a standard sound a loudness that was needlessly disagreeable, but I soon learned better, and, as experiment followed experiment, both the design of the experiments and the experimenter's skill improved. Without giving the matter explicit thought, I began to choose ranges of stimuli that covered as much of the continuum as possible without involving stimuli that seemed either distressingly faint or objectionably strong. As a consequence of my choosing ranges of stimuli that seemed to give agreeable and satisfactory ranges of subjective effect, there emerged from 21 experiments a remarkable correlation between the range chosen and the exponent obtained—a product moment correlation equal to −0.94.

Taking note of that high correlation, Teghtsoonian hypothesized that the variation in power law exponents is due to the differing dynamic ranges of the sense modalities. Although the turning of a correlation into a cause presents an inviting prospect, I should prefer to forego the diagnosis of cause and effect. Perhaps we need first to understand what causes dynamic range. On some continua, like taste intensity for sugar, for example, we reach a solubility limit beyond which we can produce no sweeter stimulus. The dynamic range is cut short because we run out of stimulus. On other continua, like electric shock, the production of a stronger and stronger stimulus is easily accomplished, but we run out of volunteers who will serve as subjects.

Poulton argued a related point. For him the correlation between range and exponent suggested that the experimenter "did not adequately compensate for the effects of different physical ranges. . . ." In addressing himself to stimulus ranges, Poulton directed attention to what seems to me to be the wrong side of the equation. In studies designed to compare exponents, it is not the stimulus range but the subjective range that ought to be the experimenter's primary concern. Ideally, the experimenter should make the subjective ranges equal. If he fully achieved that goal, then the correlation between range and exponent would become −1.0, a perfect negative correlation. With an imperfect correlation, equal to −0.94, it appears that my own experiments did not quite succeed in adjusting the subjective ranges to full equality.

In any case, having worked with more than a score of different continua, I can testify that the dramatic differences among the exponents become rather obvious if you look for them. In one instance we assembled a wide variety of rubber samples covering a generous range from soft to hard—a subjective range that seemed to me to be about 50 to 1. We then had to construct an indentation device to measure the physical hardness of the stimuli. As soon as that had been done, I guessed that the exponent for subjective hardness would be about three-quarters. Each of two different experiments by magnitude estimation gave 0.8 (Harper and Stevens 1964). In another instance, we sent away to a commercial laboratory for samples of liquids varying in viscosity. They arrived in jars labeled with the physical values of the viscosity. I unpacked the jars and shook them. It appeared to me obvious that the exponent must be less than 1.0, and I guessed that the exponent for apparent viscosity would turn out to be about one-half. The values determined by magnitude estimation under three different experimental procedures ranged from 0.42 to 0.46 (Stevens and Guirao 1964).

What I am trying to convey by those examples is the hypothesis that, although range effects are real, the differences among the exponents are even more real—a reality that stands out in obvious clarity when we look for it. Perhaps, after all, the nature of the sense organs has something to do with the matter.

EFFECTS OF REPETITION

The degree to which the stimulus range affects the exponent may sometimes be altered by the mode of presentation of the stimuli. The biasing effect of an unusually short range may increase with repetition, as we discovered when we tried to judge a series of grays ranging from black to white. When the grays were laid one by one on the table, the range appeared large—judged to be approximately 100 to 1 in several experiments

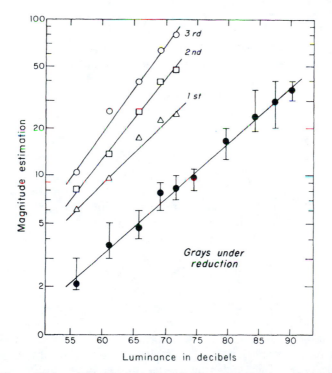

Fig. 101. The unfilled symbols show how Munsell grays, extending from black to white, are judged when they are presented entirely alone with no other visible luminance in the field of view. The luminance then covers a range of about 16 decibels, which appears subjectively rather short. On the three successive presentations of the set of stimuli, the exponent became larger. The filled symbols show the results for an extended luminance range. The exponent is 0.35, which is much lower than the value 1.2 obtained when the Munsell grays are placed one by one on a table in front of the observer.

with magnitude estimation (Stevens and Galanter 1957). On the other hand, when the observer was placed in a dark booth and allowed to view the grays through a 3-centimeter hole, so that nothing but the gray was visible—under the so-called reduction condition of viewing—the gray appeared to be a luminous patch of light, and the apparent range from black to white dropped to about 3 to 1.

In an experiment carried out with the aid of A. W. F. Huggins, I obtained the results shown in Fig. 101. The stimuli were presented three times each in irregular order to 10 observers. The three successive presentations of the grays gave the results shown by the unfilled symbols. As we see, the short range produced a steeper power function on each successive presentation. The filled symbols represent the results when the range was extended by means of two different levels of illumination applied to the grays. The slope (exponent) for the extended stimulus range is 0.35. The vertical lines through the points show the interquartile ranges. It should be remarked that the extended range was still rather short, about 33 decibels, giving a subjective range of about 15 to 1.

Our experiment with the short range of visual stimuli showed that a better approximation to the underlying magnitude function was obtained when the observer was limited to a single magnitude estimation of each stimulus. Many experimenters have assumed that more judgments are better than fewer judgments. Here we see an instance where the opposite was true.

COUNTERBALANCING FOR RANGE

Even with a single judgment—one judgment of one stimulus by each observer—a range effect may manifest itself. Under some circumstances the range effect can be canceled out in a balanced experimental design. A fair approximation to a balanced design was achieved in a study of the loudness function for a 1000-hertz tone (Stevens and Poulton 1956). Groups comprising 8 to 11 first-time observers were asked to make a single judgment, either a ratio estimation or a ratio production.

For the ratio estimations a reference stimulus was sounded and called 100, after which a second stimulus was sounded at a lower level, and the observer assigned it a number to express the apparent ratio. Different groups of observers judged different lower levels. The results, expressed in terms of the exponent implied by each ratio, are shown by the triangles in Fig. 102.

For the ratio productions the observers adjusted a special "sone potentiometer" to produce one or another fractional loudness relative to a reference standard. The exponent corresponding to the ratio productions for each group of subjects is shown by a circle in Fig. 102. The two sets of data show an approximate symmetry. Stimulus range influences both estimation and production, but in ways that resemble a mirror image. In that respect the range effect, although quite dramatic in its behavior, shows itself to be an orderly variable. Figure 102 suggests that a well balanced experiment could lead to a unique determination of the exponent. In the instance before us, the data suggest that, for the seven groups of naive listeners making their first loudness judgments, the exponent lies between 0.6 and 0.7.

In order to determine the exponent more exactly, I adjusted the two scales, top and bottom in Fig. 102, by iteration until the exponent implied by the relation between the two scales coincided with the exponent determined by the crossover of the two curves (Stevens 1971b). The exponent

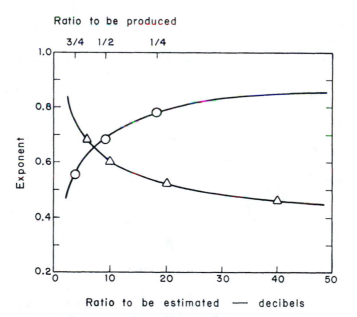

Fig. 102. The range effect in a partially balanced experiment. Each point represents a separate group of subjects who estimated (triangles) or produced (circles) a loudness ratio. When the range effect produces symmetrical functions, as is approximately true here, the exponent may be uniquely determined. It is the value that makes the exponent corresponding to the crossover point equal to the exponent implied by the relation of the scales at the top and bottom of the figure. The exponent so determined is 0.65. (From Stevens 1971b, *Psychol. Rev.*, 78, 426–450, based on data from Stevens and Poulton 1956, *J. Exp. Psychol.*, 51, 71–78. Copyright 1971 and 1956 by the American Psychological Association. Reprinted by permission.)

determined in that fashion turned out to be 0.65, a value that falls fairly close to the general consensus of many other measurements.

The crossover point in Fig. 102 corresponds approximately to the average of the two curves, and the question arises whether we should simply average the curves obtained in the two parts of the experiment. In principle we might average the two functions, but we would first face the same question that I faced in trying to determine the crossover point, namely, which values of ratio production correspond to which values of ratio estimation. Here again we might solve the problem by resort to iteration.

An interesting instance of the range effect occurred in an experiment in which both magnitude estimation and magnitude production were applied to loudness. Students in a laboratory course were instructed to try to design such an experiment. The magnitude estimations proved quite successful and resulted in the usual power function with an exponent near 0.6, but the magnitude productions gave a very large exponent, slightly greater than 1.0. For the magnitude productions the students had proceeded in the usual way and had asked each subject to adjust the loudness to match a target number spoken by the experimenter. But the numbers spoken covered the extremely wide range from 0.01 to 200, a range of 20,000 to 1. An excessively large exponent is the natural result of such a large range of target numbers. That experience points up the need to consider carefully the problem of range whenever the experimental design attempts to counterbalance magnitude estimation and magnitude production.

ON THE USE OF NUMBERS

A source of error peculiar to magnitude estimation is the tendency of observers to use round numbers, so called. At the hands of most observers the number system becomes an array of discrete values rather than a continuum. Values like 1, 2, 5, 10, and their multiples are used more often than intermediate values. The round number tendency has no great effect on a power function that is based on a group average, but it may impose a rather coarse grain on the smoothness of a power function for an individual observer.

In order to smooth out the grain, the round number tendency makes it desirable to give each observer a different modulus, preferably one of his own choosing. The objective of neutralizing the round number tendency thus becomes an additional reason for omitting the standard from experiments that use magnitude estimation.

The round number tendency causes local perturbations in the power function of the individual observer, but other factors may cause more extensive distortions. In watching observers perform magnitude estimation I have been impressed with several idiosyncracies in the use of numbers. For example, an observer may sometimes distort the low end of the scale because he fears that if he uses numbers close to one he might run out of numbers. For some people the bottom of the scale starts at one. The impression can often be dispelled by giving such a small or faint stimulus that the observer is forced into fractions.

At the other extreme, there is sometimes a tendency to perceive 100 as the top of the scale, so that the scale becomes artificially curved when values approach 100. When some observers use numbers, they act as though the ratio 1 to 2 is somehow smaller than, say, the ratio 80 to 160. Large ratios among small fractions are sometimes treated as though they were small ratios. Thus an observer may change his estimate from a hundredth to a tenth more readily than from a hundred to a thousand.

In short, despite most people's remarkable and thorough understanding of the number continuum, the use of numbers in magnitude estimation is not without interesting quirks and oddities.

Some authors have suggested that the number system itself is perceived as a power function with an exponent different from unity (Attneave 1962). In other words, like other perceptual continua, the subjective number continuum may be curved. That, of course, may be true, but the question arises, what continuum shall we compare it to in order to determine the curvature? Since in this world there are no absolutes, we must decide which continuum we will accept as the standard of straightness. A possibility suggested earlier is that we might choose apparent length as the straight continuum. If that were our choice we would then find that number is also straight, for when length is matched to number the exponent is usually close to 1.0. On the other hand, if we should choose loudness as the straight continuum, we would find the number continuum quite curved. All things considered, it appears that the number continuum stands as the best candidate for the role of the straight reference continuum.

MODULUS EQUALIZATION

For some purposes, it becomes desirable to adjust the magnitude estimations of the observers to a common modulus. Experimenters have often assumed that by presenting a standard they could assure themselves that all observers would use the same modulus. That of course is not strictly true, for it assumes that the observer perceives the standard stimulus with zero bias and zero error. Admittedly the use of a standard constrains the observers to a modulus in the vicinity of the standard but not necessarily exactly at the value of the standard.

An example from an experiment on brightness carried out in 1958 is shown by the upper function in Fig. 103. The observer sat close to a large screen illuminated to various controllable levels. The stimulus level indicated by the cross was given first, as a standard, and the other stimuli followed in irregular order. It is clear that the power function determined by the geometric means does not happen to pass through the standard, which was called 10.

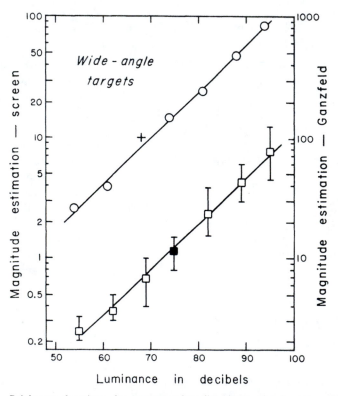

Fig. 103. Brightness functions for targets subtending large visual angles. The circles represent an experiment in which the observer viewed a large illuminated screen. The cross represents the standard presented at the outset and called 10. A nearly ideal *Ganzfeld* was used for the other experiment (squares). The black square represents the standard, called 10. In this experiment the standard level reappeared as one of the stimuli to be judged. Each stimulus was shown twice in a different irregular order to each of 10 observers. The points represent geometric means. The vertical lines represent interquartile ranges.

In an effort to achieve an even wider visual angle we devised a special pair of goggles with milk-glass lenses. When illumination was from the front by projector, the observer saw an almost completely homogeneous white field. With that arrangement we obtained the experimental results shown by the squares in Fig. 103. The standard (solid black square) was presented at the outset and called 10, but it also appeared as one of the stimuli to be judged. Used in that way, the standard lay close to the power function determined by the other values. The vertical lines mark interquartile ranges.

When no standard is given, or when each observer is given a different standard, the modulus may vary from observer to observer. In order to analyze such features as variability, it may then prove necessary to normalize the data by reducing all the individual functions to a common modulus. That has been done in two ways. In one method all the individual power functions were tied together, so to speak, at a single stimulus value (Stevens 1956a). The other method involves the procedure of allowing all the judgments to help determine the common modulus. The procedure is straightforward (Lane, Catania, and Stevens 1961). Working with the logarithms of the data, we first determine the grand mean of all judgments of all stimuli by all observers. We next determine the mean of each observer's judgments of all stimuli. We then add the difference between the grand mean and each observer's mean to that observer's judgments. In other words, we make each observer's mean coincide with the grand mean.

That procedure of modulus equalization eliminates one component of the variability in an experiment—the component due to variation in the modulus—sometimes called the intercept variability. After that component has been eliminated, it may be instructive to study the variability in the slopes (exponents) of the functions. If desired, the component due to slope or exponent variability can also be eliminated, leaving the residual random component of the variability.

ADDITIVE CONSTANTS

The power law is sometimes written with an additive constant ϕ_0 in order to bring the zero of the subjective scale ψ into coincidence with the absolute threshold on the stimulus scale ϕ. The formula then becomes

$$\psi = k(\phi - \phi_0)^\beta$$

The threshold constant enlarges the scope of the power law so that it can be shown to apply to such continua as the warmth of an aluminum object applied to the skin. Without the threshold constant the results of magnitude estimation give a curved function in log-log coordinates, as shown by the

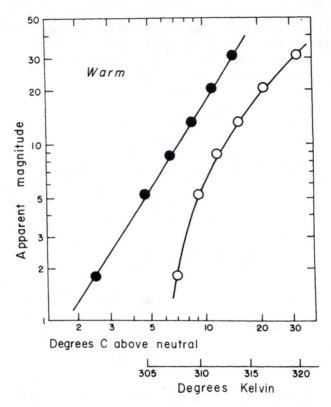

Fig. 104. Magnitude estimation of apparent warmth. Each point stands for the geometric mean of 36 estimates (12 observers). The upper abscissa, for the filled points, is a logarithmic scale of the difference in temperature between the stimulus and the physiological zero at 305.7° Kelvin (90.5° Fahrenheit). The lower abscissa, for the unfilled points, is a logarithmic scale of the absolute temperature in degrees Kelvin. (From J. C. Stevens and Stevens 1960, *J. Exp. Psychol.*, 60, 183–192. Copyright 1960 by the American Psychological Association. Reprinted by permission.)

unfilled circles in Fig. 104. When the stimulus is measured in degrees above so-called physiological zero—the neutral temperature that feels neither cold nor warm—the curve straightens out, as shown by the filled circles (J. C. Stevens and Stevens 1960). The formula for apparent warmth W then becomes

$$W = k(T - 305.7)^{1.6}$$

The temperature T is expressed in degrees Kelvin on the so-called absolute scale, which is a ratio scale.

Interestingly enough, when the same aluminum stimuli were made to feel cold, the exponent changed. For cold on the skin the exponent was 1.0.

Again the power function form was obtained only when the cold stimulus was measured as difference from physiological zero.

Sensations of warmth can also be aroused by radiant heat, as from the sun or a heat lamp. The sensation grows as a power function of the intensity of the radiant energy, provided a threshold constant is employed in the formula. A most interesting series of experiments by J. C. Stevens and his associates has shown how subjective warmth varies with such factors as the duration of the irradiation and the area of the body exposed. The power function holds under all conditions tested, but the threshold constant and the exponent both undergo systematic changes when the experimental parameters are varied.

Pain due to irradiation of a small area of the skin also follows a power function, provided a threshold constant is used, as does also the experienced degree of discomfort created by warmth and by cold applied to the entire body (J. C. Stevens, Adair, and Marks 1970).

There seems to be an obvious need for a translation constant to bring the effective zero of the temperature scale to the value at which warmth or cold begins. On other continua the need for a threshold constant may be less obvious. The need is less obvious, for example, with loudness, partly because the threshold is very low. Nevertheless a threshold constant has sometimes proved useful with loudness (Scharf and J. C. Stevens 1961).

The use of a threshold constant has proved especially helpful in describing the brightness functions when the eye has been adapted to high levels of luminance (see Fig. 26). After exposure for a few minutes to a high level of luminance, the threshold of the eye moves up by a large factor. Dimly lighted objects then become invisible, as everyone knows. When the eye becomes highly light-adapted, the formula for the visual power function requires a larger value of the constant ϕ_0 to translate the starting point to the new higher threshold.

Some investigators have preferred to write the power law equation with the constant on the left-hand side of the equation: $\psi - \psi_0 = \phi^\beta$. Although I once entertained the view that a masking noise might affect the perception of loudness by subtracting a certain number of sones (Stevens and Davis 1938), I later found that subtracting a value such as ψ_0 on the left-hand side of the equation does not describe the perceived loudness of the masked signal. Instead, a power transformation is needed, with a larger exponent, as illustrated, for example, in Fig. 25. A similar kind of power transformation is needed to describe the brightness function under masking by glare (simultaneous) contrast, as shown in Fig. 23.

Whether to subtract a constant ψ_0 from the sensation or a constant ϕ_0 from the stimulus is not a question that can be settled by mere fitting, because both forms of the equation can often be fitted fairly well to the kinds of imperfect data that experiments inevitably produce (Marks and J. C. Stevens 1968). The decision to apply the translation constant to the stimulus or to the sensation probably must be made on other grounds. The accumulated evidence has forced a change in my own view, so that when a translation is called for, I now favor translation on the stimulus axis.

Others disagree, however. D. H. Krantz (1972), an eminent theorist in mathematical psychophysics, said that for visual brightness the constant ϕ_0 has no "convenient interpretation," because, as he put it, "the interpretation as a luminance 'threshold' is nonsense, since the 'threshold' is a statistical fiction, and since . . . the values of $[\phi_0]$ rarely correspond to directly measured 'thresholds' " (p. 676). It must be agreed that the threshold is a statistical fiction—but only in the same sense that a person's stature is a statistical fiction: if you try repeatedly to measure a man's size very exactly, you encounter a slightly different value on each try. Krantz's second reason for questioning the use of the threshold constant ϕ_0 raises an issue of greater substance, however, for it is important to know whether the ϕ_0 that results in the best approximation to a power function also coincides with the threshold as conventionally measured. In general, the coincidence between the two has proved quite satisfactory, at least in certain sensory domains—those involving vision, hearing, and various kinds of thermal stimuli. The constant that straightens out the graph of the function in log-log coordinates usually coincides fairly well with the threshold measured independently in other experiments.

As we have seen, however, when a threshold shift is caused by the inhibiting effect created by masking or glare, or even by certain kinds of hearing loss, the simple additive constant does not describe the resulting function. A power transformation is then in order.

As a general rule, it appears that the additive constant ought to be avoided if possible. It should be used only when its need can be justified. Authors have occasionally used an additive constant to straighten experimental curves with no justification other than the appearance of the lines. In one instance, the removal of additive constants revealed an interesting transitivity among cross-modality matches—a transitivity that had been obscured by the additive constants (Stevens 1969).

ON BELIEVING ONE'S DATA

Students sometimes ask how I explain the results obtained by one or another investigator whose views differ from mine about the form of the psychophysical power law. I first confess that I try as little as possible to "explain results." Results have a way of explaining themselves after additional experiments have brought to light the sources of error and bias that may disturb a given outcome. Much of the confusion and the working at cross purposes in science seems to arise from the isolated experiment, the published study that stands unsupported and uncorrected by a multiple set of checks and counterbalancing investigations. Of course, the experiments themselves do not perform the mischief; rather it is the tendency of each experimenter to believe his own data that injects the noise into scientific harmony. One's own data occupy a privileged and honored status. Seldom does an experimenter put more faith in the other man's finding. Most of the time he ought to, though—we all ought to.

An inevitable result of our becoming better informed about the sources of systematic errors in psychophysics, and the consequent need for multiple, balanced experiments, ought to be to make experimenters less willing to base a psychophysical function on a single method or procedure. That has not always been the effect, however. Some authors have dutifully compiled a review of the known experimental biases, and then have tried to devise a single new experiment to bypass all the known hazards. Two examples are of interest because they produced such different results.

In one study, each of 720 observers was asked to make only a single ratio judgment in a procedure designed "to produce loudness estimates free from known biases . . ." (Warren 1970). The observer heard two loudnesses. If the louder one is called 100, he was told, what should the other one be called? The author decided that the stimulus ratio that elicited the estimate 50—in other words, a 2-to-1 ratio of loudness—was the key value. That stimulus ratio turned out to be about 6 decibels. If 2-to-1 loudness corresponds to a sound pressure change of 6 decibels, the exponent of the power function becomes 1.0, a value that happened to meet the requirements of the author's theory.

In another experiment 242 observers also made ratio estimations saying how many times louder one tone was than another (McRobert, Bryan, and Tempest 1965). The experiment had been designed, said the authors, "to minimize bias and context effects." The pooled results gave an exponent equal to 0.42. Despite the claims of minimum bias, the value of the exponent falls far below the sone scale exponent, which is 0.67 when measured in terms of sound pressure.

It is interesting that the exponent of the sone scale lies about midway between the values produced by the two foregoing "unbiased" experiments, both of which used large numbers of observers. Large numbers do not protect against systematic errors.

At the other extreme, a small number of observers can also prove misleading. Saunders (1972) used only two observers in an experiment designed, among other things, to study "the validity of magnitude estima-

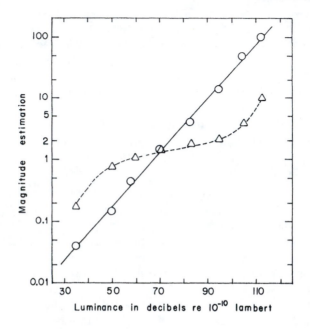

Fig. 105. Magnitude estimations given by two observers. One observer gave an excellent power function, as shown by the circles describing a straight line in the log-log coordinates. The other observer gave the results shown by the triangles. The extreme departure from a power function was presumably caused by an idiosyncratic use of numbers. (Data from Saunders 1972.)

tions of luminosity. . . ." One observer gave judgments that accord nicely with a power function, as shown by the circles in Fig. 105. The other observer gave the judgments represented by the triangles, which plainly do not describe a power function. From other procedures carried out in the experiments, it appears that the visual systems of both observers may in fact operate with rather similar characteristics. We may conclude, then, that the two observers used numbers in rather different ways. Of course, the occurrence of an occasional idiosyncratic use of numbers is precisely why the behavior of the typical (median) observer interests us more than the behavior of any one particular observer.

What do we conclude from the fact that one observer happened not to produce a power function? Saunders concluded that the difference between the observers seems "to invalidate the hypothesis that Psychophysical Laws can be derived directly from magnitude estimation scaling." He went on to say, "This seems to refute not only the Power Law of Stevens but models of the visual process based on the assumption of these laws."

I suppose the power law would indeed be a fragile principle if it could be refuted by the number-matching behavior of an author who served as his own observer. But before a serious decision on that question could be in order, it would be appropriate to know more about the matching behavior of that particular observer. How would he behave in other cross-modality experiments, such as magnitude production, matching between loudness and brightness, matching between handgrip and brightness, and so on? Although a scientist might find it a heady experience to be able to refute a widely documented law, perhaps such an author ought to reserve his decision until he finds out what the evidence from a battery of counterbalanced experiments can tell him.

In the meantime it may be of interest to consider the brightness judgments made by 166 students in a classroom experiment carried out in 1971 by my colleague, R. J. Herrnstein. He used a set of projector slides that are now manufactured commercially for use in classroom demonstrations of the method of magnitude estimation. The slides enable the instructor to project spots of light onto a white screen. Each slide produces a different light intensity on the screen. In the fairly darkened classroom a spot with a luminance of about 78 decibels was presented first and called 100. After that each member of the class wrote down a number to signify his or her impression of the brightness of each stimulus as it appeared. The stimuli were presented in irregular order, but the order was, of course, the same for all the observers. Despite the far from ideal conditions in the classroom, the geometric means for the 166 students described a rather good power function, as shown in Fig. 106. The line through the points has the slope (exponent) 0.33. The downturn at the bottom end suggests that the observers were not fully dark adapted and that the equation for their power function could use a threshold constant ϕ_0.

Inasmuch as the data in Fig. 106 were gathered locally, and since they accord well with the cube root rule that I advocated in 1953 for the brightness function, there emerges an understandable predilection for me to take the results seriously. On the other hand, I am aware that the excellent agreement with the cube root law is, like the outcome of each single experiment, the result of the interplay of factors and forces that bias things this way and that. Specifically, the factors that produce the regression effect were presumably operating to lower the exponent, while both the state of light adaptation and the relatively short stimulus range were operating to raise the exponent. Those were only three of the possible factors that interacted to produce the outcome shown in Fig. 106. An interplay of errors and biases afflicts all experiments, whether in physics or in psychophysics. Each experimental outcome bears the marks of contextual bias and systematic error.

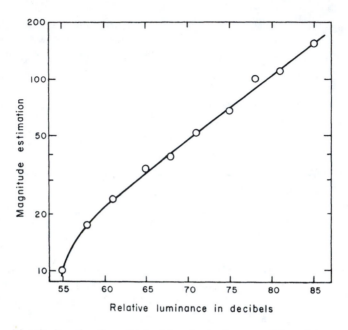

Fig. 106. Magnitude estimations obtained in a large classroom. The points are geometric means for 166 observers who assigned numbers to the brightness of spots of light projected on a large screen. A stimulus at about 78 decibels was presented first and called 100, after which the other stimuli were given in irregular order. The slope (exponent) is ⅓.

Although some theorists seem impelled to reject the idea that there exists any binding and lawful relation between stimulus and response, other psychophysicists seem prepared to acknowledge that Fechner posed a valid question when he inquired into the relation between sensation and the intensity of the physical configuration that gives rise to it. Those who believe that no psychophysical laws are possible and who reject the nomothetic imperative find their belief nurtured by the ease with which an experiment can be made to yield contrary and discordant results. And those who believe that sensation obeys discoverable laws find their faith reinforced by the results of numerous experiments that accord with the principle that equal stimulus ratios produce equal sensation ratios. That simple invariance stands as the primary psychophysical law. The measurement procedures that have been devised for its quantification suffer from an overlay of contextual factors that bias the outcome of each particular experiment. But those biasing factors seem also to obey rules that can be discovered, and those rules in turn enable us to discern better the underlying simplicities of the unlawful substrate.

References

Akman, D. D., and A. Normandeau. The measurement of crime and delinquency in Canada. *Br. J. Criminol.*, 1967, 7, 129–149.

Anderson, N. H. Cross-task validation of functional measurement. *Percept. Psychophys.*, 1972, 12, 389–395.

Attneave, F. Perception and related areas. In S. Koch (Ed.), *Psychology: a study of a science.* Vol. 4, pp. 619–659. New York: McGraw-Hill, 1962.

Beck, C., and B. S. Rosner. Magnitude scales and somatic evoked potentials to percutaneous electrical stimulation. *Physiol. Behav.*, 1968, 3, 947–953.

Beck, J., and W. A. Shaw. Ratio-estimations of loudness-intervals. *Am. J. Psychol.*, 1967, 80, 59–65.

Békésy, G. v. Über das Fechnersche Gesetz und seine Bedeutung für die Theorie der akustischen Beobachtungsfehler und die Theorie des Hörens. *Ann. Physik*, 1930, 7, 329–359. English translation in Békésy 1960, pp. 238 ff.

Békésy, G. v. A new audiometer. *Acta Otolaryngol.*, 1947, 35, 411–422. Reprinted in Békésy 1960, pp. 81 ff.

Békésy, G. v. *Experiments in hearing.* New York: McGraw-Hill, 1960.

Békésy, G. v. Mach band type lateral inhibition in different sense organs. *J. Gen. Physiol.*, 1967a, 50, 519–532.

Békésy, G. v. *Sensory inhibition.* Princeton, N.J.: Princeton Univ. Press, 1967b.

Békésy, G. v. Mach bands measured by a compensation method. *Vision Res.*, 1972, 12, 1485–1497.

Berglund, B., U. Berglund, G. Ekman, and T. Engen. Individual psychophysical functions for 28 odorants. *Percept. Psychophys.*, 1971, 9, 379–384.

Bernoulli, D. Exposition of a new theory on the measurement of risk. Originally published in Latin in 1738. Translation in *Econometrica*, 1954, 22, 23–35.

Björkman, M. Some relationships between psychophysical parameters. *Rep. Psychol. Lab., Univ. Stockholm,* 1958, No. 65.

Björkman, M. Variability data and direct quantitative judgment for scaling subjective magnitude. *Rep. Psychol. Lab., Univ. Stockholm,* 1960, No. 78.

Blackwell, H. R., Psychophysical thresholds: experimental studies of methods of measurement. Ann Arbor: Univ. Michigan, *Eng. Res. Inst., Bull.* No. 36, Jan. 1953.

Bond, B., and S. S. Stevens. Cross-modality matching of brightness to loudness by 5-year-olds. *Percept. Psychophys.*, 1969, 6, 337–339.

Borg, G., H. Diamant, L. Ström, and Y. Zotterman. The relation between neural and perceptual intensity: a comparative study on the neural and psychophysical response to taste stimuli. *J. Physiol. Lond.*, 1967, 192, 13–20.

Boring, E. G. The stimulus-error. *Am. J. Psychol.*, 1921, 32, 449–471.

Boring, E. G. The psychology of controversy. *Psychol. Rev.*, 1929, 36, 97–121.

Boring, E. G. Isochromatic contours. *Am. J. Psychol.*, 1937, 49, 130–134.

Boudreau, J. C. Stimulus correlates of wave activity in the superior-olivary complex of the cat. *J. Acoust. Soc. Am.*, 1965, 37, 779–785.

Brentano, F. *Psychologie vom empirischen Standpunkt.* Th. 1. Leipzig: Dunker und Hunblot, 1874.

Campbell, N. R. *Symposium: Measurement and its importance for philosophy.* Aristotelian Soc., Suppl. Vol. 17. London: Harrison and Sons, 1938.

Carroll, J. B. Measurement properties of subjective magnitude estimates of word frequency. *J. Verbal Learn. Verbal Behav.*, 1971, 10, 722–729.

Chapanis, A., and R. M. Halsey, Luminance of equally bright colors. *J. Opt. Soc. Am.*, 1955, 45, 1–6.

Clark, B., and J. D. Stewart. The power law for the perception of rotation by airline pilots. *Percept. Psychophys.*, 1972, 11, 433–436.

Cohen, J., and W. Little. Neural model for the Stevens power law. *Percept. Psychophys.*, 1971, 10, 269–270.

Corson, W. H. Conflict and cooperation in East-West crises: dynamics of crisis interaction. Unpublished doctoral dissertation, Harvard Univ., 1970.

Cramer, G., 1728. Letter to Nicholas Bernoulli, 1732. Quoted in note appended to Bernoulli 1738.

Cross, D. V. Sequential dependencies and regression in psychophysical studies. *Percept Psychophys.*, 1973, 14, 547–552.

Davis, H., C. Bowers, and S. K. Hirsh. Relations of the human vertex potential to acoustic input: loudness and masking. *J. Acoust. Soc. Am.*, 1968, 43, 431–438.

Davis, H., S. S. Stevens, et al. *Hearing aids: an experimental study of design objectives.* Cambridge, Mass.: Harvard Univ. Press, 1947.

Dawson, W. E. An experimental analysis of judgments of sensory difference. Unpublished doctoral dissertation, Harvard Univ., 1968.

Dawson, W. E., and R. P. Brinker, Validation of ratio scales of opinion by multimodality matching. *Percept. Psychophys.*, 1971, 9, 413–417.

Delboeuf, J. *Etude psychologique. Recherches théoriques et expérimentales sur la mesure des sensations et spécialement des sensations de lumière et de fatigue.* Brussels, 1873, 115 pp.

Delbrück, M. A physicist's renewed look at biology: twenty years later. *Science,* 1970, 168, 1312–1315.

Derbyshire, A. J., and H. Davis. The action potentials of the auditory nerve. *Am. J. Physiol.*, 1935, 113, 476–504.

DeValois, R. L., G. H. Jacobs, and A. E. Jones. Effects of increments and decrements of light on neural discharge rate. *Science,* 1962, 136, 986–988.

Easter, S. S., Jr. Excitation in the goldfish retina: evidence for a non-linear intensity code. *J. Physiol. Lond.*, 1968, 195, 253–271.

Ebbinghaus, H. Über negative Empfindungswerte. *Z. Psychol.*, 1890, 1, 320–334.

Eisler, H. Empirical test of a model relating magnitudes and category scales. *Scand. J. Psychol.*, 1962, 3, 88–96.

Ekman, G. Discriminal sensitivity on the subjective continuum. *Acta Psychol.*, 1956, 12, 233–243.

Ekman, G. Two generalized ratio scaling methods. *J. Psychol.*, 1958, 45, 287–295.

Ekman, G. Weber's law and related functions. *J. Psychol.*, 1959, 47, 343–352.

Ekman, G. Measurement of moral judgment: a comparison of scaling methods. *Percept. Mot. Skills*, 1962, 15, 3–9.

Ekman, G., and T. Künnapas. Subjective dispersion and the Weber fraction. *Rep. Psychol. Lab., Univ. Stockholm*, 1957, No. 41.

Ekman, G., and T. Künnapas. Note on direct and indirect scaling methods. *Psychol. Rep.*, 1960, 6, 174.

Ekman, G., and T. Künnapas. Measurement of aesthetic value by "direct" and "indirect" methods. *Scand. J. Psychol.*, 1962a, 3, 33–39.

Ekman, G., and T. Künnapas. Scales of aesthetic value. *Percept. Mot. Skills*, 1962b, 14, 19–26.

Ekman, G., and T. Künnapas. A further study of direct and indirect scaling methods. *Scand J. Psychol.*, 1963a, 4, 77–80.

Ekman, G., and T. Künnapas. Scales of conservatism. *Percept. Mot. Skills*, 1963b, 16, 329–334.

Ekman, G., and T. Künnapas. Scales of masculinity and femininity: a further study of direct and indirect scaling methods. *Rep. Psychol. Lab., Univ. Stockholm*, 1963c, No. 162.

Ekman, G., and L. Sjöberg. Scaling. *Ann. Rev. Psychol.*, 1965, 16, 451–474.

Elsner, W. Power laws for the perception of rotation and the oculogyral illusion. *Percept. Psychophys.*, 1971, 9, 418–420.

Engen, T., and D. H. McBurney. Magnitude and category scales of the pleasantness of odors. *J. Exp. Psychol.*, 1964, 68, 435–440.

Fechner, G. T. *Elemente der Psychophysik, 1860.* Vol. I available in English translation as *Elements of psychophysics*. New York: Holt, Rinehart and Winston, 1966.

Fechner, G. T. *In Sachen der Psychophysik*. Leipzig, 1877.

Final report on quantitative estimates of sensory events. *Adv. Sci.*, 1940, No. 2, 331–349.

Finnie, B., and R. D. Luce. Magnitude-estimation, pair-comparison and successive-interval scales of attitude items. Philadelphia: Department of Psychology, University of Pennsylvania, Memorandum MP-9 [1960].

Fletcher, H. Auditory patterns. *Rev. Mod. Physics*, 1940, 12, 47–65.

Fletcher, H. *Speech and hearing in communication*. New York: D. Van Nostrand, 1953.

Fletcher, H., and W. A. Munson. Loudness, its definition, measurement and calculation. *J. Acoust. Soc. Am.*, 1933, 5, 82–108.

Fletcher, H., and W. A. Munson. Relation between loudness and masking. *J. Acoust. Soc. Am.*, 1937, 9, 1–10.

Franzén, O., and K. Offenloch. Evoked response correlates of psychophysical magnitude estimates for tactile stimulation in man. *Exp. Brain Res.*, 1969, 8, 1–18.

Fullerton, G. S., and J. Mck. Cattell. *On the perception of small differences*. Philadelphia: University of Pennsylvania Press, 1892.

Fuortes, M. G. F., and A. L. Hodgkin. Changes in time scale and sensitivity in the ommatidia of *Limulus. J. Physiol.*, 1964, 172, 239–263.

Galanter, E. The direct measurement of utility and subjective probability. *Am. J. Psychol.*, 1962, 75, 208–220.

Garner, W. R. An informational analysis of absolute judgments of loudness. *J. Exp. Psychol.*, 1953, 46, 373–380.

Garner, W. R. A technique and a scale for loudness measurement. *J. Acoust. Soc. Am.*, 1954, 26, 73–88.

Garner, W. R., and G. A. Miller. Differential sensitivity to intensity as a function of the duration of the comparison tone. *J. Exp. Psychol.*, 1944, 34, 450–463.

Geiger, P. H., and F. A. Firestone. The estimation of fractional loudness. *J. Acoust. Soc. Am.*, 1933, 5, 25–30.

Green, D. M., and J. A. Swets. *Signal detection theory and psychophysics*. New York: Wiley, 1966.

Guirao, M., and S. S. Stevens. The measurement of auditory density. *J. Acoust. Soc. Am.*, 1964, 36, 1176–1182.

Ham, L. B., and J. S. Parkinson. Loudness and intensity relations. *J. Acoust. Soc. Am.*, 1932, 3, 511–534.

Hamblin, R. L. Mathematical experimentation and sociological theory: a critical analysis. *Sociometry*, 1971, 34, 423–452.

Harper, R., and S. S. Stevens. Subjective hardness of compliant materials. *Quart J. Exp. Psychol.*, 1964, 16, 204–215.

Harper, R. S., and S. S. Stevens. A psychological scale of weight and a formula for its derivation. *Am. J. Psychol.*, 1948, 61, 343–351.

Harrington, T., and M. M. Merzenich. Neural coding in the sense of touch: human sensations of skin indentation compared with the responses of slowly adapting mechanoreceptive afferents innervating the hairy skin of monkeys. *Exp. Brain Res.*, 1970, 10, 251–254.

Hartline, H. K., and C. H. Graham. Nerve impulses from single receptors in the eye. *J. Cell. Comp. Physiol.*, 1932, 1, 277–295.

Hawkins, J. E., Jr., and S. S. Stevens. The masking of pure tones and of speech by white noise. *J. Acoust. Soc. Am.*, 1950, 22, 6–13.

Hellman, R. P., and J. J. Zwislocki. Loudness determinations at low sound frequencies. *J. Acoust. Soc. Am.*, 1968, 43, 60–64.

Helmholtz, H. v. Zählen und Messen erkenntnisstheoretisch betrachtet. In *Philosophische Aufspätze. Eduard Zeller gewidmet*. Leipzig: Fues's Verlag, 1887, pp. 17–52. Reprinted in *Gesammelte Abh.*, 1895, 3, 356–391.

Helson, H. *Adaptation level theory*. New York: Harper & Row, 1964.

Herrnstein, R. J., and E. G. Boring. *A source book in the history of psychology*. Cambridge, Mass.: Harvard Univ. Press, 1965.

Hilgard, E. R. Pain as a puzzle for psychology and physiology. *Am. Psychol.*, 1969, 24, 103–113.

Horeman, H. W. Relation between brightness and luminance under induction. *Vision Res.*, 1965, 5, 331–340.

Indow, T. [An example of motivation research applied to product design.] Published in Japanese in *Chosa To Gijutsu*, 1961, No. 102, 45–60.

Indow, T., and S. S. Stevens. Scaling of saturation and hue. *Percept. Psychophys.*, 1966, 1, 253–272.

James, W. *The principles of psychology*. New York: Henry Holt, 1890.

Jastrow, J. The psycho-physic law and star magnitude. *Am. J. Psychol.*, 1887, 1, 112–127.

Jones, B. D., and R. Shorter. The ratio measurement of social status: some cross-cultural comparisons. *Soc. Forces*, 1972, 50, 499–511.

Jones, F. N., and M. J. Marcus. The subject effect in judgments of subjective magnitude. *J. Exp. Psychol.*, 1961, 61, 40–44.

Judd, D. B. Basic correlates of the visual stimulus. In S. S. Stevens (Ed.), *Handbook of experimental psychology*. New York: Wiley, 1951, pp. 811–867.

Kahneman, D. L., and J. Beatty. Pupillary responses in a pitch-discrimination task. *Percept. Psychophys.*, 1967, 2, 101–105.

Keidel, W. D., and M. Spreng. Neurophysiological evidence for the Stevens power function in man. *J. Acoust. Soc. Am.*, 1965, 38, 191–195.

Koh, S. D. Scaling musical preferences. *J. Exp. Psychol.*, 1965, 70, 79–82.

Krantz, D. H. Visual scaling. In L. M. Hurvich and D. Jameson (Eds.), *Handbook of sensory physiology*. Vol. VII/4: Visual psychophysics, Chap. 26. New York: Springer-Verlag, 1972.

Künnapas, T., and U. Künnapas. On the mechanism of subjective similarity for unidimensional continua. *Rep. Psychol. Lab., Univ. Stockholm*, 1971, No. 342.

Künnapas, T., and M. Sillén. Measurement of "political" preferences: a comparison of scaling methods. *Rep. Psychol. Lab., Univ. Stockholm*, 1964, No. 172.

Künnapas, T., and I. Wikström. Measurement of occupational preferences: a comparison of scaling methods. *Percept. & Mot. Skills*, 1963, 17, 611–694.

Land, E. H. The retinex. *Am. Sci.*, 1964, 52, 247–264.

Lane, H. L., A. C. Catania, and S. S. Stevens. Voice level: autophonic scale, perceived loudness, and the effects of sidetone. *J. Acoust. Soc. Am.*, 1961, 33, 160–167.

Licklider, J. C. R. Basic correlates of the auditory stimulus. In S. S. Stevens (Ed.), *Handbook of experimental psychology*. New York: Wiley, 1951, pp. 985–1039.

Loewenich, V. v., and P. Finkenzeller. Reizstärkenabhängigkeit und Stevenssche Potenzfunktion beim optisch evozierten Potential des Menschen. *Pflügers Arch. Ges. Physiol.*, 1967, 293, 256–271.

Luce, R. D. Detection and recognition. In R. D. Luce, R. R. Bush, and E. Galanter (Eds.), *Handbook of mathematical psychology*, Vol. I, Chap. 3. New York: Wiley, 1963.

Mach, E. *The analysis of sensations (and the relation of the physical to the psychical)*. Republication of 1906 English edition, which was a translation of the 5th German edition. New York: Dover, 1959.

MacKay, D. M. Psychophysics of perceived intensity: a theoretical basis for Fechner's and Stevens' laws. *Science*, 1963, 139, 1213–1216.

McRobert, H., M. E. Bryan, and W. Tempest. Magnitude estimation of loudness. *J. Sound Vib.*, 1965, 2, 391–401.

Mansfield, R. J. W. Intensity relations in vision: analysis and synthesis of a nonlinear sensory system. Unpublished doctoral dissertation, Harvard Univ., 1970.

Marks, L. E. Stimulus-range, number of categories, and form of the category scale. *Am. J. Psychol.*, 1968, 81, 467–479.

Marks, L. E., and J. C. Stevens. Individual brightness functions. *Percept. Psychophys.*, 1966, 1, 17–24.

Marks, L. E., and J. C. Stevens. The form of the psychophysical function near threshold. *Percept. Psychophys.*, 1968, 4, 315–318.

Menninger, K. *A cultural history of numbers.* Cambridge, Mass.: The M.I.T. Press, 1969.

Merkel, J. Die Abhängigkeit zwischen Reiz und Empfindung. *Phil. Stud.*, 1888, 4, 541–594; 1889, 5, 245–291, 499–557.

Miller, G. A., and W. G. Taylor. The perception of repeated bursts of noise. *J. Acoust. Soc. Am.*, 1948, 20, 171–182.

Moon, P. *The scientific basis of illuminating engineering.* Rev. ed. New York: Dover, 1961 (1936).

Moskowitz, H. R. Scales of intensity for single and compound tastes. Unpublished doctoral dissertation, Harvard Univ., 1968.

Mountcastle, V. B., G. F. Poggio, and G. Werner. The neural transformation of the sensory stimulus at the cortical input level of the somatic afferent system. In R. W. Gerard and J. W. Duyff (Eds.), *Information processing in the nervous system.* Amsterdam: Excerpta Medica Foundation, 1962, pp. 196–217.

Mountcastle, V. B., W. H. Talbot, and H. H. Kornhuber. The neural transformation of the mechanical stimuli delivered to the monkey's hand. In *Ciba Foundation Symposium, Touch, heat and pain.* London: Churchill, 1966, pp. 325–345.

Mueller, C. G. Frequency of seeing functions for intensity discrimination at various levels of adapting intensity. *J. Gen. Physiol.*, 1951, 34, 463–474.

Newhall, S. M. A method of evaluating the spacing of visual scales. *Am. J. Psychol.*, 1950, 63, 221–228.

Newman, E. B., J. Volkmann, and S. S. Stevens. On the method of bisection and its relation to a loudness scale. *Am. J. Psychol.*, 1937, 49, 134–137.

Onley, J. W., C. L. Klingberg, M. J. Dainoff, and G. B. Rollman. Quantitative estimates of saturation. *J. Opt. Soc. Am.*, 1963, 53, 487–493.

Panek, D. W., and S. S. Stevens. Saturation of red: a prothetic continuum. *Percept Psychophys.*, 1966, 1, 59–66.

Peck, R. E. The application of thymometry to the measurement of anxiety. *Int. J. Neuropsychiat.*, 1966, 2, 337–341.

Piéron, H. *La sensation, guide de vie.* Edition nouvelle. Paris: Librairie Gallimard, 1955. An earlier edition appears in English as *The sensations, their functions, processes and mechanisms.* New Haven, Conn.: Yale Univ. Press, 1952.

Piéron, H. La psychophysique de Fechner, son rôle dans l'évolution de la psychologie et sa place dans la science actuelle. *Rev. Suisse Psychol. Pure Appl.*, 1960, 19, 5–25.

Piéron, H. La psychophysique. In *Traité de psychologie expérimentale.* II: Sensation et motricité, Chap. 5. Paris: Presses Univ. de France, 1963.

Pinneo, L. R., and R. G. Heath. Electrophysiology of the human visual system in perception of flicker, fusion and brightness. *Bull. Tulane Univ. Med. Fac.*, 1966, 25, 255–266.

Plateau, J. A. F. Sur la mesure des sensations physiques, et sur la loi qui lie l'intensité de ces sensations à l'intensité de la cause excitante. *Bull. Acad. Roy. Belg.*, 1872, 33, 376–388.

Plattig, K. H. Subjektive Schwellen- und Intensitätsabhängigkeitsmessungen am elektrischen Geschmack. *Pflügers Arch. Ges. Physiol.*, 1967, 294, 76.

Pollack, I. The effect of white noise on the loudness of speech of assigned average level. *J. Acoust. Soc. Am.,* 1949, 21, 255–258.

Pollack, I. Iterative techniques for unbiased rating scales. *Quart. J. Exp. Psychol.,* 1965, 17, 139–148.

Poulton, E. C. The new psychophysics: six models for magnitude estimation. *Psychol. Bull.,* 1968, 69, 1–19.

Pradhan, P. L., and P. J. Hoffman. Effect of spacing and range of stimuli on magnitude estimation judgments. *J. Exp. Psychol.,* 1963, 66, 533–541.

Purdy, D. M. Chroma as a function of retinal illumination. Unpublished doctoral dissertation, Harvard Univ., 1929.

Purdy, D. M., The Bezold-Brücke phenomenon and contours for constant hue. *Am. J. Psychol.,* 1937, 49, 313–315.

Raffel, R. A. Cross-modality matching: sound to light. Honors thesis, Harvard Univ., 1972.

Rainwater, L. Personal communication, 1971.

Ratliff, F. *Mach bands.* San Francisco: Holden-Day, 1965.

Reynolds, G. S., and S. S. Stevens. The binaural summation of loudness. *J. Acoust. Soc. Am.,* 1960, 32, 1337–1344.

Richardson, L. F., and J. S. Ross. Loudness and telephone current. *J. Gen. Psychol.,* 1930, 3, 288–306.

Robinson, D. W. The subjective loudness scale. *Acustica,* 1957, 7, 217–233.

Sachs, M. B., J. Nachmias, and J. G. Robson. Spatial-frequency channels in human vision. *J. Opt. Soc. Am.,* 1971, 61, 1176–1186.

Saunders, J. E. The validity of magnitude estimations of luminosity and the measurement of the relative effects of preadaptation and contrast. *Vision Res.,* 1972, 12, 689–698.

Savage, C. W. *The measurement of sensation.* Berkeley: Univ. California Press, 1970.

Savage, L. J. *The foundations of statistics.* New York: Wiley, 1954.

Scharf, B. and J. C. Stevens. The form of the loudness function near threshold. In *Proc. 3rd Int. Congr. Acoust.* Amsterdam: Elsevier, 1961, pp. 80–82.

Schouten, J. F. The residue revisited. In R. Plomp and G. F. Smoorenburg (Eds.), *Frequency analysis and periodicity detection in hearing.* Leiden: A. W. Sijthoff, 1970, pp. 41–58.

Sellin, T., and M. E. Wolfgang. *The measurement of delinquency.* New York: Wiley, 1964.

Shapiro, B. J. The subjective scaling of relative word frequency. Unpublished doctoral dissertation, Harvard Univ., 1967.

Shinn, A. M., Jr. An application of psychophysical scaling techniques to the measurement of national power. *J. Polit.,* 1969, 31, 932–951.

Stevens, J. C. A comparison of ratio scales for the loudness of white noise and the brightness of white light. Unpublished doctoral dissertation, Harvard Univ., 1957.

Stevens, J. C., E. R. Adair, and L. E. Marks. Pain, discomfort, and warmth as functions of thermal intensity. In J. D. Hardy, J. A. J. Stolwijk, and A. P. Gagge (Eds.), *Physiological and behavioral temperature regulation.* Springfield, Ill.: C. C Thomas, 1970, pp. 892–904.

Stevens, J. C., and M. Guirao. Individual loudness functions. *J. Acoust. Soc. Am.,* 1964, 36, 2210–2213.

Stevens, J. C., and J. D. Mack. Scales of apparent force. *J. Exp. Psychol.,* 1959, 58, 405–413.

Stevens, J. C., J. D. Mack, and S. S. Stevens. Growth of sensation on seven continua as measured by force of handgrip. *J. Exp. Psychol.,* 1960, 59, 60–67.

Stevens, J. C., and L. E. Marks. Cross-modality matching of brightness and loudness. *Proc. Nat. Acad. Sci.,* 1965, 54, 407–411.

Stevens, J. C., and S. S. Stevens. Warmth and cold: dynamics of sensory intensity. *J. Exp. Psychol.,* 1960, 60, 183–192.

Stevens, J. C., and S. S. Stevens. Brightness function: effects of adaptation. *J. Opt. Soc. Am.,* 1963, 53, 375–385.

Stevens, S. S. Tonal density. *J. Exp. Psychol.,* 1934a, 17, 585–592.

Stevens, S. S. The volume and intensity of tones. *Am. J. Psychol.,* 1934b, 46, 397–408.

Stevens, S. S. The attributes of tones. *Proc. Nat. Acad. Sci.,* 1934c, 20, 457–459.

Stevens, S. S. The relation of pitch to intensity. *J. Acoust. Soc. Am.,* 1935, 6, 150–154.

Stevens, S. S. A scale for the measurement of a psychological magnitude: loudness. *Psychol. Rev.,* 1936, 43, 405–416.

Stevens, S. S. On the theory of scales of measurement. *Science,* 1946, 103, 677–680.

Stevens, S. S. Mathematics, measurement, and psychophysics. In S. S. Stevens (Ed.), *Handbook of experimental psychology.* New York: Wiley, 1951, pp. 1–49.

Stevens, S. S. On the brightness of lights and the loudness of sounds. *Science,* 1953, 118, 576. [Abstract]

Stevens, S. S. Pitch discrimination, mels, and Kock's contention. *J. Acoust. Soc. Am.,* 1954, 26, 1075–1077.

Stevens, S. S. Decibels of light and sound. *Physics Today,* 1955a, 8, 12–17.

Stevens, S. S. On the averaging of data. *Science,* 1955b, 121, 113–116.

Stevens, S. S. The measurement of loudness. *J. Acoust. Soc. Am.,* 1955c, 27, 815–820.

Stevens, S. S. The direct estimation of sensory magnitudes—loudness. *Am. J. Psychol.,* 1956a, 69, 1–25.

Stevens, S. S. Calculation of the loudness of complex noise. *J. Acoust. Soc. Am.,* 1956b, 28, 807–832.

Stevens, S. S. Concerning the form of the loudness function. *J. Acoust Soc. Am.,* 1957a, 29, 603–606.

Stevens, S. S. On the psychophysical law. *Psychol. Rev.,* 1957b, 64, 153–181.

Stevens, S. S. Adaptation-level vs. the relativity of judgment. *Am. J. Psychol.,* 1958, 71, 633–646.

Stevens, S. S. Measurement, psychophysics and utility. In C. W. Churchman and P. Ratoosh (Eds.), *Measurement: definitions and theories.* New York: Wiley, 1959a, pp. 18–64.

Stevens, S. S. Cross-modality validation of subjective scales for loudness, vibration, and electric shock. *J. Exp. Psychol.,* 1959b, 57, 201–209.

Stevens, S. S. Review: L. L. Thurstone's *The measurement of values. Contemp. Psychol.,* 1959c, 4, 388–389.

Stevens, S. S. Tactile vibration: dynamics of sensory intensity. *J. Exp. Psychol.,* 1959d, 57, 210–218.

Stevens, S. S. On the new psychophysics. *Scand. J. Psychol.,* 1960, 1, 27–35.

Stevens, S. S. The psychophysics of sensory function. In W. A. Rosenblith (Ed.), *Sensory communication.* Cambridge, Mass.: The M.I.T. Press, 1961a, pp. 1–33.

Stevens, S. S. To honor Fechner and repeal his law. *Science,* 1961b, 133, 80–86.

Stevens, S. S. Duration, luminance, and the brightness exponent. *Percept. Psychophys.,* 1966a, 1, 96–100.

Stevens, S. S. Power-group transformations under glare, masking, and recruitment. *J. Acoust. Soc. Am.,* 1966b, 39, 725–735.

Stevens, S. S. Matching functions between loudness and ten other continua. *Percept. Psychophys.,* 1966c, 1, 5–8.

Stevens, S. S. A metric for the social consensus. *Science,* 1966d, 151, 530–541.

Stevens, S. S. Tactile vibration: change of exponent with frequency. *Percept. Psychophys.,* 1968a, 3, 223–228.

Stevens, S. S. Ratio scales of opinion. In D. K. Whitla (Ed.), *Handbook of measurement and assessment in behavioral sciences.* Reading, Mass.: Addison-Wesley, 1968b, pp. 171–199.

Stevens, S. S. On predicting exponents for cross-modality matches. *Percept. Psychophys.,* 1969, 6, 251–256.

Stevens, S. S. Neural events and the psychophysical law. *Science,* 1970, 170, 1043–1050.

Stevens, S. S. Sensory power functions and neural events. *In Handbook of Sensory physiology,* Vol. I. New York: Springer-Verlag, 1971a, pp. 226–242.

Stevens, S. S. Issues in psychophysical measurement. *Psychol. Rev.,* 1971b, 78, 426–450.

Stevens, S. S. Perceived level of noise by Mark VII and decibels (E). *J. Acoust. Soc. Am.,* 1972a, 51, 575–601.

Stevens, S. S. A neural quantum in sensory discrimination. *Science,* 1972b, 177, 749–762.

Stevens, S. S. Perceptual magnitude and its estimation. In E. Carterette and M. Friedman (Eds.), *Handbook of perception,* Vol. 2. New York: Academic Press, in press.

Stevens, S. S., and H. Davis. Psychophysiological acoustics: pitch and loudness. *J. Acoust. Soc. Am.,* 1936, 8, 1–13.

Stevens, S. S., and H. Davis. *Hearing: its psychology and physiology.* New York: Wiley, 1938.

Stevens, S. S., H. Davis, and M. H. Lurie. The localization of pitch perception on the basilar membrane. *J. Gen. Psychol.,* 1935, 13, 297–315.

Stevens, S. S., and A. L. Diamond. Effect of glare angle on the brightness function for a small target. *Vision Res.,* 1965, 5, 649–659.

Stevens, S. S., and E. H. Galanter. Ratio scales and category scales for a dozen perceptual continua. *J. Exp. Psychol.,* 1957, 54, 377–411.

Stevens, S. S., and H. B. Greenbaum. Regression effect in psychophysical judgment. *Percept. Psychophys.,* 1966, 1, 439–446.

Stevens, S. S., and M. Guirao. Loudness, reciprocality, and partition scales. *J. Acoust. Soc. Am.,* 1962, 34, 1466–1471.

Stevens, S. S., and M. Guirao. Subjective scaling of length and area and the matching of length to loudness and brightness. *J. Exp. Psychol.,* 1963, 66, 177–186.

Stevens, S. S., and M. Guirao. The scaling of apparent viscosity. *Science,* 1964, 145, 1157–1158.

Stevens, S. S., and M. Guirao. Loudness functions under inhibition. *Percept. Psychophys.,* 1967, 2, 459–465.

Stevens, S. S., M. Guirao, and A. W. Slawson. Loudness, a product of volume times density. *J. Exp. Psychol.,* 1965, 69, 503–510.

Stevens, S. S., and J. R. Harris. The scaling of subjective roughness and smoothness. *J. Exp. Psychol.,* 1962, 64, 489–494.

Stevens, S. S., C. T. Morgan, and J. Volkmann. Theory of the neural quantum in the discrimination of loudness and pitch. *Am. J. Psychol.,* 1941, 54, 315–335.

Stevens, S. S., and E. C. Poulton. The estimation of loudness by unpracticed observers. *J. Exp. Psychol.,* 1956, 51, 71–78.

Stevens, S. S., M. S. Rogers, and R. J. Herrnstein. Apparent reduction of loudness: a repeat experiment. *J. Acoust. Soc. Am.,* 1955, 27, 326–328.

Stevens, S. S., and J. Volkmann. The relation of pitch to frequency: a revised scale. *Am. J. Psychol.,* 1940a, 53, 329–353.

Stevens, S. S., and J. Volkmann. The quantum of sensory discrimination. *Science,* 1940b, 92, 583–585.

Stevens, S. S., J. Volkmann, and E. B. Newman. A scale for the measurement of the psychological magnitude pitch. *J. Acoust. Soc. Am.,* 1937, 8, 185–190.

Teas, D. C., D. H. Eldredge, and H. Davis. Cochlear responses to acoustic transients: an interpretation of whole-nerve action potentials. *J. Acoust. Soc. Am.,* 1962, 34, 1438–1459.

Teghtsoonian, M. A. The judgment of size. *Am. J. Psychol.,* 1965, 78, 392–402.

Teghtsoonian, R. On the exponents in Stevens' law and the constants in Ekman's law. *Psychol. Rev.,* 1971, 78, 71–80.

Terrace, H. S., and S. S. Stevens. The quantification of tonal volume. *Am. J. Psychol.,* 1962, 75, 596–604.

Thalmann, R. Cross-modality matching in the study of abnormal loudness functions. *Laryngoscope,* 1965, 75, 1708–1726.

Thurstone, L. L. Fechner's law and the method of equal appearing intervals. *J. Exp. Psychol.,* 1929, 12, 214–224. Reprinted in Thurstone 1959, pp. 92–99.

Thurstone, L. L. *The measurement of values.* Chicago: Univ. Chicago Press, 1959.

Thurstone, L. L., and E. J. Chave. *The measurement of attitudes.* Chicago: Univ. Chicago Press, 1929.

Titchener, E. B. *Experimental psychology,* Vol. II, Part II (Instructor's manual). New York: Macmillan, 1923.

Torgerson, W. S. Distances and ratios in psychophysical scaling. *Acta Psychol.,* 1961, 19, 201–205.

Underwood, B. J. *Experimental psychology.* 2nd ed. New York: Appleton-Century-Crofts, 1966.

Vaughan, H. G., L. D. Costa, and L. Gilden. The functional relation of visual evoked response and reaction time to stimulus intensity. *Vision Res.,* 1966, 6, 645–656.

Versace, J. *Measurement of ride comfort.* Automotive Engineering Congress and Exposition, Detroit, Mich., Jan. 14–18, 1963.

Walsh, J. W. T. *Photometry.* 3rd ed. New York: Dover, 1958.

Warren, R. M. Elimination of biases in loudness judgments for tones. *J. Acoust. Soc. Am.,* 1970, 48, 1397–1403.

Welch, R. E., Jr. The use of magnitude estimation in attitude scaling: constructing a measure of political dissatisfaction. *Soc. Sci. Quart.,* 1971, 76–87.

Wever, E. G., and K. E. Zener. The method of absolute judgment in psychophysics. *Psychol. Rev.,* 1928, 35, 466–493.

Whalen, A. D. *Detection of signals in noise.* New York: Academic Press, 1971.

Whittle, L. S., S. J. Collins, and D. W. Robinson. The audibility of low-frequency sounds. *J. Sound Vib.,* 1972, 21, 431–448.

Woodworth, R. S. *Experimental psychology.* New York: Henry Holt, 1938.

Wyszecki, G., and W. S. Stiles. *Color science: concepts and methods, quantitative data and formulas.* New York: Wiley, 1967.

Yilmaz, H. Perceptual invariance and the psychophysical law. *Percept. Psychophys.,* 1967, 2, 533–538.

Youtz, R. E. P., and S. S. Stevens. On the pitch of frequency-modulated tones. *Am. J. Psychol.,* 1938, 51, 521–526.

Zurmühl, G. Abhängigkeit der Tonhöhenempfindung von der Lautstärke und ihre Beziehung zur Helmholtzchen Resonanztheorie des Hörens. *Z. Sinnesphysiol.,* 1930, 61, 40–86.

Zwicker, E., G. Flottorp, and S. S. Stevens. Critical band width in loudness summation. . *J. Acoust. Soc. Am.,* 1957, 29, 548–557.

Brief Table
of
Decibels
and
Common Logarithms

A decibel, like a decilog, is a tenth of a logarithmic unit. Hence, the number of decibels N is given by the equation $N = \log P/P_0$, where P is some form of power and P_0 is any desired reference value. The power P may refer to light energy or to sound energy.

The table gives the number of decibels corresponding to various ratios of power. The table can also be used for ratios of sound pressure. Enter the table with the sound pressure ratio, find the decibel value, and then double it. The doubling is necessary because sound power is proportional to the sound pressure squared.

To use the table for three-place logarithms, divide the decibel value by ten.

For ratios greater than ten, add 10 decibels for each power of ten. Examples: a ratio of 100 is 20 decibels; 1000 is 30 decibels; 230 is 23.62 decibels; 4500 is 36.53 decibels.

Ratio	Decibels	Ratio	Decibels
1.0	0.0	1.5	1.76
1.1	0.41	1.6	2.04
1.2	0.79	1.7	2.30
1.3	1.14	1.8	2.55
1.4	1.46	1.9	2.79

Ratio	Decibels	Ratio	Decibels
2.0	3.01	6.0	7.78
2.1	3.22	6.1	7.85
2.2	3.42	6.2	7.92
2.3	3.62	6.3	7.99
2.4	3.80	6.4	8.06
2.5	3.98	6.5	8.13
2.6	4.15	6.6	8.20
2.7	4.31	6.7	8.26
2.8	4.47	6.8	8.33
2.9	4.62	6.9	8.39
3.0	4.77	7.0	8.45
3.1	4.91	7.1	8.51
3.2	5.05	7.2	8.57
3.3	5.19	7.3	8.63
3.4	5.31	7.4	8.69
3.5	5.44	7.5	8.75
3.6	5.56	7.6	8.81
3.7	5.68	7.7	8.86
3.8	5.80	7.8	8.92
3.9	5.91	7.9	8.98
4.0	6.02	8.0	9.03
4.1	6.13	8.1	9.08
4.2	6.23	8.2	9.14
4.3	6.33	8.3	9.19
4.4	6.43	8.4	9.24
4.5	6.53	8.5	9.29
4.6	6.63	8.6	9.34
4.7	6.72	8.7	9.40
4.8	6.81	8.8	9.44
4.9	6.90	8.9	9.49
5.0	6.99	9.0	9.54
5.1	7.08	9.1	9.59
5.2	7.16	9.2	9.64
5.3	7.24	9.3	9.68
5.4	7.32	9.4	9.73
5.5	7.40	9.5	9.78
5.6	7.48	9.6	9.82
5.7	7.56	9.7	9.87
5.8	7.63	9.8	9.91
5.9	7.71	9.9	9.96

Table Relating
Pitch in Mels
to
Frequency in Hertz

The pitch of a 1000-hertz tone, 40 decibels above threshold, is defined as 1000 mels.

Frequency	0	10	20	30	40	50	60	70	80	90
0		12	29	46	62	78	95	111	127	144
100	161	177	193	208	223	237	250	264	277	289
200	301	312	323	334	347	358	369	379	389	399
300	409	419	429	440	450	460	470	480	490	499
400	508	518	528	538	547	556	565	574	584	593
500	602	611	620	629	638	647	655	664	673	682
600	690	699	707	716	724	732	741	750	759	767
700	775	783	791	799	808	816	824	832	840	847
800	854	861	868	876	884	891	899	906	914	922
900	929	937	944	951	959	966	973	980	987	994
1,000	1000	1007	1014	1020	1026	1032	1038	1044	1050	1056
1,100	1062	1069	1075	1081	1087	1093	1099	1106	1112	1118
1,200	1124	1130	1136	1142	1148	1154	1160	1166	1172	1178
1,300	1183	1189	1194	1200	1205	1211	1217	1223	1228	1234
1,400	1240	1245	1250	1256	1262	1268	1273	1279	1285	1290
1,500	1296	1301	1307	1313	1318	1323	1329	1334	1340	1345
1,600	1350	1356	1362	1368	1373	1378	1383	1388	1393	1398
1,700	1403	1408	1413	1418	1423	1428	1433	1438	1443	1448
1,800	1453	1458	1463	1468	1472	1477	1482	1487	1491	1496
1,900	1500	1505	1509	1513	1518	1522	1527	1531	1536	1541

Frequency	0	10	20	30	40	50	60	70	80	90
2,000	1545	1550	1554	1559	1563	1568	1572	1577	1581	1586
2,100	1590	1595	1600	1604	1608	1612	1617	1622	1626	1631
2,200	1636	1640	1645	1650	1654	1659	1663	1668	1672	1677
2,300	1681	1686	1690	1695	1700	1704	1708	1712	1717	1721
2,400	1726	1730	1735	1740	1745	1750	1754	1758	1762	1767
2,500	1771	1776	1780	1784	1789	1793	1797	1801	1805	1809
2,600	1813	1817	1821	1825	1829	1833	1837	1841	1845	1849
2,700	1852	1856	1860	1864	1868	1872	1875	1879	1883	1887
2,800	1890	1894	1898	1902	1906	1910	1913	1917	1920	1924
2,900	1928	1931	1934	1938	1941	1945	1949	1952	1955	1959
3,000	1962	1966	1969	1972	1976	1979	1982	1985	1988	1991
3,100	1994	1997	2000	2003	2006	2009	2012	2015	2018	2021
3,200	2025	2029	2032	2035	2038	2041	2044	2047	2050	2053
3,300	2056	2059	2062	2065	2068	2071	2074	2077	2080	2083
3,400	2086	2089	2092	2095	2098	2101	2104	2107	2110	2113
3,500	2116	2119	2122	2125	2128	2131	2134	2137	2140	2143
3,600	2146	2149	2152	2155	2158	2161	2164	2167	2170	2173
3,700	2176	2179	2181	2183	2186	2189	2192	2195	2198	2201
3,800	2203	2206	2209	2211	2213	2216	2219	2221	2223	2226
3,900	2229	2231	2233	2236	2238	2240	2242	2244	2246	2248
4,000	2250	2252	2255	2258	2261	2264	2267	2270	2273	2276
4,100	2279	2281	2283	2286	2289	2292	2295	2297	2300	2302
4,200	2304	2307	2309	2311	2313	2316	2318	2320	2322	2325
4,300	2328	2330	2332	2334	2337	2339	2341	2343	2345	2348
4,400	2350	2352	2354	2356	2358	2360	2362	2364	2366	2368
4,500	2370	2372	2374	2376	2378	2381	2383	2385	2387	2390
4,600	2393	2395	2397	2399	2401	2404	2406	2408	2410	2412
4,700	2414	2416	2418	2420	2422	2425	2427	2429	2431	2433
4,800	2436	2438	2440	2442	2444	2447	2449	2451	2453	2455
4,900	2457	2459	2461	2463	2465	2468	2470	2472	2474	2476
5,000	2478									
5,500	2572									
6,000	2657									
6,500	2735									
7,000	2800									
7,500	2858									
8,000	2911									
9,000	3000									
10,000	3075									

Relation between Stimulus Level in Decibels and Perceived Magnitude in Sones or Brils

One sone is defined as the loudness of a critical band of noise centered on 3150 hertz at a sound pressure level of 32 decibels above the reference level $20\,\mu N/m^2$.

One bril is defined as the brightness of a 5-degree target seen when the luminance level is 40 decibels above the reference level 10^{-10} lambert (or $0.32\,\mu cd/m^2$). The two reference levels, visual and auditory, are both near the respective absolute thresholds.

To obtain number of brils, you must first subtract 8 decibels from the stimulus level before entering the table.

A single table serves for loudness and brightness because both attributes approximate cube-root functions of stimulus power (energy flow).

Decibels	0	0.1	0.2	0.3	0.4	0.5	0.6	0.7	0.8	0.9
10	0.181	0.182	0.184	0.185	0.187	0.188	0.190	0.191	0.193	0.194
11	0.196	0.197	0.199	0.201	0.202	0.204	0.205	0.207	0.209	0.210
12	0.212	0.214	0.215	0.217	0.219	0.221	0.222	0.224	0.226	0.228
13	0.230	0.231	0.233	0.235	0.237	0.239	0.241	0.243	0.244	0.246
14	0.248	0.250	0.252	0.254	0.256	0.258	0.260	0.262	0.264	0.267
15	0.269	0.271	0.273	0.275	0.277	0.279	0.282	0.284	0.286	0.288
16	0.290	0.293	0.295	0.297	0.300	0.302	0.304	0.307	0.309	0.312
17	0.314	0.316	0.319	0.321	0.324	0.326	0.329	0.332	0.334	0.337
18	0.339	0.342	0.345	0.347	0.350	0.353	0.356	0.358	0.361	0.364
19	0.367	0.370	0.372	0.375	0.378	0.381	0.384	0.387	0.390	0.393
20	0.396	0.399	0.402	0.406	0.409	0.412	0.415	0.418	0.422	0.425
21	0.428	0.431	0.435	0.438	0.442	0.445	0.448	0.452	0.455	0.459
22	0.463	0.466	0.470	0.473	0.477	0.481	0.484	0.488	0.492	0.496
23	0.500	0.504	0.507	0.511	0.515	0.518	0.523	0.527	0.531	0.536
24	0.540	0.544	0.548	0.552	0.557	0.561	0.565	0.570	0.574	0.579
25	0.583	0.588	0.592	0.597	0.601	0.606	0.611	0.615	0.620	0.625
26	0.630	0.635	0.640	0.645	0.649	0.655	0.660	0.665	0.670	0.675
27	0.680	0.686	0.691	0.696	0.702	0.707	0.712	0.718	0.724	0.729
28	0.735	0.740	0.746	0.752	0.758	0.764	0.770	0.775	0.781	0.788
29	0.794	0.800	0.806	0.812	0.818	0.825	0.831	0.838	0.844	0.851
30	0.857	0.864	0.871	0.877	0.884	0.891	0.898	0.905	0.912	0.919
31	0.926	0.933	0.940	0.947	0.955	0.962	0.970	0.977	0.985	0.992
32	1.00	1.01	1.02	1.02	1.03	1.04	1.05	1.06	1.06	1.07
33	1.08	1.09	1.10	1.10	1.11	1.12	1.13	1.14	1.15	1.16
34	1.17	1.18	1.18	1.19	1.20	1.21	1.22	1.23	1.24	1.25

Decibels	0	0.1	0.2	0.3	0.4	0.5	0.6	0.7	0.8	0.9
35	1.26	1.27	1.28	1.29	1.30	1.31	1.32	1.33	1.34	1.35
36	1.36	1.37	1.38	1.39	1.40	1.41	1.42	1.44	1.45	1.46
37	1.47	1.48	1.49	1.50	1.52	1.53	1.54	1.55	1.56	1.58
38	1.59	1.60	1.61	1.62	1.64	1.65	1.66	1.68	1.69	1.70
39	1.72	1.73	1.74	1.76	1.77	1.78	1.80	1.81	1.82	1.84
40	1.85	1.87	1.88	1.90	1.91	1.92	1.94	1.95	1.97	1.98
41	2.00	2.02	2.03	2.05	2.06	2.08	2.10	2.11	2.13	2.14
42	2.16	2.18	2.19	2.21	2.23	2.24	2.26	2.28	2.30	2.32
43	2.33	2.35	2.37	2.39	2.41	2.42	2.44	2.46	2.48	2.50
44	2.52	2.54	2.56	2.58	2.60	2.62	2.64	2.66	2.68	2.70
45	2.72	2.74	2.76	2.78	2.81	2.83	2.85	2.87	2.90	2.92
46	2.94	2.96	2.98	3.01	3.03	3.06	3.08	3.10	3.13	3.15
47	3.18	3.20	3.22	3.25	3.27	3.30	3.32	3.35	3.38	3.40
48	3.43	3.46	3.48	3.51	3.54	3.56	3.59	3.62	3.65	3.68
49	3.70	3.73	3.76	3.79	3.82	3.85	3.88	3.91	3.94	3.97
50	4.00	4.03	4.06	4.09	4.12	4.16	4.19	4.22	4.25	4.29
51	4.32	4.35	4.39	4.42	4.46	4.49	4.52	4.56	4.60	4.63
52	4.67	4.70	4.74	4.78	4.81	4.85	4.89	4.92	4.96	5.00
53	5.04	5.08	5.12	5.16	5.20	5.24	5.28	5.32	5.36	5.40
54	5.44	5.49	5.53	5.57	5.61	5.66	5.70	5.74	5.79	5.83
55	5.88	5.92	5.97	6.02	6.06	6.11	6.16	6.20	6.25	6.30
56	6.35	6.40	6.45	6.50	6.55	6.60	6.65	6.70	6.75	6.81
57	6.86	6.91	6.96	7.02	7.07	7.13	7.18	7.24	7.29	7.35
58	7.41	7.46	7.52	7.58	7.64	7.70	7.76	7.81	7.88	7.94
59	8.00	8.06	8.12	8.19	8.25	8.32	8.38	8.44	8.51	8.58

	8.64	8.71	8.78	8.84	8.91	8.98	9.05	9.12	9.19	9.26
60	8.64	8.71	8.78	8.84	8.91	8.98	9.05	9.12	9.19	9.26
61	9.33	9.40	9.48	9.55	9.62	9.70	9.77	9.85	9.93	10.0
62	10.1	10.2	10.2	10.3	10.4	10.5	10.6	10.6	10.7	10.8
63	10.9	11.0	11.1	11.1	11.2	11.3	11.4	11.5	11.6	11.7
64	11.8	11.8	11.9	12.0	12.1	12.2	12.3	12.4	12.5	12.6
65	12.7	12.8	12.9	13.0	13.1	13.2	13.3	13.4	13.5	13.6
66	13.7	13.8	13.9	14.0	14.1	14.3	14.4	14.5	14.6	14.7
67	14.8	14.9	15.0	15.2	15.3	15.4	15.5	15.6	15.8	15.9
68	16.0	16.1	16.2	16.4	16.5	16.6	16.8	16.9	17.0	17.1
69	17.3	17.4	17.6	17.7	17.8	18.0	18.1	18.2	18.4	18.5
70	18.7	18.8	19.0	19.1	19.2	19.4	19.5	19.7	19.9	20.0
71	20.2	20.3	20.5	20.6	20.8	21.0	21.1	21.3	21.4	21.6
72	21.8	21.9	22.1	22.3	22.5	22.6	22.8	23.0	23.2	23.3
73	23.5	23.7	23.9	24.1	24.3	24.4	24.6	24.8	25.0	25.2
74	25.4	25.6	25.8	26.0	26.2	26.4	26.6	26.8	27.0	27.2
75	27.4	27.7	27.9	28.1	28.3	28.5	28.7	29.0	29.2	29.4
76	29.6	29.9	30.1	30.3	30.6	30.8	31.0	31.3	31.5	31.8
77	32.0	32.2	32.5	32.7	33.0	33.3	33.5	33.8	34.0	34.3
78	34.6	34.8	35.1	35.4	35.6	35.9	36.2	36.5	36.8	37.0
79	37.3	37.6	37.9	38.2	38.5	38.8	39.1	39.4	39.7	40.0
80	40.3	40.6	40.9	41.3	41.6	41.9	42.2	42.6	42.9	43.2
81	43.5	43.9	44.2	44.6	44.9	45.3	45.6	46.0	46.3	46.7
82	47.0	47.4	47.8	48.1	48.5	48.9	49.3	49.6	50.0	50.4
83	50.8	51.2	51.6	52.0	52.4	52.8	53.2	53.6	54.0	54.4
84	54.9	55.3	55.7	56.1	56.6	57.0	57.5	57.9	58.4	58.8

Decibels	0	0.1	0.2	0.3	0.4	0.5	0.6	0.7	0.8	0.9
85	59.3	59.7	60.2	60.6	61.1	61.6	62.1	62.5	63.0	63.5
86	64.0	64.5	65.0	65.5	66.0	66.5	67.0	67.5	68.1	68.6
87	69.1	69.7	70.2	70.7	71.3	71.8	72.4	73.0	73.5	74.1
88	74.7	75.2	75.8	76.4	77.0	77.6	78.2	78.8	79.4	80.0
89	80.6	81.3	81.9	82.5	83.2	83.8	84.4	85.1	85.8	86.4
90	87.1	87.8	88.4	89.1	89.4	90.5	91.2	91.9	92.6	93.3
91	94.1	94.8	95.5	96.3	97.0	97.8	98.5	99.3	100	101
92	102	102	103	104	105	106	106	107	108	109
93	110	111	111	112	113	114	115	116	117	118
94	119	119	120	121	122	123	124	125	126	127
95	128	129	130	131	132	133	134	135	136	137
96	138	139	140	141	143	144	145	146	147	148
97	149	150	152	153	154	155	156	158	159	160
98	161	163	164	165	166	168	169	170	172	173
99	174	176	177	178	180	181	182	184	185	187
100	188	190	191	193	194	196	197	199	200	202
101	203	205	206	208	210	211	213	214	216	218
102	219	221	223	225	226	228	230	232	233	235
103	237	239	241	243	244	246	248	250	252	254
104	256	258	260	262	264	266	268	270	272	274
105	276	279	281	283	285	287	290	292	294	296
106	299	301	303	306	308	310	313	315	318	320
107	323	325	328	330	333	335	338	340	343	346
108	348	351	354	356	359	362	365	368	370	373
109	376	379	382	385	388	391	394	397	400	403

110	406	409	413	416	419	422	426	429	432	436
111	439	442	446	449	453	456	460	463	467	470
112	474	478	481	485	489	493	496	500	504	508
113	512	516	520	524	528	532	536	540	545	549
114	553	557	562	566	570	575	579	584	588	593
115	597	602	606	611	616	621	625	630	635	640
116	645	650	655	660	665	670	676	681	686	691
117	697	702	707	713	718	724	730	735	741	747
118	752	758	764	770	776	782	788	794	800	806
119	813	819	825	832	838	845	851	858	864	871
120	878	885	891	898	905	912	919	926	934	941

Author Index

Subject Index